Dissecting a C# Application

Inside SharpDevelop

Christian Holm

Mike Krüger

Bernhard Spuida

Wrox Press Ltd. ®

Dissecting a C# Application

Inside SharpDevelop

© 2003 Wrox Press

First Printed February 2003

Published by Wrox Press Ltd.,
Arden House, 1102 Warwick Road, Acocks Green,
Birmingham, B27 6BH
United Kingdom
Printed in the United States of America
ISBN 1-86100-817-1

Trademark Acknowledgments

Wrox has endeavored to provide trademark information about all the companies and products mentioned in this book by the appropriate use of capitals. However, Wrox cannot guarantee the accuracy of this information.

Credits

Authors
Christian Holm
Mike Krüger
Bernhard Spuida

Commissioning Editor
Dan Kent

Technical Editors
Arun Nair
Veena Nair

Managing Editor
Louay Fatoohi

Project Manager
Charlotte Smith

Indexer
Andrew Criddle

Proofreader
Chris Smith

Lead Technical Reviewer
Christoph Wille

Technical Reviewers
Natalia Bortniker
Jeroen Frijters
Gavin McKay
Markus Palme
David Schultz
Erick Sgarbi
Jon Shute
Gavin Smyth
Poul Staugaard
Helmut Watson

Production Coordinator
Neil Lote

Production Assistant
Paul Grove

Cover
Natalie O' Donnell

About the Authors

Christian Holm

Christian started his writing career in mid-2000, writing technical articles for AspHeute.com, which has grown to the largest German-centric developer platform for Active Server Pages and Microsoft .NET-related technology. His focus shifted from classic ASP to .NET when he was introduced to Microsoft's .NET vision shortly after it was introduced to the public at the Professional Developers Conference 2000 in Orlando.

Since that time he has eagerly adapted the rich features of the .NET technology for his business and additionally revealed the attained .NET experience to the developers reading his articles at AspHeute.com. In 2001 he got in touch with Wrox Press to write his first chapter for the *Professional .NET Framework* book. Since then he has worked for Wrox on freelance basis as a technical editor.

> *I would like to thank everybody involved in this project at Wrox, especially Charlotte Smith and Daniel Kent, for their great support on this book project and the technical editors, especially Arun Nair, for their valuable comments on my drafts. I would also like to thank all the project managers, who gave me the opportunity to review their projects.*

Mike Krüger

Mike Krüger currently studies computer science at the Freie Universität-Berlin Germany. He has over 10 years of software development experience ranging from C64 assembly/basic language development to object-oriented systems written in C#, C++, or Java.

Currently, Mike focuses 100% of his efforts on the development of SharpDevelop. He enjoys the development in C# very much as it is his first C# and Windows project. He has also written software for the Linux operating system before he started with SharpDevelop.

Mike lives in Berlin, Germany with his girlfriend, Andrea. He loves playing computer games, watching science fiction TV series and reading books. You can contact Mike at mike@icsharpcode.net.

> *First, I would like to thank my girlfriend, Andrea, who had the idea of starting the SharpDevelop project. She helped me a lot in the development with ideas and source code (she wrote the C# parser without much help). I love you!*
>
> *I would also like to thank all the people who helped to develop SharpDevelop. It is a community effort. We have translators, people who write add-ins and bug fixes, and many people who help with their feedback to make each new release much better than the former one. I would thank especially Christoph Wille who believed in the project almost from its beginnings and without whom SharpDevelop wouldn't be as sophisticated as it now is.*

Bernhard Spuida

Bernhard Spuida works for AGS – Applied Geo-systems technology – as developer and researcher in geophysical data acquisition, processing, and visualization. He has been programming for 20 years, having worked in fields ranging from 3D graphics to databases and real-time data acquisition on platforms ranging from VAX to PCs and SUNs.

Currently, he works on remote operation of geophysical equipment, in situ pre-processing of data, and processing workflow management. He sees .NET as a technology holding great potential in his current fields of work. He writes and translates articles for the German-language ASPHeute programmer's forum and its English language section.

He also is member of the SharpDevelop core team, where he mostly manages documentation and – due to his extensive knowledge of human languages – is deeply involved in the localization effort.

Bernhard shares his time between Leoben, Austria where works, Pfronten, Germany where his family lives, and field work in places too numerous to mention. When not working, you will quite probably catch him reading a book on some strange topic, golfing or refereeing an ASP golf tournament. You can contact him either at bernhard@icsharpcode.net or at bspuida@ags-geosys.com.

I would like to thank Veronika and little Chiara for just being. You always are with me, no matter where I may be.

Further thanks go to the great folk in the Perl and ASP golf communities. You always surprise me with wonderful things that can be done with code of which I am sure the inventors of the languages never thought. And I thought that after so many years I knew all the tricks…

And of course, my family: my parents for taking me to see the world so early in my life. You gave me my love for travel, languages, learning, and books. I hope my teaching you golf can repay this in at least a small way. And my nephew Karim who at three years of age makes me rediscover the world whenever I play with him.

TABLE OF CONTENTS

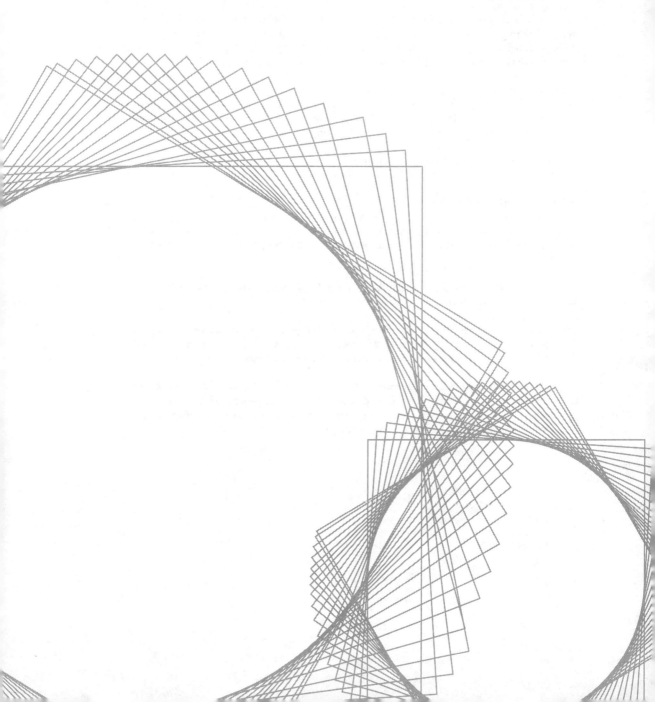

Table of Contents

Table of Contents

Table of Contents

Table of Contents

INTRODUCTION

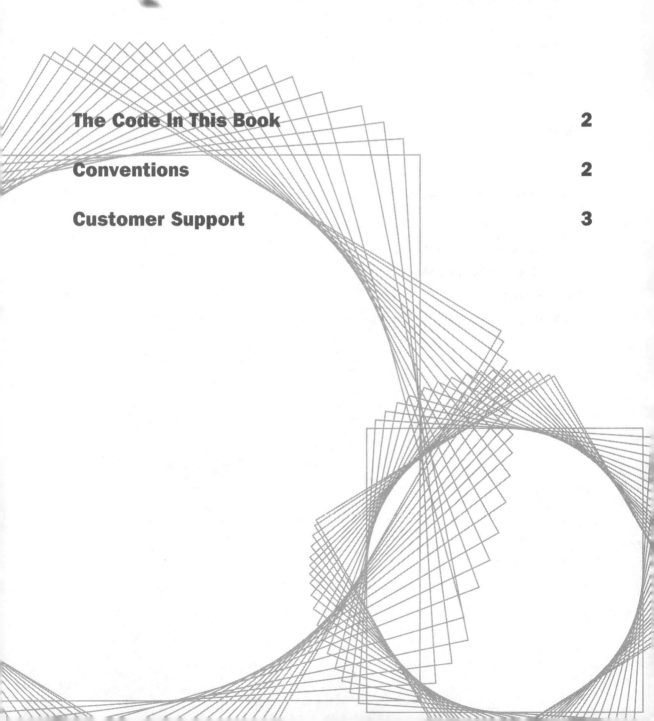

Introduction

The SharpDevelop project started as a "one man show" in September of 2000, just a few months after Microsoft released an Alpha of what was to become .NET 1.0 in early 2002. SharpDevelop is Mike Krüger's brainchild, and he got started because he was disappointed with current programming languages, and did want to try out the new programming language C#. As there was no really good programming editor aside from betas of Visual Studio .NET – which he didn't have access to – he just started to program what he needed.

The SharpDevelop core team – who wrote this book – consists of programmers who came aboard during the Beta of .NET because they wanted to see how "real" Microsoft's new platform was and how good or bad an experience it would be to program with it. Your best bet to learn a new platform is to test it with an ambitious "proof of concept" project, and that is what SharpDevelop initially was: pounding .NET and C# to see if it is viable in real-world applications.

Today, SharpDevelop is a full-featured Integrated Development Environment that leverages the features of C# and .NET, and we can say that both met or exceeded our expectations for building powerful real-world applications.

Over the course of more than two years of development, we learned a lot about this platform. This book is about sharing our experience in building real applications using .NET and C#. You will learn about design issues and decisions made, techniques and technologies used, as well as background information on features of SharpDevelop that you won't usually find in everyday applications.

SharpDevelop is an evolving open-source application, with new features being added over time that are not covered in this book. The code accompanying this book is available on the Wrox press web site. You can always get the latest C# source code from http://www.icsharpcode.net/, compare it with the code for this book and learn how code evolves and how we and our contributors implement new features.

The SharpDevelop team

The Code in This Book

All of the code in this book is taken from the 0.92 beta release of SharpDevelop.

We have tried to present the code in a form similar to the actual source files. Sometimes, because of our desire to fit as much information into the book as possible, we have had to reformat the code slightly to make it more concise.

Some things that we have done to make code more concise are:

- ❑ Removing lengthy comments
- ❑ Replacing XML comments with standard comments
- ❑ Removing whitespace
- ❑ Collapsing multiple closing braces onto single lines
- ❑ Placing long lists of parameters onto single lines

We encourage you to look at the original source files in the code download for a true view of the coding style used in the SharpDevelop project.

Conventions

We've used a number of different styles of text and layout in this book to help differentiate between different kinds of information. Here are examples of the styles we used and an explanation of what they mean.

Code has several styles. If it's a word that we're talking about in the text – for example, when discussing a for (...) loop, it's in this font. If it's a block of code that can be typed as a program and run, then it's also in a gray box:

```
if (categoryTable  == null )
```

Sometimes we'll see code in a mixture of styles, like this:

```
if (categoryTable  == null )
{
  categoryTable = GetChildCategories(-1);
  System.Web.HttpContext.Current.Cache["categories"] = categoryTable;
}
```

In cases like this, the code with a white background is code we are already familiar with; the line highlighted in gray is a new addition to the code since we last looked at it.

Advice, hints, and background information come in this type of font.

> **Important pieces of information come in boxes like this.**

Bullets appear indented, with each new bullet marked as follows:

- **Important Words** are in a bold type font.

- Words that appear on the screen, or in menus like the Open or Close, are in a similar font to the one you would see on a Windows desktop.

- Keys that you press on the keyboard, like *Ctrl* and *Enter*, are in italics.

Customer Support

We always value hearing from our readers, and we want to know what you think about this book: what you liked, what you didn't like, and what you think we can do better next time. You can send us your comments, either by returning the reply card in the back of the book, or by e-mail to feedback@wrox.com. Please be sure to mention the book title in your message.

How to Download the Sample Code for the Book

When you visit the Wrox web site, www.wrox.com, locate the title through our Search facility or by using one of the title lists. Click Download Code on the book's detail page, or on the Download item in the Code column for title lists.

The files that are available for download from our site have been archived using WinZip. When you've saved the archives to a folder on your hard drive, you need to extract the files using a decompression program such as WinZip or PKUnzip. When you extract the files, the code will be extracted into separate folders for each chapter of this book, so ensure your extraction utility is set to use folder names.

Errata

We've made every effort to make sure that there are no errors in the text or in the code. However, no one is perfect and mistakes do occur. If you find an error in one of our books, such as a spelling mistake or a faulty piece of code, we would be very grateful to hear about it. By sending in errata you may save another reader hours of frustration, and, of course, you will be helping us to provide even higher quality information. Simply e-mail the information to support@wrox.com – your information will be checked and, if correct, posted to the errata page for that title, and used in reprints of the book.

To find errata on the web site, go to www.wrox.com, and simply locate the title through our Advanced Search or title list. Click the Book Errata link below the cover graphic on the book's detail page.

E-Mail Support

If you wish to query a problem in the book with an expert who knows the book in detail, then e-mail support@wrox.com with the title of the book and the last four numbers of the ISBN in the subject field of the e-mail. A typical e-mail should include the following things:

- The **title of the book**, the **last four digits of the ISBN** (8171), and the **page number** of the problem.

- Your **name**, **contact information**, and the **problem** in the body of the message.

We need the above details to save your time and ours – we *never* send unsolicited junk mail. When you send an e-mail message, it will go through the following chain of support:

❑ Customer Support – Your message is delivered to our customer support staff, who are the first people to read it. They have files on most frequently asked questions and will answer anything general about the book or the web site immediately.

❑ Editorial – Deeper queries are forwarded to the technical editor responsible for that book. They have experience with the programming language or particular product, and are able to answer detailed technical questions on the subject.

❑ The Authors – Finally, in the unlikely event that the editor cannot answer your problem, they will forward the request to the author. Wrox authors are glad to help support their books. They will e-mail the customer and the editor with their response, and again all readers should benefit.

The Wrox support process can only offer support for issues that are directly pertinent to the content of our published title. Support for questions that fall outside the scope of normal book support is provided via the community lists of our http://p2p.wrox.com/ forum.

p2p.wrox.com

For author and peer discussion, join the P2P mailing lists. Our unique system provides **programmer to programmer**™ contact on mailing lists, forums, and newsgroups, all in addition to our one-to-one e-mail support system. If you post a query to P2P, you can be confident that the many Wrox authors and other industry experts who are present on our mailing lists are examining it. At p2p.wrox.com, you will find a number of different lists that will help you not only while you read this book, but also as you develop your own applications. Particularly appropriate to this book are the aspx and the aspx_professional lists.

To subscribe to a mailing list, just follow these steps:

1. Go to http://p2p.wrox.com/.

2. Choose the appropriate category from the left menu bar.

3. Click on the mailing list you wish to join.

4. Follow the instructions to subscribe, and fill in your e-mail address and password.

5. Reply to the confirmation e-mail you receive.

6. Use the subscription manager to join more lists and set your e-mail preferences.

Why This System Offers the Best Support

You can choose to join the mailing lists, or you can receive them as a weekly digest. If you don't have the time (or the facility) to receive the mailing lists, then you can search our online archives. Junk and spam mails are deleted, and your own e-mail address is protected by the Lyris system. Queries about joining or leaving lists, and any other general queries about lists, should be sent to listsupport@p2p.wrox.com.

CHAPTER 1

Features at a Glance

Before we start looking at the code that implements SharpDevelop, we need to have a clear idea about what features Sharp Develop provides. The aim of this chapter is to run through the key features that we will be looking at later in the book.

Although SharpDevelop is free of charge and free for you to adapt as per your needs, it sports all the features of its full-blown commercial counterparts such as Delphi/Kylix or Visual Studio. When writing code in SharpDevelop, we get syntax highlighting, code completion, method insight, XML based project management, and we can even design Windows Forms!

In the course of our discussions, we will be covering the following topics:

- ❑ Customizing SharpDevelop
- ❑ Customization for Coding using various languages
- ❑ Managing Projects
- ❑ Creating Windows Forms

Before we start looking at goodies such as syntax highlighting or project management, we will discuss the customization of SharpDevelop's user interface to fit our personal requirements. The next section, *Customizations for Coding*, will then introduce us to using templates and wizards, which saves us from having to write most of the general code structures encountered in daily practice. We will also talk about other desirable features, such as code completion, method insight, a powerful search and replace, and so on.

Another important feature of a full-featured IDE is project management. We will be discussing project management in SharpDevelop. Last, but not least, we will be covering the Windows Forms designer that helps us to easily create Windows Forms.

The idea behind SharpDevelop

Yet another IDE? You might well ask this. Our answer is: Why not? Some time ago, Microsoft proposed a new software architecture called 'Windows Next Generation Services', which then became .NET. It looked like a good idea from the start. So once we got wind of this new architecture, we were curious and wanted to see what could actually be done with this platform as soon as we could get hold of one of the early betas. These betas only contained command-line tools, so doing our own proper development tool seemed like a good idea. Mike decided try doing just that. After a modest start, implementing something akin to Notepad, things took off.

With Free/Open Source implementations of the Microsoft .NET architecture on which SharpDevelop runs and on which we developed it happening as this book is written, there will some day be one IDE for multiple platforms – OS and hardware-wise. The Eclipse project is aimed towards this goal too, but the approach taken is different as it is based on Java integrating other languages into the IDE. We aim to use .NET and its free implementations as a platform for integrating development, including non-.NET platforms such as Java or the GNU Compiler Collection. If you have a programming language you want to use and a compiler/interpreter for it, you can 'plug it in' and develop using SharpDevelop!

Chapter 2 has a discussion of the history of SharpDevelop in terms of design decisions. If you are interested in seeing a full evolutionary tree of the SharpDevelop IDE please refer either to the Change Log (Help | About and then click on the ChangeLog tab) or online at http://www.icsharpcode.net/OpenSource/SD/Changes.asp.

SharpDevelop Software Requirements

As a developer, you are strongly advised to run SharpDevelop either on Microsoft Windows 2000 or Microsoft Windows XP. Other Windows platforms such as Microsoft Windows NT4 or Microsoft Windows 9x are not recommended, as the .NET Runtime offers only limited support. For example, if you intend to develop ASP.NET applications and use Windows NT4, you need the Windows NT Option Pack. Developing ASP.NET applications on Windows 9x is not possible, as the .NET Runtime and/or other Windows components do not offer full support.

Since SharpDevelop relies on the Microsoft .NET Runtime you have to install the free downloadable .NET package. Therefore, either the redistributable .NET Runtime or the .NET Framework Software Development Kit must be installed prior running the SharpDevelop IDE. As the .NET Framework SDK installation has several benefits compared to the redistributable package, (for example, it has comprehensive documentation for developers) the .NET Framework SDK installation is recommended.

You might now ask what the hardware requirements are. SharpDevelop will run on slower PCs, but if you want to use resource-consuming features such as Code Completion and hate lags, you should be equipped with a modern CPU, enough RAM (more than 128 MB), and for best viewing experience, a resolution of 1024x768 pixels is recommended.

Now, it's time to present the features of the SharpDevelop IDE. The next section of this chapter provides you with a brief tour to get you acquainted with the most important features of the IDE.

SharpDevelop's Panels and Views

After SharpDevelop has launched you will see several panels. If SharpDevelop was started for the first time, the panels are in their default alignment:

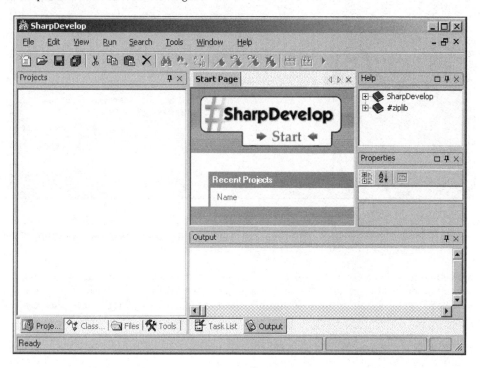

On the left-hand side at the botom you can see a tabbed panel that includes Project Scout (Projects tab), and the tabs of the Class Scout (Classes tab), File Scout (Files tab) and the Tool Scout (Tools tab). The Project Scout displays the contents of a Combine (a collection of linked projects) or project. Using the context menu, you can set the properties of the Combine or projects. The Class Scout lists all classes and class members of a project hierarchically. The Class Scout makes navigation through your project's class members very easy, as double clicking on a member jumps to the location where it was declared.

The Project Scout and the Class Scout are discussed later in this chapter and at source code level in Chapter 13. The File Scout lists directories and files, and opens files as you double-click them. In other words, it is a simple file manager. The Tool Scout contains several handy tools, which are accessed by clicking on the appropriate tab. Clicking on a tab reveals a list view of contained items. For instance, if you click on the Clipboard ring tab, you can easily paste previously copied code snippets into your source code. However, there's more. The Tool Scout offers an ASCII table, C# documentation tags, and license headers that can be inserted into your files:

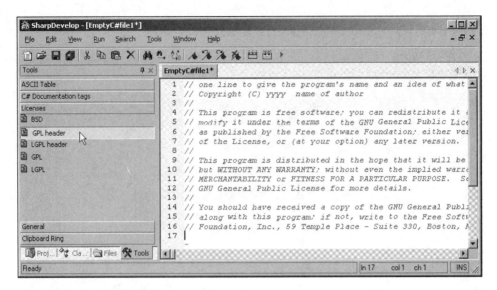

If a Windows Forms project is opened and you are in the design view, you see the Forms tab in the Tool Scout. The Forms tab lists all Windows Form Controls that can be dragged and dropped into the design view. The design view itself is described later in this section.

If you need help, you can access SharpDevelop's built-in help either by choosing one of the entries of the help menu or clicking on the entries of the help pad. Help pad's default location is on the right-hand side of SharpDevelop's main window. You can expand the topics by clicking on the plus sign and double-click on the entry. The page is opened in SharpDevelop's main window:

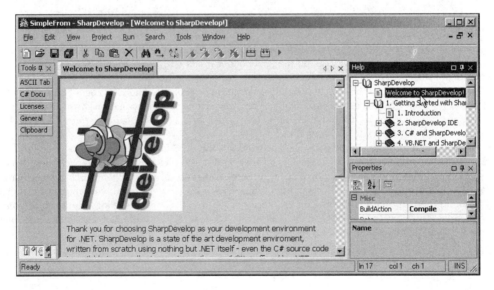

The **Properties** pad's default location is at the right-hand side below the **Help** pad (see previous screenshot). The properties pad contains a list of the properties of the currently opened item. For example, if a file is currently visible in the main window, the pad lists the respective properties of the file or if a Windows Form Control is selected you can edit the control's properties:

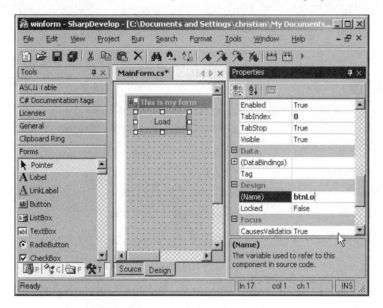

The **Task List** pad and the **Output** pad contain a listing of build errors and compiler messages, respectively.

These two pads' default location is at the bottom:

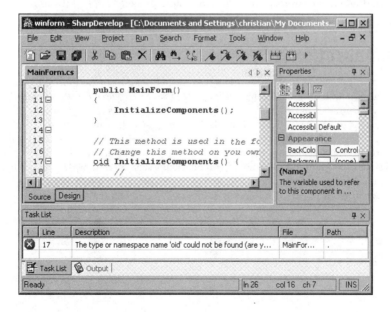

This was just a glance at the pads in SharpDevelop. For more in-depth information on pads please refer to Chapter 13.

Before we move on to the next section, a few words on the Editor view and the Design view. The Editor view is the standard view where you write your source code. The Design view is accessible when working on a Windows Forms project and let's you drag and drop controls from the Tool Scout to a Windows Form.

Limitations

SharpDevelop comes with a broad range of features. However, some might ask what features are not included in the IDE. The following list contains some common IDE features that are not currently provided:

❑   Debugging support

❑   Windows Installer projects to build .msi files

❑   Database and business process modeling tools

❑   Application stress test tools

Customizing SharpDevelop

Before we start writing code we want to customize the UI to our needs and preferences, as this allows us to get the maximum benefit. SharpDevelop allows several customizations to fit our needs. We won't be discussing the entire range of the customisation options, like changing screen layout, changing the tool bar, and so on. Rather, we will focus our attention to customizing some of the more important features of SharpDevelop.

Internationalization

Any competitive application needs to implement internationalization support; SharpDevelop was built with this design aspect in mind. The default language that SharpDevelop starts up with is English (represented as International English). However, apart from English, SharpDevelop supports many other languages, as well. These include French, German, Japanese, and others.

SharpDevelop also supports non-Latin languages like Japanese, Russian, Korean, and so on. If our operating system is configured to use non-Latin character sets, then SharpDevelop will automatically display these character sets correctly. For instance, if you prefer Japanese as your UI language your customized SharpDevelop will look something like this:

Support for internationalization is a daunting task that must not be underestimated. This feature affects the application's core and, hence, has to be integrated into the application's structure from beginning. Although, to some extent, internationalization design aspects are discussed in the Microsoft .NET Framework SDK documentation, (search for "Internationalization" and/or "Satellite Assemblies"), there are sometimes good reasons to reconsider these suggestions and fit the design to the application.

In Chapter 7, we will be getting an in-depth view on planning internationalization support for an application, and about implementing this feature programmatically.

The next entry in the Option panel is Visual Style; this settings dialog deals with the visual appearance of the SharpDevelop IDE.

Defining the Appearance

Different programmers – different preferences! As we know, in any document-based application there are two possible ways to work with documents. On the one hand, there is the Multiple-Document Interface (MDI), on the other there is Single-Document Interface (SDI).

Under MDI, every document resides in the same instance of the application and is accessed by clicking on the appropriate tab of the document interface. Thus, an MDI application has a main window containing multiple MDI child windows inside it.

The SDI interface starts a new instance of the application for each document, so that there is only one window, which contains the respective document.

From the Visual Style option, we can select either the Multiple Document Layout Manager or the Single Document Layout Manager. The choice is purely a matter of personal preference.

These two distinct styles are managed by the LayoutManager, which is described in greater detail in Chapter 6.

Customizations for Coding

Writing code is hard work. We therefore expect a bit of support for easing repetitive tasks, such as completing and/or inserting chunks of code, highlighting keywords, and so on. Programmers favor less typing and using shortcuts over retyping commonly used code constructs. SharpDevelop offers a wide range of features for making the coding process more efficient and easier.

Getting Started with Templates

In this section, we will cover code templates and wizards. These utilities help us to reduce the amount of effort involved in writing recurring snippets of code. As the results of these utilities provide the basic constructs, all that is left to do is to fill in the gaps.

Assuming we have a C# file open, we just have to type in the shortcut for the desired template. For instance, typing `forb` and then pressing the space key will provide us with a basic skeleton of the `for` statement. This skeleton would look like:

```
for (; ; ) {
}
```

The only task left for the programmer, as mentioned before, is to fill the gaps of the skeleton with meaningful values.

If we are not sure of a template's shortcut text, we can type *Ctrl+J,* when the caret (the keyboard cursor) is active in the edit view. This will pop up a listbox containing the complete list of template constructs available to us. From within this list, we can then select the desired template.

The templates are not hard-coded. If necessary we can edit, add, or remove these templates.

Object-oriented programming languages require classes. As classes tend to get complex, an easy way of safely defining them is always appreciated. SharpDevelop provides us with a class wizard that offers several options to save us from having to write standard code.

The class wizard is available from the **File Wizard** panel; under this panel it is listed as **New Class Wizard**. To bring up the **File Wizard** panel click on File | New | File… menu.

In this screen, we can define the base class and its access modifiers, add it to a project, and of course set its name.

The pages that follow allow implemented interfaces to be selected along with formatting options, license text, and more.

Changing Syntax Highlighting

Black and white code listings are harder to read and understand than code listings in which the key words are highlighted. SharpDevelop offers us several modes for highlighting our code.

Syntax highlighting is applied in the editor view (the area where you write your code). SharpDevelop comes with several built-in modes of syntax highlighting for different languages.

Chapter 9 will explain the highlighting strategy in detail.

Code Completion and Method Insight

As we write code, we make use of class members, such as methods or properties. It would be quite helpful if we have a list of the available class members handy. This avoids typing mistakes and in cases where a large number of classes and their members are involved (for example, the .NET Base Class Library) code completion makes coding a lot easier.

A simple example is writing code to display some text to the console. When we finish writing `Console` and type the dot operator '.', a list pops up with all available members of the `Console` class:

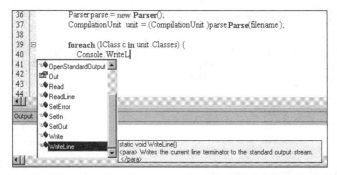

The help bubble, next to the listbox, offers a short description of the active element of the list. To read more about code completion refer to Chapter 13. The engine used to obtain the completion data is described in Chapter 12.

Method insight allows us to view the parameter list of methods of the BCL as well as for the methods in the user-defined classes. This helps to maintain the correct parameter order and thus avoids introduction of manual errors. The following screenshot shows a simple example of method insight:

```
dbconn.cs*                                              ◁ ▷ ✕
13
14
15    class DBConnection
16    {
17        public static void Main(string[] args)
18        {
19            string strConn ="Initial Catalog=Northwind;Data Sour
20            string strSecuritySetting = "Integrated Security=SSI
21            int nTimeout = 10;
22            DBConn MyDbConn = new DBConn();
23            MyDbConn.Connector(strConn,str|
24        }
              void DBConn.Connector (string DbConn, string SecuritySetting, int TimeOut)
25    }
26  }
27
```

The help bubble next to the code completion list displays the return type of the `Connector` method plus its parameter list. You can read more about method insight and its implementation in Chapter 13.

Bookmarks

SharpDevelop's bookmark management allows us to easily manage bookmarks in our source code. Bookmarks can be toggled by:

- ❑ Clicking on the Toggle Bookmark option available from the Search menu
- ❑ Clicking on the flag button located on the standard toolbar
- ❑ Pressing *Ctrl+F2* after placing the caret at the desired line

A dark green background represents a bookmarked line. Moving back and forth between the bookmarks is made possible by the navigational keys or buttons respectively. In Chapter 10, we will cover the bookmarking feature in detail.

Search and Replace Functionality

SharpDevelop's search and replace functionality comprises various features, ranging from the usual searching of strings to the use of Regular expressions or Wildcard search. The design strategy behind the search functionality is covered in detail in Chapter 10.

The Find dialog is accessed from the Search menu, through the binocular button of the standard toolbar, or through its shortcut, *Ctrl+F*:

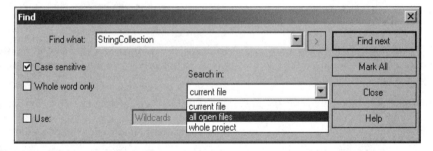

The Mark All button highlights all the results found for the designated search target. The search target offers the option to search in the current file, all open files, or the whole project.

The Replace dialog box offers, as the name suggests, the option to replace the findings with a new string.

Compiling the Code

After writing the code, the next logical step is to compile it. In SharpDevelop, we can compile a combine, a project, or just a single file. We will be talking about combines in a minute. To start compilation, we can use the commands available in the Run menu or click on the buttons shown in the following screenshot:

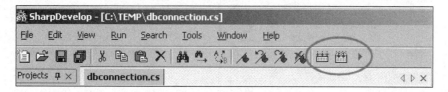

During compilation, if any errors occurred then the Task List (the output window) will display these errors. By simply clicking on the error listing, we can jump to the line of our code concerned.

Managing Projects

A feature that makes an IDE complete is the facility for managing our projects. SharpDevelop offers several features to achieve this goal.

Combines and Projects – What's in a Name?

A combine can contain one or more projects, thus it can be thought of as an 'uberproject', the mother of all projects. This name was chosen to avoid any conflicts with existing trademarks. The contents of a combine (or project) are displayed in the Project Scout. An overview of the Project Scout is given in the *Navigating the Project* section of this chapter.

Navigating the Project

Navigating through a project is as easy as using the Windows file explorer. The tree view of the Project Scout displays the content of a project and the Class Scout lists all the classes of the currently opened project.

The Project and Class Views of the World

Typical views of the Project Scout and Class Scout will be similar to these screenshots:

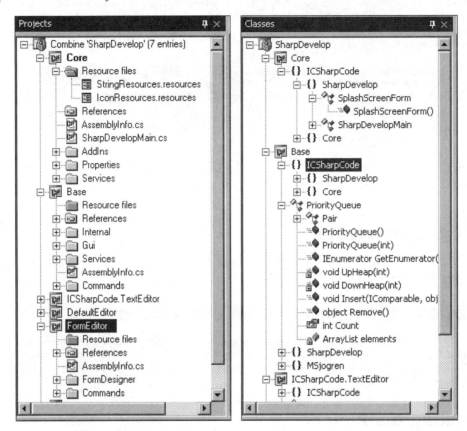

The Project Scout allows easy navigation and assignment of various settings of its items by right-clicking on the entry – a file, project, or combine.

The class view is also displayed as a tree view. A typical view of the Class Scout is as shown above.

The Class Scout gives us a detailed overview of the various classes involved in our project. To find out more about this feature implementation please refer to Chapter 14.

Creating Windows Forms

SharpDevelop features a built-in Windows Forms designer. Using this designer we can easily add controls to a Windows Form, edit their properties, and even format them. Everything starts with a new project or, as mentioned before, we can create a single file without a project. As the implementation of a Forms designer is no trivial task, the final three chapters of the book are devoted to this interesting topic.

Adding Controls to Windows Forms

Let's assume that we want to create a new C# project, for this click on File | New | Combine.... The New Project dialog box pops up – select the Windows forms project entry under the C# node, then provide a name for the project and click on OK. When the new Windows Form project is loaded, two new tabs appear below the editor view – the Source tab and the Design tab. Clicking on the Source tab shows the source code view of a general Windows form structure.

As we are interested in the Designer, click on the Design tab located next to the Source tab. Additionally, click on the Tools tab to access the available Windows Form Controls. We should now see a window that looks something like this:

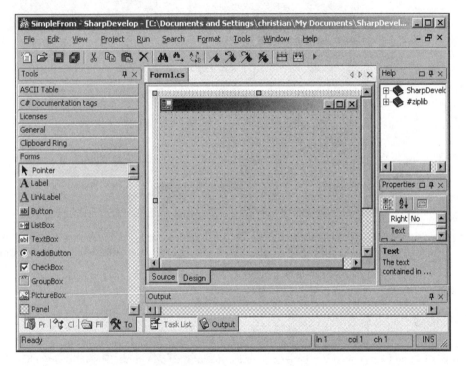

The Tool Scout, selected by the Tools tab, allows us to click and drag Windows Form Controls onto the previously created blank form. After we have some Controls on the form, we will need to edit their properties.

Properties and Formatting of Controls

To format a Control, right-click on the Control and we will see the Control's formatting options. The context menu allows aligning Controls, setting the tab order, and so on:

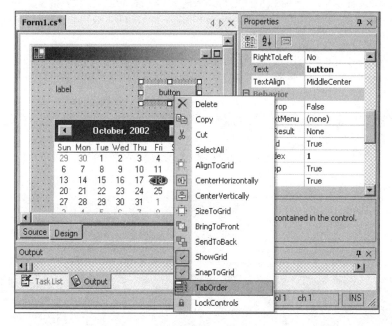

The Control's properties are located on the left on the default setting. Of course, we can rearrange the panels as SharpDevelop supports Window docking. The property panel allows us to edit the Controls in a very intuitive way.

Summary

In this chapter we breezed through the major and most prominent features of the SharpDevelop IDE. As this was just an overview, this chapter presented no source code at all. The following chapters will explain the presented features in far more detail, and will discuss the design decisions and technical aspects involved, by revealing and stepping through the source code.

CHAPTER 2

2

Designing the Architecture

In this chapter, we will be looking at the history of SharpDevelop and its basic design concepts. Also, we will be discussing the practices used in the SharpDevelop development process. Some of our practices and methods might seem unusual, but we want to tell the truth about our development process; at some places it's quite contrary to the procedures prescribed for an ideal development process but we will explain why this is. This chapter lays the foundation for understanding the succeeding chapters and, in any case, it's good to know how a technology was developed. We will be presenting some complex structures in this book, so understanding the thinking behind the processes at work is necessary.

History of Architectural Design Decisions

In this section, we will step backward in time to the early days of SharpDevelop. This will be helpful to us in understanding the current design of SharpDevelop. Miguel de Icaza (the founder of Gnome and the Mono project) once said that, "One day you have to tell the whole story." Now that day has come for SharpDevelop.

Mono is a cross platform .NET implementation; refer to www.go-mono.com for more information

The Early Stages

It all began in September 2000 when Mike Krüger came across the PDC version of the .NET framework Microsoft just had released. He had some experience in programming under Linux but had never written a Windows application before. When he saw C#, he thought that C# was a better language than Java and decided to write an IDE for it since at that time a good, free IDE was missing for this language.

The unofficial version is that he had just too much time (which has since dramatically changed) and was looking for a bigger programming project to spend this time on.

The initial programming of SharpDevelop began with a Windows text editor, which was customized for C# highlighting. After a short design phase (1-2 days) the development of SharpDevelop began.

Initially, there was just a main MDI window with a .NET rich textbox, which was able to open text files. It could load and save the text and run the `csc.exe` (the C# compiler) over the file and then execute the output file it generated.

It didn't take long to realize that the limits of this rich textbox weren't acceptable for an IDE project; therefore, the next step was to write an integrated editor, with facility for syntax highlighting. It took two weeks to complete a simple editor and a basic project management tool with a tree view showing all project files, and to make the whole system stable enough to develop SharpDevelop using SharpDevelop itself.

Building SharpDevelop with SharpDevelop

The first editor was relative simple. Text was represented as a simple `ArrayList` that contained strings. Each string was a line of text. The lines were generated using the `System.IO.StreamReader` class.

Before this data structure was chosen, other data structures, such as storing the lines in a list, were considered. The list-based structure would solve the line insertion penalty. If a line is inserted into an `ArrayList`, all other elements have to be moved back one element to make room for the element to be inserted. This wouldn't be a problem with list-based data structure where a line insertion operation consumes constant time.

However, the list-based structure suffers in other areas, such as getting the correct line object from a line number or offset. To get the real line, it would have taken linear time (the same time as line insertion in an array). A decision was made to have the 'slow' part happening during insertion, as we thought it was more important to get a specific line fast than making the insertion of lines efficient. Therefore, it seemed natural for us to work with the `ArrayList` structure.

We didn't want to optimize the editor for large files – we only wanted to have a source code editor capable of working on files having less than 10,000 lines. Another approach would have been to store the text in a linear data structure that handled lines by itself. Other editors have taken this approach and we were aware of it, but we didn't find any good literature to help us with this issue.

If we insert a character into a line it shouldn't take much time, because this affects only a single line. But making the whole buffer linear would have taken too much insertion penalty for every operation. The array for the buffer is much larger than the array for just lines; hence, it makes an insertion slower. Therefore, we decided to use the line-based structure.

The first editor split the line into words and these words had colors assigned to them. The words got a default color (black) and then were compared with the C# keywords. This way, some basic syntax highlighting was added to the IDE.

One of our earliest considerations was the syntax-highlighting problem. It was clear to us that built-in syntax highlighting would cause more problems than it solved. Built-in highlighting would not be customizable without recompiling the whole project. It provides no easy way of extending the syntax highlighting for new languages other than changing the source code. We chose to define the syntax highlighting in XML, since this enabled us to move this part out of the IDE; it also enabled us to support syntax highlighting for other programming languages than C#.

We looked at the implementation of syntax highlighting in other editors and determined the different features implemented in them. Our first XML definitions were the way it is now. It looks a bit like the definitions used in JEdit (http://www.jedit.org). In Chapter 9, we will be discussing these definition files in detail.

In spite of studying other editors, we didn't change the syntax highlighting definitions; only some minor issues were addressed (like renaming the tags according to our changed XML naming scheme – the first version had upper case tag names whereas now we use camel casing). But, the overall structure didn't change much. With this matter of syntax highlighting settled, there was still another major issue left– the text editor was extremely slow.

The limiting factor for our editor's speed was the drawing routine, which re-drew the entire editor window whenever the text was scrolled, even if it was by a single line. The text area repainted the whole text for each scrolling operation. No smart drawing was used. This was sluggish on most machines.

This problem was solved by having the system redraw only those regions that had changed. This was done by using a control that knew the size of the whole text. This control got moved around on the panel. The .NET Framework paints only the region that has changed and takes care of fast scrolling.

This speeded up the editor a lot, but in turn created another problem – the control size limit of 32,768 pixels. With the Courier font at 10 points, the editor control was limited to 2,178 lines. The editor could load more lines, but the control cut them off.

With this limit, SharpDevelop ran for about one and a half years. For the development of SharpDevelop this was enough; as all SharpDevelop code files are smaller than 2,000 lines this limit of the editor posed no real problem.

Later, we switched back to self-drawing; the drawing routines are faster in newer .NET versions, but slower than the old 2178 lines version. The text editor will be discussed in Chapter 11.

However, back to our story, SharpDevelop was first made public in August 2000 through an announcement in the Microsoft .NET newsgroups. It got a lot of positive feedback and therefore, the development continued.

The design direction changed a bit away from a C#-only IDE to a more general development environment. But even now, C# is the best-supported language under the IDE. This is not due to design decisions, it is just that there are not so many people working on support for the other languages. In early 2001 an add-in (also known as plug-in) infrastructure was introduced.

The first add-in structure was for menu commands defined in external dynamic link libraries using XML. This was a very limited solution and add-ins could only be used to plug into a special add-in menu. Another separate add-in API was implemented to allow the extension of editor commands.

During 2001, SharpDevelop got support for internationalization. The internationalization model has not changed since then. A key string is used to identify the string in the internationalization database. The internationalization data is generated out of a database and is written into resource files. There is a resource handler class that handles the different languages and returns the localized string. Detail on internationalization in SharpDevelop can be found in Chapter 7.

Correcting Bad Design Decisions

In December 2001, the editor's data structure was changed from a simple `ArrayList` with strings to a linear model. The editor was almost rewritten from scratch and this time the objective was to separate the editor's code from the IDE's code, more than before. The old editor was a monolithic monster. Fortunately, large parts of the old editor's code could be reused and translated into the new model.

The decision to switch to the new model was made because by then we had found the literature on text editor programming; besides, we had also looked at the implementation of text models in other editors. With this, the problem of having to perform too many copy operations when using a linear model was also solved.

The old line-based structure had some problems. It copied too many strings and had some complicated algorithms for insertion/replace and so on, which took too much time. The performance was poor in the old model. Now, the text editor data structure was turned into a separate layer underneath the control and the simple `ArrayList` was dismissed. In Chapter 8, we will delve deeper into the new data structure.

Now, the editor itself keeps track of where a line begins or ends. To find a line from an offset (this is a common operation as the model is offset based, but the display is not) it takes O(log n) time. (For example: there are roughly 20 operations for finding a line, if there are one million lines in our list.) The lines are stored in a sorted list and the search is done using the binary search algorithm. This makes the operation necessary for finding a line from a given position nearly as fast as in the line-based model. In this model it was simple, as the line number was equal to the array list position.

In January 2002, we solved one of the biggest issues in the whole development process – the add-in problem.

Our dream was to have add-ins that could be extended by other add-ins. For example, we wanted to have an add-in that could browse assemblies. This object browser should be in an external assembly and just plug into SharpDevelop. But it should also be possible for other developers to extend this object browser. It should be possible to insert a command into the object browser's context menu or do other similar things.

The AddIn tree solved this problem and much more. The AddIn tree is capable of defining add-ins using an XML format as glue code, which might be placed almost anywhere using a path model.

Once we started using this structure development sped up. We could safely add new extendable components, without breaking other parts of the source code. We could throw away bad components without harming the project.

The XML definition of our AddIn tree was also inspired by Eclipse, it has a similar definition but eclipse works differently from the way SharpDevelop does. See www.eclipse.org for more details on Eclipse.

We will be discussing the AddIn tree in Chapter 3.

The development of a C# Parser began in 2001 but the development process was quite slow. It took a lot of time, not because it was too difficult, but because it was done in our spare time (the spare time left besides the time we sacrificed to SharpDevelop).

We chose not to use the CodeDOM facilities of the .NET Framework because we need to get information about the position of types, methods, etc. Using CodeDOM would have forced us to extend each CodeDOM class with custom properties. Our own parser tree layer has proven to be helpful; we use it for more than just the parser.

The first time code completion worked in SharpDevelop was in Spring 2002.

Unfortunately, we did not think about a general parse tree. We needed a parse tree that was abstracted from the parser in SharpDevelop. This meant that we had to change the parser output. The parser wasn't rewritten – a new abstract layer was created, which took the reflection API and our own parser tree layer as an example of how to develop a .NET class model. Then interfaces were defined for all .NET class features and an abstract implementation for them was written to make it easier to implement this layer.

After this, the parser was restructured to fit in with the new structure and it worked quite well, even though the parser wasn't written with flexibility in mind. After the long development phase, the parser was relatively stable and capable of parsing source code at a high level.

We will be looking at the parser in Chapter 12.

Now it is even possible to plug-in any sort of parsers and have working code completion and method insight for the languages that those parsers generate a parse tree for.

The Design Decisions

There were clear design requirements for the application. SharpDevelop should be easy to deploy. Just copy and run the project. This approach to software deployment is known as 'Xcopy deployment', as is used with MS .NET technology.

We didn't want to use an installer, nor did we need one. We had a strong Linux background where the installer concept is perceived as being a bit strange because we were used to simply downloading, compiling, and running software. Besides, we couldn't find any good open source installers that would solve our problems. However, now we are using an installer, respecting the Windows traditions, but it is always an option to just download the .zip file with the source code, build it, and run SharpDevelop without needing any installer support.

The IDE should not assume that any special drive or directory exists. It should only assume that there is a SharpDevelop application folder, nothing more. The .NET environment is aware of the location of the user's application folder and it takes care to see that it exists and is in the right place (with write permission). All options and other data that are to be written somewhere should be stored in the user's application data folder, as SharpDevelop should run in a multi-user environment without hassles. Therefore, every user has an independent copy of the standard option files, which they can change without affecting any other user.

Another important goal was the 'do not touch the registry' design decision. SharpDevelop should not create registry keys or assume that some registry keys exist. It should use the registry as a workaround only if there is no other feasible alternative. This allows easy copy and run installation, and will also allow easier porting to systems that do not have a registry.

Another important decision was to use XML for every data file, and to move as much data from the code to XML as possible. XML is a powerful format that allows easy conversion using XSLT. It adds a lot of extra flexibility to SharpDevelop and is used whenever possible in SharpDevelop development.

Fortunately, the .NET platform makes it extremely easy for us to use XML in our applications. In fact, the NET platform relies on XML for its applications. More importantly XML helps us in cleaning up code; often the code is bloated with information that could be easily stored in a separate file. In this code many properties are being set, and objects are created without doing anything with them. They just have to be stored somewhere. All these are signs of code that could be written with XML instead.

A good example is the GUI code where buttons, forms, group boxes, and other controls are defined. Each of these has properties assigned to it, information on where it is, which label it has, and other details. This code doesn't really add functionality to a program. It just defines the way something looks. XML is a good way to collect all this data in a file. So we began to use XML to reduce the actual code size.

Currently some panels and dialogs that are defined by Windows Forms depend upon the XML format. Most forms are still missing; one of our next steps will be to design a better XML format for dialogs and panels. We plan to use a format that works with Layout management. SharpDevelop should run under a wide range of operating systems (currently it is only Windows based) with different languages. For the time being, the dialogs and panels may look a bit strange when big fonts are used or when a non-standard screen resolution is chosen. Some (human) languages use rather lengthy strings in labels and these are cut off.

Another important issue is the use of the MVC model in SharpDevelop.

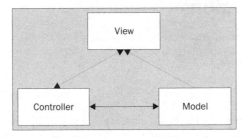

As we can see from the diagram, the controller is between the view and the model and it communicates with both of them. The view needs to display the data. Therefore, it needs to read the model. It does not need to make changes to the model so this communication is one-way.

For example, the text editor (in this chapter we won't go into implementation details, but this is a good example) has a data model called the 'document'. In this model, text is stored, which is broken up into lines. We use edit actions to change this text and a Control (in Windows Forms terms) to display our text.

The Control that displays the text represents the view in our MVC model. The edit actions correspond to the controller (even if they are implemented using more than one class) and the model is implemented by the document layer. The edit actions see to it that the view is updated and even call for redisplay for some actions. The document layer, however, doesn't know anything about the view. All these parts are independent of each other. We have tried to apply this model to the whole project.

This is especially important if we want to be able to switch the GUI API. History has shown us that GUI APIs come and go. If you know a bit about Java you may have noticed that Java AWT (the first version of a Java GUI framework) was replaced by Java Swing, and some time back IBM released SWT (the most recent Java GUI toolkit from IBM).

This could easily happen with the .NET platform, too. In fact, there is no reason why it shouldn't. Therefore, in our design we took care to provide for this eventuality. Even if we always use the same GUI API, it is a good idea to make the view 'switchable'. In this way, it is possible to change the view, if so desired, or even to develop several different views for the same data. As a bonus, this model helps to think in terms of components, thereby, leading to a component-oriented approach.

Designing Component-Exchangeability

SharpDevelop aims to allow configuration changes on the fly, such as switching the user interface language at run time or altering the layout at run time. This had led to a component-oriented approach in which the components interact with each other through a common model.

We have designed a model that allows us to change components as we desire. For example, we may remove the class browser without breaking anything in SharpDevelop. This was done using a component model that is tree based. All components are loosely coupled, making SharpDevelop programming a bit like using Lego building blocks.

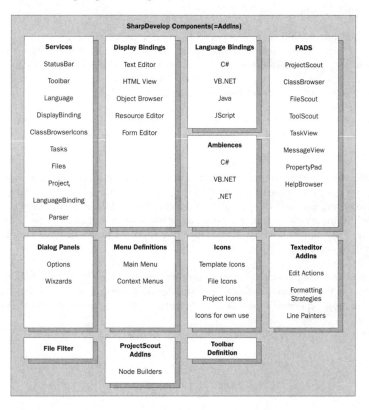

This is a quick overview of the SharpDevelop components. As you can see, we have quite a huge number of components that form the SharpDevelop project. With our add-in system, we can manage all these components, and we believe that it is general enough to add all the future components we will need as well.

Best Practices

During the development of SharpDevelop, we've found some practices that we considered very helpful. In the following sections we'll step through two of them – pattern oriented design and general coding guidelines. Our aim is to present information about the design process that you may find useful.

Being aware of the best practices used during a development process helps a lot in ensuring that the process is smooth and avoids many potential pitfalls.

Design Patterns

In this section we will give a brief overview of the design patterns used in developing SharpDevelop. We began to use design patterns relatively late in the development process, as we weren't aware of the benefits they provide for our design process. Design Patterns try to solve the flexibility problem, but not through inheritance. Inheritance does this at the compile time (it is not possible to change the type of a class during run time). Using Design Patterns enables us to change the behaviour of an object at run time.

If you have further interest in design patterns and design-pattern-driven design, we recommend you to look at the book *Design Patterns* from Gamma, Helm, Johnson and Vlissides (ISBN 0-201-63361-2). Even though the book does not contain C# examples, the concepts behind patterns are described very well. However, in this book we have explained the necessary patterns with care, so even if you don't have an in-depth knowledge of design patterns you can easily understand them.

Design Patterns are neither voodoo nor boring theory. Design Patterns provide a list of common solutions that are used in real-world applications, and have been proven to be useful in a number of different projects.

Apart from the better structure and enhanced flexibility that the pattern-oriented approach provides to SharpDevelop, we found design patterns useful for better understanding of the structure, without having to use UML. However, note that design patterns do not replace UML. In fact, they complement each other well. UML is important for understanding complex systems but in case the UML diagrams are missing, patterns make life a bit easier. Knowledge of patterns is useful and knowing how to apply them to our projects is a good thing.

The patterns listed here are not exactly same as they are given in the *Design Patterns* book. Instead, they are described the way as they are used in SharpDevelop. We do not redefine patterns but it might be possible to see the same pattern explained a bit differently in other texts. But the concept is always the same.

We will be looking at following patterns:

❏ Singleton

❏ Factory

❑ Decorator

❑ Strategy

❑ Memento

❑ Proxy

Singleton

The singleton pattern is the pattern-oriented way of creating global variables. The singleton ensures that there is only one instance of the singleton class during run time. It provides us with a global access point to it as well. Lately, most singletons in SharpDevelop are being replaced by services, but the service manager itself follows the singleton pattern, as well as some other classes of minor importance.

We use the singleton pattern when we are sure that we need only one instance of an object during the run time of our application.

An example of the singleton pattern is as given:

```
class ExampleSingleton
{
  public void PrintHello()
  {
    System.Console.WriteLine("Hello World!");
  }

  ExampleSingleton()
  {
  }

  static ExampleSingleton  exampleSingleton = new ExampleSingleton();

  public static ExampleSingleton Singleton {
    get {
      return exampleSingleton;
    }
  }
}
```

Note that, the singleton object has only private constructors. This ensures that an object cannot be created from our singleton class outside the singleton class; thereby allowing us to ensure that there is only ever one such object.

Factory

The factory pattern creates an object out of several possible classes. For example, when we are working with an interface and we have more than one implementation for it, we can use a factory to create an object that implements the interface; the factory can select the implementation that it returns to us.

A factory is useful when the creation of an object should be abstracted from the end product (for example, in cases where a constructor won't be good enough):

```csharp
public interface IHelloPrinter
{
    void PrintHello();
}

public class EnglishHelloPrinter : IHelloPrinter
{
    public void PrintHello()
    {
        System.Console.WriteLine("Hello World!");
    }
}

public class GermanHelloPrinter : IHelloPrinter
{
    public void PrintHello()
    {
        System.Console.WriteLine("Hallo Welt!");
    }
}

public class HelloFactory
{
    public IHelloPrinter CreateHelloPrinter(string language)
    {
        switch (language) {
            case "de":
                return new GermanHelloPrinter();
            case "en":
                return new EnglishHelloPrinter();
        }
        return null;
    }
}
```

In this example you need to create an object from `HelloFactory` and this factory creates a `IHelloPrinter` given a language. This adds a bit more flexibility to the design.

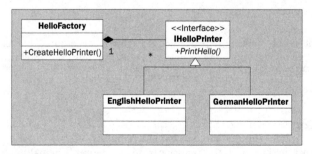

This is the UML diagram for our example. With this pattern, we can easily add new concrete `HelloPrinter` classes to our `HelloFactory` that can be created without letting the users of the factory know that other implementations are added. The classes that use `HelloPrinter` classes only need to know the factory class.

Decorator

The decorator pattern adds functionality to an object at run time. The decorator inherits from an interface; it extends and implements all methods in this interface. It receives an object that implements this interface in the constructor and delegates all calls that the original interface exposes to the object it received through the constructor.

The decorator can add a number of functions that the original interface doesn't have. This is useful for adding functionality on the fly. In SharpDevelop we have classes that convert our internal abstract layer for classes, methods, etc. into a human readable string. A decorator is used to extend these classes so that they can return human-readable strings for the .NET Framework reflection classes too. Classes that convert the reflection classes to the SharpDevelop model are implemented separately. This helps us to reduce the code duplication.

Another approach would have been to implement the reflection conversion decorator as an abstract base class leaving the conversion methods abstract and have all converters implement them. This approach, however, forces the conversion classes to inherit from a single base class. Also, this does not leave much flexibility in the inheritance tree, as .NET supports only single inheritance. The design pattern approach is superior to this.

Imagine that some of the language converters need some different conversion methods. Then we can simply write another decorator, which adds these methods without making the inheritance tree more complex.

This example uses the factory example as a base to demonstrate the decorator pattern:

```csharp
public interface IHelloPrinterDecorator : IHelloPrinter
{
  void PrintGoodbye();
}

public abstract class AbstractHelloPrinterDecorator : IHelloPrinterDecorator
{
  IHelloPrinter helloPrinter;

  public AbstractHelloPrinterDecorator(IHelloPrinter helloPrinter)
  {
    this.helloPrinter = helloPrinter;
  }

  public void PrintHello()
  {
    helloPrinter.PrintHello();
  }

  public abstract void PrintGoodbye();
}

public class EnglishHelloPrinterDecorator : AbstractHelloPrinterDecorator
{
  public EnglishHelloPrinterDecorator(IHelloPrinter helloPrinter)
   : base(helloPrinter)
  {
  }
```

```
   public override void PrintGoodbye()
   {
     System.Console.WriteLine("Good bye!");
   }
}

public class GermanHelloPrinterDecorator : AbstractHelloPrinterDecorator
{
   public GermanHelloPrinterDecorator(IHelloPrinter helloPrinter)
   : base(helloPrinter)
   {
   }

   public override void PrintGoodbye()
   {
     System.Console.WriteLine("Auf Wiedersehen!");
   }
}
```

We let the decorator inherit from an abstract base class too, but the decorator code is more static (in the sense that it won't change) than the `HelloPrinter` classes.

The `IHelloPrinterDecorator` adds a `PrintGoodbye` method to our classes to extend their functionality. There are two implementations of the decorator, which we can apply to the simple `HelloPrinter` classes to give them a new method.

You can use even a German decorator with an English hello printer, but this might cause some strange effects.

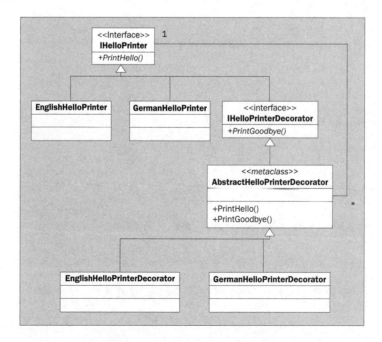

In this diagram, we can see that the real `HelloPrinter` classes can inherit from another class without problems. Other decorators can be added to it without problems. The `HelloPrinters` can change their decorator at run time and extend their functionality dynamically.

Strategy

The strategy pattern is one of the most frequently used ones in SharpDevelop. With this pattern we can encapsulate algorithms and change them at run time. For example in our search algorithm, we use a searching strategy. We have two implementations for normal text search and regular expression search and we can change the behavior of our search object at run time. This pattern is in contrast to the decorator where we change the skin; with strategy, we change the guts!

Let's look at an example to demonstrate this:

```
using System;

public interface IHelloStrategy
{
   string GenerateHelloString();
}

public class EnglishHelloStrategy : IHelloStrategy
{
  public string GenerateHelloString()
  {
    return "Hello World!";
  }
}

public class GermanHelloStrategy : IHelloStrategy
{
  public string GenerateHelloString()
  {
    return "Hallo Welt!";
  }
}

public class HelloPrinter
{
   IHelloStrategy helloStrategy;

   public IHelloStrategy HelloStrategy {
     get {
       return helloStrategy;
     }
     set {
       helloStrategy = value;
     }
   }

   public void PrintHello()
   {
     if (helloStrategy != null) {
```

```
        Console.WriteLine(helloStrategy.GenerateHelloString());
      }
   }
}
```

As we can see, it is similar to the factory pattern but the factory pattern alters the object at creation time, whereas the strategy can be switched on the fly.

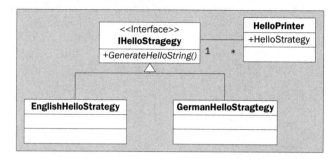

In the diagram, we see that the `HelloPrinter` has a special strategy and that a strategy can be applied to a number of `HelloPrinters` to give them the functionality.

The strategy pattern is useful to encapsulate algorithms for which we know a bad but easy-to-implement solution and a good but difficult to implement solution. We can implement the bad but easy solution first and test our code with this bad solution. With this pattern we can later implement the better solution without changing the code calling the algorithm.

Memento

A memento simply stores the state of an object to restore it later. For example, we use mementos in SharpDevelop to store the state of the workbench and to store information about the file (like highlighting, caret position, or the currently used bookmarks in the document).

Memento's are used in places where the objects should not expose their internal state to the outer world using public members. Some other good reasons to use mementos would be to allow the user to save the state of the workbench at run time and to allow them to switch between several former saved states.

Here's an example of implementing a memento:

```
public class OurObjectMemento
{
   int    internalState;
   string anotherState;

   public int InternalState {
      get {
         return internalState;
      }
   }

   public string AnotherState  {
```

```
      get {
        return anotherState;
      }
    }

    public OurObjectMemento(int internalState, string anotherState)
    {
      this.internalState = internalState;
      this.anotherState  = anotherState;
    }
  }

  public class OurObject
  {
    int     internalState = 0;
    string anotherState   = "I know nothing";

    public OurObjectMemento CreateMemento()
    {
      return new OurObjectMemento(internalState, anotherState);
    }

    public void RestoreMemento(OurObjectMemento memento)
    {
      this.internalState = memento.InternalState;
      this.anotherState  = memento.AnotherState;
    }

    public void DoStuff()
    {
      internalState = 42;
      anotherState  = "I know the question too";
    }

    public void PrintState()
    {
      System.Console.WriteLine("current state is {0}:{1}",internalState,
                               anotherState);
    }
  }
```

As we see, the memento itself exposes all internal variables from our `OurObject`. In SharpDevelop, all mementos can convert themselves to XML (and back). This makes the object state persistent.

Proxy

The proxy pattern is used when we need to handle objects that take a lot of time to create, are complex, or take too much memory. The proxy pattern allows us to postpone the creation of the 'big' object until it is actually used.

In SharpDevelop, proxies are used to represent the classes of the .NET runtime. These proxy classes only have the name of the real classes, take much less memory, and are faster to load. They do not contain information about the class members; hence, when these are requested, the real class must be loaded.

This example uses the factory pattern as well:

```csharp
public class HelloPrinterProxy : IHelloPrinter
{
  string language;
  IHelloPrinter printer = null;

  public HelloPrinterProxy(string language)
  {
    this.language = language;
  }

  public void PrintHello()
  {
    if (printer == null) {
      printer = new HelloFactory().CreateHelloPrinter(language);
      if (printer == null) {
        throw new System.NotSupportedException(language);
      }
    }
    printer.PrintHello();
  }
}
```

This `HelloPrinterProxy` class creates the actual printer object when the `PrintHello` method is called for the first time. If we have a case where we need many objects (in our case from `IHelloPrinter`) that would take up many resources and only some of them are actually ever used, proxies should be used.

Now imagine that the `HelloPrinters` are remote objects and we store them in a hash table, where the key is the language that the printer can print. Now imagine the `HelloPrinters` receiving their strings from a remote server. Further let's assume that every creation of a `HelloPrinter` consumes 5 MB of RAM. In such a scenario it makes sense to store the `HelloPrinter` proxy classes in the hashtable. Besides, it is generally the case that only one `HelloPrinter` is needed in the application:

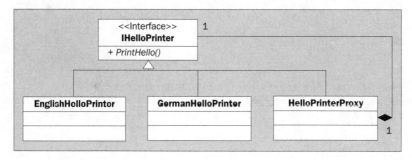

As we can see from the diagram, the proxy class is just an implementation of the interface that the actual big class implements. The classes that use HelloPrinters don't know the difference between the proxy implementation and the real ones.

This concludes our discussions on patterns. In the next section we'll be learning about the SharpDevelop coding style.

Coding Style Guideline

As is all always the case, we found it quite useful to have strict guidelines regarding the coding style. It has helped to enhance the readability of the code and in reducing the time required for understanding complicated parts. All examples in this book are written according to this style guide.

It contains various guidelines for various important aspects like:

- ❑ File Organization
- ❑ Indentation
- ❑ Comments
- ❑ Declaration
- ❑ Statements
- ❑ Whitespace
- ❑ Naming Conventions

For an in depth coverage of our coding style guideline, you can refer to the `CodingStyleGuide.pdf` file. This file is included along with the distribution of SharpDevelop and can be found in the `SharpDevelop\doc` directory.

Now let's look at another interesting topic – the tools that we have used for tracking and removing bugs in SharpDevelop.

Defect Tracking and Testing

For an open source project, it is sometimes forgotten that software should not be released until it has been reasonably tested and debugged enough to qualify as practical and usable software. There have been quite a few open source projects out there that seem to have missed out on this principle. What is even worse is that a large number of the reported bugs get never fixed. This is not because the programmers are evil; it happens because they do not observe decent bug tracking practices.

Fortunately, times have changed a bit and most projects now use advanced defect tracking and testing techniques. SharpDevelop does so too.

Bug Tracker

One important tool, which we have used for SharpDevelop, is the bug tracker. It is an online application to which every team member can submit bugs:

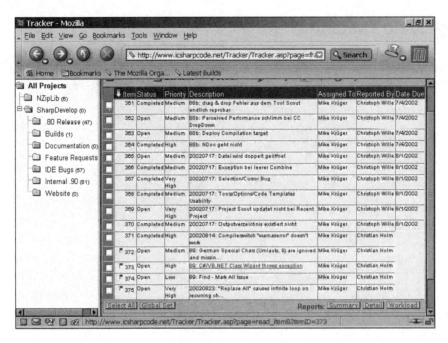

Whenever we had some spare time, these bugs were then resolved. The bug tracker is a tool that only team members can access.

Prior to the bug tracker era, the bugs were filed on paper, but paper always tends to get lost. This application version of bug tracking is much more robust than the paper version. It also takes too much time to put all submitted bugs on paper. With a bug tracker, one can just cut and copy the submitted bugs to a centralized database. We can even attach images, and track the bug's history.

Before each release, it is our goal to fix as many bugs from the tracker, as we can manage.

Let's now discuss the testing strategies that we used during the development of SharpDevelop.

Unit Tests

For a GUI application, it is more difficult to apply unit tests, but they too profit from unit testing. One important lesson we had to learn during the SharpDevelop project was that code should be written with tests in mind. It is difficult to apply tests to code that was not written with tests in mind.

SharpDevelop is an application that does not have many unit tests. This is due to the fact that it was necessary to write a new unit test application (#Unit) that can handle loading assemblies from different directories, as the SharpDevelop assemblies are not all located in one directory. However, even with these few tests written much time was saved. Bugs were found that would have not been found so easily otherwise. For example, sometimes, when the text area has changed the change broke a part of the text area (maybe the line representation) and often these bugs appear only on few cases like an 100% empty file. The unit tests do check this case and others too. Manual tests can easily overlook one case, but automatic unit tests don't.

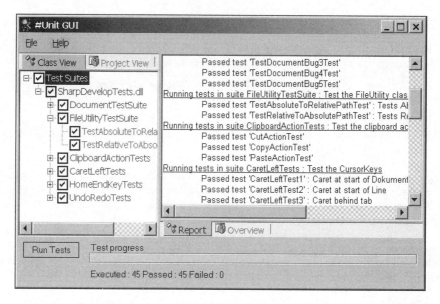

Lately, unit tests have been written for the document model and the edit actions. Writing unit tests is a good way to prevent bugs from being reintroduced, and to make sure that the functions work as specified.

We had wanted to write a unit test for every bug found, but this has proven to be a difficult task, as many bugs are GUI-related and unit testing for GUI code is generally difficult. For example, the caret gets incorrectly drawn as it is drawn 3 pixels above the line. Now, this type of bug can only be verified visually. However, we are trying to extend our unit test suite to make SharpDevelop more robust than it is now. Besides, this would also gives an extra layer of safety, even if code is restructured.

For the rest of the chapter, we will be discussing restructuring and other SharpDevelop practices. Some of them are unusual, but keep in mind that the SharpDevelop development team is small. Only one person has written the majority of the code (and read too much of the design patterns book and about refactoring practices!).

Refactor Frequently

Refactoring is the most important practice we have used in the development of SharpDevelop. If you want to read more about refactoring, we recommend you to read *Refactoring: Improving the Design of Existing Code* by Martin Fowler and others (ISBN 0-201-48567-2).

Refactoring consists of a list of simple rules that can be applied to a program's source code to enhance its structure, without having to break the program. These rules range from simple renaming to redesigning of the object structure.

One day, I was asked if there were some aspects of the design for which we would have preferred to choose another path. All I can say in answer to this question is, "If there is, we would choose the other path now." There is nothing wrong in taking an unknown approach. If a project is started with a development team that hasn't done something similar in nature before, it is natural to make wrong decisions, or at least some that are not as good as they might be.

During the development of SharpDevelop we had made many bad design decisions, some of them are:

❑ We started out by using a 'wrong' data structure for developing the text editor. We had used an `ArrayList` of lines, but now we have opted for a linear block model.

❑ Earlier in the process, the text editor was built into SharpDevelop; now it is a component which can be used in other applications too.

❑ Initially, the overall structure was fragmented, and we had various kinds of XML formats describing the connections between components; now we have the AddIn tree, which solves many of our old problems.

I could give many more examples. The point is that, whenever we felt that we had taken the wrong approach we simply restructured our design, even if it meant we had to restructure a large part of the project. It is not as much work as it first seems to be and in the long run it helped us a lot and didn't even hurt anybody (not even Clownfish, which is our mascot).

Sometimes, because of refactoring, we had to remove a feature from SharpDevelop, but it always got re-implemented again later in much better quality and in less time. Some parts were structured on a whiteboard; some parts have evolved from first tries. But every part has needed refactoring.

Design and Refactoring

Below I have listed some of our experiences with refactoring. Note that this list isn't a hard guideline that we used for every case. However, it does give a very good idea about how the program evolved. Here is a list of our refactoring rules:

❑ If you don't understand a method, break it down into smaller ones and give them proper relevant names.

❑ Favor readable/understandable code over code with more performance.

❑ Don't design too much today; tomorrow it will be so much easier.

❑ No amount of refactoring is too much.

❑ Use Assertions wherever possible.

❑ Solve each problem at its root.

❑ Last but not least an important rule: Eat your own dog food.

If You Don't Understand a Method, Break it into Smaller Ones

The SharpDevelop project manager always complains that there aren't enough comments in the SharpDevelop source code. However, the code is commented (but not necessarily in the manner he wishes). Now you might ask how this contradiction arises.

It's quite simple. The interfaces and services that people use are commented in the .NET way with XML comment tags. But the implementations are not commented very well.

For each method, we attempted to find a good name that explains what the method does. If someone doesn't understand a method, it is either a sign of a bad name or a too lengthy method, which should be further broken down.

Commenting is just as important, but it is more important to comment how the methods interact with each other or how the code works. Giving all methods XML documentation tags results often in just copying the method name, and gives a bad explanation such as this:

```
// This method returns back the user name.

string GetUserName()
{
  return userName;
}
```

This style of comment is fine when you know that you need this method, or when you write a library that other people use, or when you only want to provide XML documentation for your project, and you don't want to write documentation manually.

If a method isn't easy to understand, it should be considered harmful and refactored. C# is a language that is relatively easy to read. We have had enough experiences, where the methods often got cut off into different methods or that they ended up being thrown away.

Again, if every method were to have extensive documentation, then the development process would take much more time than it normally does.

The comments on how the method does things should be done through developer comments (that is, non-documentation comments). Programmers can refer to these comments when they change something later on.

More important is general documentation about the infrastructure, how classes interact with each other, or some UML drawings of the infrastructure. In SharpDevelop, we've used UML drawings only on the whiteboard and very few actually have seen the outside world. Hopefully, this book will change this by providing us with a decent documentation on the way things are done in the SharpDevelop project.

Favor Readable Code Over Code with Better Performance

I know some people would love to kill me for saying this, but let me explain myself. When I began programming (in the late 80s), a good programmer was a programmer who could optimize the code in a such way that people who learn coding in this century wouldn't have imagined it to be possible. But this optimization had a cost – maintainability.

We often find that a method isn't quite understandable, because the programmer optimized it for performance rather than readability. In this case, some performance should be sacrificed to enhance code maintainability. Let's illustrate this point with an example from the SharpDevelop source code.

The SharpDevelop's `SaveFile` method can be written like this:

```
public void SaveFile(string fileName)
{
  ... // some stuff

  string lineTerminator = null;
  switch (lineTerminatorStyle) {
    case LineTerminatorStyle.Windows:
```

```
          lineTerminator = "\r\n";
          break;
        case LineTerminatorStyle.Macintosh:
          lineTerminator = "\r";
          break;
        case LineTerminatorStyle.Unix:
          lineTerminator = "\n";
          break;
    }

    foreach (LineSegment line in Document.LineSegmentCollection) {
      stream.Write(Document.GetText(line.Offset, line.Length));
      stream.Write(lineTerminator);
    }

    ... // close stream etc.
  }
```

In this code listing, concentrate on the part that is responsible for determining the line terminator for different operating systems. We have an enumeration giving the line terminator style. But we need some code that gives us the byte representation for the line terminator styles.

At first sight, this approach isn't easily understandable (now try to imagine 100 methods like this, where we need to read the code twice). If there is a bug in the code that prevents us from getting the correct line terminator, we can't even write a unit test for this bug. It might accidentally be reintroduced in the source code. Remember, no code is small enough to be bug free.

A better approach is to put the switch statement into its own method:

```
string GetLineTerminatorString(LineTerminatorStyle lineTerminatorStyle)
{
  switch (lineTerminatorStyle) {
    case LineTerminatorStyle.Windows:
      return "\r\n";
    case LineTerminatorStyle.Macintosh:
      return "\r";
    case LineTerminatorStyle.Unix:
      return "\n";
  }
  return null;
}
```

This enhances readability considerably. We have a self-describing variable for the switch, and have also encapsulated the switch in a method that can be unit tested. Generally, smaller chunks of code are more understandable (and writing unit tests for them is easier).

Now, we can set the string with this method, but we create a temporary variable that is only used once in the code:

```
string lineTerminator = GetLineTerminatorString(lineTerminatorStyle);
foreach (LineSegment line in Document.LineSegmentCollection) {
```

```
    stream.Write(Document.GetText(line.Offset, line.Length));
    stream.Write(lineTerminator);
}
```

Now imagine that we have 5-6 lines of code between the `lineTerminator` = statement and the `foreach` statement; this reduces code maintainability (and this can happen when someone does not take care when inserting some lines in the code). Temporary variables are good in many cases, but they are often used excessively.

Instead, the SharpDevelop code implements in the following way:

```
foreach (LineSegment line in Document.LineSegmentCollection) {
    stream.Write(Document.GetText(line.Offset, line.Length));
    stream.Write(GetLineTerminatorString(lineTerminatorStyle));
}
```

Now, we have saved a line but at the cost of performance. Let's look at some practical numbers – I saved a file with 10,000 lines on my notebook, the optimized version of this code took about the same amount of time as the readable/less-optimized version. This is an important lesson – don't optimize when there is no need for it.

If you aren't sure what is faster, try it out and compare the timings. The compiler and the runtime do a lot of optimization for us, so never assume that you might do it faster. Always be sure to test it using exemplary test cases. Even if the readable version is not as fast as the optimized version, we should only optimize it if there is a real need for optimization. In other words, optimize only in critical sections. A profiler can help us in finding these critical sections.

Don't Design too Much Today; Tomorrow it Will be so Much Easier

This is another practice people won't believe, but for the SharpDevelop project it has worked. Maybe you know the old Spathi (a race in Star Control II, a computer game from 1992) saying, "Don't let me die today, tomorrow it would be so much better."

This rule is my version of this saying. It's not because I dislike working on design (in fact I do a lot of designing), but I also know that requirements will always change. Therefore, we shouldn't try to make the code much more flexible or general than it needs to be. We also know that programmers learn more over time, therefore a simple design that works is enough for the moment. If needed, we can always refactor the code later.

Don't confuse simple design with bad design; simple designs are not bad. A simple design is a design that solves our needs now; we can always refactor toward a more sophisticated design later on (should the need arise). But be careful, if you know some reason why your simple design would fail, don't use it.

No Amount of Refactoring is too Much

Often refactoring seems to be impossible or too great a challenge and, therefore, refactoring is avoided. However impossible it may seem, we can always break the refactoring process into little steps, each of which can be done separately, without breaking the whole program. Even if refactoring means much work now, it always means less work later on. More importantly, even if refactoring seems to be a lot of work, in reality it isn't; often it just seems to be much more work than it actually is.

Of course, the unit tests for the code refactored must be ported over to the new structure too, or new unit tests must be written. But in many cases this is very easy.

Use Assertions Wherever Possible

Another practice that helped us a lot in the design and implementation is the use of assertions inside the code. .NET provides an `Assert` method, which checks whether an expression is `true` and if not, it will display an error message box containing the stack trace (the user can decide if the application should continue or be stopped).

Every time a variable ought to have a specific value or a comment might be useful for reporting the variable value at this point, an assertion does this better. The `Debug.Assert` method is only called when the `DEBUG` symbol is defined (in the debug build). In the release build, these assertions won't be called.

```
Example of an assertion in SharpDevelops open file method :
public void OpenFile(string fileName)
{
  Debug.Assert(fileUtilityService.IsValidFileName(fileName));
  …
}
```

This example checks whether the filename is valid and if it is not, a message box appears showing the stack trace and we see the bad code, which gave us an invalid filename. These checks should be done before the `OpenFile` method is called. The checks are done in the GUI code to determine whether a filename is valid or not.

By the way, the function that checks the filename for validity is very valuable. Therefore, it is listed here under the best practices. It is a good example of being a little finicky about what the user might input or functions may think is a valid filename:

```
public bool IsValidFileName(string fileName)
{
  if (fileName == null || fileName.Length == 0 || filename.Lengt >= 260) {
    return false;
  }

  // platform independent : check for invalid path chars
  foreach (char invalidChar in Path.InvalidPathChars) {
    if (fileName.IndexOf(invalidChar) >= 0) {
      return false;
    }
  }
}
```

```
// platform dependent : Check for invalid file names (DOS)
// this routine checks for follwing bad file names :
// CON, PRN, AUX, NUL, COM1-9 and LPT1-9
string nameWithoutExtension =
        Path.GetFileNameWithoutExtension(fileName);
if (nameWithoutExtension != null) {
    nameWithoutExtension = nameWithoutExtension.ToUpper();
}
if (nameWithoutExtension == "CON" ||
    nameWithoutExtension == "PRN" ||
    nameWithoutExtension == "AUX" ||
    nameWithoutExtension == "NUL") {
  return false;
}

char ch = nameWithoutExtension.Length == 4 ?
        nameWithoutExtension[3] : '\0';

return !((nameWithoutExtension.StartsWith("COM") ||
        nameWithoutExtension.StartsWith("LPT")) &&
      Char.IsDigit(ch));
}
```

Assertions and check functions are a valuable practice. Unit tests round out the security issues even more. It is always good to strive for robust and secure code.

Solve Each Problem at its Root

This is another important practice that most people don't follow. When a bug pops up somewhere, it might go deeper than just the place where it was first seen. If bugs are fixed at a higher layer and not at their root, then they will turn up where ever the culprit lower-level layer is being used, and ultimately, we will be forced to apply a work around to every piece of code that uses this layer. This kind of bug fixes makes the resulting code hard to understand and every time the buggy code is used, the developers introduce a bug in the code they are currently writing.

Another interesting point is about implementing features. If a feature needs to be implemented, it might be better to put it in a new place, because other parts of the application might need this too, and we can easily share it. The same that is true for bugs, applies to new features as well.

For example, we happened to insert a file watcher into SharpDevelop. The contributor who implemented the file watcher feature put it into the text area code; and it worked, but only for the text area. The object browser, resource editor, or other display bindings were unable to make use of it.

A much better place to include it would have been in the abstract base class implemented by a display binding. If an editor (or viewer) needs the file watcher features, it can just implement this class and turn it on (or off) and all parts of the application can profit from the file watcher feature. One reason for doing it in this sloppy way was because the person didn't think about the other display bindings. Another reason was the lack of proper communication, within the project team

I know that it is hard to post to the mailing list something like, "I'll implement a file watcher and want to put it in the text area." This is mainly because developers don't want to look dumb. But discussing technical issues and overall design should not be considered dumb. Developers do this when they are at the same place. But curiously, this doesn't happen when they work in different places, and have instant messengers and e-mail to share thoughts. This is the reason why all contributions to the main IDE are overseen by the main developer, who knows the overall structure better than anyone else.

Eat Your Own Dog Food

SharpDevelop was a good application to develop, because it itself was being used in the development process for the whole time. It is good to actually use the program that you write. If a program is seen from the user's point of view, UI glitches and missing features (bugs as well) are more apparent.

SharpDevelop has been used since the very first few weeks to develop SharpDevelop. This helped us a lot in improving the features and in fine-tuning them, something that we might have otherwise neglected. This is one practice that makes open source software successful. The programmers who write the stuff usually are their own users too.

Unfortunately, many programmers out there just change their program's behavior instead of improving the code. For example, in SharpDevelop one of the all time worst features was Search and Replace. It's because the developer who developed this feature almost never used it; he did all search and replace operations with ultra edit, as ultra edit had powerful searching features.

Another feature that frequently broke down in SharpDevelop was the template completion window; this window comes up when you press *Ctrl+J*. This happened frequently because the SharpDevelop code developers do not use templates, and hence it was low on their priority list. Later on, this problem was solved by using the same completion window that was used for code completion.

In earlier days, when SharpDevelop had no active VB .NET contributor, the VB .NET support group developed random features too. We have some beta testers, but no tester uses all features of the IDE, and there are some features that no tester ever uses. Lately, we discovered problems with the New Class Wizard, because no tester or core developer actively uses this wizard.

All these examples prove that it is important to view the product from the user's perspective. Bug reports from users are helpful, but we certainly don't want to let all the testing be done by our users. We want to ship a stable product.

Summary

In this chapter, we have discussed the beginnings of SharpDevelop.

We have seen some major design decisions that were made for SharpDevelop, and which are essential for the understanding of the whole structure. We have learned about design patterns and what the MVC model is.

In the *Best Practices* section, we discussed the coding style and it's importance. We also learned about refactoring and about defect tracking and testing. With this knowledge, we can now go on to the next chapter, where we will be discussing the add-in implementation in detail.

CHAPTER 3

3

Implementing the Core

In this chapter, we will learn about the structure that forms the basis of SharpDevelop. As in most applications, the core of SharpDevelop is the executable but unlike most apps it provides only a few basic services in addition to its main task, which is to load and build the so-called AddIn tree. In Chapter 2, we saw the main idea behind the AddIn tree and its history. Add-ins are also called plug-ins, but for the purposes of our discussions we will be using the term add-ins.

In this chapter, we will be discussing the AddIn tree structure it's implementation. We will also be learning about the mechanism of object creation inside the AddIn tree. This chapter is essential for the understanding of the interaction between SharpDevelop and the AddIn tree. After discussing the AddIn tree, we will also look at how SharpDevelop manages property persistence.

The core infrastructure is separated from the rest of the code and can be found in the `src\SharpDevelop\Core` directory. The whole add-in system is in this folder in the subfolder `AddIns` but we encourage you to read the sections about the add-in system before you try to read the source code.

The AddIn Tree

The AddIn tree is a simple tree data structure. There is only one AddIn tree for each instance of SharpDevelop. This is the reason for implementing it by using the singleton design pattern (as seen in Chapter 2).

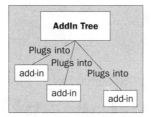

This diagram will give us the basic idea of add-ins; add-ins just plug into the tree and the tree contains the whole system. Physically, an add-in is defined by an XML file and a set of DLLs that are referenced by the XML. The DLLs provide the code, while the XML defines how and where it plugs into the AddIn tree.

We will now take a closer look at the AddIn tree:

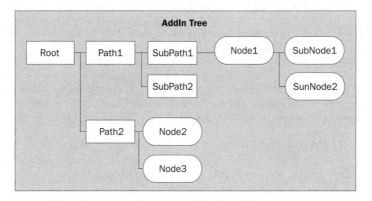

In the above diagram we have two different objects in the tree: nodes and paths.

The AddIn tree is a tree that "binds them all". The add-ins are the nodes of the AddIn tree (the paths are not 'really' add-ins because they have no use other than to structure the tree). The IDE changes its behavior according to what these nodes define. The path to the nodes is structured like a file system. If we want to access SubNode2 we have to specify the location as /Path1/SubPath1/Node1/SubNode2. We see that Node1 is like a path but we will see the difference between a path and a node later. For now, we will just say that nodes are paths that contain definitions of behavior.

All SharpDevelop parts that use the AddIn tree must know the path from which they can obtain the required nodes. For example, the SharpDevelop Options dialog has the path /SharpDevelop/Dialogs/OptionsDialog. In this path, and its sub-paths, only dialog panels are stored. The dialog now grabs all panels from this sub-tree and inserts them into a tree view where they are displayed. In other words, the add-in that defines a particular path also gets to define the (runtime) interface of the nodes that can be inserted below it:

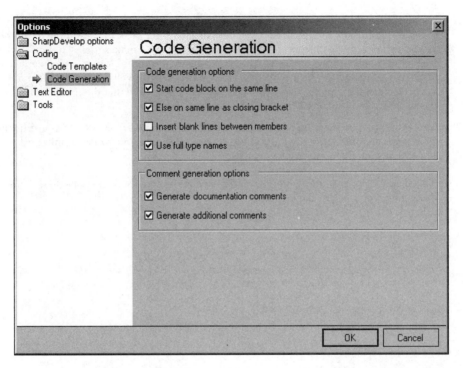

In the left side of the Options panel, in the tree view, we can see our AddIn tree nodes. The folders represent empty nodes and the other tree-view nodes without the folder icon (for example, Code Generation) are the nodes that contain panels (in this case all subnodes of this node are ignored). To add new panels, add-ins just have to insert the correct nodes into the path, and the dialog will show them. All visible elements in SharpDevelop (and most invisible ones too; for example, keyboard commands in the text editor, like cursor keys, are implemented as nodes in the add-in tree) are defined by nodes.

Advantages of Using the AddIn Tree

The AddIn tree has quite a few advantages over the other design approaches:

❑   It allows extension of existing add-ins by other add-ins. The main problem when add-ins are to be extended by add-ins lies in the fact that the existing add-ins have to be informed when the other add-ins perform an action (like building a context menu). This is required because the add-in that want to extend the other must extend the 'actions' of the other add-in and some sort of communication must happen between them. This is the main issue solved with the add-in structure. Unfortunately, this is the hardest one to explain because most people have never encountered this problem or they have not thought about this grade of flexibility (even if they have written an add-in system for their programs).

❑ Another advantage of the AddIn tree is that the `assembly` files containing the executable code need not reside in one directory. They can be stored in any location the developer wants to, and the add-in system will manage the file loading. This makes it easy to implement a "copy and remove" deployment of add-ins. Just copy the add-in folder, which contains an XML definition and the required assemblies, to the SharpDevelop `AddIns` folder and it will work. Remove the directory and the add-in is taken out! Note that the .NET standard is to put all the assemblies into one `bin` directory.

❑ Also with this approach, the add-ins don't have to implement their own add-in structure, as all the add-ins are based on only one system – The AddIn tree. We can customize just any functionality via the same narrow interface.

Now, we will take a look at how deeply the add-in is rooted in the application. Let's begin with the method that runs everything. This method can be found inside the `src\SharpDevelop\Core\SharpDevelopMain.cs` file:

```
public class SharpDevelopMain
{
  static SplashScreenForm splashScreen = null;
  static string[] commandLineArgs = null;

  public static SplashScreenForm SplashScreen {
    get {
      return splashScreen;
    }
  }

  public static string[] CommandLineArgs {
    get {
      return commandLineArgs;
    }
  }

  [STAThread()]
  public static void Main(string[] args)
  {
    commandLineArgs = args;
    bool noLogo = false;

    foreach (string arg in args) {
      if (arg.ToUpper().EndsWith("NOLOGO")) {
        noLogo = true;
      }
    }

    if (!noLogo) {
      splashScreen = new SplashScreenForm();
      splashScreen.Show();
    }

    ArrayList commands = null;
    try {
      ServiceManager.Services.
```

```
        InitializeServicesSubsystem("/Workspace/Services");

    commands = AddInTreeSingleton.AddInTree.GetTreeNode
      ("/Workspace/Autostart").BuildChildItems(null);

    for (int i = 0; i < commands.Count - 1; ++i) {
      ((ICommand)commands[i]).Run();
    }
  } catch (XmlException e) {
    MessageBox.Show("Could not load XML :\n" + e.Message);
    return;
  } catch (Exception e) {
    MessageBox.Show("Loading error, please reinstall :\n" + e.ToString());
    return;
  } finally {
    if (splashScreen != null) {
      splashScreen.Close();

    }
  }

  // run the last autostart command, this must be
  // the workbench starting command
  if (commands.Count > 0) {
    ((ICommand)commands[commands.Count - 1]).Run();
  }

  // unloading services
  ServiceManager.Services.UnloadAllServices();
  }
}
```

First, the Main method initializes the splash screen. This is not overly important, but while we do the real work, that of building the AddIn tree, the user will at least see something.

The try...catch block is rather important. A call is made to the AddIn tree to obtain the tree node /Workspace/Autostart, and then it builds all child items from this node. Later on we will see how this is done.

After this, the for statement casts these built child items into the ICommand interface and the Run method is called (except for the last one).

After the try...catch block, the last command is started. We start it separately to ensure that the splash screen is closed when the last command starts. This last command fires up the workbench form (the main window) of the IDE and runs the message loop.

Note that, in this code listing, we do not see any Windows.Forms code, or where the tip of the day pop-up is launched (this pops up when SharpDevelop starts). Nor do we see the code completion wizard startup code (this wizard is started at the first time SharpDevelop is launched). All of this is done with the help of the AddIn tree. As per our design principles, SharpDevelop does not embed any GUI layer in the Core, giving a good extensibility for any further use of other toolkits. The GUI layer is only implemented when is actually needed by the application.

It is possible to build a completely different application on top of the AddIn tree by just putting other Run commands in the tree. This application can then benefit from the AddIn tree, just as SharpDevelop does. The AddIn tree was not part of SharpDevelop from the start. It started its life as a subsystem of SharpCvs (formerknown as NCvs), and afterwards it was ported over to SharpDevelop and SharpDevelop was refactored to take advantage of this new add-in system. SharpCvs was part of the SharpDevelop distribution but now it is no longer part of it because the project was discontinued and no longer maintained.

When the last Run command returns, the application message loop is assumed to have ended and it is time to clean up; this is achieved through service unloading. We will be taking a detailed look at services in Chapter 5.

Now we will delve deeper into the add-in structure and have a look at the superstructure of the AddIn tree.

The AddIn Tree Superstructure

The AddIn tree is defined by an interface that exposes all the functionality that is used by the rest of the application. To get an overview of the functionality provided by this structure, we will take a look at the IAddInTree interface. It can be found in src\SharpDevelop\Core\AddIns\IAddInTree.cs.

```
public interface IAddInTree
{
  // Returns the default condition factory.
  ConditionFactory ConditionFactory {
    get;
  }

  // Returns the default codon factory.
  CodonFactory CodonFactory {
    get;
  }

  // Returns a collection of all loaded add-ins.
  AddInCollection AddIns {
    get;
  }


  // Returns a TreeNode corresponding to <code>path</code>.
  IAddInTreeNode GetTreeNode(string path);

  // Inserts an AddIn into the AddInTree.
  void InsertAddIn(AddIn addIn);

  // Removes an AddIn from the AddInTree.
  void RemoveAddIn(AddIn addIn);

  // This method does load all codons and conditions in the given assembly.
  Assembly LoadAssembly(string assemblyFile);
}
```

At first, the AddIn tree has the `ConditionFactory` and `CodonFactory` objects. We will be looking at codons in detail later on in this chapter. For now, we will just say that these factories create our AddIn tree node contents. The next property is the `AddIns` property, which is also discussed later in this chapter.

After the `AddIns` property, the method that is really important for us is the `GetTreeNode` method. This is the only method needed by the add-ins to use the AddIn tree. The other methods (and properties) are currently only used internally in the core assembly.

The `InsertAddIn` and `RemoveAddIn` methods may be useful for implementing an add-in manager in the IDE; however, currently they are not used. Now that we know about the most important method of the `IAddInTree` interface, let's look at the definition of an add-in file.

Add-in Definition

We will begin this section by examining a simple add-in file:

```
<AddIn name = "Typed Collection Wizard"
    author = "Mike Krueger"
    copyright = "GPL"
    url = "unknown"
    description = "Creates a typed collection"
    version = "1.0.0">

    <Runtime>
      <Import assembly="TypedCollectionWizard.dll"/>
    </Runtime>

    <Extension path = "/SharpDevelop/Templates/File/TypedCollection">
      <DialogPanel id = "CollectionGenerator"
        label = "Typed Collection"
        class = "TypedCollectionGenerator.TypedCollectionWizardPanel"/>
    </Extension>
  </AddIn>
```

This is a typical SharpDevelop add-in definition, and is written in XML. The root node has attributes about the add-in, these attributes are not currently used in any code but we use them to carry information about the add-in.

The `<Runtime>` node contains information about the assemblies that are required for this add-in to work. This is usually a list of assemblies that contain the classes used in the definition file. After that, an `<Extension>` node is defined, which has a `path` attribute and one child.

In this case, the child is a dialog panel, which has some attributes. This child will be placed under the `/SharpDevelop/Templates/File/TypedCollection` path in the add-in tree. We will call this child a 'codon'. In other words, unlike `<Runtime>` and `<Extension>`, the `<DialogPanel>` node type is not defined by the AddIn tree. Rather it is defined by a mechanism that we called a codon.

We chose the name codon, because other terms that we used had misleading meanings and implications. For example, initially they were called as modules, but this term was misleading and created problems when we tried to explain the concept. Therefore, we decided to choose another name that isn't used anywhere else in computing. The <DialogPanel> node produces an instance of an object type that has its attributes defined by a codon. For reasons of brevity, we sometimes use the term codon to mean the XML node as well.

Objects from this codon class get stored in the tree structure and represent the codon XML nodes at run time and are also called codons. But this rather liberal usage of the term is not a problem since, from the context of our discussion, it is quite clear which codon is meant. In cases where this is confusing, we will use the term 'codon XML node' for the XML nodes, 'codon class' for the class representation, and 'codon objects' for the objects created in the add-in tree at run time.

As we can see, a codon is just an implementation of the ICodon interface, found in the src\SharpDevelop\Core\AddIns\Codons\ICodon.cs file:

```
public interface ICodon
{

  // returns the add-in in which this codon object was declared
  AddIn AddIn {
    get;
    set;
  }

  // returns the name of the xml node of this codon. (it is the same
  // for each type of codon (the name of the XML tag inside
  // the add-in file))
  string Name {
    get;
  }

  // returns the ID of this codon object.
  string ID {
    get;
  }

  // returns the Class which is used in the action corresponding to
  // this codon (may return null, if no action for this codon is
  // given)
  string Class {
    get;
  }

  // Insert this codon after all the codons defined in this string
  // array
  string[] InsertAfter {
    get;
    set;
  }

  // Insert this codon before the codons defined in this string array
  string[] InsertBefore {
```

```
      get;
    }

    // Creates an item (=object) with the specified sub items and
    // the current Condition status for this item.
    object BuildItem(object owner, ArrayList subItems,
                    ConditionFailedAction action);
}
```

All codons know their `AddIn` (the object representation for the definition file). Each codon class must have a unique name. This name is the same as the name of the codon XML node and it must be attached to the codon class with the custom attribute `CodenNameAttribute`. It defines the name of the codon XML node. The `AbstractCodon` base class (see below) uses `CodenNameAttribute` to implement the get property (not shown) as required by interface `ICodon`.

The `ID` is the name of the codon object inside the tree (codons are referenced by their `ID`), therefore no two codons can have the same `ID` when they are stored under the same AddIn tree path. This ID comes from the XML attribute `CollectionGenerator` of the DialogPanel, which we saw before.

The other attributes are `Class`, `InsertAfter`, and `InsertBefore`. These attributes are not required for a codon XML node definition but they get used frequently. Not all codon classes use the `Class` attribute but `InsertAfter/InsertBefore` is used to arrange the codons on the same level.

For some codons, such as dialog panels, this may make sense, while for others like display bindings (these create views for the IDE; we see display bindings in Chapter 6) the arrangement is not important.

The only method that a codon must have is the `BuildItem` method. In our dialog panel codon example, the codons do not implement the control directly – instead they create new panels. This is done with a call to the `BuildItem` method.

Codons can define additional attributes, the values of which they obtain from the XML definition, and can apply them to the objects that they build. The AddIn tree puts these build codons together so that they can be used outside the tree structure.

Now we will take a look at the manner in which a codon class flags the add-in system that it has attributes that need to be read from the codon XML node. One approach would be to use attribute names that are equal to field names in the object. However, this would not give much flexibility; what to do if some field names are not set in the XML? Or what about fields that should not be able to be set inside the XML node? Therefore another approach was chosen – flagging fields by using attributes.

We use the custom attributes feature of C# to define which attributes a codon has, because we need to make it explicit when a codon has mandatory attributes. For example, all codons must have the `ID` attribute defined, so they can be named. Besides the required attribute issue, it is not good if all class fields are treated as potential XML attributes. To illustrate how this works we will look at the abstract implementation, which can be found under `src\SharpDevelop\Core\AddIns\Codons\AbstractCodon.cs`:

```
public abstract class AbstractCodon : ICodon
{
    [XmlMemberAttributeAttribute("id", IsRequired=true)]
```

```
      string id = null;

      [XmlMemberAttributeAttribute("class")]
      string myClass = null;

      [XmlMemberArrayAttribute("insertafter")]
      string[] insertafter = null;

      [XmlMemberArrayAttribute("insertbefore")]
      string[] insertbefore = null;

      // Canonical get/set properties for all attributes seen above are taken
      // out.

      // Creates an item with the specified sub items and the current
      // Condition status for this item.
      public abstract object BuildItem(object owner, ArrayList subItems,
                                       ConditionFailedAction action);
}
```

We can see that `XmlMemberAttributeAttribute` or `XmlMemberArrayAttribute` has been defined before each field in the `AbstractCodon` class. This attribute has one parameter, which is the attribute name that a codon XML node may have. The attribute has an `IsRequired` property and, if it is set to `true`, all codon XML nodes that describe an instance of this class must have this attribute or the `AddIn` class which loads the codon XML node will throw an exception.

Codons have a class attribute, `CodonNameAttribute`, applied that has only one parameter – the codon name. This is the name of the codon XML node. Now that we know about codons in detail, let's look at object generation.

From Tree Node to Running Object

To understand how objects are created, we need to understand the method that is used most often inside the add-in tree:

```
IAddInTreeNode GetTreeNode(string path);
```

As we can see, this method returns an `IAddInTreeNode`. We will now take a look at this interface. It can be found under `src\SharpDevelop\Core\AddIns\IAddInTree.cs`:

```
public interface IAddInTreeNode
{
  // A hash table containing the child nodes.
  Hashtable ChildNodes {
    get;
  }

  // A codon defined in this node
  ICodon Codon {
    get;
```

```
  }

  // All conditions for this TreeNode.
  ConditionCollection ConditionCollection {
    get;
  }

  // Gets the current ConditionFailedAction
  ConditionFailedAction GetCurrentConditionFailedAction(object caller);

  // Builds all child items of this node using the <code>BuildItem</code>
  // method of each codon in the child tree.
  ArrayList BuildChildItems(object caller);

  // Builds one child item of this node using the <code>BuildItem</code>
  // method of the codon in the child tree. The sub item with the ID
  object BuildChildItem(string childItemID, object caller);
}
```

We see that the child nodes are stored in a `Hashtable`. This means that finding a particular tree node is fast. The next property is the `Codon` property. It gives us the name of the codon stored in the node. We will be looking at conditions later on.

For now, we will discuss the `BuildChildItems` and `BuildChildItem` methods.

The `BuildChildItems` method calls `BuildItem` on all child codons (if any) and returns them as an `ArrayList`. This method is defined in the `DefaultAddInTreeNode` class, which is located in the file `src\SharpDevelop\Core\AddIns\DefaultAddInTreeNode.cs`:

```
public ArrayList BuildChildItems(object caller)
{
  ArrayList items = new ArrayList();

  IAddInTreeNode[] sortedNodes = GetSubnodesAsSortedArray();

  foreach (IAddInTreeNode curNode in sortedNodes) {
    // don't include excluded children
    ConditionFailedAction action =
      curNode.GetCurrentConditionFailedAction(caller);
    if (action != ConditionFailedAction.Exclude) {
      ArrayList subItems = curNode.BuildChildItems(caller);

      object newItem = curNode.Codon.BuildItem(caller, subItems, action);

      if (newItem != null) {
        items.Add(newItem);
      }
    }
  }
  return items;
}
```

First, we obtain the child nodes as a sorted array. The child items get sorted topologically according to the `InsertAfter/InsertBefore` properties of the sub-nodes' codons. This might cause strange effects when we specify that a node should be put before a particular node. Note that by before we mean not directly before the node, but rather somewhere before that node in general. Often it is necessary to specify the items between which it should be inserted for the results that are expected. After that, the condition for the child is checked, and if it is not excluded it will be put into the items `ArrayList`.

Note that the `subItems` are created recursively with this method (called on the child) and that the codon `BuildItem` method must handle the sub-items itself. Each tree node can have sub-items and during the object creation these sub-items must be handled.

This is important because what a sub-item is isn't clear on the level of the AddIn tree node.

For example, if it is a menu item then the items must be cast to the menu item class and be put into the items menu item collection. Unfortunately, the `DefaultAddInTreeNode` does not know about the codon implementation. Only the codon does. Therefore, codons must handle their sub-items by themselves. Note that not all codons are able to handle sub-items. For example, file filter codons do not handle sub-items, these just get discarded; but it is up to the codon implementer to decide what happens (throw exception, silently discard, or do something else).

After this, the new item will be put into the `ArrayList` and the array list is returned. The `BuildChildItem` method does the same thing, except that it only builds one specific child.

Now that we know how objects are created, let's look at look at the creation of codons.

Codon Creation

To properly understand how a codon is created, we first need to look at the codon subsystem:

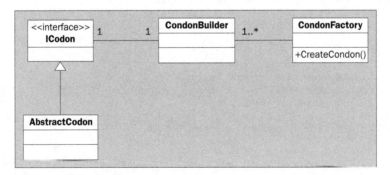

We have already seen the `ICodon` interface in the section on *Add-in Definition*. Now we will be looking at the classes responsible for the codon creation. The system allows new codons to be defined by add-ins. This ensures much more flexibility than defining a static set of codons inside the core assembly. When an assembly is imported by the add-in subsystem, it is scanned for types that have the `CodonNameAttribute` attached and are a subclass of the `AbstractCodon` class.

We decided to make the inheritance from the `AbstractCodon` class mandatory because it is easier to use this abstract class and it does not introduce any limitations to our current codon implementations. If the future proves that we were wrong with this assumption we can switch back to make a `ICodon` implementation and the `CodonNameAttribute` sufficient for a codon implementation without breaking anything.

The `AbstractCodon` class provides the basic functionality, which every codon must have. We already know that codons are XML-defined objects. The codon responsible for a specific XML node is determined by the node name. This node name and the codon name, which is given by the `CodonNameAttribute`, must be equal. The core locates the codon that has a `CodonNameAttribute`, which matches the XML node name. After that a new `CodonBuilder` is created for these types, which is handed over to the `CodonFactory`.

The codon builder (`src\SharpDevelop\Core\AddIns\Codons\CodonBuilder.cs`) builds a codon with:

```
public ICodon BuildCodon(AddIn addIn)
{
  ICodon codon;
  try {
    // create instance (ignore case)
    codon = (ICodon)assembly.CreateInstance(ClassName, true);

    // set default values
    codon.AddIn = addIn;
  } catch (Exception) {
    codon = null;
  }
  return codon;
}
```

It gets the assembly and class name in the constructor; that is all that is needed. The `CodonBuilder` reads the `CodonNameAttribute` and makes the attribute value available as a public property. The `CodonFactory` that is available under `src\SharpDevelop\Core\AddIns\Codons\CodonFactory.cs` searches for a given XML node for the correct builder. In other words, the `CreateCodon` method of `CodonFactory` takes an XML node, finds the proper `CodonBuilder`, and asks it to build the codon. A reference to the add-in needs to be carried along:

```
public class CodonFactory
{
  Hashtable codonHashtable = new Hashtable();

  public void AddCodonBuilder(CodonBuilder builder)
  {
    if (codonHashtable[builder.CodonName] != null) {
      throw new DuplicateCodonException(builder.CodonName);
    }
    codonHashtable[builder.CodonName] = builder;
  }
```

```
public ICodon CreateCodon(AddIn addIn, XmlNode codonNode)
{
    CodonBuilder builder = codonHashtable[codonNode.Name] as CodonBuilder;

    if (builder == null) {
      throw new ApplicationException("unknown condition found");
    }

    return builder.BuildCondition(addIn);
  }
}
```

The `AddCodonBuilder` method just adds a new builder to the factory, and in the `CreateCodon` method, the correct builder is taken out of the hash table that contains the `CodonBuilder`.

Conditions

Now we are ready to move on to conditions. A condition is used in the AddIn tree to indicate whether a node is active (that is, if it should be built when `BuildItem` is called). This is useful for dynamically changing the AddIn tree. Dynamic changes are used in the menus to make menu items invisible, when they aren't used or to disable menu items. All this is done using conditions:

```
< Condition openproject="*" action="Disable">
  <!-- Here may follow a menu definition (left out for this chapter) -->
</Condition>
```

(This is just an example and does not reference to a real file.)

The `<Condition>` node is a sub-node of an `<Extension>` node, which have seen. Now we will look at the `<Condition>` node; it has an action attribute that is set to `Disable`. Currently there are only three possible options for a condition – `Nothing`, `Exclude`, and `Disable`. These actions occur only when the condition evaluates to `false`.

`Nothing` does nothing, if the condition fails. If we choose this, it will be similar to not using a condition. This is only included for the sake of completeness. If no action attribute is specified, `Exclude` is the default action. It merely removes the item virtually from the AddIn tree when the `BuildItem` method is called. `Disable` tries to disable the item. The codon object must handle the disable case by itself. Only the object knows whether it can be disabled and how this happens. For example, if we disable a menu item the `Enabled` property has to be set to `false`.

From the coding viewpoint the conditions are similar to the codons:

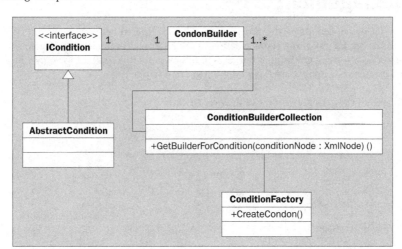

The only difference is that the `ConditionFactory` doesn't have a hash table that contains the condition builders directly, instead a `ConditionBuilderCollection` is used that stores all conditions in a collection and searches in the collection for the right condition. This is done because conditions are not differentiated by name. Instead, conditions use different attributes for identification. That means that no two different conditions can expose the same set of required attributes because the implementation must chose only one condition. This limitation makes sense – if two conditions have the same set of attributes they should mean the same thing or else more meaningful names should be chosen.

The interface is also different. For example, conditions do not need `ID` numbers or arrangement information. The interface definition can be found under `src\SharpDevelop\Core\AddIns\ Conditions\ICondition.cs`:

```
public interface ICondition
{
   // Returns the action which occurs, when this condition fails.
   ConditionFailedAction Action {
     get;
     set;
   }

   // Returns true, when the condition is valid otherwise false.
   bool IsValid(object caller);
}
```

The condition interface is small, but this is all that's needed. We will be looking at more practical aspects of conditions and codons in the next chapter. For now, this should be sufficient to introduce the next section on loading of add-in XML files and construction of the AddIn tree.

AddIn Management

The add-in management is done by the `AddIn` class, which is located under `src\SharpDevelop\Core\AddIns\AddIn.cs`. This class is a representation of the XML add-in file format, which we will be seeing in the next chapter. We will not go through this class in full, because it is similar to what we have seen – a file gets read and it is inserted into the tree. Nothing unexpected happens.

First we will need to get a short overview of the `AddIn` class:

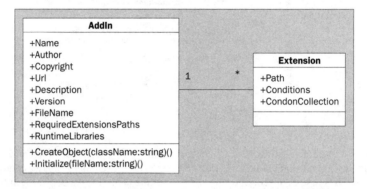

The attributes shown in the diagram above are populated from the add-in XML file that we saw in the *Add-in Definition* section. The extensions contained in the add-in XML are stored in a separate class called `Extension` that contains all extension paths and contents defined by this add-in. An extension path is just a shortcut for putting codons in the appropriate path.

For example, / is the root path and when we specify `/myPath/subPath1` the node `myPath` is created as child of the root node and this node gets a child node called `subPath`. All codons defined in this extension path are children of the `subPath1` node. We save this add-in structure to have the option of removing an add-in at run time.

Now, we will look at how the `AddIn` class gets loaded and initialized. To understand this let's examine the `Initialize` method:

```
public void Initialize(string fileName)
{
  this.fileName = fileName;
  XmlDocument doc = new XmlDocument();
  doc.Load(fileName);

  try {
    name = doc.DocumentElement.Attributes["name"].InnerText;
    author = doc.DocumentElement.Attributes["author"].InnerText;
    copyright = doc.DocumentElement.Attributes["copyright"].InnerText;
    url = doc.DocumentElement.Attributes["url"].InnerText;
    description = doc.DocumentElement.Attributes["description"].InnerText;
    version = doc.DocumentElement.Attributes["version"].InnerText;   }
  catch (Exception) {
    throw new AddInLoadException("No or malformed 'AddIn' node");
```

```
    }

    foreach (object o in doc.DocumentElement.ChildNodes) {
      if (o is XmlElement) { // skip comments
        XmlElement curEl = (XmlElement)o;

        switch (curEl.Name) {
          case "Runtime":
            AddRuntimeLibraries(Path.GetDirectoryName(fileName), curEl);
            break;
          case "Extension":
            AddExtensions(curEl);
            break;
        }
      }
    }
  }
```

First, we obtain all add-in attributes from the root node and store them. After that, the child nodes are parsed and the helper methods handle them differently:

❑ **Runtime node**
The runtime node contents get loaded into the AddIn tree. The node contains a list of assemblies that are loaded and scanned for additional codons and conditions, which get inserted into the AddIn tree factories

❑ **Extension node**
This node is used to place the codons in the tree. The extension node takes a path that will be used to insert all subnodes that describe codons into the tree under the path given.

We do have the problem of add-in dependencies. This is solved by queuing the add-in load. We try to load add-ins sequentially; if one loading fails the add-in is placed at the end of the queue and all other XML files are loaded before the add-in, which failed. If no add-in in the queue can be loaded, then we show the load errors (the thrown exceptions) that prevent the add-ins from loading.

We will now delve deeper into the `AddExtensions` method from the `AddIn` class, which is responsible for parsing any `Extension` elements, including the conditional and various codon subnodes:

```
void AddExtensions(XmlElement el)
{
  if (el.Attributes["path"] == null) {
    throw new AddInLoadException("One extension node has no path attribute
      defined.");
  }
  Extension e = new Extension(el.Attributes["path"].InnerText);
  AddCodonsToExtension(e, el, new ConditionCollection());
  extensions.Add(e);
}
```

As you can see, after checking that the extension has a path attribute, this method creates an `Extension` object based on the path and calls `AddCodonsToExtension` to populate it.

Lets look at the `AddCodonsToExtension` method.

```
void AddCodonsToExtension(Extension e, XmlElement el, ConditionCollection
conditions)
{
  foreach (object o in el.ChildNodes) {
    if (!(o is XmlElement)) {
      continue;
    }
    XmlElement curEl = (XmlElement)o;
```

After setting up a loop through the elements in the `Extension` element of our XML document, we switch on the name of each element. Some elements are ignored because their sub-trees do not contain codons and so we don't need to traverse them.

```
switch (curEl.Name) {
  case "And": // these nodes are silently ignored.
  case "Or":
  case "Not":
  case "Condition":
    break;
```

If the node is a `Conditional` node, we need to create a new `ICondition` object. If the `Conditional` element does not have the required attributes, we create a condition with a `ConditionFailedAction`:

```
case "Conditional":
  ICondition condition = null;

  // construct condition
  if (curEl.Attributes.Count == 0 || (curEl.Attributes.Count == 1 &&
    curEl.Attributes["action"] != null)) {

    condition = BuildComplexCondition(curEl);
    // set condition action manually
    if (curEl.Attributes["action"] != null) {
      condition.Action = (ConditionFailedAction)
        Enum.Parse(typeof(ConditionFailedAction),
        curEl.Attributes["action"].InnerText);
    }
```

If the condition is `null` after calling `BuildComplexCondition`, we throw an exception, as the condition must not have been formatted correctly.

```
if (condition == null) {
  throw new AddInTreeFormatException
    ("empty conditional, but no condition definition found.");
}
```

If the element does have the required attributes, we can go ahead and create the condition from the AddIn tree.

```
} else {
    condition = AddInTreeSingleton.AddInTree.
        ConditionFactory.CreateCondition(this, curEl);
    AutoInitializeAttributes(condition, curEl);
}
```

We then add the condition to the `ConditionCollection` of conditions to be traversed. After traversing the collection, we remove the last condition as it has now been traversed.

```
// put the condition at the end of the condition 'stack'
conditions.Add(condition);

// traverse the subtree
AddCodonsToExtension(e, curEl, conditions);

// now we are back to the old level, remove the condition
// that was applied to the subtree.
conditions.RemoveAt(conditions.Count - 1);
break;
```

There is one more type of element that we need to deal with – codons. As codons do not use a single element name, we use the `default` case of our `switch` statement to handle them. This means that anything that has not been dealt with previously will be treated as a codon:

```
default:
    ICodon codon = AddInTreeSingleton.AddInTree.
        CodonFactory.CreateCodon(this, curEl);
    AutoInitializeAttributes(codon, curEl);
```

Before we add the codon to the `CodonCollection` of the extension, we need to set its `InsertAfter` and `InsertBefore` properties to ensure that it is added in the correct place.

```
e.Conditions[codon.ID] = new ConditionCollection(conditions);
if (codon.InsertAfter == null &&
    codon.InsertBefore == null && e.CodonCollection.Count > 0) {
    codon.InsertAfter = new string[] {
        ((ICodon)e.CodonCollection
            [e.CodonCollection.Count - 1]).ID };
}
e.CodonCollection.Add(codon);
```

If the element has child nodes then we need to add an extension for the codon.

```
if (curEl.ChildNodes.Count > 0) {
    Extension newExtension = new Extension(e.Path + '/' + codon.ID);
    AddCodonsToExtension(newExtension, curEl, conditions);
    extensions.Add(newExtension);
```

```
            }
        break;
    }
  }
 }
}
```

If you want to go on to learn more about the AddIn tree, you can see it in action in the next chapter. For now, we will take a break from AddIns and look at property management in SharpDevelop.

Property Management in SharpDevelop

Property management is the ability to manage, save, and load all 'options' (we call them properties) that the user has altered while they use the program. Examples of properties are the UI language or recently opened files. SharpDevelop has a simple common model for this issue. We will look at how this problem was solved because it may be helpful to you for your projects.

In this section, when we speak of properties we do not mean properties in the sense of C# properties. We mean a more general concept. Our concept is simple, we have a key and a value, each key has at most **one** value.

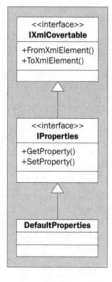

The diagram gives us an overview of the property management system. The IXmlConvertable interface is the base for the IProperties interface. Currently, there is only one implementation of the IProperties interface, called DefaultProperties.

We will see how the property system works inside SharpDevelop and how to use it for our own add-ins, having done that, we will be capable of building a system like this in our other applications too. Finally, we will discuss how to make properties persistent. The Property system is able to store simple types into properties as well as whole objects. We will also discuss the reasons for property management being so difficult and the solutions to reduce the level of complexity.

The Idea behind the IXmlConvertable Interface

SharpDevelop defines an interface called IXmlConvertable to indicate that an object can convert its contents to XML and restore its state later. Now we look at this interface located in the src\SharpDevelop\Core\Properties\IXmlConvertable.cs file:

```
public interface IXmlConvertable
{
   object FromXmlElement(XmlElement element);

   XmlElement ToXmlElement(XmlDocument doc);
}
```

As we can see the definition is quite simple; there are only two methods. The FromXmlElement method takes an XmlElement, and returns a new instance that gets initialized with the content from the element. We do not want to use .NET serialization because the object may change, but the file format does not. When the XML format changes, we may consider reading old nodes too and convert them.

.NET XML serialization was used in the first version of the code completion database (you can find more about it in *Chapter 13*) but later on it was replaced by our own routines. The code completion database stores all information (classes/members and documentation) about the .NET Framework classes into a single file.

The version that used serialization took up 90MB hard disk space and over 15 minutes to build on my notebook. The routine that was written without serialization takes only around 20MB and builds the database in 1 minute on the same machine. The hand-made solution is faster and much smaller because the file format is optimized to avoid overhead.

.NET XML serialization is good when the volume of data is less. Besides, we shouldn't spend too much time on solving the persistence issue. Now that we have learned about the IXmlConvertable interface, let's examine the IProperty interface because it extends IXmlConvertable.

Overview of the IProperties Interface

First, we will need to get an overview of the main interface – the IProperties interface. The rest of the application works with this simple interface; this is all that we need. We have functions for getting and setting properties. The IProperties interface also defines a method for cloning an IProperties object. The IProperties interface is located in the src\SharpDevelop\Core\Properties\ IProperties.cs file:

```
public interface IProperties : IXmlConvertable
{
   object GetProperty(string key, object defaultvalue);
   object GetProperty(string key);
   int GetProperty(string key, int defaultvalue);
   bool GetProperty(string key, bool defaultvalue);
   short GetProperty(string key, short defaultvalue);
```

```
    byte GetProperty(string key, byte defaultvalue);
    string GetProperty(string key, string defaultvalue);
    System.Enum GetProperty(string key, System.Enum defaultvalue);

    void SetProperty(string key, object val);

    IProperties Clone();

    event PropertyEventHandler PropertyChanged;
}
```

Let's take a closer look at the various forms of the `GetProperty` methods. The simplest form is:

```
    object GetProperty(string key);
```

This form gets a `key` and returns an `object` to us. In SharpDevelop, this method is only used for getting temporary properties.

A temporary property is simply a property that cannot be written to disk. In this case, the user (we) must know about the property type and perform all castings. The problem with a persistent object property lies in converting it into XML and back (this is discussed in the next section).

Another form of this method is:

```
    object GetProperty(string key, object defaultvalue);
```

This form takes an object and uses a default value. The default value is returned when a property with the key is not found, and the object `defaultvalue` is inserted under the key. This approach makes it easier to create a default property file. Otherwise, all properties must be changed to generate a default file. This method can be used for persistent properties also, but shorthand methods are defined for basic types that make the usage of properties easier, (basic types are `int`, `bool`, `short`, `byte`, `string`, and `enum`).

These overloaded methods will perform some casting for the user, which makes them more comfortable to use. These variants are used more often than the object-based one.

In the next section, we will see why the first form of `GetProperty` method is special and how it manages to store objects into the XML file.

The Default Implementation

Now we will look at the default implementation of the `IProperties` interface. We will be looking at the important parts only; we won't be seeing the empty default constructor or how an `OnEvent` method is defined.

This implementation is in the
`src\SharpDevelop\Core\Properties\DefaultProperties.cs` file:

```
    public class DefaultProperties : IProperties
    {
        Hashtable properties = new Hashtable();
```

As we can see, this class is based on `System.Collections.Hashtable`, this ensures a decent speed when a `get` or `set` method is used on a property. Let's look at the `GetProperty` method:

```
public object GetProperty(string key, object defaultvalue)
{
  if (!properties.ContainsKey(key)) {
    if (defaultvalue != null) {
      properties[key] = defaultvalue;
    }
    return defaultvalue;
  }

  object obj = properties[key];

  // stored an XmlElement in properties node >
  // set a FromXmlElement of the defaultvalue type at this
  // propertyposition.
  if (defaultvalue is IXmlConvertable && obj is XmlElement) {
    obj = properties[key] = ((IXmlConvertable)defaultvalue).
      FromXmlElement((XmlElement)((XmlElement)obj).FirstChild);
  }
  return obj;
}
```

The first part is simple; it just says that when the hash table cannot find the key we simply return the default value. In this case, the key is created, the default value is assigned, and the default value is returned. (But only the first time; at the second call the key will exist.)

From now on, things get more complicated. We will need to know a bit about the loading routines. The basic-types just get an XML node that has a `value` attribute. All other nodes are treated as object nodes and are not converted when the property file is loaded. Instead, they are converted when the get property method is first called. We just overwrite the values of the default value and give it back.

In SharpDevelop, when an object is to be obtained from the properties, a call like this is made:

```
myObj = GetProperty("MyRequestedKey", new DefaultObject());
```

As we can see, the default value is not used anywhere else. Therefore we can alter this during the `GetProprety` call.

You might ask why it is being done this way. We could have used another approach, by just storing the type of the `IXmlConvertable` object and using this type information to create the object with a call to `System.Reflection.Assembly.CreateInstance(string typeName)`. However, this approach doesn't work, as we do not know in which assembly the type is defined (although we might save the assembly name too). More importantly, when the property system is initialized and the property is loaded we do not want to load all assemblies and create all types because this takes too much time and memory. Therefore, they will be created on demand. Keep in mind that the property system is initialized before the AddIn tree gets loaded (because some add-ins may need properties when they load up).

Now, we will skim over the overloaded methods. They all use the basic method that returns an object and takes a default value to do their job. Even if we promised to omit the boring ones, it might be useful to see that all basic types have a `Parse` method defined, which takes a string and outputs the type.

Another method of converting strings to types would have been to use the `System.Convert` class. Unfortunately, this class provides no mechanism for converting enumeration types.

Let's now look at the code:

```
public object GetProperty(string key)
{
  return GetProperty(key, (object)null);
}

public int GetProperty(string key, int defaultvalue)
{
  return int.Parse(GetProperty(key, (object)defaultvalue).ToString());
}

public bool GetProperty(string key, bool defaultvalue)
{
  return bool.Parse(GetProperty(key, (object)defaultvalue).ToString());
}

public short GetProperty(string key, short defaultvalue)
{
  return short.Parse(GetProperty(key, (object)defaultvalue).ToString());
}

public byte GetProperty(string key, byte defaultvalue)
{
  return byte.Parse(GetProperty(key, (object)defaultvalue).ToString());
}

public string GetProperty(string key, string defaultvalue)
{
  return GetProperty(key, (object)defaultvalue).ToString();
}

public System.Enum GetProperty(string key, System.Enum defaultvalue)
{
  return (System.Enum)Enum.Parse(defaultvalue.GetType(),
    GetProperty(key, (object)defaultvalue).ToString());
}
```

These are the `get` methods described by the interface. The `Enum` version checks whether the property can be converted to `Enum` and, if not, it just returns the default value.

We mentioned earlier that it is possible to add a new value to our properties implicitly. Now, we take a look at our `SetProperty` method, which sets a property explicitly:

```
public void SetProperty(string key, object val)
{
  object oldValue = properties[key];
  if (!val.Equals(oldValue)) {
    properties[key] = val;
    OnPropertyChanged(new PropertyEventArgs(this, key, oldValue, val));
  }
}
```

This method fires the property-changed event by calling the `OnPropertyChanged` method. This is important because sometimes it is necessary to carry out an update when a specific property changes. We will look at such updates in *Chapter 7*, which deals with updating the IDE when the user switches the UI language.

The `SetProperty` method is commonly used when the user changes options in the option dialog. Generally, properties are read and silently inserted into the properties object.

Now we will take a break from wading through the source code, and will stop to investigate some practical issues with ways properties are used in SharpDevelop.

Properties at Work

One useful feature of our property framework is that the `IProperties` interface itself extends the `IXmlConvertable` interface. This allows for an interesting option – storing `IProperties` instances into properties.

This is used in several places, for example, the text editor uses this feature. The text editor has its own `IProperties` object, which holds its options (this prevents name clashes). In earlier SharpDevelop versions, the text editor made a copy of the main properties from SharpDevelop and used the local copy. That allowed the user to change the font for a single window without touching the font properties of the others. However, this feature was found unintuitive by our users (they expected that if they change the font all text areas would get updated) and was easily taken out; the object was simply assigned without calling a copy and it worked.

Without using something like the `IProperties` concept, it might have taken a lot of time to shift away from such a working model but with the properties it was extremely easy. Now we look at another part of the IDE where an `IProperties` object is used and which has nothing to do with persistence.

We will look at the Project options dialog. It can be found in the `SharpDevelop\src\SharpDevelop\Base\Gui\Dialogs\ProjectOptionsDialog.cs` file. This code snippet is taken from `ProjectOptionsDialog` constructor:

```
IProperties properties = new DefaultProperties();
properties.SetProperty("Project", project);
AddNodes(properties, optionsTreeView.Nodes, node.BuildChildItems(this));
```

First, we define a new `IProperties` object and then call the `AddNodes` method, which adds all the project configuration panels. The next important piece of code is in the `foreach` statement; in each loop the `Config` property is set to the current configuration:

```
configurationTreeNode = new TreeNode("Configurations");
configurationTreeNode.NodeFont = plainFont;

foreach (IConfiguration config in project.Configurations) {
  TreeNode newNode = new TreeNode(config.Name);
  newNode.Tag = config;
  if (config == project.ActiveConfiguration) {
    newNode.NodeFont = boldFont;
  } else {
    newNode.NodeFont = plainFont;
  }
  properties.SetProperty("Config", config);
  AddNodes(properties, newNode.Nodes,
    configurationNode.BuildChildItems(this));
  configurationTreeNode.Nodes.Add(newNode);
}
```

The node is then added to the tree view. It is not necessary to create a new `IProperties` object for each loop because all project option panels must receive their configuration at startup. In an older version, the configuration panels just got their configuration and that was all that was needed. But then a contributor needed a project configuration option that uses a property from the project itself. To implement this, one possible solution would have been to make sure that the configuration objects knew their parent (the project) and that the configuration panel just uses this property.

Instead, we chose the present approach. It is used in more places than just in the one we are looking at now. It's a very good solution since all panels just get one object and new panels can be added that need new objects without changing the old ones.

To make a property persistent in SharpDevelop we just need to put it in the main `IProperties` object. This object is obtained as follows:

```
PropertyService propertyService = (PropertyService)ServiceManager.Services.
  GetService(typeof(PropertyService));
```

The `PropertyService` implements the `IProperties` interface and is defined in the namespace `ICSharpCode.Core.Services`. We will be discussing services in Chapter 5. For now it's enough to know how to get the `IProperties` object that stores everything.

Next, we will be discussing various aspects of storing and reloading properties.

Property Persistence

The default `IProperties` implementation is able to save its contents to an XML file and read it back. Now we will take a look at an XML code snippet that was cut out of a SharpDevelop properties XML file. An entire properties file can be found in your user's application data folder under `.ICSharpCode\SharpDevelop\SharpDevelopProperties.xml` (to obtain it, you should have started SharpDevelop at least once on your system):

```
<SharpDevelopProperties fileversion="1.1">
  <Properties>
```

```
    <Property key="SharpDevelop.UI.CurrentAmbience" value="CSharp" />
    <Property
      key="ICSharpCode.SharpDevelop.Gui.ProjectBrowser.ShowExtensions"
      value="True" />
    <Property key="SharpDevelop.CreateBackupCopy" value="False" />
    <Property key="ICSharpCode.SharpDevelop.Gui.Dialogs.
      NewProjectDialog.DefaultPath" value=" C:\Documents and Settings\Wrox\
      My Documents " />
    <Property key="SharpDevelop.LineTerminatorStyle" value="Windows" />
    <XmlConvertableProperty key="SharpDevelop.Gui.MainWindow.WindowState">
      <WINDOWSTATE FULLSCREEN="False"STATE="Maximized">
        523|21|640|480
      </WINDOWSTATE>
    </XmlConvertableProperty>
  </Properties>
</SharpDevelopProperties>
```

The root node contains a version number, which is used to indicate the version. This helps to avoid version mismatch when the XML file is loaded and has a format different from the current one. SharpDevelop currently discards a file with a version number other than 1.1. If the format is changed again, we may build in a converter for old files. Generally, this is the way with the XML data files; old files are easily converted on the fly to the new format.

The next node is the `<Properties>` node, which contains all the properties. In future, beside the `<Properties>` node, we might need to add other nodes to the root node; therefore, it was done this way. This is a good tip when designing XML file formats – always allow for future extensibility by nesting collections of related elements under higher-level elements. Let's now examine the `<Property>` nodes.

All `<Property>` nodes have a primitive key-value pair (these are the 'basic-types'). The last node, however, is different: it is called `XmlConvertableProperty` and it contains a single `<WINDOWSTATE>` node. This node does not follow the current naming guidelines (it is all capitals, rather than being in camel casing) and contains other information than key-value pairs. This property is an `IXmlConvertable` object made persistent in this XML. It is from the type `WorkbenchMemento` and the implementation can be found under `src\SharpDevelop\Base\Gui\Workbench\WorkbenchMemento.cs`.

It saves the state of the workbench and is used to restore the state of the IDE on the next SharpDevelop startup. The type of the object that is made persistent is not saved with the file (we have discussed this issue already).

Now that we know what the format looks like, we will look at the source code that is responsible for reading this XML format. The `SetXmlElement` method from the `DefaultProperties` class is given the `<Properties>` node from the XML definition above and this is how it parses it:

```
protected void SetXmlElement(XmlElement element)
{
  XmlNodeList nodes = element.ChildNodes;
  foreach (XmlElement el in nodes) {
    if (el.Name == "Property") {
      properties[el.Attributes["key"].InnerText] =
```

```
            el.Attributes["value"].InnerText;
        } else if (el.Name == "XmlConvertableProperty") {
          properties[el.Attributes["key"].InnerText] = el;
        } else {
          throw new UnknownPropertyNodeException(el.Name);
        }
      }
    }

    public virtual object FromXmlElement(XmlElement element)
    {
      DefaultProperties defaultProperties = new DefaultProperties();
      defaultProperties.SetXmlElement(element);
      return defaultProperties;
    }
```

As we can see, the `XmlConvertableProperty` nodes are handled differently. The `XmlElement` is stored into the `properties` hash table. Simple properties get the value assigned directly.

The write routine that handles it must write back an unchanged `XmlElement` node because during run time it might happen that the property that contains the `XmlElement` is never read:

```
    public virtual XmlElement ToXmlElement(XmlDocument doc)
    {
      XmlElement propertiesnode = doc.CreateElement("Properties");

      foreach (DictionaryEntry entry in properties) {
        if (entry.Value != null) {
          if (entry.Value is XmlElement) { // write unchanged XmlElement back
            propertiesnode.AppendChild
              (doc.ImportNode((XmlElement)entry.Value, true));
          } else if (entry.Value is IXmlConvertable) {
            XmlElement convertableNode =
              doc.CreateElement("XmlConvertableProperty");

            XmlAttribute key = doc.CreateAttribute("key");
            key.InnerText = entry.Key.ToString();
            convertableNode.Attributes.Append(key);

            convertableNode.AppendChild(((IXmlConvertable)entry.Value).
              ToXmlElement(doc));

            propertiesnode.AppendChild(convertableNode);
          } else {
            XmlElement el = doc.CreateElement("Property");

            XmlAttribute key = doc.CreateAttribute("key");
            key.InnerText = entry.Key.ToString();
            el.Attributes.Append(key);
```

```
        XmlAttribute val = doc.CreateAttribute("value");
        val.InnerText = entry.Value.ToString();
        el.Attributes.Append(val);

        propertiesnode.AppendChild(el);
      }
    }
  }
  return propertiesnode;
}
```

We have now seen how the DefaultProperties implementation works, and why it works this way and no other.

Summary

In this chapter, we have learned what the AddIn tree is and what it does. We have also discussed codons and got an introduction to conditions. In the next chapter, we will discuss, in detail, how to define our own codons and conditions. We will also see some practical aspects of the AddIn tree, which was discussed, mostly theoretically, in this chapter.

We also saw how objects are created from the AddIn tree and learned about the loading and storing of the add-in files into the AddIn tree. Besides the AddIn tree, we have seen how the property management in SharpDevelop works and how to define our own properties inside the IDE.

CHAPTER 4

4

Building the Application with Add-ins

This chapter focuses on the way SharpDevelop application is built by using add-ins. We are already familiar with codons (we came across them in the last chapter). In this chapter we will go through all the codons and conditions that are currently defined in SharpDevelop. The outline for this chapter is:

- ❏ Working with Codons
  - ❏ The ICommand interface
  - ❏ Making Menus Work
  - ❏ Codon Overview
- ❏ Wiring up Add-ins with Conditions
  - ❏ Condition Structure
  - ❏ Defining Conditions
  - ❏ Overview of Available Conditions

In the course of our discussion, we will be discussing the creation of codons and conditions and then we will look into the creation of menus, as it is one of the most complex usages of the Addin tree.

Unless noted, all the add-in examples, in this chapter, are taken from the add-in definition for SharpDevelop, which can be found in the `src\AddIn` directory of the distribution. All the add-in files have the `.addin` extension, which is mandatory as SharpDevelop scans the `AddIn` directory and all the sub-directories for `*.addin` files.

Working with Codons

In this section we will look at all the codons defined in SharpDevelop. But before that, we need to have a little knowledge of the add-in definition for defining sub-items. We have already seen in the *From Tree Node to Running Object* section of the last chapter how sub-items should be handled from the coding viewpoint but we haven't seen the XML format nor did we consider how to define sub-items in XML. So now, let's look at a sub-item definition:

```
<Extension path = "/ExampleMenu">
  <MenuItem id = "AddMenu" label = "Add">
    <MenuItem id = "AddItem"   label = "Add item"   class ="MyAddItem">
    <MenuItem id = "AddFolder" label = "Add folder" class ="MyAddFolder">
  </MenuItem>
</Extension>
```

(Note that this snippet isn't taken from any of SharpDevelop's actual add-in files.)

The code snippet that we have just seen, is a short form of this longer version:

```
<Extension path = "/ExampleMenu">
  <MenuItem id = "AddMenu" label = "Add"/>
</Extension>
<Extension path = "/ExampleMenu/AddMenu">
  <MenuItem id = "AddItem"   label = "Add item"   class ="MyAddItem">
  <MenuItem id = "AddFolder" label = "Add folder" class ="MyAddFolder">
</Extension>
```

In SharpDevelop's add-in files, the first version is the most commonly used version, as it makes the XML files more maintainable. However, we should never forget the meaning of this abbreviated style and how a sub-menu is added explicitly. Each codon is a path in the AddIn tree too, with the ID being the path name. Therefore, it doesn't make sense to have two codons in the same path that have the same ID.

Now we will go on to see how the menu items work.

The ICommand Interface

Recall what we saw of the SharpDevelop Main() method in the section on *Advantages of Using the Addin Tree* in the last chapter. This method retrieved the ICommand objects from the AddIn tree and called a Run() method on them. Let's take a look at this interface, which can be found in the src\SharpDevelop\Core\AddIns\Codons\ICommand.cs file:

```
public interface ICommand
{
  object Owner {
    get;
    set;
  }

  void Run();
}
```

This interface is used as the base interface for menu items too. Menu items are just commands, which implement the Run() method. The Owner property is used for callback purposes. As we have already seen in the last chapter, the BuildItem() method that creates objects obtains an Owner object, which is usually the object that requests the items to be built.

For example, the open file tab context menu items receive their tab parent that has information such as the currently selected window in this manner. The currently selected window from the open file tab does not necessarily need to be the current active window from the IDE.

Now let's look at a typical command. In the last chapter we saw the Main() method of SharpDevelop and wondered why no Application.Run or window creation was defined. Let's consider the StartWorkbenchCommand() method, which starts the SharpDevelop workbench. It is defined under src\SharpDevelop\Base\Commands\AutostartCommands.cs:

```
public class StartWorkbenchCommand : AbstractCommand
{
   const string workbenchMemento = "SharpDevelop.Workbench.WorkbenchMemento";

   EventHandler idleEventHandler;
   bool isCalled = false;

   void ShowTipOfTheDay(object sender, EventArgs e)
   {
     if (isCalled) {
       Application.Idle -= idleEventHandler;
       return;
     }
     isCalled = true;
     // show tip of the day
     PropertyService propertyService =
       (PropertyService)ServiceManager.
       Services.GetService(typeof(PropertyService));

     if (propertyService.GetProperty("ICSharpCode.SharpDevelop.Gui.Dialog.
       TipOfTheDayView.ShowTipsAtStartup", true)) {
       ViewTipOfTheDay dview = new ViewTipOfTheDay();
       dview.Run();
     }
   }
}
```

You may have noticed that the ShowTipOfTheDay method has some code to ensure that it is only called once. You may also be wondering why the method uses the following line of code to remove an event handler from Application.Idle:

```
Application.Idle -= idleEventHandler;
```

We need to do this because when the tip of the day view is closed, the main window looses the focus. We need to start the tip of the day while the application is running and this dirty little hack does just that for us. It is really troublesome to get the tip of the day view running because Windows.Forms exhibits different behavior under Windows 2000 and under Windows XP and sometimes bugs will occur only under one of these operating systems. (In this case, the bug only occurred under Windows 2000.)

The next method we see starts the SharpDevelop workbench. Notice that a `ShowTipOfTheDay` event handler is added to `Application.Idle`. The `ShowTipOfTheDay` method will be put as the event handler in the idle event and will run only once because it removes itself from the event handler queue.

If SharpDevelop gets ported to other operating systems (or another API than Windows Forms) this start method is one part that must be rewritten because it depends on `Windows.Forms`.

```
public override void Run()
{
  Form f = (Form)WorkbenchSingleton.Workbench;
  f.Show();
  idleEventHandler = new EventHandler(ShowTipOfTheDay);
  Application.Idle += idleEventHandler;

  if (SharpDevelopMain.CommandLineArgs != null) {
    foreach (string file in SharpDevelopMain.CommandLineArgs) {
      switch (System.IO.Path.GetExtension(file).ToUpper()) {
        case ".CMBX":
        case ".PRJX":
          try {
            IProjectService projectService = (IProjectService)
              ICSharpCode.Core.Services.ServiceManager.
              Services.GetService(typeof(IProjectService));
            projectService.OpenCombine(file);
          } catch (Exception e) {
            Console.WriteLine
              ("unable to open project/combine {0} exception was :\n{1}",
              file, e.ToString());
          }
          break;
        default:
          try {
            IFileService fileService = (IFileService)
              ICSharpCode.Core.Services.ServiceManager.
                Services.GetService(typeof(IFileService));
            fileService.OpenFile(file);
          } catch (Exception e) {
            Console.WriteLine
              ("unable to open file {0} exception was :\n{1}",
              file, e.ToString());
          }
          break;
      }
    }
  }

  f.Focus(); // windows.forms focus workaround

  // start the parser thread
  DefaultParserService parserService = (DefaultParserService)
    ServiceManager.Services.GetService(typeof(DefaultParserService));
  parserService.StartParserThread();
```

```
      // finally run the workbench window ...
      Application.Run(f);

      // save the workbench memento in the ide properties
      PropertyService propertyService = (PropertyService)
        ServiceManager.Services.GetService(typeof(PropertyService));
      propertyService.SetProperty(workbenchMemento,
        WorkbenchSingleton.Workbench.CreateMemento());
    }
  }
```

Let's now move on to see how menus work.

Making Menus Work

A menu item from the add-in implementer's point of view doesn't have much to do with implementing a menu item (that is, with putting a .NET event handler in the `Click` event). Instead, a command is implemented that has a `Run()` method. However, the basic `ICommand` interface is not used because we need some more features from the menu item commands. To get an overview of these features, we will look at the `IMenuCommand` interface, which can be found in the file `src\SharpDevelop\Base\Internal\Codons\MenuItems\IMenuCommand.cs`.

This interface must be implemented by all SharpDevelop menu commands:

```
public interface IMenuCommand : ICommand
{
  bool IsEnabled {
    get;
    set;
  }

  bool IsChecked {
    get;
    set;
  }
}
```

The `IMenuCommand` extends the `ICommand` interface, which we have seen in the section *The ICommand Interface*. It extends this interface with two properties:

❑   `IsEnabled`
    This is used for enabling/disabling menu commands. Disabled menu commands are generally shown grayed out.

❑   `IsChecked`
    If `IsChecked` is `true`, then a checkmark is drawn in front of the menu command.

An abstract implementation, `AbstractMenuCommand`, which is commonly used can be found under `src\SharpDevelop\Base\Internal\Codons\MenuItems\AbstractMenuCommand.cs`.

This abstract implementation is the trivial implementation of the interface above; therefore, we will not be looking at it.

Now that we know what the add-in implementer must provide, let's have a look at the other side – the `MenuItem` codon. This is what SharpDevelop provides to the add-in authors.

It is defined under:
`src\SharpDevelop\Base\Internal\Codons\MenuItems\MenuItemCodon.cs`.

This codon creates the menu items out of the menu commands. We will look at the codon implementation step by step. First comes the class definition with the `CodonNameAttribute` giving the name `MenuItem` to the codon:

```
[CodonName("MenuItem")]
public class MenuItemCodon : AbstractCodon
{
```

Note that `MenuItemCodon` subclasses the `AbstractCodon` class (which we saw in Chapter 3). It inherits some basic attributes from the `AbstractCodon` class; shortly, we will see a table of all attributes regardless of how they are defined in this class or inherited from `AbstractCodon`. On top of the class definition are the `MenuItemCodon`-specific attributes:

```
[XmlMemberAttribute("label", IsRequired=true)]
string label       = null;

[XmlMemberAttribute("description")]
string description = null;

[XmlMemberAttribute("shortcut")]
string shortcut    = null;

[XmlMemberAttribute("icon")]
string icon        = null;

[XmlMemberAttribute("link")]
string link        = null;

// Canonical properties for all fields above
```

The `XmlMemberAttribute` defines the XML attribute name, which is automatically stored in the fields. Let's look at each attribute and what it means:

Name	Required	Purpose
label	yes	The label is shown as the menu text.
Class	no	The action or menu item builder for the menu codon. This attribute is inherited from the `AbstractCodon` class.
description	no	Sets a description, which describes the menu item. It is only used for the main menu items (because that is the standard in most applications) and the description is shown in the status bar when the item is selected. (If not set, the description will not be shown.)

Name	Required	Purpose
Shortcut	no	The shortcut key. When this key is pressed the menu command runs (even if the menu is not opened).
Icon	no	The name of the menu item's icon. Note that this name is not the file name. Instead, it is the resource name of the icon that which should be used (for more details refer to Chapter 7).
Link	no	A URL that is used for web sites. This is the shortcut for creating web links in a menu.
Id	yes	The ID of the menu item. (Inherited from `AbstractCodon`.)
insertbefore	no	A list (separated by commas) of menu item IDs that must be displayed before this menu item. (Inherited from `AbstractCodon`.)
insertafter	no	A list (separated by commas) of menu item IDs that get displayed after this menu item. (Inherited from `AbstractCodon`.)

If any of the attributes are not specified, default values will be used (usually empty or `null`). In the source code, the author of the codon class has given the default values of the attributes as the default values of the fields.

For example, for all attributes of the menu item codon, the default value is `null`. Only the required attributes must be specified, otherwise SharpDevelop will not load. Instead, it will point out the error in the add-in definition XML file and stop.

No add-in error is tolerated in SharpDevelop and there are no plans to change this. This is because during the startup phase the impact of the error can't be determined; for example, if a core definition part has an error it might result in unexpected behavior and errors elsewhere. To avoid these problems, we have designed SharpDevelop in such a way that after encountering an error the loading process itself will fail.

Now we will continue with our analysis of the source code by looking at the `BuildItem()` method of the menu item codon:

```
public override object BuildItem(object owner, ArrayList subItems,
  ConditionFailedAction action)
{
  SdMenuCommand newItem = null;
  StringParserService stringParserService = (StringParserService)
    ServiceManager.Services.GetService(typeof(StringParserService));
```

This part of the code gets the `StringParserService`. This service is used for parsing `${...}` style tags, which are used for internationalization (see Chapter 7). All attributes that are displayed in the user interface get parsed by the `StringParserService`.

This part of the code checks whether the link attribute was specified and sets a menu item with an event handler according to the link attribute specified:

```
        if (Link != null) {
        newItem = new SdMenuCommand(stringParserService.Parse(Label),
          new EventHandler(new MenuEventHandler(owner, Link.StartsWith("http") ?
          (IMenuCommand)new GotoWebSite(Link) : new GotoLink(Link)).Execute));
      } else {
```

If the link points to a web page (that is if it starts with `http`) then it will be displayed in the internal browser. Otherwise, it will be opened with a call to `Process.Start()`.

The `SdMenuCommand` class is a wrapper for menu items. Currently SharpDevelop uses the Magic library (http://www.dotnetmagic.com) for drawing menu items. Before Magic was used, SharpDevelop had to draw the menu items using owner drawn .NET `Windows.Forms` menu items. Magic, however, provides a better look and feel and is faster. The `Windows.Forms` menu items caused re-draws when the menu is reconstructed and on some other operations. However, these re-draws resulted in flickers. Magic is much better at handling this issue because it doesn't use the standard main menu; it implements a menu control itself.

The `SdMenuCommand` provides a thin abstraction layer on top of the menu items. It just gets a label and an event handler as constructor argument. Currently the `SdMenuCommand` merely extends the Magic menu command and builds on top of its features. In the future, the `SdMenuCommand` may be enhanced with our own features depending on which GUI libraries SharpDevelop will be ported to. Because we use this abstraction layer, it is easy to switch to other menu drawing libraries than magic.

If the menu item is not a link, the event handler of the `SdMenuCommand` must be created by using the information from the class attribute to generate an `IMenuCommand` object:

```
    object o = null;
    if (Class != null) {
      o = AddIn.CreateObject(Class);
    }
```

What happens next depends on the object `o`:

```
    if (o != null) {
      if (o is ISubmenuBuilder) {
        return ((ISubmenuBuilder)o).BuildSubmenu(owner);
      }
      if (o is IMenuCommand) {
        newItem = new SdMenuCommand(stringParserService.Parse(Label),
          new EventHandler(new MenuEventHandler(owner,
          (IMenuCommand)o).Execute));
      }
    }
```

We have two types of menu commands – standard menu commands and submenu builders. A submenu builder is a piece of code that creates menu items dynamically. This is useful for the creating the recent files menu or the list of currently open windows in the window menu. We will see submenu builders a little later in this chapter.

Now only one case is left, the menu item, which has sub-items but not the class attribute:

```
if (newItem == null) {
  newItem = new SdMenuCommand(stringParserService.Parse(Label));
  if (subItems != null && subItems.Count > 0) {
    foreach (object item in subItems) {
      if (item is MenuCommand) {
        newItem.MenuCommands.Add((MenuCommand)item);
      } else {
        newItem.MenuCommands.AddRange((MenuCommand[])item);
      }
} } } //closing braces collapsed for brevity
```

A menu item gets all sub-items (the subItems ArrayList is a parameter for the build method) that are created from the AddIn tree and adds them to the menu commands from the SdMenuCommand class.

A call to BuildItem may not give a single menu item. Instead, an array might be returned if an ISubmenuBuilder was called. Therefore, ISubmenuBuilders can't be used at the top level. All top-level items in SharpDevelops main menu and context menus are folders or menu commands.

Note that menu items that are links or have commands can't have sub-menus. If the add-in implementer defines sub-items for menu items that have a class or link attribute, the sub-menu items will be disregarded.

After the creation of the menu item, the icon for this menu is set (if the icon attribute is specified):

```
Debug.Assert(newItem != null);

if (Icon != null) {
  ImageList imgList = new ImageList();
  ResourceService resourceService = (ResourceService)
    ServiceManager.Services.GetService(typeof(ResourceService));
  imgList.Images.Add(resourceService.GetBitmap(Icon));
  newItem.ImageList  = imgList;
  newItem.ImageIndex = 0;
}
```

Next, the description is set:

```
newItem.Description = stringParserService.Parse(description);
```

Then the menu shortcut key is applied:

```
if (Shortcut != null) {
  try {
    newItem.Shortcut = (Shortcut)
      ((System.Windows.Forms.Shortcut.F1.GetType()).
      InvokeMember(Shortcut, BindingFlags.GetField, null,
      System.Windows.Forms.Shortcut.F1, new object[0]));
  } catch (Exception) {
```

```
        newItem.Shortcut = System.Windows.Forms.Shortcut.None;
      }
    }
```

Finally, the enabled/disabled status for this item is determined:

```
    newItem.Enabled = action != ConditionFailedAction.Disable;
    return newItem;
  }
```

Now we have completed the creation of a menu item in SharpDevelop. We have seen the usage of the `MenuEventHandler` class. This class is an internal class of the `MenuItemCodon` class. It is used to wrap the `IMenuCommand` action to a .NET event handler:

```
class MenuEventHandler
{
  IMenuCommand action;

  public MenuEventHandler(object owner, IMenuCommand action)
  {
    this.action       = action;
    this.action.Owner = owner;
  }

  public void Execute(object sender, EventArgs e)
  {
    this.action.Run();
  }
}
```

In the next section, we will be creating a menu from the AddIn tree.

Creating Menu Items

You might be wondering how the menu items are actually created. To understand this we will look at the default workbench implementation. It's under the `UpdateMenu()` method of the `src\SharpDevelop\Base\Gui\Workbench\DefaultWorkbench.cs`:

```
void UpdateMenu(object sender, EventArgs e)
{
  TopMenu.Style = (Crownwood.Magic.Common.VisualStyle)
    propertyService.GetProperty("ICSharpCode.SharpDevelop.Gui.VisualStyle",
      Crownwood.Magic.Common.VisualStyle.IDE);
  MenuCommand[] items = (MenuCommand[])
    (AddInTreeSingleton.AddInTree.GetTreeNode(mainMenuPath).
    BuildChildItems(this)).ToArray(typeof(MenuCommand));
  TopMenu.MenuCommands.Clear();
  TopMenu.MenuCommands.AddRange(items);

  CreateToolBars();
}
```

First the style is updated. SharpDevelop allows switching the menu item style at run time. You can choose between an Office XP style and an older 3D style. This is a Magic library setting.

After that, the menu commands are created and inserted in the top menu. Note that if it changes, for example when we open a project or switch a window, the entire menu is re-created. The speed penalty is minimal. It is much slower to actually switch the current MDI window than to recreate the menu because the recreation is just a "calculation" operation and the switch of the MDI is a redrawing operation, which takes much more time. The recreation of the menu will end in a redraw of the menu control too but magic uses double buffering, which prevents flickers. With the SharpDevelop layout manager, which does not use MDI child windows, the menu switch will work without the user noticing any delay.

In the next section, we will look at menu builders – they are the SharpDevelop way of creating dynamic menus.

Menu Item Builders

Sometimes it is not enough just to store menu items in an XML definition file. The items may need runtime information for their creation. The AddIn tree is static, as it cannot redefine its own definition after startup. For creating dynamic menus the `ISubmenuBuilder` interface was defined, which solves this problem.

The `ISubmenuBuilder` interface is simple and can be found under `src\SharpDevelop\Base\Internal\Codons\MenuItems\ISubmenuBuilder.cs`:

```
public interface ISubmenuBuilder
{
  MenuCommand[] BuildSubmenu(object owner);
}
```

Objects that implement this interface are used in SharpDevelop for:

- ❑ Displaying Recent Files / Recent Projects submenu
- ❑ In the textarea context menu where a builder displays all available syntax highlighting schemes
- ❑ The tools in the Tools menu
- ❑ The current open windows in the Window menu
- ❑ The tool windows (we call them pads) in the View menu

Now we will look at the menu builder, which creates the View menu. In the next chapter, we will see how the Recent Files / Recent Projects menus are handled. The menu item builder can be found in the file `src\SharpDevelop\Base\Commands\MenuItemBuilders.cs`:

```
public class ViewMenuBuilder : ISubmenuBuilder
{
  class MyMenuItem : SdMenuCommand
  {
    IPadContent padContent;
```

```
    bool IsPadVisible {
      get {
        return WorkbenchSingleton.Workbench.WorkbenchLayout.IsVisible
          (padContent);
      }
    }

    public MyMenuItem(IPadContent padContent) : base(padContent.Title)
    {
      this.padContent = padContent;
      this.Click += new EventHandler(ClickEvent);
      Update += new EventHandler(UpdateThisItem);
    }

    public void UpdateThisItem(object sender, EventArgs e)
    {
      Checked = IsPadVisible;
    }

    void ClickEvent(object sender, EventArgs e)
    {
      if (IsPadVisible) {
        WorkbenchSingleton.Workbench.WorkbenchLayout.HidePad(padContent);
      } else {
        WorkbenchSingleton.Workbench.WorkbenchLayout.ShowPad(padContent);
      }
    }
  }

  public MenuCommand[] BuildSubmenu(object owner)
  {
    ArrayList items = new ArrayList();
    foreach (IPadContent padContent in
      WorkbenchSingleton.Workbench.PadContentCollection) {
      items.Add(new MyMenuItem(padContent));
    }
    return (MenuCommand[])items.ToArray(typeof(MenuCommand));
  }
}
```

The BuildSubmenu item just creates a MenuCommand array that contains the MyMenuItem class, which is initialized with IPadContents taken from the workbench window. We will see all about pads, the workbench, and other GUI-related issues in Chapter 6. For now, this class is a nice example of menu item builders.

This builder solves the problem of making every tool window inside SharpDevelop hideable in the so-called View menu, where menu icons should mark a pad (tool window) as visible or not. Instead of manually providing a separate menu item for each pad that shows/hides the window, these items are auto-generated by the builder. The implementer of the tool window need not worry about the View menu. Currently, a pad can't flag that it should not be hideable but we can implement this feature (with a codon attribute) if the need arises.

Now we will look at the add-in definition of the **View** menu, which is in the
`src\AddIns\SharpDevelopCore.addin` file:

```
<MenuItem id = "View" label = "${res:XML.MainMenu.ViewMenu}">
  <MenuItem id = "ViewBuilder"
    label = ""
    class = "ICSharpCode.SharpDevelop.Commands.ViewMenuBuilder" />
  <MenuItem id = "ViewItemsSeparator" label = "-" />
  <MenuItem id = "FullScreen"
    label = "${res:XML.MainMenu.ViewMenu.FullScreen}"
    icon = "Icons.16x16.FullScreen"
    description = "${res:XML.MainMenu.ViewMenu.FullScreen.Description}"
    class = "ICSharpCode.SharpDevelop.Commands.ToggleFullscreenCommand" />
</MenuItem>
```

The top `MenuItem` is the **View** menu. Its first item is the `ViewMenuBuilder`, which we saw earlier. This item will be replaced with the contents built by the menu item builder. We have to specify the `label`, as it is a required attribute. In this case it is just set empty.

With the introduction of the menu builder, the SharpDevelop menu system was considered 'feature complete'. The next sections will give us an overview of the different codons used in SharpDevelop. We will look at each of them, to get a feel of the AddIn tree's usage inside SharpDevelop.

Codon Overview

We have seen the `MenuItem` codon in detail. In this section, we will discuss all the codons that are currently defined inside SharpDevelop. From Chapter 3, we already know the codon definition; in this chapter we will see the attributes of the codon XML node and the location of the codon class.

The Class Codon (class)

The class codon is the basic codon. It just inherits from `AbstractCodon`. Often this codon is sufficient to put a class into the path for describing something that just needs a class without any further properties. For example, it is used to insert workspace services (see Chapter 5 for details on workspace services) into the AddIn tree.

When new types of classes are inserted into the Addin tree, often the class codon is the first step in inserting them. This was the case for adding display bindings (for details, refer to Chapter 6) before they got their own codons because they needed new attributes.
Class location: `src\SharpDevelop\Core\AddIns\Codons\ClassCodon.cs`

```
<Extension path = "/Workspace/Autostart">
  <Class id = "StartWorkbenchCommand"
    class = "ICSharpCode.SharpDevelop.Commands.StartWorkbenchCommand"/>
</Extension>
```

We have seen the object creation in the last chapter, but note that the given class must have a public empty constructor, otherwise an exception will be thrown when the `BuildItem()` method is called. The caller must specify which classes or interfaces the objects must have (or implement). This makes the class attribute flexible.

The File Filter Codon (FileFilter)

The file filter codon is used to place file filters into file open and file save dialogs. Language bindings usually extend them.

Class location: `src\SharpDevelop\Base\Internal\Codons\FileFilterCodon.cs`

```
<Extension path = "/SharpDevelop/Workbench/FileFilter">
  <FileFilter id = "CSharp"
    insertbefore="AllFiles"
    name = "C# Files (*.cs)"
    extensions = "*.cs"/>
</Extension>
```

The file filter codon just builds a string in the `BuildItem()` method, which contains a standard file filter. The file filter for our example would be: `C# Files (*.cs)|*.cs`. Note that the duplicate file filters won't be filtered out.

The Icon Codon (Icon)

The icon codon is used to extend the icon database of SharpDevelop through add-ins. SharpDevelop uses a resource file to get icons but add-ins can bring their own icons into SharpDevelop (for example, to use custom icons for a project file of a specific language).

Class location: `src\SharpDevelop\Core\AddIns\Codons\IconCodon.cs`

```
<Extension path = "/Workspace/Icons">
  <Icon id = "XmlFileIcon"
    location = "icons\XmlFileIcon.png"
    extensions=".xml"/>
</Extension>
```

If we used more than one icon for an extension, the last icon that is inserted will be used. This behavior can be used to overwrite standard icons with custom ones.

The Dialog Panel Codon (DialogPanel)

The dialog panel codon is used for options dialogs and for wizard dialogs.

Class location: `src\SharpDevelop\Base\Internal\Codons\DialogPanelCodon.cs`

```
<Extension path = "/SharpDevelop/CompletionDatabaseWizard">
  <DialogPanel id = "SetupPanel"
    label = "${res:Dialog.Wizards.
      CodeCompletionDatabaseWizard.SetupPanel.Title}"
    class = "ICSharpCode.SharpDevelop.Gui.Dialogs.
```

```
        OptionPanels.CompletionDatabaseWizard.SetupPanel"/>
   </Extension>
```

All dialog panel classes must implement the `IDialogPanel` interface. It is implemented in `src\SharpDevelop\Base\Internal\Codons\IDialogPanel.cs` and it has an abstract implementation in the same directory. The dialog panel simply provides a control and a `ReceiveDialogMessage()` method, which returns a Boolean value. For actions like OK, cancel, etc., the dialog panel receives a message, which can be interrupted when `ReceiveDialogMessage` returns `false`.

Wizard panels must extend the `IWizardPanel` interface (`src\SharpDevelop\Base\Gui\Dialogs\Wizard\IWizardPanel.cs`), which extends the `IDialogPanel` with wizard-specific functions. Wizard panels can enable/disable the buttons (**Ok, Next, Finish, Cancel**) of the wizard dialog and they can tell which panel will come after the current one when the **Next** button is pressed. The dialog recalls what the previous dialog panels were and takes care of the **Previous** button itself.

The Display Binding Codon (DisplayBinding)

The display binding codon is used to put display bindings (for details refer to Chapter 6) into SharpDevelop. The display binding path is: `/SharpDevelop/Workbench/DisplayBindings`

Class location: `src\SharpDevelop\Base\Internal\Codons\DisplayBinding \DisplayBindingCodon.cs`

Example:

```
<Extension path = "/SharpDevelop/Workbench/DisplayBindings">
  <DisplayBinding id = "Text"
    insertafter = "Browser"
    supportedformats = "Text Files, Source Files"
    class = "ICSharpCode.SharpDevelop.DefaultEditor.Gui.Editor.
    TextEditorDisplayBinding"/>
</Extension>
```

This codon inserts the text editor that is used for all source files. It is inserted after the browser codon, which displays web pages. It is important to insert it after the browser because the text editor display binding 'wants' to open all files and so it must be asked last about how the file should be opened. All additional display bindings must be inserted before the `Text` display binding or they will never run.

The Language Binding Codon (LanguageBinding)

The language binding codon is used to put language bindings into SharpDevelop. The language binding path is `/SharpDevelop/Workbench/LanguageBindings`.

Class location: `src\SharpDevelop\Base\Internal\Codons\LanguageBinding \LanguageBindingCodon.cs`

```
<Extension path = "/SharpDevelop/Workbench/LanguageBindings">
  <LanguageBinding id = "CSharp"
    supportedextensions = ".cs"
    class = "CSharpBinding.CSharpLanguageBinding" />
</Extension>
```

The Toolbar Item Codon (ToolbarItem)

The toolbar item codon is used to define the SharpDevelop toolbar. The SharpDevelop toolbars are currently defined under /SharpDevelop/Workbench/ToolBar. The toolbar item codons that are directly in this path are treated as top items, which represent toolbars. All sub-items from these top items are toolbar items.

Class location: src\SharpDevelop\Base\Internal\Codons\Toolbars\ToolbarItemCodon.cs

```
<Extension path = "/SharpDevelop/Workbench/ToolBar">
  <ToolbarItem id = "Standard">
    <ToolbarItem id = "New"
      icon = "Icons.16x16.NewDocumentIcon"
      tooltip = "${res:XML.MainMenu.FileMenu.New.File.Description}"
      class = "ICSharpCode.SharpDevelop.Commands.CreateNewFile"/>
  </ToolbarItem>
</Extension>
```

This example creates a toolbar called Standard, which has one toolbar item (id="New").

Now that we have seen all the codons, let's move on to conditions – they are the second building block of the AddIn tree.

Wiring up Add-ins with Conditions

We already know that the AddIn tree definition can't be changed at run time. Theoretically, add-ins and tree-node paths might be removed but this won't help us if we want to enable/disable menu items. In the last chapter we have already seen conditions (in the section on *Conditions*) and gotten an overview of the system and know what they do in general.

In this section we will learn about:

❑ **The Condition Structure** – We will see how conditions are joined and how they get used in an add-in definition

❑ **Defining Conditions** – We will see how conditions are defined in the source code

❑ **Overview of Available Conditions** – We will be looking at all the conditions that are used into SharpDevelop

Let's start our discussions of Conditions by examining the Condition Structure.

Condition Structure

We have already seen conditions in the XML add-in definition. Now we will take a deeper look at what can be done in the definition.

The standard condition is used as follows:

```
<Extension path = "[ExtensionPath]">
  <Conditional [Attributes] [action="Disable"]>
    ...(Codons that have the condition applied)
  </Conditional>
</Extension>
```

Often conditions must be joined to form conditions having different options. For example, if we want both condition A and condition B to be true to validate codons we may do this:

```
<Extension path = "[ExtensionPath]">
  <ConditionalA>
    <ConditionalB>
      ... (Codons that have the condition A and B applied)
    </ConditionalB>
  </ConditionalA>
</Extension>
```

When we want either condition A or condition B to be true, we can use:

```
<Extension path = "[ExtensionPath]">
  <ConditionalA>
    ... (Codons that have the condition A applied)
  </ConditionalA>
  <ConditionalB>
  ... (Copy of the codons above (now they have the condition Bapplied)
  </ConditionalB>
</Extension>
```

The problem is that we can't build a codon having condition A and not condition B (thats is, condition B evaluates to false). Therefore, to build complex conditions a system of joining conditions was introduced. The following functions can be used for joining conditions:

- ❑ And – n conditions can be joined by logical AND

- ❑ Or – n conditions can be joined by logical OR

- ❑ Not – One condition can be negated

We refer to these functions as 'condition operators'.
When joining conditions, the syntax in the add-in file looks like this:

```
<Extension path = "[ExtensionPath]">
  <Conditional [action="Disable"]>
    <And>
      <Condition [Attributes]/>
```

```
        <Condition [Attributes]/>
        <Condition [Attributes]/>
        <Or>
          <Condition [Attributes]/>
          <Condition [Attributes]/>
        </Or>
        <Not>
          <Condition [Attributes]/>
        </Not>
      </And>
      ... (Codons that have the joined condition applied)
    </Conditional>
  </Extension>
```

Note that the `Conditional` node can only have one condition node applied. Otherwise, the result is unspecified. This error is currently not detected. Instead, only the first condition block is used.

The main `Conditional` XML node contains the action to be taken when this joined condition is applied. The child elements of this `Conditional` node (that is, the sub-conditions) are called `Condition`. This is so because it is valid to use a condition in a `Conditional` node without condition operators and we need to see the difference between a condition and an empty `Conditional` node:

```
<Extension path = "[ExtensionPath]">
  <Conditional [action="Disable"]>
    <Condition [Attributes]/>
      ... (Codons that have the joined condition applied)
  </Conditional>
</Extension>
```

We will see a real-world example of a complex condition at the end of this chapter.

Now that we know what conditions look like in the add-in definition, we are going on to look at how conditions are implemented in the source code.

Defining Conditions

Conditions are defined similarly to codons. Instead of a `CodonName` attribute, the condition class has a `ConditionAttribute`. However, this attribute does not receive a name. As mentioned earlier, instead of a name, the conditions are differentiated by their required attributes (therefore the set of required attributes must be unique). It is defined in this particular way because conditions only have the node name `Conditional` (or `Condition`).

Conditions are added to the condition builder of the AddIn tree, in a manner similar to codons. All runtime libraries that are defined in an add-in are automatically scanned for defined conditions. These are added to the condition builder and, after that, they can be used by the add-in (or other add-ins). If there is an attribute clash (two conditions with the same set of required attributes), the add-in implementation will throw an exception and SharpDevelop won't start. It is designed this way because the add-in implementor should be forced to write correct add-ins, conditions, and codons.

Now we will look at the simplest condition, the compare condition. It is available in the file `src\SharpDevelop\Core\AddIns\Conditions\CompareCondition.cs` and is used to compare two strings. This makes sense because the provided strings get a run through the string parser. With the `${...}` tags we can obtain a SharpDevelop property (with `${property:PROPERTYAME}`).

Codons can be disabled under special circumstances. For example, in the SharpDevelop window menu MDI-specific menu items like tile, cascade, and arrange icons are present. They are only enabled when the current layout manager is set to MDI layout and at least one window is active:

```xml
<Conditional action="Disable">
  <And>
    <Condition activewindow="*" />
    <Condition string="${property:SharpDevelop.Workbench.WorkbenchLayout}"
      equals="MDI"/>
  </And>
  ...
</Conditional>
```

Now we are going to look at the implementation of the compare condition:

```csharp
[ConditionAttribute()]
public class CompareCondition : AbstractCondition
{
  [XmlMemberAttribute("string", IsRequired=true)]
  string s1;

  [XmlMemberAttribute("equals", IsRequired=true)]
  string s2;

  public string String1 {
    get {
      return s1;
    }
    set {
      s1 = value;
    }
  }

  public string String2 {
    get {
      return s2;
    }
    set {
      s2 = value;
    }
  }

  public override bool IsValid(object owner)
  {
    StringParserService stringParserService = (StringParserService)
      ServiceManager.Services.GetService(typeof(StringParserService));
    return stringParserService.Parse(s1) == stringParserService.Parse(s2);
  }
}
```

As we can see, the conditions are using the `XmlMemberAttribute`; earlier we saw that this attribute class was called `XmlMemberAttributeAttribute`, but .NET allows us to skip the `Attribute` postfix when using attributes, therefore we don't need to specify the last `"Attribute"` when using this attribute. `XmlMemberAttributeAttribute` looks weird so `XmlMemberAttribute` is used in the codon and condition implementations.

The main difference between codons and conditions is that conditions don't build items. Instead, they have the `IsValid()` method, which determines whether the condition is successful or not. Conditions don't have shared attributes like `id`, `class`, `insertbefore`, or `insertafter`, because there is currently no need for them.

Overview of Available Conditions

This section will give us an overview of all the conditions that are currently defined in SharpDevelop. We will start with the window active condition.

Window Active Condition

This condition checks if a window is active, and if it is active checks the type. With this condition we can even check if the window contains specific a view-content (a special display binding). If we set the `activewindow` attribute to * we could check whether any window is open.

Class location: `src\SharpDevelop\Base\Internal\Conditions\WindowActiveCondition.cs`

```
<MenuItem id = "Edit" label = "${res:XML.MainMenu.EditMenu}">
  <Conditional activewindow="*" action="Disable">
    <MenuItem id = "Undo"/>
    <MenuItem id = "Redo"/>
  </Conditional>
</MenuItem>
```

To make the condition example snippets easier to understand, we have removed the `class`, `label`, and `icon` attributes from the menu items. This example activates the **Undo** / **Redo** menu items in the edit menu only if a window is active.

Window Open Condition

This condition checks whether a window is open, and if there is, the type of all open windows is checked. This can be useful for adding a menu item when a special window is open. With this condition, we can check if a window contains specific view content. Also, if we set the `openwindow` attribute to *, we can check if any window is open. It has one attribute.

Class location: `src\SharpDevelop\Base\Internal\Conditions\WindowOpenCondition.cs`

```
<Conditional action="Disable">
  <Or>
    <Condition
openwindow="ICSharpCode.SharpDevelop.DefaultEditor.Gui.Editor.ITextAreaControlProv
ider"/>
    <Condition openproject="*"/>
  </Or>
```

```
    <MenuItem id = "Find"/>
    <MenuItem id = "FindNext"/>
    <MenuItem id = "Replace"/>
</Conditional>
```

This example enables the find menu items only if a text area or project is open. It shouldn't be only open when the active window is a text area because it is possible to search in all open files. Therefore, the open window condition is used instead.

Project Active Condition

This condition checks whether a project is selected, and if so, it checks whether any project is of the given type. (By specifying * as project name it is possible to check if any project is selected). It is possible to have a project open but no selected project.

If we have a file open, which is contained in an open project, then this project gets automatically selected. Here is the attribute table for this condition:

Class location:
`src\SharpDevelop\Base\Internal\Conditions\ProjectActiveCondition.cs`

```
<Extension path =
"/SharpDevelop/Workbench/ProjectOptions/ConfigurationProperties">
  <Conditional activeproject="C#">
    <DialogPanel id = "CSharpCodeGenerationPanel"
      label = "${res:Dialog.Options.PrjOptions.
        CodeGenerationPanel.PanelName}"
      class = "CSharpBinding.CodeGenerationPanel"/>
    <DialogPanel id = "CSharpOutputOptionsPanel"
      label = "${res:Dialog.Options.PrjOptions.
        OutputOptionsPanel.PanelName}"
      class = "CSharpBinding.OutputOptionsPanel"/>
    <DialogPanel id = "CSharpRuntimeCompilerPanel"
      label = "Runtime/Compiler"
      class = "CSharpBinding.ChooseRuntimePanel"/>
  </Conditional>
</Extension>
```

In this example, dialog panels are added to the project options configuration dialog only if the active project is C#. All the language bindings will put their configuration dialogs under `/SharpDevelop/Workbench/ProjectOptions/ConfigurationProperties` and use the project active condition for making the panels available when the correct project is configured (note that only the active project can be configured).

Project Open Condition

This condition checks if a project is opened (if a project is inside the opened combine). If several projects are open, it checks all projects for the given project type and returns `true` when it is found. If * is specified as the project type, then it checks if any project is open. It returns `false` if no project is open.

Class location: `src\SharpDevelop\Base\Internal\Conditions\ProjectOpenCondition.cs`

We saw an example of this condition in the earlier section on the window open condition.

Combine Open Condition

With this condition you can check if a combine is opened (or not). There is only one condition that checks if a combine is open. There is no difference between combine types, because a combine in SharpDevelop is just a container for projects and all projects must be in a combine.

Class location: `src\SharpDevelop\Base\Internal\Conditions\CombineOpenCondition.cs`

```
<MenuItem id = "Close">
  <Conditional iscombineopen="True" action="Disable">
    <MenuItem id = "CloseCombine"/>
  </Conditional>
</MenuItem>
```

This example is taken from the SharpDevelop **File** menu and the menu item `CloseCombine` is only enabled if a combine is open.

Owner State Condition

This condition is used to make the add-in definition a bit shorter for cases where the menu items need to know something about the object that creates them.

Class location: `src\SharpDevelop\Base\Internal\Conditions\OwnerStateCondition.cs`

The owner state is an enumeration. The owner must implement the owner state interface, which is in the same file as the condition. The owner must set this enum according to what it defines as internal state.

```
public interface IOwnerState {
  System.Enum InternalState {
    get;
  }
}
```

For example the **Open** File tab uses the following, which is located in the `src\SharpDevelop\Base\Gui\Components\OpenFileTab.cs` file:

```
public class OpenFileTab : Crownwood.Magic.Controls.TabControl, IOwnerState
{
  readonly static string contextMenuPath =
    "/SharpDevelop/Workbench/OpenFileTab/ContextMenu";

  [Flags]
  public enum OpenFileTabState {
    Nothing             = 0,
    FileDirty           = 1,
    ClickedWindowIsForm = 2,
    FileUntitled        = 4
  }

  OpenFileTabState internalState = OpenFileTabState.Nothing;

  public System.Enum InternalState {
    get {
      return internalState;
    }
  }
}
// ... rest of the OpenFileTab definition
```

We will skip the complete listing and focus only on the owner state. The internal state is set before the context menu is created. The `OpenFileTabState` flags mean the following:

- `FileDirty` – Set when the selected file is dirty (when the file content has changed since the last save).

- `ClickedWindowIsForm` – Set when the clicked window is a `System.Windows.Forms.Form`; this is useful for maximize/minimize operations, which only makes sense on forms.

- `FileUntitled` – Only set when the selected file is untitled. This is only the case for new, unsaved files.

Now we will look at the context menu definition in the add-in file (`AddIns\SharpDevelopCore.addin`):

```
<Extension path  = "/SharpDevelop/Workbench/OpenFileTab/ContextMenu">
  <MenuItem id = "Close"/>
  <MenuItem id = "CloseSeparator" label = "-" />

  <Conditional action="Disable">
    <And>
      <Condition ownerstate="FileDirty"/>
      <Not>
        <Condition ownerstate="FileUntitled"/>
      </Not>
    </And>
    <MenuItem id = "Save"/>
  </Conditional>
```

```
    <MenuItem id = "SaveAs"/>
    <MenuItem id = "SaveSeparator" label = "-" />

    <Conditional action="Disable">
      <Not>
        <Condition ownerstate="FileUntitled" />
      </Not>
      <MenuItem id = "CopyPathName"/>
    </Conditional>

    <Conditional ownerstate="ClickedWindowIsForm">
      <MenuItem id = "WindowSeparator"  label =   "-" />
      <MenuItem id = "Restore"/>
      <MenuItem id = "Minimize"/>
      <MenuItem id = "Maximize"/>
    </Conditional>
  </Extension>
```

As we can see, the owner state conditions are used almost everywhere. The Save menu item is disabled if the file is not dirty or if it is untitled. The CopyPathName item copies the file name to the clipboard; this makes sense only if the file has a name. The Restore/Minimize/Maximize items are only enabled when a form is clicked.

Alternatively, we might have defined more than one context menu path, for example /SharpDevelop/Workbench/OpenFileTab/ContextMenu/ClickedWindowIsForm, and this path would be taken if the clicked window was a form. However, with this approach we must provide path names for each combination:

/SharpDevelop/Workbench/OpenFileTab/ContextMenu/ClickedWindowIsFormAndIsUntitl ed,

/SharpDevelop/Workbench/OpenFileTab/ContextMenu/ClickedWindowIsFormAndIsDirty,

and so on. This would be 2^3=8 path combinations containing mostly the same items with little variation (like a disabled "Save" item). The owner state approach is much shorter.

Summary

In this chapter, we have discussed the menu item codon in detail. We learned about the menu item builder and can now extend menus in SharpDevelop with our own items. We got an overview of all the codons used in SharpDevelop. We also looked into conditions and learned about creating new conditions.

In the next chapter, we will have an overview of the workspace services. Along with the Addin tree, services are the underpinnings of SharpDevelop.

CHAPTER 5

5

Providing Functionality with Workspace Services

In this chapter we will be discussing the topic of services in SharpDevelop. We will learn what a service is and how it is defined. Then, we will go on to see the various services that are available to the programmers in the IDE. After reading this chapter, we will be in a position to appreciate the bonuses that the service concept delivers in conjunction with the AddIn tree and why we have used services instead of other alternatives such as singleton classes or static definitions.

Implementation Considerations

Initially, we only had the AddIn tree and SharpDevelop depended on it alone to provide functionality. However, menu commands and other actions needed classes that provided functions, like OpenFile, or a place where the compiler output could be written. Sometimes it was necessary to know when some event takes place (for example an event needs to be defined somewhere to inform other parts of the IDE when a project is opened).

These functions could be defined in the main window, but then this class would start growing bigger and bigger with each new event, ultimately becoming impossible to maintain.

We solved this problem by defining classes that only had static members, and which all the other objects needing their service could access. These classes defined events for their methods too. Other objects can be informed through the static classes when an event occurs (like the project opening).

But there were too many (over 10) of these static helper classes, and it was difficult to locate them in the source tree. Another problem with these static helper classes arose – they were hard to replace. Also, there was no way an add-in could extend one of these helper classes, as they were statically inserted into the source.

This problem was solved by introducing a services layer, which builds on the AddIn tree under these classes. The classes are no longer static, instead they are created once and then can be accessed, wherever needed, through a singleton helper class.

Now, most of these old static classes have been converted to services. However, there are some exceptions; classes that are only used in subsystems and which don't seem to have any practical use outside these subsystems still use the original design.

Let's now look at what a service must provide to fit into the service structure.

Requirements for Services

The main requirement for a service is that it provides support to other parts of the application. They 'serve' as helper classes. Beside that, all services must implement the IService interface, which can be found under src\SharpDevelop\Core\Services\IService.cs:

```
public interface IService
{
  // Is true when the service did already initialize, false otherwise.
  bool IsInitialized {
    get;
  }

  // This method is called after the services are loaded.
  void InitializeService();

  // This method is called before the service is unloaded.
  void UnloadService();

  event EventHandler Initialize;
  event EventHandler Unload;
}
```

The IService interface has only two basic methods and one property:

❑ InitializeService – Instead of the constructor, services should initialize themselves in this method .

❑ UnloadService – In this method the service should free all acquired resources.

❑ IsInitialized – This flags if the InitializeService method has been called.

For both of the methods, events are defined that fire when these methods are executed.

Like many other interfaces there already exists an abstract implementation of this interface called AbstractService, which is defined in the same path and namespace.

Next, we will see how services are managed and where the InitializeService and UnloadService methods get called. We will also see how to access the services in order to use them.

The ServiceManager

The ServiceManager class stores all the services that are available at run time, and provides a single access point to these services. To ensure that there is only a single service manager, it follows the singleton pattern we discussed in Chapter 2. All objects that require some service must request the required service from the ServiceManager.

The service manager performs service initialization and unloading too. It is defined in the file src\SharpDevelop\Core\Services\ServiceManager.cs:

```
public class ServiceManager
{
  ArrayList serviceList        = new ArrayList();
  Hashtable servicesHashtable  = new Hashtable();

  static ServiceManager defaultServiceManager = new ServiceManager();

  // Gets the default ServiceManager
  public static ServiceManager Services {
    get {
      return defaultServiceManager;
    }
  }

  // Don't create ServiceManager objects, only have ONE per application.
  private ServiceManager()
  {
  }

  // This method initializes the service system to a path inside the
  // AddIn tree. This method must be called ONCE.
  public void InitializeServicesSubsystem(string servicesPath)
  {
    // add 'core' services
    AddService(new PropertyService());
    AddService(new ResourceService());
    AddService(new StringParserService());
    AddService(new FileUtilityService());

    // add AddIn tree services
    AddServices((IService[])AddInTreeSingleton.AddInTree.GetTreeNode
      (servicesPath).BuildChildItems(this).ToArray(typeof(IService)));

    // initialize all services
    foreach (IService service in serviceList) {
      service.InitializeService();
    }
  }

  // Calls UnloadService on all services.
  //This method must be called ONCE.
  public void UnloadAllServices()
  {
```

```
    foreach (IService service in serviceList) {
      service.UnloadService();
    }
  }

  protected void AddService(IService service)
  {
    serviceList.Add(service);
  }

  protected void AddServices(IService[] services)
  {
    foreach (IService service in services) {
      AddService(service);
    }
  }

  // Requests a specific service, may return null if this service is not
  // found.
  public IService GetService(Type serviceType)
  {
    IService s = (IService)servicesHashtable[serviceType];
    if (s != null) {
      return s;
    }

    foreach (IService service in serviceList) {
      if (serviceType.IsInstanceOfType(service)) {
        servicesHashtable[serviceType] = service;
        return service;
      }
    }
    return null;
  }
}
```

The InitializeServicesSubsystem and UnloadAllServices methods will be called in the Main method of SharpDevelop (for a listing of the main method refer to Chapter 3).

All the services defined in the core are added directly to the service manager, as other services may be dependent on them. They are usable by all other services. Note that in the current model, some services may work before the InitializeService method is called (this depends on the service because some services may not need to be initialized to do their work). To solve the dependency problem we introduced the Initialize method, which gets called when all services are accessible through the service manager. However this might not be helpful if the services aren't initialized; in this case you've to get the service, check if it has been initialized (through the IsInitialized flag) and if not, wait for this event (using the Initialize event). To avoid this problem, SharpDevelop guarantees that all 'core' services are up and running when other services get loaded.

The services are stored in parallel in an ArrayList and a Hashtable. The ArrayList is used to run through all available services. This is useful for initialization and unloading.

Now a question arises – why isn't the `Hashtable` used to run through all the services? The answer is relatively simple. When a service added to the table, the type under which the service will be requested is not known. It may be any interface that the service object implements, the type itself, or a base type of the service object. We can't just initialize the services when they are added because of the dependency problem (all services must be available to the service initialization).

Assume that instead of iterating through the `servicesList` we used this loop:

```
// initialize all services
foreach (IService service in servicesHashtable.Values) {
  service.InitializeService();
}
```

If a service requests another service under a type that is not stored in the `Hashtable`, the table will change and the `foreach` loop will fail. Alternatively, we could choose to store all subtypes and interfaces into the hash table, but this was not implemented since it is not necessary to have all the types available in the `Hashtable`. There would be many objects under `System.Object` too and a hash table operates faster with fewer objects in it (admittedly, this is a weak argument counting the numbers of the services we have).

Using this method, the service will be put into the hash table the first time it is requested. The services are allowed to expose several types so this might not be a clean way of doing a service subsystem and this may change in future versions (but for now it works). One argument against this 'flexibility' is that a specific service will only be requested under one type in SharpDevelop. The `GetService` method first looks into the hash table, and if the service isn't found there it looks in the `serviceList`. If the service is still not found, it puts it into the hash table and returns the `service` object. If it is not found there, it returns `null`. The hash table acts as a speed improvement, nothing more.

Now that we know how and where services are requested, let's look at how services are added to the AddIn tree.

Defining Services

All services are put into the AddIn tree by using a class codon (for details on codons refer to Chapter 4) under the path `/Workspace/Services`. Currently the extension node in `AddIns\SharpDevelopCore.addin` is:

```
<Extension path = "/Workspace/Services">
  <Class id    = "ProjectService"
         class = "ICSharpCode.SharpDevelop.Services.DefaultProjectService"/>
  <Class id    = "FileService"
         class = "ICSharpCode.SharpDevelop.Services.DefaultFileService"/>
  <Class id    = "ParserService"
         class = "ICSharpCode.SharpDevelop.Services.DefaultParserService"/>
  <Class id    = "TaskService"
         class = "ICSharpCode.SharpDevelop.Services.TaskService"/>
  <Class id    = "StatusBarService"
         class =
            "ICSharpCode.SharpDevelop.Services.DefaultStatusBarService"/>
  <Class id    = "ToolbarService"
```

```
            class = "ICSharpCode.SharpDevelop.Services.ToolbarService"/>
    <Class id    = "LanguageService"
            class = "ICSharpCode.SharpDevelop.Services.LanguageService"/>
    <Class id    = "ClassBrowserIconsService"
            class =
              "ICSharpCode.SharpDevelop.Services.ClassBrowserIconsService"/>
    <Class id    = "LanguageBindingService"
            class =
              "ICSharpCode.SharpDevelop.Services.LanguageBindingService"/>
    <Class id    = "DisplayBindingService"
            class = "ICSharpCode.SharpDevelop.Services.DisplayBindingService"/>
    <Class id    = "AmbienceService"
            class = "ICSharpCode.SharpDevelop.Services.AmbienceService"/>
</Extension>
```

All services must implement the `IService` interface or else SharpDevelop won't load (we will get an error message). To add a new service simply implement the `IService` interface (or extend the abstract implementation `AbstractService`, which lies in the same directory) and add a class codon pointing to the new service class to the services path.

Common Services at your Service

In this section, we will look at all services that are currently defined in SharpDevelop. Note that unless explicitly mentioned, the default implementation is in the same directory as the service interface, and is called `DefaultXXXService`, while the interface is called `IXXXService` (some services are accessible through interfaces).

We will discuss some of the services in detail, but most of them are described briefly as they are either covered in the other chapters or their implementation isn't interesting enough to discuss them here.

Let's begin with the services defined in the `Core` project of SharpDevelop (therefore they're called 'core' services). They're inside the core because they don't have SharpDevelop-specific dependencies. They include:

❑ **File Utility Service** – For common file operations and providing icons for files

❑ **Property Service** – Service for accessing the global properties of SharpDevelop

❑ **Resource Service** – The localization manager

❑ **StringParser Service** – The service for defining properties inside strings

After the core services we cover the other services (they are inside the base project of SharpDevelop) as well:

❑ **Ambience Service** – Formats type and member information to the user preferences and provides access to the code generation style

❑ **ClassBrowserIcons** Service – The service which makes it easier to get the icons for types and members

❏ **File Service** – Handles SharpDevelop file functions that are too high level for the File Utility Service (like open/close file inside the IDE)

❏ **Project Service** – Keeps track of the current open projects and combines

❏ **Parser Service** – Access layer to the parser, which is used for code completion and the class browser

File Utility Service

The file utility service is one of the most important services in SharpDevelop. Without it, SharpDevelop would not be as stable as it is because it provides many file checking functions. It is used for common file operations and providing icons.

This service contains helper functions for commonly used functionality, that is not present in the System.IO.Path class, and some other additional file-related functions. It provides the access point to file and project icons too. The service can be found under src\SharpDevelop\Core\Services\ FileUtilityService\FileUtilityService.cs:

```
public class FileUtilityService : AbstractService
{
  public ImageList ImageList {
    get;
  }
  public Bitmap GetBitmap(string name);

  public Image GetImageForProjectType(string projectType);
  public int   GetImageIndexForProjectType(string projectType);

  public Image GetImageForFile(string fileName);
  public int   GetImageIndexForFile(string fileName);
```

The methods above handle the icons. An ImageList containing all icons can be accessed through the ImageList property. Now let's look at what these methods do:

❏ GetBitmap - With this method, SharpDevelop grabs bitmaps out of the bitmap pool. Using this function bitmaps from the SharpDevelop resource file and from AddIn tree-defined icons can be accessed because they share the same 'naming system'.

❏ GetImageForProjectType - Returns an image for a specific project type. Each project must have a type that identifies its language. For example all C# projects have the type "C#" (case sensitive). It returns a generic project file icon if the project type does not have an icon attached to.

❏ GetImageIndexForProjectType – Returns an index in the ImageList property for a specific project type.

❏ GetImageForFile – Returns an image for a file. If no icon is found an 'unknown file' icon will be returned.

❏ GetImageIndexForFile – Returns an index in the ImageList property for a specific file. If no icon is found the index of an 'unknown file' icon will be returned.

After these, some functions are defined that use native calls:

```
class NativeMethods {
  [DllImport("kernel32.dll", SetLastError=true)]
  public static extern int GetVolumeInformation(string volumePath,
        StringBuilder volumeNameBuffer,
        int volNameBuffSize,
        ref int volumeSerNr,
        ref int maxComponentLength,
        ref int fileSystemFlags,
        StringBuilder fileSystemNameBuffer,
        int fileSysBuffSize);

  [DllImport("kernel32.dll")]
  public static extern DriveType GetDriveType(string driveName);
} // end of native methods class

public string VolumeLabel(string volumePath)
{
  try {
    StringBuilder volumeName  = new StringBuilder(128);
    int dummyInt = 0;
    NativeMethods.GetVolumeInformation(volumePath, volumeName, 128,
        ref dummyInt, ref dummyInt, ref dummyInt, null, 0);
    return volumeName.ToString();
  } catch (Exception) {
    return String.Empty;
  }
}

public DriveType GetDriveType(string driveName)
{
  return NativeMethods.GetDriveType(driveName);
}
```

The VolumeLabel and GetDriveType functions are used in the file scout to determine the type and name of a drive. The DriveType enum is defined in the same file; we won't bother looking at it here.

Now let's look at a method that provides the names of all the files in a directory (and optionally all subdirectories too) back into a StringCollection. This method is used whenever specific files are to be loaded, like the *.addin files in the SharpDevelop AddIn directory:

```
public StringCollection SearchDirectory(string directory,
    string filemask, bool searchSubdirectories)
{
    StringCollection collection = new StringCollection();
    SearchDirectory
        (directory, filemask, collection, searchSubdirectories);
    return collection;
}
```

```
public StringCollection SearchDirectory(string directory, string filemask)
{
    return SearchDirectory(directory, filemask, true);
}

void SearchDirectory(string directory, string filemask, StringCollection
collection, bool searchSubdirectories)
{
  try {
    string[] file = Directory.GetFiles(directory, filemask);
    foreach (string f in file) {
      collection.Add(f);
    }
    if (searchSubdirectories) {
      string[] dir = Directory.GetDirectories(directory);
      foreach (string d in dir) {
        SearchDirectory(d, filemask, collection, searchSubdirectories);
      }
    }
  } catch (Exception e) {
    MessageBox.Show("Can't access directory " + directory + " reason:\n" +
                    e.ToString(),
                    "Error", MessageBoxButtons.OK, MessageBoxIcon.Error);
  }
}
```

A message box is displayed when the `SearchDirectory` method cannot access a specific directory.

Next, we will look at the helper methods, which convert relative paths to absolute paths and vice-versa. These methods are used during project save, where all file names get stored relative to the project file location:

```
public string AbsoluteToRelativePath(string baseDirectoryPath,
                                      string absPath);
public string RelativeToAbsolutePath(string baseDirectoryPath,
                                      string relPath);
```

Then, we have some validation methods defined:

```
public bool    IsValidFileName(string fileName);
public bool    TestFileExists(string filename);
public bool    IsDirectory(string filename);
public string  GetDirectoryNameWithSeparator(string directoryName);
```

Here's what these methods do:

❑ `IsValidFileName` – Returns `true` if the given file name is valid. We have already seen this function in Chapter 2. Note that this method is platform dependent.

❑ `TestFileExists` – Tests whether a file having the given file name exists, and displays a warning message box if not. It returns `true` if the file exists and `false` otherwise. This method is used whenever the user has to be informed that a file can't be loaded, as it's nonexistent.

- ❏ `IsDirectory` – Returns `true` if the file given by filename is a directory, otherwise `false` is returned.

- ❏ `GetDirectoryNameWithSeparator` – This method returns a directory name that has a separator attached at the end. If the user enters a directory name, they may or may not attach the path separator. Instead of validating every directory usage for whether it has a separator at the end this method does the job for us.

Now we will look at the methods that make the SharpDevelop file save routines safe:

```
public FileOperationResult ObservedSave(SaveFileDelegate saveFile,
    string fileName, string message, FileErrorPolicy policy);
```

This method has overloads that take following arguments:

```
SaveFileDelegate saveFile, string fileName, FileErrorPolicy policy
SaveFileDelegate saveFile, string fileName
NamedFileOperationDelegate saveFileAs, string fileName, string message,
    FileErrorPolicy policy
NamedFileOperationDelegate saveFileAs, string fileName,
    FileErrorPolicy policy
NamedFileOperationDelegate saveFileAs, string fileName
```

Now we look at the `ObservedLoad` method, which works the same way:

```
public FileOperationResult ObservedLoad(FileOperationDelegate saveFile,
                                 string fileName,
                                 string message,
                                 FileErrorPolicy policy);
```

This method has overloads that take the following arguments:

```
FileOperationDelegate saveFile, string fileName, FileErrorPolicy policy
FileOperationDelegate saveFile, string fileName
NamedFileOperationDelegate saveFileAs, string fileName, string message,
    FileErrorPolicy policy
NamedFileOperationDelegate saveFileAs, string fileName,
    FileErrorPolicy policy
NamedFileOperationDelegate saveFileAs, string fileName);
}
```

All these save/load methods are used to make the save/load methods safer by placing them in a `try...catch` block and display an error message if they fail. Every time files are saved or loaded the following errors can occur:

- ❏ **Write Protected** – The save operations fails

- ❏ **Not accessible** – The save/load operations may fail according to the current user's permissions

- ❏ **Network connection lost** – The save/load operations fail after they have started

These errors are gracefully handled with the save/load methods used by SharpDevelop. It is annoying to wrap a `try...catch` statement around our code whenever a file operation is being performed. The methods display a message box when an error occurs, containing a standard message (this message can be replaced with a more sophisticated message). Alternatively, a message box is displayed that allows the user chose between:

❑ **Retry** – The save operation is tried again

❑ **Ignore** – The failed operation is ignored

❑ **Choose other location** – Allows the user to select another location for saving the file (it is available only for named file save operations)

❑ **Show Exception** – The thrown exception is shown, which helps to understand the reason why the save operation failed

All save operations inside SharpDevelop are wrapped with an observed save. Save operations that the user can retry, like a file save, are wrapped with a message box. All other save operations that are performed in the background, like project file save or property save, are wrapped with a more sophisticated message box.

We will now move on to look at the enumerations and delegates that are used by the methods that we discussed above. The delegate that these methods get must point to the function that performs the file operation:

```
public enum FileErrorPolicy {
   Inform,
   ProvideAlternative
}

public enum FileOperationResult {
   OK,
   Failed,
   SavedAlternatively
}

public delegate void FileOperationDelegate();

public delegate void NamedFileOperationDelegate(string fileName);
```

The `FileOperationDelegate` is used for file operations that do not take a file name as argument. In this case, the **Choose location** button at the error message box will not be available (for load operations it is never available). The user can only use retry/ignore and look at the exception that caused the error.

Next, we consider the `ObservedSave` method that takes a `SaveFileAsDelegate` in detail. All other methods work in a similar way:

```
public SaveFileResult ObservedSave(SaveFileAsDelegate saveFileAs, string fileName,
string message, SaveFilePolicy policy)
{
   try {
     saveFileAs(fileName);
```

```
        return SaveFileResult.OK;
    } catch (Exception e) {
      switch (policy) {
        case SaveFilePolicy.Inform:
          using (SaveErrorInformDialog informDialog = new
SaveErrorInformDialog(fileName, message, e)) {
            informDialog.ShowDialog();
          }
          break;
        case SaveFilePolicy.ProvideAlternative:
          restartlabel:
          using (SaveErrorChooseDialog chooseDialog = new
SaveErrorChooseDialog(fileName, message, "Error while saving", e, true)) {
            switch (chooseDialog.ShowDialog()) {
              case DialogResult.OK:
                using (SaveFileDialog fdiag = new SaveFileDialog()) {
                  fdiag.OverwritePrompt = true;
                  fdiag.AddExtension     = true;
                  fdiag.CheckFileExists = false;
                  fdiag.CheckPathExists = true;
                  fdiag.Title            = "Choose alternate file name";
                  fdiag.FileName         = fileName;
                  if (fdiag.ShowDialog() == DialogResult.OK) {
                    return ObservedSave
                      (saveFileAs, fdiag.FileName, message, policy);
                  } else {
                    goto restartlabel;
                  }
                }
              case DialogResult.Retry:
                return ObservedSave(saveFileAs, fileName, message, policy);
              case DialogResult.Ignore:
                return SaveFileResult.Failed;
            }
          }
          break;
      }
    }
    return SaveFileResult.Failed;
}
```

We have seen the entire file service and now know how file operations are made secure inside SharpDevelop. These methods are simple and make the program much more robust.

Now we will move on to the next service, which handles the global properties in SharpDevelop.

Property Service

The property service is just an `IProperties` object, like we saw in the *Property Management in SharpDevelop* section of Chapter 3. This service is used to access the properties that are global in SharpDevelop. It is defined under `src\SharpDevelop\Core\Services\PropertyService.cs`. This service loads and saves its contents to a property file. Beside that, it has a `ConfigDirectory` property defined. This points to the directory in which all SharpDevelop data must be saved. Currently this is set to:

```
System.Environment.GetFolderPath(Environment.SpecialFolder.ApplicationData)+
                    Path.DirectorySeparatorChar+".ICSharpCode"+
                    Path.DirectorySeparatorChar+"SharpDevelop"+
                    Path.DirectorySeparatorChar;
```

This service is used wherever properties must be made persistent (refer to Chapter 3 for more information on property persistence).

Resource Service

The resource service is used for internationalization (for details, refer to Chapter 7) and icons. Dialogs set their labels directly using the resource service (except XML defined dialogs, see Chapter 17). Other than that, bitmaps that are defined in resource files should be got using the `FileUtilityService` class instead because the resource service can only access the bitmaps defined in the SharpDevelop resource files and the `FileUtilityService` can access these and bitmaps from the AddIn tree too. The service is defined under `src\SharpDevelop\Core\Services\ResourceService.cs`:

```
public class ResourceService : AbstractService
{
  public string GetString(string name);

  public Icon GetIcon(string name);
  public Bitmap GetBitmap(string name);
}
```

The `GetIcon` method returns the same image as the `GetBitmap` method but in another format (as `System.Drawing.Icon` class). Icons are used to set the icon of a `System.Windows.Forms.Form`.

Note that most internationalization is done through the `StringParserService` class, which we will be discussing next.

String Parser Service

The string parser helps us with internationalization and tags in strings. For example, if a message needs to display a file name the message text may be:

```
string msg = "Can't load file {0}.";
```

In addition, with `String.Format` the message could be displayed with:

```
DisplayMessage(String.Format(msg, filename));
```

These solution would work but for each string that is displayed the translators must know what {0}, {1} etc. is and sometimes this can lead to confusion (the original language message contains some clues to what {x} means but maybe too few to be sure). Therefore, SharpDevelop uses ${...} tags (this style gets used by many other programs too) to clarify this:

```
string msg = "Can't load file ${FileName}.";
```

We need some sort of parser to replace the ${...} tags with the file name. This parser is implemented as a service called the string parser service. The `StringParserService` class is defined under `src\SharpDevelop\Core\Services\StringParserService.cs`. We will examine its code in Chapter 7; for now we will only look at the declarations:

```
public class StringParserService : AbstractService
{
  public PropertyDictionary Properties {
    get;
  }
  public string Parse(string input);
  public string Parse(string input, string[,] customTags);
}
```

In the `Properties` dictionary, custom properties can be written and are then available in all following `Parse` calls.

Note that all tags are case insensitive ${FileName} is the same as ${FILENAME} or ${FiLeNaMe}

The `Parse` method has two variants. One of them takes custom tags that are saved into a `string[,]` array. For example:

```
string msg = stringParserService.Parse("Can't load file ${FileName}.", new
string[,] {
  {"FileName", fileName}
});
```

This snippet would set a tag called `FileName` for the input string. The string parser only replaces the tags it knows about. If an unknown tag is found in the string, it is copied to the output string untouched. Custom tags have a higher priority than global properties. The string parser service knows about the following global tags:

❑ `Date` – Gives back the current date. Almost any string displayed in SharpDevelop is parsed with the stringparser service. The `Date` tag is used mostly in file templates, in which the creation date is inserted.

❑ `Time` – returns the current time.

- ❏ `env:[EnvironmentVariableName]` – with this tag, all environment variables (`System.Environment.GetEnvironmentVariables()`) can be accessed. For example, `${env:SystemRoot}` would be transformed to `C:\WINNT` on my system because the environment variable `SystemRoot` has this value.

- ❏ `res:[ResourceName]` – used for internationalization. With this tag resource strings can be loaded out of the resource database (for details refer Chapter 7).

- ❏ `property:[PropertyName]` – allows global properties, which are all SharpDevelop options, to be accessed.

The `StringParserService` is the last service defined in the `Core`. Now we will move on to the `Base` project, which provides higher-level services for the IDE.

In the core are the core services and the AddIn tree so there is no need to limit ourselves to using the core to develop an IDE. It is possible to do anything else with it. Inside the base project are the underpinnings of the IDE, there are most commands, the project management system, and so on. This is the heart of the IDE part in SharpDevelop.

Ambience Service

The ambience service provides some look and feel options for the user. It doesn't provide GUI look and feel, rather it wraps code generation options or 'ambiences'. We will look at what an ambience is after we have seen the service implementation. It is available in the file `src\SharpDevelop\Base\Services\AmbienceService\AmbienceService.cs`:

```
public class AmbienceService : AbstractService
{
  public IProperties CodeGenerationProperties {
    get;
  }
  public bool GenerateDocumentComments {
    get;
  }
  public bool GenerateAdditionalComments {
    get;
  }
  public bool UseFullyQualifiedTypenames {
    get;
  }
  public AmbienceReflectionDecorator CurrentAmbience {
    get;
  }
  public event EventHandler AmbienceChanged;
}
```

The first four properties are used for code generation. The user can chose the preferred code generation method from the options dialog and the code is formatted using that information. We will look at code generation options in Chapter 17. For now it is enough to know that the code generation properties are just put into an `IProperties` object and that these properties are easy-to-use wrappers.

121

We should pay attention to the `CurrentAmbience` property. It returns an
`AmbienceReflectionDecorator` object, which inherits from `IAmbience` found under
`src\SharpDevelop\Base\Services\AmbienceService\IAmbience.cs`.

Ambiences are used to format information about classes and reflection according to the preferred visual
style of the user. Look at the following screenshots to get an impression of what they do:

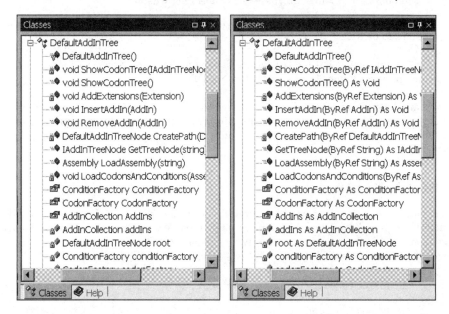

With the C# ambience shown on the left the methods and fields are printed in C# style (type first; look
at the method parameters and return values). The VB.NET ambience shown on the right prints the
names in VB.NET style (name As Type).

Ambiences are used in the object browser and code completion/method insight windows as well. They
provide a look and feel for the user and they have rich formatting options, as we can see in the file
`src\SharpDevelop\Base\Services\AmbienceService\IAmbience.cs`:

```
[Flags]
public enum ConversionFlags {
  None                 = 0,
  ShowParameterNames   = 1,
  UseFullyQualifiedNames = 2,
  ShowModifiers        = 4,
  ShowInheritanceList  = 8,
  ShowAccessibility    = 16,

  StandardConversionFlags = ShowParameterNames |
                            UseFullyQualifiedNames |
                            ShowModifiers,
  All = ShowParameterNames |
        ShowAccessibility |
        UseFullyQualifiedNames |
```

```
        ShowModifiers |
        ShowInheritanceList
}

public interface IAmbience
{
  ConversionFlags ConversionFlags {
    get;
    set;
  }

  string Convert(IClass c);
  string Convert(IIndexer c);
  string Convert(IField field);
  string Convert(IProperty property);
  string Convert(IEvent e);
  string Convert(IMethod m);
  string Convert(IParameter param);
}
```

The `Convert` methods are used to convert a type representation to a printable (human readable) string. The conversion flags do the following:

- ❑ `ShowParameterNames` – show the name of the method parameters. If this flag is not set, only the type will be displayed.

- ❑ `UseFullyQualifiedNames` – use the fully qualified name instead of a short name. For example `System.Windows.Forms.Button` is fully qualified, the short name is `Button`.

- ❑ `ShowModifiers` – show all modifiers, except accessibility modifiers.

- ❑ `ShowInheritanceList` – show the base types of a class.

- ❑ `ShowAccessibility` – shows all modifiers that change the accessibility.

The `IAmbience` interface defines converters for all classes that are defined in the abstract parser layer (refer to Chapter 12). The `AmbienceReflectionDecorator` class just extends these converters to all reflection classes; it is used to display reflection information like in the object browser.

Class Browser Icons Service

The class browser icons service is used to get the icons for types and type members. It is implemented as a service because icons for types and members are used in many locations including:

- ❑ In the class browser

- ❑ In the code completion window

- ❑ In the object browser

To reduce code duplication, the class browser icon service is used in these cases. The class is defined under src\SharpDevelop\Base\Services\ClassBrowserIcons \ClassBrowserIconsService.cs:

```
public class ClassBrowserIconsService : AbstractService
{
  public ImageList ImageList { get; }

  public int CombineIndex { get; }
  public int NamespaceIndex { get; }
  public int LiteralIndex { get; }
  public int ClassIndex { get; }
  public int StructIndex { get; }
  public int InterfaceIndex { get; }
  public int EnumIndex { get; }
  public int MethodIndex { get; }
  public int PropertyIndex { get; }
  public int FieldIndex { get; }
  public int DelegateIndex { get; }
  public int EventIndex { get; }

  public int InternalModifierOffset { get; }
  public int ProtectedModifierOffset { get; }
  public int PrivateModifierOffset { get; }

  public int GetIcon(IMethod method);
  public int GetIcon(IProperty method);
  public int GetIcon(IField field);
  public int GetIcon(IEvent evt);
  public int GetIcon(IClass c);

  public int GetIcon(MethodBase methodinfo);
  public int GetIcon(PropertyInfo propertyinfo);
  public int GetIcon(FieldInfo fieldinfo);
  public int GetIcon(EventInfo eventinfo);
  public int GetIcon(System.Type type);
}
```

As we see, the class browser service exposes the image list containing all icons and the offsets to specific icons through properties. For all icon indices, except `Combine`, `Namespace`, and `Literal`, icons are defined that reflect their modifier. Therefore, if an icon for an `internal struct` should be displayed the correct icon has the image index `StructIndex + InternalModifierOffset`. In most cases, the user of this service just uses the `GetIcon` methods that give back the correct icon for all abstract parser layer classes and all reflection classes.

File Service

The file service doesn't have much to do with the file utility service, which we have seen before. The file service is responsible for:

❑ Common file operations like open, rename, remove, or create a new file. It is important to use the service for rename or remove operations as it raises an event for them, and all other components can update their status. For example, when we rename a file that is open, the window containing the open file is renamed as well.

❑ Storing the `RecentOpen` object, which contains the recently opened files and projects.

The service is defined under `src\SharpDevelop\Base\Services\File\IFileService.cs`:

```
public interface IFileService
{
   RecentOpen RecentOpen {
     get;
   }
```

The `RecentOpen` class is defined in `src\SharpDevelop\Base\Services\File\RecentOpen.cs` and holds all our recently opened projects and files (up to 10 files and 10 projects).

It is stored into the SharpDevelop properties (therefore `RecentOpen` implements `IXmlConvertable`) and the `RecentOpen` object itself listens to the file service's file open event and the project open event from the project service. A menu item builder builds recent file/recent project menus out of the `RecentOpen` contents.

Now let's look at the main file handling methods:

```
void OpenFile(string fileName);
void NewFile(string defaultName, string language, string content);
IWorkbenchWindow GetOpenFile(string fileName);
```

- ❑ `OpenFile` – opens the file whose name is given by fileName (i.e, it shows the file in the workbench window). This method displays an error message if something goes wrong, like file not found, read error or access denied.

- ❑ `NewFile` – opens a new file with a given name, language and file content in the work bench window

- ❑ `GetOpenFile` – gets an opened file by name, returns null, if the file is not open.

Now we will take look at the file operations that are performed using the service:

```
void RemoveFile(string fileName);
void RenameFile(string oldName, string newName);
```

These methods perform the following tasks:

- ❑ `RemoveFile` – removes a file from all open project and physically too.

- ❑ `RenameFile` – renames a file physically (all file names used will be updated too).

These functions simply call these event handlers:

```
event FileEventHandler FileRenamed;
event FileEventHandler FileRemoved;
```

The methods `RemoveFile` and `RenameFile` first perform the physical operation (remove and rename) and afterwards fire the appropriate events. (The event handlers will do the remove from/rename in the project). If the operation fails, a message box with the error will be displayed and the event handler will not be called. The project service listens to these events and updates the project file information. The `RecentOpen` object updates its information too. This ensures that all parts get informed when a file is renamed or removed inside the IDE.

Now that we know how files are handled through the file service, we will look at how projects and combines are handled through the project service.

Project Service

SharpDevelop works on combines. As seen in Chapter 1, a combine is a container for projects and combines. Projects contain source files that are compiled to an assembly.

The project service is responsible for handling the root combine. It compiles projects too and it provides many events that are used in SharpDevelop. The `IProjectService` interface is found under `src\SharpDevelop\Base\Services\Project\IProjectService.cs`:

```
public interface IProjectService
{
  IProject CurrentSelectedProject {
    get;
    set;
  }

  Combine CurrentSelectedCombine {
    get;
    set;
  }

  // Gets the root combine, if no combine is open it returns null.
  Combine CurrentOpenCombine {
    get;
  }
```

These properties provide access to the current combine and make the following properties available:

❑ `CurrentSelectedProject` – the project containing the current open file or that file which is currently selected in the project scout (as seen in Chapter 4)

❑ `CurrentSelectedCombine` – the combine containing the current selected project

❑ `CurrentOpenCombine` – this is the root combine, which contains all open projects and combines

You might wonder why the `CurrentSelected*` properties can be set. The answer is relatively simple: the service does not know about them; it just manages them. The project scout sets them and the service should not communicate with a GUI component because this would make the service depend on a certain pad (in this case the project scout).

Now we will look at the methods and properties used for compilation:

```
bool NeedsCompiling {
   get;
}
```

This property returns `true` if an open project is dirty (modified). This indicates that during a compile run something will be compiled.

```
void OnStartBuild();
void OnEndBuild();
```

The `OnStartBuild`/`OnEndBuild` methods fire the associated events to inform the IDE when a build occurs. The build is usually threaded and therefore it is nice to know when a build has ended. For example, the IDE will be switched to the task view at the `EndBuild` event when it contains errors.

Now to the compile methods:

```
void CompileCombine();
void RecompileAll();
void CompileProject(IProject project);
void RecompileProject(IProject project);
```

These methods do the following:

❑ `CompileCombine` – compiles all dirty projects in the root combine (and sub-combines).

❑ `RecompileAll` – compiles any project in the root combine and forces recompilation. Recompilation is done with another method than compilation in the project subsystem, as there may be some (programming) languages that need to complete some tasks, like removing the executables or providing a forced overwrite switch to the compiler, before recompilation.

❑ `CompileProject` – compiles just a given project

❑ `RecompileProject` – recompiles a given project.

We must know how to set a project as dirty to mark that it is to be compiled in the next compile run. This is done with the following methods:

```
void MarkFileDirty(string filename);
void MarkProjectDirty(IProject project);
```

Note that all dirty projects will be compiled when the user clicks on compile.

Sometimes it is necessary for us to know the name of the output file produced by a project after the compile run. If a language produces more than one output file (as Java does) the name of the main file should be returned.

There are two methods for getting it:

```
string GetOutputAssemblyName(IProject project);
string GetOutputAssemblyName(string fileName);
```

SharpDevelop is capable of compiling files on a per file basis. Therefore, two methods are defined that do the same – one for a project and one for a file.

Now we will look at the methods that handle combine persistence:

```
void OpenCombine(string filename);
void SaveCombine();
void CloseCombine();
```

❏   OpenCombine – opens a new root combine. This method closes the old root combine automatically (if any was open).

❏   SaveCombine – saves the whole root combine on disk (all projects and sub-combines are saved too).

❏   CloseCombine – closes the active root combine. After this method call all projects are closed.

Now we will examine a special method that saves the preferences from a combine:

```
void SaveCombinePreferences();
```

This method saves the whole state of the IDE to restore it the next time the combine is opened. We will now look at the default implementation, which is taken from src\SharpDevelop\Base\Services\Project\DefaultProjectService.cs.

It would be nice to have a little understanding of the SharpDevelop GUI layer, but you can understand this method even without knowledge about the GUI layer:

```
void SaveCombinePreferences(Combine combine, string combinefilename)
{
  PropertyService propertyService =
  (PropertyService)ServiceManager.Services.GetService
    (typeof(PropertyService));
  string directory = propertyService.ConfigDirectory + "CombinePreferences";
  if (!Directory.Exists(directory)) {
    Directory.CreateDirectory(directory);
  }
```

This first part just creates a CombinePreferences directory in the application data folder in the .ICSharpCode\SharpDevelop path if it does not exist. In this path the combine preferences are saved. They are saved independently from the combine file, as it is annoying to have somebody else's settings open up while using the IDE. This could easily happen in team development when the combine file is shared among a number of people.

Then the root node will be created:

```
string combinepath = Path.GetDirectoryName(combinefilename);
XmlDocument doc = new XmlDocument();
doc.LoadXml("<?xml version=\"1.0\"?>\n<UserCombinePreferences/>");

XmlAttribute fileNameAttribute = doc.CreateAttribute("filename");
fileNameAttribute.InnerText = combinefilename;
doc.DocumentElement.Attributes.Append(fileNameAttribute);
```

Note that the combine will be identified through its file name, which is stored in the `filename` attribute of the root node.

Now all files that are currently open are stored:

```
XmlElement filesnode = doc.CreateElement("Files");
doc.DocumentElement.AppendChild(filesnode);

foreach (IViewContent content in
WorkbenchSingleton.Workbench.ViewContentCollection) {
    if (content.ContentName != null) {
      XmlElement el = doc.CreateElement("File");

      XmlAttribute attr = doc.CreateAttribute("filename");
      attr.InnerText = fileUtilityService.AbsoluteToRelativePath(combinepath,
content.ContentName);
      el.Attributes.Append(attr);

      filesnode.AppendChild(el);
    }
  }
```

After that, all pads (such as the class browser or project scout) store their mementos (refer the section on *Design Patterns* in Chapter 2) into the XML:

```
XmlElement viewsnode = doc.CreateElement("Views");
doc.DocumentElement.AppendChild(viewsnode);

foreach (IPadContent view in WorkbenchSingleton.Workbench.PadContentCollection)
{
    if (view is IMementoCapable) {
      XmlElement el = doc.CreateElement("ViewMemento");

      XmlAttribute attr = doc.CreateAttribute("class");
      attr.InnerText = view.GetType().ToString();
      el.Attributes.Append(attr);

el.AppendChild(((IMementoCapable)view).CreateMemento().ToXmlElement(doc));

      viewsnode.AppendChild(el);
    }
  }
```

Now an `IProperties` object will be created to store other information that is not stored in it at this point. Currently only the active window is stored:

```
IProperties properties = new DefaultProperties();
properties.SetProperty("ActiveWindow",
WorkbenchSingleton.Workbench.ActiveWorkbenchWindow == null ? "" :
WorkbenchSingleton.Workbench.ActiveWorkbenchWindow.ViewContent.ContentName);

XmlElement propertynode = doc.CreateElement("Properties");
doc.DocumentElement.AppendChild(propertynode);

propertynode.AppendChild(properties.ToXmlElement(doc));

fileUtilityService.ObservedSave(new NamedFileOperationDelegate(doc.Save),
directory + Path.DirectorySeparatorChar + combine.Name + ".xml",
FileErrorPolicy.ProvideAlternative);
}
```

This completes it. All these values will be loaded and set the next time the combine is opened.

Now we will continue with our project service:

```
ProjectReference AddReferenceToProject(IProject prj, string filename);
ProjectFile AddFileToProject(IProject prj, string filename,
    BuildAction action);
ProjectFile RetrieveFileInformationForFile(string fileName);
```

These methods are used to make it easier to handle project files and project references:

❑   `AddReferenceToProject` – adds a reference to a given project. It returns the `ProjectReference` object, which will be created and inserted into the project.

❑   `AddFileToProject` – adds a file to the project with a given `BuildAction` (`Nothing/Compile/EmbedAsResource/Exclude`). It returns the `ProjectFile` object, which will be created and inserted into the project.

❑   `RetrieveFileInformationForFile` – searches through all open projects for the project that contains the given file. The `ProjectFile` object from the project containing this file will be returned. This method returns `null` if no project contains the given file.

More information about the `ProjectFile` and `ProjectReference` classes can be obtained in the SharpDevelop source code. The project layer is defined in the directory `src\SharpDevelop\Base\Internal\Project`:

```
void RenameProject(string oldName, string newName);
void RemoveFileFromProject(string fileName);
```

❑   `RenameProject` – renames a project (the project must be open).

❑   `RemoveFileFromProject` – removes the specified file from its project. The project must be open (somewhere in the tree of the root combine) otherwise it can't be removed from the project. If the same file is in more than one open project it will be removed from all of them. This function will not remove a file physically from disk.

Finally, the events that are called by the respective methods are defined:

```
// Called before a build run
event EventHandler StartBuild;

// Called after a build run
event EventHandler EndBuild;

// Called after a new root combine is opened
event CombineEventHandler CombineOpened;

// Called after a root combine is closed
event CombineEventHandler CombineClosed;

// Called after the current selected project has changed
event ProjectEventHandler CurrentProjectChanged;

// Called after the current selected combine has changed
event CombineEventHandler CurrentSelectedCombineChanged;

// Called after a project got renamed
event ProjectRenameEventHandler ProjectRenamed;
}
```

This completes our discussion on project handling in SharpDevelop. Now we will look at projects from another perspective – the logical structure.

Parser Service

The parser service is important for the class browser and method insight. It manages all the installed parsers (currently there is only a C# parser implemented for SharpDevelop). It is responsible for providing the Resolve method, which tells SharpDevelop what type a specific expression has (this is used for code completion and method insight). We will be discussing parsers and the innermost workings of this service in Chapter 12.

For now let's take a look at the interface, which is defined under src\SharpDevelop\Base\Services\ParserService\IParserService.cs.

```
public interface IParserService
{
    IParseInformation ParseFile(string fileName);
    IParseInformation ParseFile(string fileName, string fileContent);

    IParseInformation GetParseInformation(string fileName);

    IParser GetParser(string fileName);

    // Default Parser Layer dependent functions
    IClass    GetClass(string typeName);
    string[]  GetNamespaceList(string subNameSpace);
    ArrayList GetNamespaceContents(string subNameSpace);
    bool      NamespaceExists(string name);
```

```
    // Resolves an expression.
    // The caretLineNumber and caretColumn are 1 based.
    ResolveResult Resolve(string expression, int caretLineNumber, int caretColumn,
string fileName);

    void AddReferenceToCompletionLookup(IProject project, ProjectReference
reference);
    event ParseInformationEventHandler ParseInformationChanged;
}
```

The `ParseFile` functions return an `IParseInformation` object (the class is defined in the same file). A parse information contains a dirty compilation unit (a parse tree for a single file) and a valid compilation unit. Note that if you communicate with the parser all offsets are 1-based. This has historical reasons (many parsers are 1-based).

The dirty compilation unit is set when the parser returned errors during parsing and the valid compilation unit is only set when the parsing was successful (therefore the valid compilation unit is error free). Code completion and method insight must merge this information to get the expected results (for details refer Chapter 12).

```
public interface IParseInformation
{
    ICompilationUnitBase ValidCompilationUnit {
        get;
    }
    ICompilationUnitBase DirtyCompilationUnit {
        get;
    }
    ICompilationUnitBase BestCompilationUnit {
        get;
    }
    ICompilationUnitBase MostRecentCompilationUnit {
        get;
    }
}
```

The `BestCompilationUnit` returns the most error free compilation unit, this is usually the valid compilation unit (if it exists) otherwise it is the dirty compilation unit.

The `MostRecentCompilationUnit` property returns the last compilation unit that was compiled. That is mostly the dirty compilation unit (because a file in progress is seldom error free) but sometimes (if no dirty compilation unit is set) it returns the valid compilation unit.

Now that we have covered the important services in SharpDevelop, let's briefly discuss the remaining ones.

Other Services

Beside the services we have already discussed in this chapter there are a few other, less important services defined in SharpDevelop which we will only describe briefly:

- ❑ Status Bar Service – displays the status bar messages.

- ❑ Language Service – provides access to all supported natural spoken languages. All the languages to which the SharpDevelop UI can be switched and the codepage they use are accessible through this service (for details refer to Chapter 7).

- ❑ Task Service – stores the tasks that are displayed in the task window. Common tasks are compiler errors or search results.

- ❑ Toolbar Service – builds the SharpDevelop tool bars out of the AddIn tree. There are plans to extend this service so that it can build general toolbars from an AddIn tree path. However, this must wait until floating toolbars for .NET are available. (The Magic Library, www.dotnetmagic.com, plans to provide them.)

- ❑ Language Binding Service – makes all of the language bindings (links to external compilers) accessible through file name (language bindings can compile and 'run' files) or project type (they compile and run projects too).

- ❑ Display Binding Service – provides an access point to all installed display bindings (refer to Chapter 6).

Summary

In this chapter, we learned about the service concept in SharpDevelop and how it used in the IDE. We have seen the service manager, where the services are inserted into the AddIn tree and accessed. We also got an overview of all the services available inside SharpDevelop.

Now that we have a good understanding of what can be done inside SharpDevelop, let's move on to the next (and last) part of the basic structure – the GUI layer.

CHAPTER 6

6

The User Interface

In this chapter, we will learn about the way SharpDevelop handles the GUI. As we know, SharpDevelop uses the MVC (model-view-controller) concept, which means, in the underlying parts, the GUI is abstracted. With SharpDevelop, we planned in advance to make the GUI abstract to allow easy switching of GUI APIs (for example, from Windows Forms to GTK# or QT#). This abstraction has many benefits:

- ❑ It provides a clean model for all commands to work with

- ❑ The abstraction layer helps in applying workarounds to some Windows Forms' bugs

- ❑ The abstracted Layout Manager helps provide a new look and feel (like adding floating pads) to the Workbench IDE without making any major code changes for switching the look and feel of the IDE

Before we dive into the details, let's look at how the overall interaction takes place in the GUI layer:

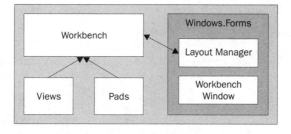

The abstract GUI layer is simple. We have a Workbench that contains views and pads, similar to a container. The views are windows having editable content, like text. Pads, on the other hand, are tool windows, like the Project Scout.

However, note that the Workbench doesn't know how to display the views and pads on the screen. The views may be stored in an MDI area or a tab control, or be floating around. The Workbench does not care how the views are displayed. Anything concerned with the GUI API resides in the Layout Manager. In contrast to the Workbench, the views and pads know how to display their content.

The Layout Manager handles the GUI and provides an implementation of the Workbench window too (therefore, it is implemented using the GUI Toolkit). A Workbench window contains a view and handles basic window operations like selecting a window. It doesn't know the positioning of the window or how it is displayed.

Display Management

In this section, we will look at the source code of the various parts of the abstract GUI layer and how to use the abstract GUI layer to display HTML inside SharpDevelop. The standard GUI objects we will look at are:

- ❑ Workbench windows
- ❑ Views
- ❑ Pads

Finally, we will look at the integrated HTML Help Viewer, which is a real implementation of views and pads.

The Workbench Window

The Workbench window maps the basic window functions to an interface. To make the GUI work, SharpDevelop need not know much about a window or how it is implemented. All that is needed for the GUI actions to work are that the window must:

- ❑ Have a title
- ❑ Have a close method
- ❑ Have a way to be selected
- ❑ Trigger events to indicate a change or a window action

Note that these requirements evolved from the earlier SharpDevelop versions that didn't have an abstracted GUI layer. In the former implementation, the window had only a few functions that are now abstracted.

How it is represented and displayed doesn't matter to the Workbench, as this job is done in the Layout Manager. The interface for the Workbench window is defined in the `src\SharpDevelop\Base\Gui\IWorkbenchWindow.cs` file:

```
// The IWorkbenchWindow is the basic interface to a window, which
// shows a view (represented by the IViewContent object).
public interface IWorkbenchWindow
{
```

```
// The window title.
string Title {
  get;
  set;
}

// The current view content, which is shown inside this window
IViewContent ViewContent {
  get;
}

// Closes the window
//  if force == true it closes the window without asking the user, even
//if the content is dirty.
void CloseWindow(bool force);

// Brings this window to the front and sets the user focus to this
// window.
void SelectWindow();

// Is called when the window is selected.
event EventHandler WindowSelected;

// Is called when the window is deselected.
event EventHandler WindowDeselected;

// Is called when the title of this window changes.
event EventHandler TitleChanged;

// Is called after the window closes.
event EventHandler CloseEvent;
}
```

As we can see, the interface provides only the basic functionality. Later, in the *Layout Managers* section, we will look at an implementation of this interface.

Now, let's take a look at views.

Views

The underlying part of the GUI layer is the views. A view usually contains an editor or a 'viewer' that is able to edit (or display) a file, for example, the text editor or the resource editor. Basically, it is just a panel that is displayed in an MDI window or on a tab page. We will begin with a look at the IViewContent interface, which is the interface that the views expose to the outer world. It can be found in the src\SharpDevelop\Base\Gui\IViewContent.cs file:

```
public interface IViewContent : IDisposable
{
  Control Control {
    get;
  }
```

The following property has a control (Windows.Forms) as its value. Currently, the interface is based on Windows Forms. At a later stage, the Control property might return a more generic object or another abstract representation to get rid of the Windows.Forms dependency, but which one of these cannot be predicted.

This property returns the Workbench window in which the view is currently displayed:

```
IWorkbenchWindow WorkbenchWindow {
  get;
  set;
}
```

The WorkbenchWindow has a reference to the view too.

The name untitled is chosen when the IsUntitled property is true:

```
string UntitledName {
  get;
  set;
}

string ContentName {
  get;
  set;
}
bool IsUntitled {
  get;
}
```

The ContentName usually points to the file or URL that the view displays, but actions should not generally assume this. For untitled files, the ContentName property is null.

```
bool IsDirty {
  get;
  set;
}

bool IsReadOnly {
  get;
}

bool IsViewOnly {
  get;
}
```

These properties achieve the following:

❑ IsDirty
   If this property is true it indicates that the content needs to be saved (this is a 'dirty' file), and a '*' sign is displayed after the window title to inform the user about the 'dirty' state. When the file is closed, the window will prompt the user to save the file.

❏ `IsReadOnly`
If this property is `true`, it indicates that the content can't be written into (because it is write-protected). A '+' sign after the window title is displayed for write-protected files, which are never dirty.

❏ `IsViewOnly`
This property is a bit like the `IsReadOnly` property with the exception that no '+' sign is displayed and that, on views, no load or save operations can occur. This type of view is the one that we will use to build our HTML help viewer.

The `RedrawContent` method is called to re-initialize the content, which is more than just repainting, unlike what the name suggests. It is about refreshing all information that might have changed (for example, in the case of a user interface switch). The content is not empty but the view should get all Addin Tree information again. The following listing is an excerpt from this method:

```
    void SaveFile();
    void SaveFile(string fileName);
    void LoadFile(string fileName);
    event EventHandler ContentNameChanged;
    event EventHandler DirtyChanged;
}
```

The first three methods perform the save and load operations for the view, followed by two events that signal the change of the `ContentName` property and the `IsDirty` flag. The `SaveFile` method that doesn't take a parameter should save the file with the filename that was specified during the last load or save operation.

The `AbstractViewContent` implements all those and makes it easier to develop views. If a view has the `IsViewOnly` flag set, it need not overwrite the `SaveFile` and `LoadFile` methods, as they are never called. Note that, in that case, `SaveFile` or `LoadFile` throw a `NotImplementedException`.

Pads

Pads are tool windows inside SharpDevelop. Tool windows are a bit different from views, as they can hide themselves and only one tool window of a type can be open, at a time. Tool windows usually don't show file contents; instead, they help the user do their job.

SharpDevelop currently implements the following pads:

❏ **Project Scout** – Displays the file structure in all currently open projects

❏ **Class Scout** – Displays the namespace structure of the currently open combine

❏ **Task List** – Displays compiler errors and search results, and enables the user to jump to the error or search result position

❏ **Property Scout** – Used in the forms designer to display (and alter) properties of GUI objects

❑ **File Scout** – An Explorer-like component for displaying the file structure

❑ **Tool Scout** – Provides an Outlook-like sidebar used to drag-and-drop code snippets and to put objects on the forms designer

❑ **Output Pad** – Displays compiler messages

❑ **Help Scout** – Displays the SharpDevelop help file and can open help topics using the internal browser, the implementation of which we will look at in Chapter 7

A pad is similar to a view with some exceptions as follows:

❑ Pads can't be added by the user at run time. Currently, there is a fixed count of pads attached to the Workbench (although with the current structure, it would be possible to add or remove pads at run time, this makes no sense, as the user will want instant access to any pad).

❑ Pads are always visible – they can't be closed; only hidden. This reduces the time needed to pop up the pad when it is made visible.

❑ Pads can't be untitled; they always have a unique name. They have an icon that is shown by the IDE.

❑ Pads are not displayed in the Workbench window. The Layout Manager is responsible for showing the pads. We have used the Magic library to show the pads in a docking content window.

We will take a closer look at the `IPadContent` interface, as any pad must implement this interface. The definition of the `IPadContent` interface can be found in the `src\SharpDevelop\Base\Gui\IPadContent.cs` file:

```csharp
// The IPadContent interface is the basic interface to all "tool" windows
// in SharpDevelop.
public interface IPadContent : IDisposable
{
  // Returns the title of the pad.
  string Title {
    get;
  }

  // Returns the icon of the pad, which may be null if the pad has no
  // icon defined.
  Bitmap Icon {
    get;
  }

  // Returns the Windows.Control for this pad.
  Control Control {
    get;
  }
```

```
    // Re-initializes all components of the pad; that is, reloads the
    //Addin Tree and localization information, and then redraws the content.
    void RedrawContent();

    // Is called when the title of this pad has changed.
    event EventHandler TitleChanged;

    // Is called when the icon of this pad has changed.
    event EventHandler IconChanged;
}
```

Now that we have looked at both views and pads, let's look at an implementation that uses both of them.

Views and Pads Applied – An Integrated HTML Help Viewer

In this section, we will learn how to implement a view and a pad. For the purpose of our discussion, we will examine the HTML help system in SharpDevelop. We will look at the following topics in detail:

❑ The HTML view
    We will look at an example of a real `IViewContent` implementation in action.

❑ Navigating the help file
    We will look at a pad that uses the HTML view content to display information.

The following screenshot shows the HTML help navigator:

The HTML View

The HTML View is an IViewContent implementation. We will look at how the Internet Explorer control is wrapped to the IViewContent interface and how this view is used to display HTML pages inside SharpDevelop.

To begin with, we must wrap the SHDocVw ActiveX control to a managed component. Fortunately, this is an easy task with the aximp utility that is shipped with the .NET SDK. This command-line tool wraps an ActiveX component to a .NET Windows.Forms class.

At the command prompt, execute the following command:

```
aximp C:\WINDOWS\system32\shdocvw.dll
```

This will create two files, SHDocVw.dll and AxSHDocVw.dll. The AxSHDocVw.dll contains the wrapped ActiveX control we need. We need to reference these two files in our project.

Now we have to rename the SHDocVw.dll file (this assembly contains the wrapped COM interfaces) to Interop.SHDocVw.dll (or to any other name other than SHDocVw.dll). If we don't, it will produce strange side effects under .NET when we run our application on Windows 2000. For example, in our case, the **Open file** dialog wasn't able to access the My Documents directory. We could not determine what exactly caused this problem.

Next, we need to wrap the basic ActiveX control to something more useful. In SharpDevelop, the control may show navigation buttons when used as a normal browser. However, we use this control to display our help files too, and in **Help** file view mode, the navigation buttons must disappear.

The control is implemented in the src\SharpDevelop\Base\Gui\BrowserDisplayBinding\HtmlViewPane.cs file:

```
public class HtmlViewPane : UserControl
{
  AxWebBrowser axWebBrowser = null;

  ToolBar toolBar      = new ToolBar();
  TextBox urlTextBox   = new TextBox();

  bool isHandleCreated = false;
  string lastUrl       = null;

  public AxWebBrowser AxWebBrowser {
    get {
      return axWebBrowser;
    }
  }
}
```

The `AxWebBrowser` is the wrapped ActiveX component that the `aximp` tool creates. Our HTML view will look like:

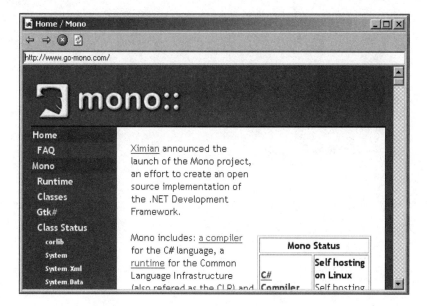

First, we initialize the control with the toolbar and the URL textbox. The constructor has a single parameter that indicates whether the navigation bar with the buttons and the text field should be displayed or not:

```
public HtmlViewPane(bool showNavigation)
{
  Dock = DockStyle.Fill;
  Size = new Size(500, 500);

  if (showNavigation) {
    for (int i = 0; i < toolBarButtons.Length; ++i) {
      ToolBarButton toolBarButton = new ToolBarButton();
      toolBarButton.ImageIndex    = i;
      toolBar.Buttons.Add(toolBarButton);
    }

    ResourceService resourceService = (ResourceService)
      ServiceManager.Services.GetService(typeof(ResourceService));
    toolBar.ImageList = new ImageList();
    toolBar.ImageList.Images.Add
      (resourceService.GetBitmap("Icons.16x16.BrowserBefore"));
    toolBar.ImageList.Images.Add
      (resourceService.GetBitmap("Icons.16x16.BrowserAfter"));
    toolBar.ImageList.Images.Add
      (resourceService.GetBitmap("Icons.16x16.BrowserCancel"));
    toolBar.ImageList.Images.Add
      (resourceService.GetBitmap("Icons.16x16.BrowserRefresh"));
```

```
    toolBar.Appearance = ToolBarAppearance.Flat;
    toolBar.Dock = DockStyle.Top;
    toolBar.ButtonClick += new
      ToolBarButtonClickEventHandler(ToolBarClick);

    Controls.Add(toolBar);

    urlTextBox.Location  = new Point(0, 24);
    urlTextBox.Size      = new Size(Width, 24);
    urlTextBox.KeyPress += new KeyPressEventHandler(KeyPressEvent);
    urlTextBox.Anchor    = AnchorStyles.Left | AnchorStyles.Right |
      AnchorStyles.Top;

    Controls.Add(urlTextBox);
  }

  axWebBrowser = new AxWebBrowser();
  axWebBrowser.BeginInit();
  if (showNavigation) {
    int height = 48;
    axWebBrowser.Location = new Point(0, height);
    axWebBrowser.Size     = new Size(Width, Height - height);
    axWebBrowser.Anchor   = AnchorStyles.Left | AnchorStyles.Right |
  AnchorStyles.Bottom | AnchorStyles.Top;
  } else {
    axWebBrowser.Dock = DockStyle.Fill;
  }
  axWebBrowser.HandleCreated +=
    new EventHandler(this.CreatedWebBrowserHandle);
  axWebBrowser.TitleChange    +=
    new DWebBrowserEvents2_TitleChangeEventHandler(TitleChange);

  Controls.Add(axWebBrowser);
  axWebBrowser.EndInit();
}
```

Note that the toolbar buttons are handled differently as compared to normal buttons in the .NET Framework. The toolbar buttons don't have a click or activate event attached to them; instead, the toolbar control fires an event that has an `int` value (equal to the button position) when a toolbar button is clicked.

Therefore, we just initialize these with a `for` statement. The web browser control is handled like any other .NET Windows Forms control.

The `ToolBarClick` event handler delegates all actions to the ActiveX control wrapper:

```
void ToolBarClick(object sender, ToolBarButtonClickEventArgs e)
{
  try {
    switch(toolBar.Buttons.IndexOf(e.Button)) {
      case 0:
        axWebBrowser.GoBack();
```

```
          break;
      case 1:
          axWebBrowser.GoForward();
          break;
      case 2:
          axWebBrowser.Stop();
          break;
      case 3:
          axWebBrowser.CtlRefresh();
          break;
   }
} catch (Exception) {
    // Please ignore any errors (although not a good coding practice)
}
}
```

Now we will look at some more event handling methods:

```
void TitleChange(object sender, DWebBrowserEvents2_TitleChangeEvent e)
{
  urlTextBox.Text = axWebBrowser.LocationURL;
}

void KeyPressEvent(object sender, KeyPressEventArgs ex)
{
  if (ex.KeyChar == '\r') {
    Navigate(urlTextBox.Text);
  }
}
```

Note that pressing the return key in the Windows Forms textbox control is represented as \r instead of \n. A \n is used as line terminator for any other Windows Forms controls I know about, but the textbox behaves a little strangely.

```
public void CreatedWebBrowserHandle(object sender, EventArgs evArgs)
{
  isHandleCreated = true;
  if (lastUrl != null) {
    Navigate(lastUrl);
  }
}
```

We can navigate to an URL page in the AxWebBrowser only after the handle of the Internet Explorer control is created. Therefore, we need to save the URL that is requested before the handle is created. The isHandleCreated field indicates the handle creation.

The heart of our control is the Navigate method. It checks whether the handle is created and if not, it stores the URL into the lastUrl field. After that it puts the URL into the textbox and it wraps the Navigate method from the AxWebBrowser object to a friendlier one:

```
public void Navigate(string name)
{
  if (!isHandleCreated) {
    lastUrl = name;
    return;
  }
  urlTextBox.Text = name;
  object arg1 = 0;
  object arg2 = "";
  object arg3 = "";
  object arg4 = "";
  try {
    axWebBrowser.Navigate(name, ref arg1, ref arg2, ref arg3, ref arg4);
  } catch (Exception e) {
    Console.WriteLine(e.ToString());
  }
}
```

The `Navigate` method of the `AxWebBrowser` takes many command-line arguments but we don't bother with them.

Now, we must override the `Dispose` method to ensure the timely disposal of the ActiveX control:

```
protected override void Dispose(bool disposing)
{
  base.Dispose(disposing);
  if (disposing) {
    axWebBrowser.Dispose();
  }
}
```

Finally, we have a fully functional user control that we can easily wrap to an `IViewContent` interface by extending the `AbstractViewContent` class (which makes the implementation of the interface much simpler):

```
public class BrowserPane : AbstractViewContent
{
  HtmlViewPane htmlViewPane;
```

The view implementation just uses the `HtmlViewPane`. The view needs to implement some properties, which are defined in the `IViewContent` interface:

```
public override Control Control {
  get {
    return htmlViewPane;
  }
}
```

```
public override bool IsDirty {
  get {
    return false;
  }
  set {
  }
}

public override bool IsViewOnly {
  get {
    return true;
  }
}
```

Note that the Control property is abstract, and that the IsDirty and IsViewOnly properties are declared virtual in the AbstractViewContent class. We overwrite the IsDirty and IsViewOnly properties because we want only a simple view, which is never dirty (giving back false ensures that it is never marked as dirty).

Now we implement the constructors, one of which flags if the navigation bar should be shown. The default constructor just shows the navigation bar:

```
protected BrowserPane(bool showNavigation)
{
  htmlViewPane = new HtmlViewPane(showNavigation);
  htmlViewPane.AxWebBrowser.TitleChange +=
    new DWebBrowserEvents2_TitleChangeEventHandler(TitleChange);
}

public BrowserPane() : this(true)
{
}
```

We need to dispose the HtmlViewPane instance. This is important; otherwise we may produce a memory leak (remember that the underlying control is a COM component):

```
public override void Dispose()
{
  htmlViewPane.Dispose();
}
```

Lastly, we override the LoadFile method, which just navigates the HtmlViewPane to a URL, and the TitleChange event, which sets the name of the view to the title of the HTML page currently viewed. This name will be taken as the window title:

```
public override void LoadFile(string url)
{
  htmlViewPane.Navigate(url);
}
```

```
      void TitleChange(object sender, DWebBrowserEvents2_TitleChangeEvent e)
      {
        ContentName = e.text;
      }
    }
```

The implementation of the `BrowserPane` view is very straightforward, as all the important work is done in the `HtmlViewPane`.

With the HTML view complete, we may concentrate on navigating the HTML help file. You must have noticed that `AbstractViewContent` helps us greatly in implementing a view for SharpDevelop. We have to bother with only some details and most of the coding is straightforward.

Navigating the Help File

How does SharpDevelop display its internal help? We are using the standard `.chm` format for this task. However, we have applied a few tricks as well. The `.chm` format itself is not really useful when we want to develop a custom help viewer, as we need to get the contents of the help file for displaying them. We will look at how that is done, in this section.

The browser itself, implemented as a pad, is defined in the `src\SharpDevelop\Base\Gui\Pads\HelpBrowser\HelpBrowser.cs` file:

```
public class HelpBrowser : AbstractPadContent
{
  static readonly string helpPath = Application.StartupPath +
                                    Path.DirectorySeparatorChar + ".." +
                                    Path.DirectorySeparatorChar + "doc" +
                                    Path.DirectorySeparatorChar + "help" +
                                    Path.DirectorySeparatorChar;

  static readonly string helpFileName = helpPath + "HelpConv.xml";

  Panel      browserPanel = new Panel();
  TreeView   treeView     = new TreeView();

  public override Control Control {
    get {
      return browserPanel;
    }
  }

  public HelpBrowser() : base("${res:MainWindow.Windows.HelpScoutLabel}",
    "Icons.16x16.HelpIcon")
  {
    treeView.Dock       = DockStyle.Fill;
    treeView.ImageList  = new ImageList();
    ResourceService resourceService = (ResourceService)
      ServiceManager.Services.GetService(typeof(ResourceService));
```

```
        treeView.ImageList.Images.Add
          (resourceService.GetBitmap("Icons.16x16.HelpClosedFolder"));
        treeView.ImageList.Images.Add
          (resourceService.GetBitmap("Icons.16x16.HelpOpenFolder"));

        treeView.ImageList.Images.Add
          (resourceService.GetBitmap("Icons.16x16.HelpTopic"));
        treeView.BeforeExpand   += new TreeViewCancelEventHandler(BeforeExpand);
        treeView.BeforeCollapse +=
          new TreeViewCancelEventHandler(BeforeCollapse);
        treeView.DoubleClick += new EventHandler(DoubleClick);
        browserPanel.Controls.Add(treeView);

        LoadHelpfile();
    }
```

This is the initial setup of the tree view. What is more interesting is how we load the help file and generate that nice tree of help topics:

```
    // Parses the xml tree and generates a TreeNode tree out of it.
    void ParseTree(TreeNodeCollection nodeCollection, XmlNode parentNode)
    {
      foreach (XmlNode node in parentNode.ChildNodes) {
        switch (node.Name) {
          case "HelpFolder":
            TreeNode newFolderNode = new
              TreeNode(node.Attributes["name"].InnerText);
            newFolderNode.ImageIndex = newFolderNode.SelectedImageIndex = 0;
            ParseTree(newFolderNode.Nodes, node);
            nodeCollection.Add(newFolderNode);
            break;
          case "HelpTopic":
            TreeNode newNode = new
              TreeNode(node.Attributes["name"].InnerText);
            newNode.ImageIndex = newNode.SelectedImageIndex = 2;
            newNode.Tag = node.Attributes["link"].InnerText;
            nodeCollection.Add(newNode);
            break;
        }
      }
    }

    void LoadHelpfile()
    {
      XmlDocument doc = new XmlDocument();
      doc.Load(helpFileName);
      ParseTree(treeView.Nodes, doc.DocumentElement);
    }
```

The LoadHelpfile method loads the help file, and the ParseTree method recursively parses the nodes defined in the XML file and generates the TreeNode objects from the XML definition. We will get back to this interesting XML file shortly.

Let's look at the event-handling methods for displaying a help topic:

```
HelpBrowserWindow helpBrowserWindow = null;

void HelpBrowserClose(object sender, EventArgs e)
{
  helpBrowserWindow = null;
}

void DoubleClick(object sender, EventArgs e)
{
  TreeNode node = treeView.SelectedNode;
  if (node.Tag != null) {
    string navigationName = "mk:@MSITStore:" + helpPath +
      node.Tag.ToString();
    if (helpBrowserWindow == null) {
      helpBrowserWindow = new HelpBrowserWindow();
      WorkbenchSingleton.Workbench.ShowView(helpBrowserWindow);
      helpBrowserWindow.WorkbenchWindow.CloseEvent +=
        new EventHandler(HelpBrowserClose);
    }
    helpBrowserWindow.LoadFile(navigationName);
  }
}
void BeforeExpand(object sender, TreeViewCancelEventArgs e)
{
  if (e.Node.ImageIndex < 2) {
    e.Node.ImageIndex = e.Node.SelectedImageIndex = 1;
  }
}

void BeforeCollapse(object sender, TreeViewCancelEventArgs e)
{
  if (e.Node.ImageIndex < 2) {
    e.Node.ImageIndex = e.Node.SelectedImageIndex = 0;
  }
}
}
```

The methods perform the following tasks:

❑ HelpBrowserClose
This method is called when the help browser view closes. It sets the helpBrowserWindow to null to indicate that a new help browser window must be created when the next help topic is selected.

❑ DoubleClick
This method opens the help view in the Workbench, and sets its content to point to the new help topic. If a view is already open, it just sets the new content and reuses the existing view.

❑ BeforeExpand and BeforeCollapse
These methods switch the open and close icons for the folders, respectively.

The view content that this pad displays is simple. As we already have the BrowserPane, we can just subclass it and reuse the code we have already written. The only difference is that the help browser view has no navigation bar, but this can be turned off using the protected constructor from the base class. The HelpBrowserPane is in the same file as the help browser:

```
public class HelpBrowserPane : BrowserPane
{
  public HelpBrowserPane() : base(false)
  {
    ContentName = "Help";
  }
}
```

We don't use the .hhc format which represents the table of contents (TOC), because the .hhc file is in HTML format and needs to be tweaked a bit to become a valid XML file that can be parsed by the .NET XML parser.

The original .chm table of contents file is converted to an XML TOC file by an external utility, HelpBrowserApp, that is shipped with SharpDevelop. It is available in the src\Tools\HelpBrowserApp directory. It simply converts the .hhc file into an XML representation.

Here's an example of the XML format used:

```
<HelpCollection>
  <HelpFolder name="SharpDevelop">
    <HelpTopic name="Welcome to SharpDevelop!"
             link="SharpDevelop.chm::/pr01.html" />
    <HelpFolder name="1. Getting Started with SharpDevelop">
      <HelpTopic name="1. Introduction"
               link="SharpDevelop.chm::/ch01s01.html" />
    </HelpFolder>
  </HelpFolder>
</HelpCollection>
```

We use HelpFolder nodes as a folder. A help topic that has a name and a link is passed to the Navigate method of our HTML view. This help file is the output of the help parser, and we need a description file that tells our parser which files to convert:

```
<HelpCollection>
  <HelpFile hhc="SharpDevelop.hhc" chm="SharpDevelop.chm"/>
  <HelpFolder name="#ziplib">
    <HelpFile hhc="031SharpZipLib.hhc" chm="031SharpZipLib.chm" />
  </HelpFolder>
</HelpCollection>
```

The parser converts the HelpFile nodes from this file and loads the .hhc file specified in the hhc attribute. It generates the tree defined in the .hhc file, from this definition.

The conversion from .hhc is done using regular expressions. We need to add some closing tags with specific opening tags to convert from HTML to XML. The .chm attribute is needed to construct the correct link (that is, set the link attributes).

We can look at an `.hhc` example file in the `doc\help` folder, named `SharpDevelop.hhc`:

```
<HTML>
<HEAD>
</HEAD>
  <BODY>
<OBJECT type="text/site properties">
  <param name="ImageType" value="Folder">
</OBJECT>
<UL>
<LI> <OBJECT type="text/sitemap">
    <param name="Name" value="SharpDevelop">
    <param name="Local" value="index.html">
  </OBJECT><UL><LI> <OBJECT type="text/sitemap">
    <param name="Name" value="Welcome to SharpDevelop!">
    <param name="Local" value="pr01.html">
  </OBJECT><LI> <OBJECT type="text/sitemap">
    <param name="Name" value="1. Getting Started with SharpDevelop">
    <param name="Local" value="ch01.html">
  </OBJECT><LI> <OBJECT type="text/sitemap">
    <param name="Name" value="2.1.6. Properties Scout">
    <param name="Local" value="ch01s02s01s06.html">
  </OBJECT></UL><LI> <OBJECT type="text/sitemap">
    <param name="Name" value="2.2. Code Window">
    <param name="Local" value="ch01s02s02.html">
  </OBJECT></UL></UL>
</BODY>
</HTML>
```

This is a sample `.hhc` file that is not XML compliant. To make it XML compliant, we need to generate the closing `</LI>` tags. The `<param>` tags are not closed either. The tool that converts this file to XML uses the following method to convert files that have this `.hhc` format:

```
void MakeXmlCompliant()
{
  StringBuilder strFixup = new StringBuilder(Regex.Replace
    (hhcFileContents, "(?'start'<param\\s[^>]*)(?'end'\"/?>)",
    "${start}\"/>"));

  strFixup.Replace("</OBJECT></UL>", "</OBJECT></LI></UL>");
  strFixup.Replace("</OBJECT><LI>", "</OBJECT></LI><LI>");
  strFixup.Replace("</OBJECT><UL><LI>", "</OBJECT></LI><UL><LI>");
  hhcFileContents = strFixup.ToString();
}
```

The first `Replace` method uses a regular expression that closes only the `param` tags. Closing the `<LI>` tags is done with the standard `Replace` method because the `.hhc` files are auto-generated and the format is fixed. Now, we have a file that can be loaded correctly with the XML classes of .NET, and we can generate a well-formed XML document for loading the help tree.

Layout Managers

We will now switch gears and discuss the Layout Manager system, which is responsible for displaying views and pads. They do all the 'dirty' work that needs to be done while using GUI libraries.

Before diving into the code, let's look at the working of the Layout Manager. This will give us an idea of how it looks. We will look at the MDI Layout Manager, which puts the Workbench windows in an MDI area where the windows can be maximized, minimized, or arranged:

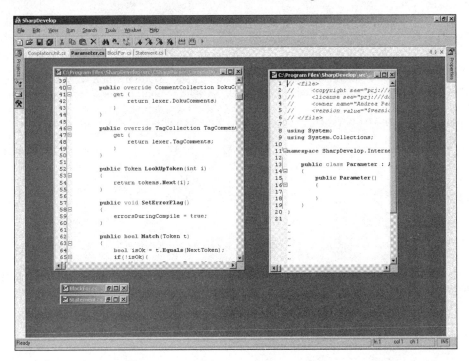

We also have a Layout Manager for handling SDI layout, which puts the windows into a tab page. We plan to use a feature of the Magic library that allows docking of the views too, like docking the pads (but, currently, this is not the top priority task). The new Layout Manager will look like the current SDI Layout Manager; but in the new tab area, tab pages can be rearranged creating new tab controls, which can contain other tab pages that share the same area. This simulates MDI features like tiling horizontally or vertically using tab controls and docking.

As usual, let's look at the interface that must be implemented by all Layout Managers. It is called `IWorkbenchLayout` and it is defined in the `src\SharpDevelop\Base\Gui\IWorkbenchLayout.cs` file:

```
public interface IWorkbenchLayout
{
    IWorkbenchWindow ActiveWorkbenchwindow {
        get;
    }
```

One of the important functionalities that a Layout Manager must have is to enable marking one window as the active Workbench window. This window is the one that contains the user focus.

The Layout Manager is capable of being attached to (or detached from) a Workbench by setting the Workbench back to the original uninitialized state. The detach operation removes all Workbench windows attached to the views.

After this call, the views will get new Workbench windows when a new Layout Manager is attached to their Workbench.

```
void Attach(IWorkbench Workbench);
void Detach();
```

Now we will look at the functions that handle the pads. The ShowPad method will be used the first time a pad is attached to the Layout Manager. The ActivatePad method makes a pad visible (if necessary) and puts it to the front. The HidePad method hides a pad (after this call the given pad is invisible but it does exist and will not be disposed). The IsVisible method checks if a specific pad is, currently, not hidden.

```
void ShowPad(IPadContent content);

void ActivatePad(IPadContent content);

void HidePad(IPadContent content);

bool IsVisible(IPadContent padContent);
```

Despite it's name, the RedrawAllComponents method does not update the display. The Layout Manager should refresh its Addin Tree information, update its localization data, and then do a redraw. This has nothing to do with the common repainting operation:

```
void RedrawAllComponents();
```

The last method shows a new view. This call is used when a new view is created and is made visible. This method attaches a Workbench window to the view. Lastly, this interface defines an event that is fired when the ActiveWorkbenchwindow property changes:

```
IWorkbenchWindow ShowView(IViewContent content);

event EventHandler ActiveWorkbenchWindowChanged;
}
```

The MDI Layout Manager is implemented in the src\SharpDevelop\Base\Gui\Workbench\ Layouts\MdiWorkbenchLayout.cs file:

```
// This is a Workspace with a single document interface.
public class MdiWorkbenchLayout : IWorkbenchLayout
{
  static string defaultconfigFile;
  static PropertyService propertyService = (PropertyService)
    ServiceManager.Services.GetService(typeof(PropertyService));
  static string configFile = propertyService.ConfigDirectory +
    "MdiLayoutConfig.xml";
  Form wbForm;

  DockingManager dockManager;
  ICSharpCode.SharpDevelop.Gui.Components.OpenFileTab tabControl =
    new ICSharpCode.SharpDevelop.Gui.Components.OpenFileTab();

  static MdiWorkbenchLayout()
  {
    PropertyService propertyService = (PropertyService)
      ServiceManager.Services.GetService(typeof(PropertyService));
    string language =
      propertyService.GetProperty("CoreProperties.UILanguage").ToString();
    // Filter out region codes (for example DE-de will be DE, currently
    // we don't support region codes
    if (language.IndexOf('-') > 0) {
      language = language.Split(new char[] {'-'})[0];
    }

    defaultconfigFile = Application.StartupPath +
            Path.DirectorySeparatorChar + ".." +
            Path.DirectorySeparatorChar + "data" +
            Path.DirectorySeparatorChar + "options" +
            Path.DirectorySeparatorChar + "Layouts" +
            Path.DirectorySeparatorChar + language +
            Path.DirectorySeparatorChar + "LayoutConfig.xml";

    if (!File.Exists(defaultconfigFile)) {
      defaultconfigFile = Application.StartupPath +
            Path.DirectorySeparatorChar + ".." +
            Path.DirectorySeparatorChar + "data" +
            Path.DirectorySeparatorChar + "options" +
            Path.DirectorySeparatorChar + "Layouts" +
            Path.DirectorySeparatorChar + "LayoutConfig.xml";
    }
  }
}
```

First, the path of the default configuration file is set. This configuration file is used for setting the docking state of the pads. It is in XML format and is a feature of the Magic library, which generates a configuration file for the dockstate of the pads. If the configurations aren't set properly, then the layout will be garbled (all pads will auto-dock to the left side). This should never happen because the default config file will be loaded; but if it is missing, it won't disturb the application:

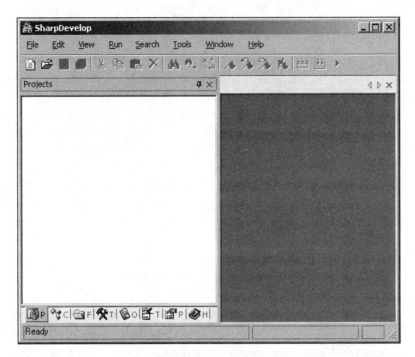

We have to provide a separate configuration file for each language, as Magic identifies the docked controls by their name. If it is unable to find a language-specific configuration file, a default configuration file is used, created by us. We just create a layout that we feel is handy, and put our configuration file for the default layout in the distribution.

Resuming our discussion of the MDI Layout Manager, let's look at the `ActiveWorkbenchwindow` property:

```
public IWorkbenchWindow ActiveWorkbenchwindow {
  get {
    if (tabControl.SelectedTab == null) {
      return null;
    }
    return (IWorkbenchWindow)tabControl.SelectedTab.Tag;
  }
}
```

This property returns the active Workbench window. Only the Layout Manager can determine where it is and how it is represented.

Now we'll look at the `Attach` method that attaches the Layout Manager to the Workbench (look at the diagram at the beginning of this chapter). As we can switch the Layout Manager at run time, this method is quite interesting. Note that, in this code snippet, the Workbench itself inherits from `System.Windows.Forms.Form`:

```
public void Attach(IWorkbench Workbench)
{
  wbForm = (Form)Workbench;
  wbForm.Controls.Clear();
  wbForm.IsMdiContainer = true;

  tabControl.Dock = DockStyle.Top;
  tabControl.ShrinkPagesToFit = true;
  tabControl.Appearance =
    Crownwood.Magic.Controls.TabControl.VisualAppearance.MultiDocument;
  tabControl.Size = new Size(10, 24);
  wbForm.Controls.Add(tabControl);

  dockManager = new DockingManager(wbForm, VisualStyle.IDE);

  Control firstControl = null;

  IStatusBarService statusBarService = (IStatusBarService)
    ICSharpCode.Core.Services.ServiceManager.Services.GetService
      (typeof(IStatusBarService));
  wbForm.Controls.Add(statusBarService.Control);

  foreach (ToolBar toolBar in ((DefaultWorkbench)Workbench).ToolBars) {
    if (firstControl == null) {
      firstControl = firstControl;
    }
    wbForm.Controls.Add(toolBar);
  }

  ((DefaultWorkbench)Workbench).TopMenu.Dock = DockStyle.Top;
  wbForm.Controls.Add(((DefaultWorkbench)Workbench).TopMenu);

  ((DefaultWorkbench)Workbench).TopMenu.MdiContainer = wbForm;
  wbForm.Menu = null;
  dockManager.InnerControl = tabControl;
  dockManager.OuterControl = statusBarService.Control;

  foreach (IViewContent content in Workbench.ViewContentCollection) {
    ShowView(content);
  }

  foreach (IPadContent content in Workbench.PadContentCollection) {
    ShowPad(content);
  }

  tabControl.SelectionChanged += new EventHandler(ActiveMdiChanged);

  try {
    if (File.Exists(configFile)) {
      dockManager.LoadConfigFromFile(configFile);
    } else if (File.Exists(defaultconfigFile)) {
      dockManager.LoadConfigFromFile(defaultconfigFile);
    }
```

```
    } catch (Exception) {
      Console.WriteLine
        ("can't load docking configuration, version clash ?");
    }
    RedrawAllComponents();
}
```

When switching the Layout Managers, the `Detach` method is called first. This method restores the Workbench window to its former state:

```
public void Detach()
{
  if (dockManager != null) {
    dockManager.SaveConfigToFile(configFile);
  }

  foreach (DefaultWorkspaceWindow f in wbForm.MdiChildren) {
    f.TakeOffContent();
    f.ViewContent = null;
    f.Controls.Clear();
    f.Close();
  }

  tabControl.TabPages.Clear();
  tabControl.Controls.Clear();

  if (dockManager != null) {
    dockManager.Contents.Clear();
  }

  ((DefaultWorkbench)wbForm).TopMenu.MdiContainer = null;
  wbForm.IsMdiContainer = false;
  wbForm.Controls.Clear();
}
```

If our Layout Manager is set to a Workbench, we'll now look into the problem of showing the various pads:

```
Hashtable contentHash = new Hashtable();

public void ShowPad(IPadContent content)
{
  if (contentHash[content] == null) {
    IProperties properties = (IProperties)
      propertyService.GetProperty("Workspace.ViewMementos", new
        DefaultProperties());
    content.Control.Dock = DockStyle.None;
    Content newContent;
    if (content.Icon != null) {
      ImageList imgList = new ImageList();
      imgList.Images.Add(content.Icon);
      newContent = dockManager.Contents.Add
        (content.Control, content.Title, imgList, 0);
```

```
    } else {
      newContent = dockManager.Contents.Add
        (content.Control, content.Title);
    }
    contentHash[content] = newContent;
  } else {
    Content c = (Content)contentHash[content];
    if (c != null) {
      dockManager.ShowContent(c);
    }
  }
}

public bool IsVisible(IPadContent padContent)
{
  Content content = (Content)contentHash[padContent];
  if (content != null) {
    return content.Visible;
  }
  return false;
}

public void HidePad(IPadContent padContent)
{
  Content content = (Content)contentHash[padContent];
  if (content != null) {
    dockManager.HideContent(content);
  }
}

public void ActivatePad(IPadContent padContent)
{
  Content content = (Content)contentHash[padContent];
  if (content != null) {
    content.BringToFront();
  }
}
```

These functions handle pads and work with the Magic library's dock controls to handle the pad state.

The RedrawAllComponents method in the Layout Manager must renew all information that might have possibly changed. The Layout Manager doesn't call Redraw on the views or pads, as this is the task of the Workbench. We defined the Workbench to implement it this way because there would be code duplication if all Layout Managers called Redraw on pads and views:

```
public void RedrawAllComponents()
{
  tabControl.Style = (Crownwood.Magic.Common.VisualStyle)
    propertyService.GetProperty
      ("ICSharpCode.SharpDevelop.Gui.VisualStyle",
        Crownwood.Magic.Common.VisualStyle.IDE);
```

```
        // redraw correct pad content names (language may have changed)
        foreach (IPadContent content in
          ((IWorkbench)wbForm).PadContentCollection) {
          Content c = (Content)contentHash[content];
          if (c != null) {
            c.Title = c.FullTitle = content.Title;
          }
        }
      }
```

The next method, ShowView, is the equivalent of ShowPad, for views. It shows a view as a DefaultWorkspaceWindow in the MDI area of the main window (we will look at the DefaultWorkspaceWindow later in this section):

```
    public IWorkbenchWindow ShowView(IViewContent content)
    {
      DefaultWorkspaceWindow window = new DefaultWorkspaceWindow(content);

      content.Control.Visible = true;

      if (wbForm.MdiChildren.Length == 0 ||
        wbForm.ActiveMdiChild.WindowState == FormWindowState.Maximized) {
          ((Form)window).WindowState = FormWindowState.Maximized;
      }
      window.TabPage = tabControl.AddWindow(window);
      ((Form)window).MdiParent = wbForm;
      ((Form)window).Show();
      window.Closed += new EventHandler(CloseWindowEvent);

      return window;
    }
```

Now we need to do some event handling:

```
    public void CloseWindowEvent(object sender, EventArgs e)
    {
      DefaultWorkspaceWindow f = (DefaultWorkspaceWindow)sender;
      if (f.ViewContent != null) {
        ((IWorkbench)wbForm).CloseContent(f.ViewContent);
      }
    }


    void ActiveMdiChanged(object sender, EventArgs e)
    {
      if (ActiveWorkbenchWindowChanged != null) {
        ActiveWorkbenchWindowChanged(this, e);
      }
    }

    public event EventHandler ActiveWorkbenchWindowChanged;
}
```

Writing a Layout Manager is an annoying task, and we have often found that bugs break into some of the Layout Managers. However, we have a single point of failure when something 'strange' is going on in the GUI. The good thing about Layout Managers is that they are relative simple, small, and help to improve the design of the other parts (the view or pad model is really nice to program with). Only the Layout Manager knows about the implementation details of the windows it provides, so each Layout Manager must provide an implementation of IWorkbenchWindow.

In the past, we have had a floating Layout Manager that used the same workspace window as the MDI Layout Manager. The floating Layout Manager was discarded because very few users ever used it.

The workspace window is implemented in the
src\SharpDevelop\Base\Gui\Workbench\Layouts\DefaultWorkspaceWindow.cs file:

```csharp
public class DefaultWorkspaceWindow : Form, IWorkbenchWindow
{
  IViewContent content;

  EventHandler setTitleEvent = null;
  Crownwood.Magic.Controls.TabPage tabPage = null;

  public Crownwood.Magic.Controls.TabPage TabPage {
    get {
      return tabPage;
    }
    set {
      tabPage = value;
    }
  }

  public string Title {
    get {
      return Text;
    }
    set {
      Text = value;
      string fileName = content.ContentName;
      if (tabPage != null) {
        tabPage.Title = value;
      }
      if (fileName == null) {
        fileName = content.UntitledName;
      }
      if (fileName != null) {
        FileUtilityService fileUtilityService = (FileUtilityService)
          ServiceManager.Services.GetService(typeof(FileUtilityService));
        int index = fileUtilityService.GetImageIndexForFile(fileName);
        this.Icon = System.Drawing.Icon.FromHandle
          (((Bitmap)fileUtilityService.ImageList.Images[index]).GetHicon());
      }
      OnTitleChanged(null);
    }
  }
}
```

```
public IViewContent ViewContent {
  get {
    return content;
  }
  set {
    content = value;
  }
}

public DefaultWorkspaceWindow(IViewContent content)
{
  this.content = content;
  content.WorkbenchWindow = this;
  content.Control.Dock = DockStyle.Fill;
  Controls.Add(content.Control);

  setTitleEvent = new EventHandler(SetTitleEvent);
  content.ContentNameChanged += setTitleEvent;
  content.DirtyChanged      += setTitleEvent;
  SetTitleEvent(null, null);
}
```

The Layout Manager sets the tab page for the window. If a title change occurs, the window sets the name of the tab too. An alternative would have been to let the tab listen to the `TitleChanged` event; but the former approach was a bit easier because it doesn't require us to extend the tab, or to remove event handlers when a window closes.

The `SetTitleEvent` sets the title of the window. If the content is untitled, this method retrieves the default `untitledname` and constructs a name that has the `<untitledname>Number` form. It searches through all windows in the Workbench to find the first 'free' number and acquires it:

```
string myUntitledTitle = null;
public void SetTitleEvent(object sender, EventArgs e)
{
  if (content == null) {
    return;
  }
  string newTitle = "";
  if (content.ContentName == null) {
    if (myUntitledTitle == null) {
      string baseName =
        Path.GetFileNameWithoutExtension(content.UntitledName);
      int     number = 1;
      bool    found  = true;
      while (found) {
        found = false;
        foreach (IViewContent windowContent in
          WorkbenchSingleton.Workbench.ViewContentCollection) {
            string title = windowContent.WorkbenchWindow.Title;
            if (title.EndsWith("*") || title.EndsWith("+")) {
              title = title.Substring(0, title.Length - 1);
          }
```

```
                    if (title == baseName + number) {
                        found = true;
                        ++number;
                        break;
                    }
                }
            }
            myUntitledTitle = baseName + number;
        }
        newTitle = myUntitledTitle;
    } else {
        newTitle = WindowState == FormWindowState.Minimized ?
            Path.GetFileName(content.ContentName) : content.ContentName;
    }

    if (content.IsDirty) {
        newTitle += "*";
    } else if (content.IsReadOnly) {
        newTitle += "+";
    }

    if (newTitle != Title) {
        Title = newTitle;
    }
}

protected override void OnResize(EventArgs e)
{
    base.OnResize(e);
    SetTitleEvent(null, null);
}
```

Like the Workbench layout, the window is able to detach the content. After this method call, the content can be inserted in a new Workbench window:

```
public void DetachContent ()
{
    content.ContentNameChanged -= setTitleEvent;
    content.DirtyChanged        -= setTitleEvent;
}
```

Now, we will look at the closing methods. The window pops up a message box that asks the user if the window can be safely closed:

```
protected override void OnClosing(CancelEventArgs e)
{
    base.OnClosing(e);
    if (!forceClose andand ViewContent != null andand ViewContent.IsDirty) {
        ResourceService resourceService = (ResourceService)
            ServiceManager.Services.GetService(typeof(ResourceService));
        DialogResult dr = MessageBox.Show
            (resourceService.GetString("MainWindow.SaveChangesMessage"),
```

```
                resourceService.GetString("MainWindow.SaveChangesMessageHeader") +
                  " " + Title + " ?", MessageBoxButtons.YesNoCancel,
                  MessageBoxIcon.Question);
         switch (dr) {
           case DialogResult.Yes:
             Activate();
             if (content.ContentName == null) {
               while (true) {
                 new ICSharpCode.SharpDevelop.Commands.SaveFileAs().Run();
                 if (ViewContent.IsDirty) {
                   DialogResult result = MessageBox.Show
                     ("Do you really want to discard your changes ?",
                       "Question", MessageBoxButtons.YesNo,
                         MessageBoxIcon.Question,
                           MessageBoxDefaultButton.Button2);
                   if (result == DialogResult.Yes) {
                     break;
                   }
                 } else {
                   break;
                 }
               }
             } else {
               ViewContent.SaveFile();
             }
             break;
           case DialogResult.No:
             // set view content dirty = false, because I want to prevent
             //double checks, if Close() is called twice.
             ViewContent.IsDirty = false;
             break;
           case DialogResult.Cancel:
             e.Cancel = true;
             return;
       }
     }
}

protected override void OnClosed(EventArgs e)
{
  base.OnClosed(e);
  OnWindowDeselected(e);
  OnCloseEvent(null);
}

bool forceClose = false;
public void CloseWindow(bool force)
{
  forceClose = force;
  Close();
}
```

Another issue that we had to deal with was that of selection. Selection (bringing an MDI window to the front and making it the focus) is a problem with Windows Forms, and was a hard task to solve. As `Activate` and `Select` do not always work, we didn't find a good scheme, but when we call `Focus` on the control that the view gives us, the selection seems to work fine. The current implementation that focuses on the control that the window contains does work in SharpDevelop:

```
public void SelectWindow()
{
  if (tabPage  != null) {
    tabPage.Select();
  }

  Activate();
  Select();
  content.Control.Focus();
}

protected override void OnGotFocus(EventArgs e)
{
  base.OnGotFocus(e);
  OnWindowSelected(e);
}

protected override void OnDeactivate(EventArgs e)
{
  base.OnDeactivate(e);
  OnWindowDeselected(e);
}
```

The related events are defined at the bottom of this class, and are the events we must provide because we implement the `IWorkbenchWindow` interface:

```
protected virtual void OnTitleChanged(EventArgs e)
{
  if (TitleChanged != null) {
    TitleChanged(this, e);
  }
}

protected virtual void OnCloseEvent(EventArgs e)
{
  if (CloseEvent != null) {
    CloseEvent(this, e);
  }
}

public virtual void OnWindowSelected(EventArgs e)
{
  if (WindowSelected != null) {
    WindowSelected(this, e);
  }
}
```

```
public virtual void OnWindowDeselected(EventArgs e)
{
  if (WindowDeselected != null) {
    WindowDeselected(this, e);
  }
}

public event EventHandler WindowSelected;
public event EventHandler WindowDeselected;
public event EventHandler TitleChanged;
public event EventHandler CloseEvent;
}
```

Now that we have studied the existing implementation of the user interface, let's take a look at the potential changes that could be made in the future.

The Current and Future Implementation

Currently, the abstracted GUI layer handles the various requirements well. It allows us to implement much of the code without having to know about Windows Forms, and this improves the API portability, which was the goal of the GUI layer. The big GUI layer we have seen here won't change much in the future versions, but it will be completed with a part that abstracts the GUI on a deeper level – the dialog level.

Currently dialogs are tied to Windows Forms, and are not portable to other APIs. We did port some dialogs and panels over to XML, but this is only the first step in making them portable. We will discuss the current XML format in Chapter 17 within the *The XML Forms Persistence Format* section. We are planning for a system that has:

❑ An abstract representation of GUI elements
This will be done through interfaces and an abstract factory that creates the GUI elements.

❑ Layout management for GUI elements
SharpDevelop is a localized application and often we have to deal with the problem that the labels or buttons are displayed too small. Therefore, the only way to solve this is to use layout management.

❑ An XML representation for dialogs and panels
XML is more maintainable than source code. It should be possible to use the abstract layer from source too, but XML dialogs make the source code smaller, easier to debug, and simpler to make changes to (will not require recompiles too).

❑ A non-GUI implementation of the abstract layer
This will be used for unit testing of the dialogs and panels. Currently, not much code of SharpDevelop is covered by unit tests. Securing dialogs and panels would be a big step forward.

Summary

In this chapter, we learned about the abstract GUI layer that is used to represent the SharpDevelop superstructure, and what benefits the GUI layer brings to the application, and how it is implemented.

We looked at the `IViewContent` interface, and implemented it to produce an HTML view using the Internet Explorer ActiveX control.

We implemented the `IPadContent` interface and examined what a pad is, as opposed to a view. We learned how the help viewer inside SharpDevelop is implemented.

We learned what a Layout Manager is, and how it manages the views and pads to construct the actual layout of the IDE. We saw that it was easy to switch a Layout Manager to apply a new SharpDevelop look and feel on the fly.

We looked at the implementation of a workspace window that the Layout Manager uses. We have examined how the workspace window is required beside the views, to make the GUI layer work in the way that we designed it to work.

In the next chapter, we will learn how internationalization is implemented in SharpDevelop.

CHAPTER 7

7
Internationalization

As your software grows popular, you will probably want to offer it in different languages and adapt it to different culture sets. The core idea of internationalization is to create a persistent look and feel for our customers, no matter what language they use. Although the .NET Framework offers great support for localization, we needed to implement it with expandability in mind. The support for internationalization, or in other words, the attempt to enable porting our software to other languages begins with its architectural design.

Right since the first stable beta builds, SharpDevelop was designed with internationalization in mind. Before we investigate how SharpDevelop handles this daunting task, we must first have a general idea of what design strategy to apply while developing a localizable application.

GUI-driven software is affected by internationalization in two major ways:

❑ First, the layout must be capable of resizing menus, dialog boxes, and so on, for fitting the different character sets and/or special characters

❑ Second, localizable resources should never be hard-coded, and the language packs should be able to easily migrate into the application using localized resource files

The localizable resources comprise of localized resource strings, screen and window positions, constants, filenames, paths, and even images. The resource strings, especially, deserve an extra amount of attention, as it is through them that our software communicates with the user. Resource strings change from language to language leading to several tricky situations; for example the same sentence may vary in length across two diverse languages, thereby affecting the length parameter of the resource string.

Why should these kinds of problems bother us? Well, if we define a screen area that is too small, the translated equivalent text might exceed the limits of the component (for example, a textbox, label, or similar), and the text may become unreadable, as demonstrated in the following screenshot:

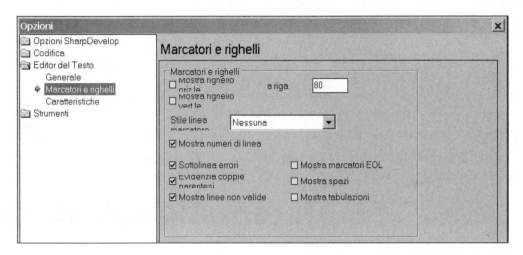

The Italian translation contains more words than the English original, hence the truncation of labels.

Another issue, which needs to be mentioned, is string concatenation. Developers often join words together to form strings (for example, error messages). This may work in the case of one particular language; but since the word order and the words, in general, can have dissimilar forms (singular, plural, gender, and so on), it may cause meaningless combinations for other languages.

With localization comes the need to support different character sets. This topic affects both the GUI and the strings – dialog boxes have to be resized, the read direction may have to be reversed, and the appropriate character set has to be selected.

For example, if you want to add Western European languages to your application, you should use the internationally standardized ISO-8859-1 character set (for details, you can refer to http://www.htmlhelp.com/reference/charset). This character set contains all characters necessary to type and display Western European languages, and complies with 7-bit devices, which normally ignore the eighth bit, as it's an 8-bit superset of ASCII. Keep in mind that such 7-bit devices will turn 8-bit character sets into garbage; so do consider this when coding. However, no modern Windows platform has these issues.

On the other hand, we can use the 16-bit Unicode (ISO-10646) character set which is an extension of ISO-8859-1 to wide characters. Due to its capabilities, most of the languages (including Asian) can be encoded. More importantly, .NET uses Unicode internally and the compilers support it fully. Unicode's major drawback is that it is not supported by certain operating systems. Some older systems may have trouble when they encounter Unicode in their software. Keep in mind that these systems are not supported by .NET.

After this brief overview of design of localized software, you might wonder how SharpDevelop handles this internationalization task. In this chapter, we will not only show you its implementation in the IDE, but also demonstrate how easy it is to translate SharpDevelop to your preferred language.

Let's start our discussion by looking at the working of the localization engine, after which we'll explain the techniques for enabling hassle-free and instant language switching system.

To bring SharpDevelop to a global audience, besides English, several languages are already built-in. No matter what language is used, we intend to ensure usability for the user. Our internationalization strategy is based on the motivation to encourage native speakers to perform these translations. Hence, we offer a unified and easy-to-use web application where translators can add new languages and also build language resource files offline.

Handling Internationalization in SharpDevelop

Depending on your preferred language (or the requirement of your project) you can change the language settings by navigating the menu to the UI Language panel. This action will switch the menu language immediately to the newly selected one, without the need to restart SharpDevelop.

Before we move to the next section, where the redrawing event chain is explained in detail, let us talk about the flag view (where we get to see the flags of the respective countries). But first, we look at the code in the
src\SharpDevelop\Base\Services\Language\LanguageService.cs file:

```
public class LanguageService : AbstractService
{
  string languagePath = Application.StartupPath +
                    Path.DirectorySeparatorChar + ".." +
                    Path.DirectorySeparatorChar + "data" +
                    Path.DirectorySeparatorChar + "resources" +
                    Path.DirectorySeparatorChar + "languages" +
                    Path.DirectorySeparatorChar;

  ImageList languageImageList = new ImageList();
  ArrayList languages        = new ArrayList();

  public ImageList LanguageImageList {
    get { return languageImageList; }
  }
}

public ArrayList Languages {
  get { return languages; }
}

public LanguageService()
{
  LanguageImageList.ImageSize = new Size(46, 38);

  XmlDocument doc = new XmlDocument();
  doc.Load(languagePath + "LanguageDefinition.xml");

  XmlNodeList nodes = doc.DocumentElement.ChildNodes;

  foreach (XmlElement el in nodes) {
    languages.Add(new Language(el.Attributes["name"].InnerText,
      el.Attributes["code"].InnerText, LanguageImageList.Images.Count));
```

```
        LanguageImageList.Images.Add(new Bitmap(languagePath +
           el.Attributes["icon"].InnerText));
    }
}
```

We assign the hard-coded path information to a string variable named `languagePath`. Then we have to initialize an `ImageList` (which holds the flag images) and an `ArrayList` (which holds the appropriate language name). These variables function as properties and get their values, as assigned in the constructor of the `LanguageService` class.

Within the constructor, the `LanguageDefinition.xml` file (in the `\Data\Resources\Languages` directory) is parsed to retrieve the available language information using the path information provided by the `languagePath` string variable. The language code, and its representative flag are extracted according to the structure of the `LanguageDefinition.xml` file, the language name.

The next listing shows us a snippet of the XML file:

```
<Languages>
  <Languages name="U.S. English" code="en-us" page="" icon="usa.png" />
  <Languages name="International English" code="en" page="" icon="uk.png" />
  <Languages name="German" code="de" page="" icon="germany.png" />
  ...
</Languages>
```

After retrieving the language entries, the `ListView` box within the **Option** dialog must be filled up. This is done by the constructor of the `IDEOptionPanel` class located in the `src\SharpDevelop\Base\Gui\Dialogs\OptionPanels\IDEOptions\SelectCulturePanel.cs` directory.

The following snippet gives us the relevant lines of code:

```
public IDEOptionPanel()
{

  LanguageService languageService = (LanguageService)
    ServiceManager.Services.GetService(typeof(LanguageService));
  listView.Location          = new Point(8, 8);
  listView.Size              = new Size(136, 200);
  listView.LargeImageList    = languageService.LanguageImageList;
  listView.ItemActivate     += new EventHandler(ChangeCulture);
  listView.Sorting           = SortOrder.Ascending;
  listView.Activation        = ItemActivation.OneClick;
  listView.BorderStyle       = flat ? BorderStyle.FixedSingle :
    BorderStyle.Fixed3D;
  listView.Anchor = (System.Windows.Forms.AnchorStyles.Top |
                    (System.Windows.Forms.AnchorStyles.Left |
                     System.Windows.Forms.AnchorStyles.Right));

  foreach (Language language in languageService.Languages) {
    listView.Items.Add(new ListViewItem(new string[] {language.Name,
      language.Code}, language.ImageIndex));
```

```
    }

    this.Controls.Add(listView);
    ..
    }
```

Although changing languages is naturally easy, there has to be some mechanism under the hood to provide such usability. In the next section, we will show an approach for enabling localization support without compromising on ease of use. This section covers redrawing the GUI, accessing the resource files and replacing localized strings.

Redrawing with Events

After we have confirmed the choice of language, the whole GUI has to be redrawn as per the new settings. A chain of events is necessary to redraw all the components involved. Before we step through this process, let's take a look at the following diagram:

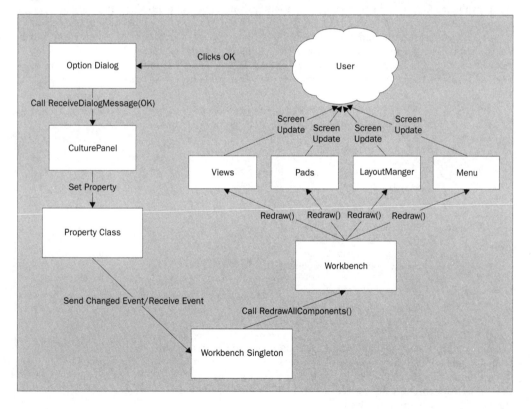

This simplified flowchart shows us the sequence from the user's click to the redrawn GUI.
After the user confirms their selection by pressing the **OK** button, the `AcceptEvent` method (located in the `TreeViewOptions.cs` file under `src\SharpDevelop\Base\Gui\Dialogs`) triggers a `DialogResult.OK` message. The message is received by the `ReceiveDialogMessage` method located in the `src\SharpDevelop\Base\Gui\Dialogs\OptionPanels\IDEOptions\SelectCulturePanel.cs` file:

```
public override bool ReceiveDialogMessage(DialogMessage message)
{
  if (message == DialogMessage.OK) {
    if (SelectedCulture != null) {
      propertyService.SetProperty(uiLanguageProperty, SelectedCulture);
    }
  }
  return true;
}
```

If this evaluates to `true`, the `SetProperty` method is invoked, which resides in the `src\SharpDevelop\Core\Properties\DefaultProperties.cs`. This method triggers the `OnPropertyChanged` method and provides the `PropertyEventArgs` object with the new attributes – the spoken language and its culture setting. This property change is handled by the `TrackPropertyChanges` method of the `WorkBenchSingleton` class in `src\SharpDevelop\Base\Gui\Workbench\WorkbenchSingleton.cs`:

```
static void TrackPropertyChanges(object sender,
ICSharpCode.Core.Properties.PropertyEventArgs e)
{
  if (e.OldValue != e.NewValue) {
    switch (e.Key) {
      case workbenchLayoutProperty:
        SetWbLayout();
        break;

      case "SharpDevelop.UI.CurrentAmbience":
      case "ICSharpCode.SharpDevelop.Gui.VisualStyle":
      case "CoreProperties.UILanguage":
        workbench.RedrawAllComponents();
        break;
    }
  }
}
```

When selecting a new language in the **Options** panel, the current setting (`e.OldValue`) certainly differs from the new one. Nothing happens if the user clicks on the language already in use. The attribute of interest here is the `CoreProperties.UILanguage` property. A change in this property (evaluated by the `switch` statement) causes a redraw of the GUI, or in other words, it triggers the `RedrawAllComponents` method.

The `WorkbenchSingleton` class inherits the `DefaultWorkbench` class. Hence, you find the `RedrawAllComponents` method in the base class (src\SharpDevelop\Base\Gui\Workbench\DefaultWorkbench.cs):

```
public void RedrawAllComponents()
{
  UpdateMenu(null, null);

  foreach (IViewContent content in workbenchContentCollection) {
    content.RedrawContent();
  }

  foreach (IPadContent content in viewContentCollection) {
    content.RedrawContent();
  }

  layout.RedrawAllComponents();
}
```

Now let's look at what happens to the **Files** tab label. Using the English language, the label reads **Files**. If we change it, for example, to German the tab label reads **Dateien** – how is this achieved?

Within the `FileScout` class (src\SharpDevelop\Base\Gui\Pads\FileScout.cs) there is a property named `Title`, which assigns the tab label according to the selected language. The assignment is done by means of the `ResourceService`, which is explained in detail in the next section:

```
public string Title {
get {
  return resourceService.GetString("MainWindow.Windows.FileScoutLabel");
  }
}
```

But how is the tab label actually changed? As seen before, the `DefaultWorkbench` class fires the `RedrawContent` method. For the `FileScout` class, the following steps are performed to change the tab label:

```
public void RedrawContent()
{
  OnTitleChanged(null);
  OnIconChanged(null);
}
```

In the snippet above, the `OnTitleChanged` method is called, whereas `OnIconChanged` is a new event handler. Note that it's the `OnTitleChanged` handler that actually performs the change:

```
protected virtual void OnTitleChanged(EventArgs e)
{
  if (TitleChanged != null) {
    TitleChanged(this, e);
  }
}
```

Now that we know how to redraw the GUI after changing the language settings, we must access the appropriate resource file.

Accessing Resources

The Microsoft .NET documentation suggests that we should use Satellite Assemblies for localizing an application. Following the suggested scheme, the resource files are compiled to assemblies using Microsoft's Assembly Linker (`Al.exe`) tool (refer to the .NET Framework SDK documentation for more information).

This scheme represents the decentralized resource management model and has its drawbacks. Each language and its additional subcultures should be stored in individual subdirectories. As more languages are added to an application, the directory tree grows bigger and this also results in an increased number of `.dll` files. To avoid this problem, we chose a centralized resource management system for SharpDevelop. Although each language is separately stored in a resource file (`StringResources.[Language identifier].resources`) located in the `\data\resources` path, we do not create a Satellite Assembly for each language, instead we dynamically load the language strings each time the language settings are changed. The beauty of centralized management is that there is no redundant code, and add-ins can have their own resources, which are loaded centrally from the AddIn tree.

Now that we know about these benefits, we must make them accessible to our application. As SharpDevelop is based on services, we utilize the Resource service that builds on the `ResourceService.cs` and the `ResourceNotFoundException.cs` files. Both files can be found in the `src\SharpDevelop\Core\Services` directory.

Let's take a look at the `ResourceServices` class (under `ResourceService.cs`) first. This class is responsible for performing the following tasks:

- Changing the settings (`ChangeProperty` method)
- Loading appropriate language strings (`LoadLanguageResources` method)
- Loading new icons (`GetIcon` method)
- Loading new bitmaps (`GetBitmap` method)
- Throwing an exception if a string is not found (`GetString` method)

As we are more interested in the action performed on switching to a different language, we will look at the methods that deal with retrieving the language strings. First, the `ChangeProperty` method is invoked:

```
void ChangeProperty(object sender, PropertyEventArgs e)
{
  if (e.Key == uiLanguageProperty && e.OldValue != e.NewValue)
  {
    LoadLanguageResources();
  }
}
```

If there is a valid change in the UI language, the `LoadLanguageResources` method is called:

```
void LoadLanguageResources()
{
  PropertyService propertyService = (PropertyService)
    ServiceManager.Services.GetService(typeof(PropertyService));
  string language = propertyService.GetProperty
    (uiLanguageProperty, Thread.CurrentThread.CurrentUICulture.Name);

  localStrings = Load(stringResources, language);
  if (localStrings == null && language.IndexOf('-') > 0) {
    localStrings =
      Load(stringResources, language.Split(new char[] {'-'})[0]);
  }

  localIcons = Load(imageResources, language);
  if (localIcons == null && language.IndexOf('-') > 0) {
    localIcons = Load(imageResources, language.Split(new char[] {'-'})[0]);
  }
}
```

This method loads the strings and localized icons. The loading action is performed by the `Load` method:

```
Hashtable Load(string name, string language)
{
  string fname = resourceDirectory + Path.DirectorySeparatorChar +
    name + "." + language + ".resources";

  if (File.Exists(fname)) {
    Hashtable resources = new Hashtable();
    ResourceReader rr = new ResourceReader(fname);
    foreach (DictionaryEntry entry in rr) {
      resources.Add(entry.Key, entry.Value);
    }
    rr.Close();
    return resources;
  }
  return null;
}
```

These code snippets assume that all strings are loaded properly. However, while coding, translations under development may remain incomplete. To ensure proper handling of such occurrences, SharpDevelop first reloads the English language. The beauty of this is that, if there is no appropriate language string, we can at least read an English entry. In rare cases, where even this routine fails, a `ResourceNotFoundException` exception is thrown:

```
public string GetString(string name)
{
  if (localStrings != null && localStrings[name] != null) {
    return localStrings[name].ToString();
  }
```

```
    string s = strings.GetString(name);

    if (s == null) {
       throw new ResourceNotFoundException("string >" + name + "<");
    }

    return s;
}
```

The `ResourceNotFoundException` class conveys the error message in its constructor, and is found in `src\SharpDevelop\Core\Services\ResourceNotFoundException.cs`:

```
public class ResourceNotFoundException : Exception
{
   public ResourceNotFoundException(string resource) : base("Resource not
   found : " + resource) {
   }
}
```

Now, we will look at the process of replacing the old language strings with the chosen ones, performed by a service named `StringParserService`. You can access the source code of this service by navigating to the `Src\SharpDevelop\Core\Services\StringParserService.cs` file.

To give you an idea what the replaceable strings look like, we will take a peek at the C# template file. Full coverage of this topic is given in Chapter 3 and Chapter 5. This XML file contains information about an empty C# file. Among lots of other information we find two localized strings – the template `Name` and its `Description`:

```
<?xml version="1.0" ?>
<Template Originator="Mike Krueger" Language="C#" Created="3/09/2001"
LastModified="3/09/2001">
  <TemplateConfiguration>
      <Name>${res:Templates.File.C#.EmptyC#File.Name}</Name>
      <Icon>C#.File.CSFileIcon</Icon>
      <Category>C#</Category>
      <LanguageName>C#</LanguageName>
      <Description>${res:Templates.File.C#.EmptyC#File.Description}</Description>
   </TemplateConfiguration>
   <TemplateFiles>
      <File DefaultExtension=".cs" DefaultName="EmptyC#file">
        <![CDATA[ // created on ${Date} at ${Time}]]>
      </File>
   </TemplateFiles>
   <FileOptions />
</Template>
```

Depending on the selected language, the appropriate string is filled in; for example, in case of English, it will look like:

```
<Name>Empty C# File</Name>
<Description>creates an empty C# file</Description>
```

If we had selected German, this would be:

```
<Name>Leere C# Datei</Name>
<Description>erzeugt eine leere C# Datei</Description>
```

You might wonder what makes the CDATA section of the XML template file necessary. Actually, this section is replaced by the StringParser service, and resembles a timestamp. The service replaces the ${Date} and ${Time} section with the current date and time values, resulting in the line:

```
// created on 04/09/2002 at 15:15
```

The service parses the current strings and replaces them if the appropriate string match is found. The Parse method takes a string variable named input and a string array named custom_tags as parameters. By means of regular expressions, and if and switch constructs, the input string data is evaluated. The return value is the new translated language string:

```csharp
public string Parse(string input, string[,] custom_tags)
{
  string output = input;
  if (input != null) {
    const string pattern = @"\$\{([^\}]*)\}";
    foreach (Match m in Regex.Matches(input, pattern)) {
      if (m.Length > 0) {
        string token        = m.ToString();
        string propertyName = m.Groups[1].Captures[0].Value;
        string propertyValue = null;
        switch (propertyName.ToUpper()) {
          case "DATE": // current date
            propertyValue = DateTime.Today.ToShortDateString();
            break;
          case "TIME": // current time
            propertyValue = DateTime.Now.ToShortTimeString();
            break;
          default:
            propertyValue = null;
            if (custom_tags != null) {
              for (int j = 0; j < custom_tags.GetLength(0); ++j) {
                if (propertyName.ToUpper() == custom_tags[j, 0].ToUpper()) {
                  propertyValue = custom_tags[j, 1];
                  break;
                }
              }
            }
            if (propertyValue == null) {
              propertyValue = properties[propertyName.ToUpper()];
            }
            if (propertyValue == null) {
              int k = propertyName.IndexOf(':');
              if (k > 0) {
                switch (propertyName.Substring(0, k).ToUpper()) {
                  case "RES":
                    ResourceService resourceService = (ResourceService)
```

```
            ServiceManager.Services.GetService
                (typeof(ResourceService));
            propertyValue = Parse(resourceService.GetString
                (propertyName.Substring(k + 1)), custom_tags);
            break;
          case "PROPERTY":
            PropertyService propertyService = (PropertyService)
             ServiceManager.Services.GetService
                (typeof(PropertyService));
            propertyValue = propertyService.GetProperty
                (propertyName.Substring(k + 1)).ToString();
            break;
          }
        }
      }
      break;
    }
    if (propertyValue != null) {
      output = output.Replace(token, propertyValue);
    }
    }
  }
  }
  return output;
  }
}
```

But what if your native language is not among these, or you want to add a new language? The rest of the chapter comprises utilities for translators and developers, who may want to import or export their own language resources or compile resource files, and gives a fundamental idea of how to build an easily manageable, collaborative solution in accordance with the motto "Translations – anytime, anywhere".

Managing Translations

This section presents a classic ASP (Active Server Pages) web application accessible only to SharpDevelop's translators, which manages all the SharpDevelop transactions. As it is a proprietary application, only code snippets are provided, which will give the reader an idea of how to implement such a service.

For those who ask why no ASP.NET example application is provided in this book, the answer is that an ASP.NET application ready for deployment was still under development. This application allows translators to enter translations in two ways:

❏ **Online Mode**
In this mode, translation is done with a common list and forming views into the translations

❏ **Offline Mode**
Here, translation is done by downloading an XML file, and then uploading it after the translations have been performed

Both methods share one commonality – the translator can download an XML file and create a resource file from it using the translation builder utility found in the `src\tools\translationbuilder\tbuilder.cs` file.

In this way, the translators can test their translations by integrating them with the running application anytime, without requiring a SharpDevelop team member to build the entire resource file collection from the database (refer to the *Generating Resource Files from the Database* section for a description of this process).

Lets look at the online translation application used by the translators and the generation of resource files, and then move on to discuss the ways in which the team can build the resource files from the translation database.

The Translation Web Application

This section will give us an idea of the design of the online translation component. The web application uses ASP and features logon security, easy user and translation management with statistics, and the ability to download or upload language files. As our motto is "Translations – anytime, anywhere", there are three basic requirements that influence the design process:

❑ **Online mode** – The online mode part presents an example of a web application that uses ASP to deliver maximum performance and usability.

❑ **Offline mode** – If a translator does not have an Internet connection as an option, the offline mode section rounds up the 'Anywhere, anyplace' motto. This section covers prerequisites to be able to work offline and introduces a little gadget, the `tbuilder` utility. The `tbuilder` utility is the missing link to compile the XML file containing the language strings into resource files, after which these strings are used by the application. A detailed example of use of the `tbuilder` tool is provided in the *Generating Resource Files from XML* section.

❑ **Localization implication** – Lastly, there is the character set issue for foreign languages. Some languages, such as Japanese or Russian, use non-Latin character sets. If our web application is not able to handle these, then we will run into trouble. Handling these foreign characters just like Latin ones results in displaying garbage. A peek under the hood of the ASP web application shows us how to take care of foreign characters.

The application is accessed at the entry point (Home), where the translator chooses the language they wish to edit. A translator has privileges only to edit their assigned language and can only view other languages. After the language selection, they list the localizable strings at the List Translation page. This page accesses the database and retrieves the appropriate strings.

The translator is able to add or modify the language strings in the List Translation page. If the translator wishes to work offline, they can download the XML file (at the XML Download page) to their local machine. The XML file contains everything that they need to translate the original English strings to the desired language. After translation work is complete, they navigate to the Offline Translating page and paste the modified XML source into an input field. The submission process will upload the content of the input field and merge it with the database.

Localization Implications

Internationalization also means that the application, in this case – the web-based front-end, can handle non-Latin character sets and code pages, without which the user will see a garbage output in the application's windows.

Windows 2000 and applications of the same generation can handle 16-bit Unicode; but if you happen to use older systems like the Windows 9x generation, you are out of luck and will have to upgrade to the 2000 version. To enable Unicode compliance in your dynamic web pages, you have to perform the following steps (some seem redundant while using ASP; but when you have to support many browsers, you start to get a bit wary):

❑ Use @CODEPAGE and Session.CodePage to interpret localized (latin, non-latin) strings.

❑ Use the ADO Stream Object to retrieve Unicode formatted strings from an SQL 2000 or Access 2000 database.

❑ Use the HTML <META HTTP-EQUIV> tag to set the appropriate code page.

❑ Write XML documents as Unicode formatted

❑ If you use the FileSystemObject, you must set the appropriate attribute for the file stream to Unicode.

We are now ready to retrieve Unicode data from our database, or display Unicode languages correctly.

Compiling to Resource Files

In the offline mode, there are two ways to generate resource files:

❑ From XML by translators

❑ From the database by the team

Generating Resource Files from XML

To achieve platform independence, we chose XML to store the native language strings. A translator can download the XML file from the web application:

The downloaded file will be saved as a file named resources.xml. It will look like the following snippet (this string is in German):

```
<?xml version-"1.0" encoding-"windows-1252" ?>
<translation language="de">
 <resource name="_Internal.Bogus.Translation.Test">
     <![CDATA[ Das ist ein Test]]>
   </resource>

 <resource name="CompilerResultView.DescriptionText">
  <![CDATA[ Beschreibung]]>
   </resource>
```

```
<resource name="CompilerResultView.FileText">
 <![CDATA[ Datei]]>
  </resource>

<resource name="CompilerResultView.LineText">
 <![CDATA[ Zeile]]>
  </resource>

<resource name="Dialog.About.DialogName">
 <![CDATA[ Über SharpDevelop]]>
  </resource>
```

After we have downloaded the XML file from the web application, we have to compile it to a resource file. The tbuilder utility (located in the \bin directory) generates a valid language resource file with the filename StringResources.<language code>.resources.

All that is left for us to do is to copy this file to the \data\resources directory (while SharpDevelop is not active, because the availability check of resource files is done during SharpDevelop's loading procedure).

The generation is performed by using the ResourceWriter class of the System.Resources namespace. Let's take a peek into the payload of the TranslationBuilder class of the tbuilder utility. The point of interest here is the Assemble method:

```
static void Assemble(string pattern)
{
  string[] files = Directory.GetFiles(Directory.GetCurrentDirectory(),
  pattern);

  foreach (string file in files) {
    if (Path.GetExtension(file).ToUpper() == ".XML") {
      try {
        XmlDocument  doc = new XmlDocument();
        doc.Load(file);
        string resfilename = "StringResources." +
          doc.DocumentElement.Attributes["language"].InnerText +
            ".resources";
        ResourceWriter rw = new ResourceWriter(resfilename);

        foreach (XmlElement el in doc.DocumentElement.ChildNodes) {
          rw.AddResource(el.Attributes["name"].InnerText, el.InnerText);
        }

        rw.Generate();
        rw.Close();
      }
      catch (Exception e) {
      Console.WriteLine("Error while processing " + file + " :");
      Console.WriteLine(e.ToString());
    }
  }
} } }
```

After we load the XML from the web application into the XMLDocument object named simply doc, we have to assign an appropriate name for the generated resource file. As the resource file takes the form StringResources.<language code>.resources, where the abbreviation for the language is extracted from the language attribute of the XML file.

This filename combination is then assigned to a string variable named resfilename and a new ResourceWriter object (rw) is instantiated.

As we have seen in the code listing, our ResourceWriter object takes the filename of the resource file as parameter. As our source file has an XML format, we iterate through it using a foreach statement. Resource entries are defined as name and value pairs, similar to the entries in a hash table. The AddResource method of the ResourceWriter class adds entries to the resource file and must be called at least once to successfully generate a valid resource file. After adding to the ResourceWriter object all the entries found, the Generate method is called to write the entries into a file stream.

The next section covers an all-in-one solution to extract a language XML file from a database and output a resource file.

Generating Resource Files from the Database

Lastly, there's the Assemble utility, which creates resources out of a database. This utility can be found in \src\Tools\Assemble. As the OLE DB .NET Data Providers are flexible, we get high performance support for Microsoft SQL databases, JET compatible databases, and even Oracle databases.

Now let's get to the core and look at the application's MainClass (in Main.cs). The MainClass has two methods besides its entry point. In all, it has the Main method, the Open method, and the ConvertIllegalChars method.

The Open method's functionality is solely to open a connection to a database, using a suitable .NET Data Provider. The following lines of code are straightforward and refer to an MS Access database:

```
static void Open()
{
  string connection = "Provider=Microsoft.Jet.OLEDB.4.0;Data Source=" +
    Application.StartupPath + Path.DirectorySeparatorChar +
      "LocalizeDb.mdb;
  myConnection = new OleDbConnection(connection);
  myConnection.Open();
}
```

The ConvertIllegalChars method masks escape sequences such as a newline (\n), carriage return (\r), and so on, to well formed resource-file-compatible characters:

```
static string ConvertIllegalChars(string str)
{
  StringBuilder newString = new StringBuilder();
  for (int i = 0; i < str.Length; ++i) {
    switch (str[i]) {
      case '\r':
        break;
      case '\n':
```

```
        newString.Append("\\n");
        break;
      case '"':
        newString.Append("\\\"");
        break;
      case '\\':
        newString.Append("\\\\");
        break;
      default:
        newString.Append(str[i]);
        break;
    }
  }
  return newString.ToString();
}
```

Using the `StringBuilder` class makes string operations simple. In the `Main` method we handle parameter input and retrieve the language from the database:

```
public static void Main(string[] args)
{
  Open();
  string lang = "PrimaryResLangValue";
  StreamWriter writer = null;

  foreach (string param in args) {
    string par = param;
    if (par.StartsWith("/F:")) {
      par = par.Substring(3);
      writer = new StreamWriter(par, false, new UTF8Encoding());
    }
    if (par.StartsWith("/T:")) {
      par = par.Substring(3);
      lang = par;
    }
  }

  OleDbCommand myOleDbCommand =
    new OleDbCommand("SELECT * FROM Localization", myConnection);
  OleDbDataReader reader = myOleDbCommand.ExecuteReader();
  while (reader.Read()) {
    string val = ConvertIllegalChars(reader[lang].ToString()).Trim();
    if (val.Length > 0) {
      string str = reader["ResourceName"].ToString() + " = \"" + val + "\"";
      if (writer == null) {
        Console.WriteLine(str);
      } else {
        writer.WriteLine(str);
      }
    }
  }
  reader.Close();
  if (writer != null) {
```

```
    writer.Close();
  }
  myConnection.Close();
}
```

The `Assemble` utility accepts two parameters `/F` and `/T`.

The `/F` switch assigns the filename of the resource file and the `/T` switch refers to the translation language to extract. After assigning these we can extract the language string from the database, using an `OleDB` command. The `OleDB` command executes a SQL `select` statement against the database. In this case, we only need to fetch the data for read-only purposes, so we use the `OleDBDataReader`, a read-only and forward-only data reader, to retrieve the data.

For example, to retrieve the German language version from the database, issue the following command at the command prompt:

assemble /T:lang-de /F:StringResources.de.res

This command generates a `StringResources.de.res` file shown in the following snippet:

```
CompilerResultView.DescriptionText = "Beschreibung"
CompilerResultView.FileText = "Datei"
CompilerResultView.LineText = "Zeile"
Dialog.About.DialogName = "Über SharpDevelop"
Dialog.About.label1Text = "Version"
Dialog.About.label2Text = "Build"
Dialog.About.label3Text = "Autoren"
Dialog.Componnents.RichMenuItem.LoadFileDescription = "Lade Datei ${File}"
Dialog.Componnents.RichMenuItem.LoadProjectDescription = "Lade Projekt ${Project}"
Dialog.Componnents.RichMenuItem.NoRecentFilesString = "letzte Dateien"
Dialog.Componnents.RichMenuItem.NoRecentProjectsString = "letzte Projekte"
Dialog.DirtyFiles.DialogName = "Ungespeicherte Dateien speichern ?"
Dialog.DirtyFiles.DirtyFiles = "Ungespeicherte Dateien"
Dialog.DirtyFiles.DiscardAllButton = "Alle &Verwerfen"
Dialog.DirtyFiles.Files = "Dateien"
Dialog.DirtyFiles.SaveAllButton = "&Alle speichern"
```

Summary

This chapter taught us the dos and don'ts for making an application available to a global community. We learned how SharpDevelop handles the built-in internationalization support. Our discussion included pointers on resource management aspects, managing localized resources within an application, and accessing them programmatically.

Then we examined the issues involved in building an online/offline solution for internationalization, that supports Unicode and thus non-Latin characters anywhere and anytime.

In Chapter 8, we will discuss the document management features of SharpDevelop and their implementation, focussing on the internal representation of editable text.

CHAPTER 8

8

Document Management

In this chapter, we will look at the various issues concerned with managing documents in the SharpDevelop IDE. In this chapter's context, the term 'document management' means handling the internal representation of the text to be edited. The efficient management of text is important to ensure that the users can use the IDE conveniently. A bad text representation will slow down the editor's user interface and alienate the users.

In this chapter, we will discuss:

- ❑ Text representation
- ❑ Representing lines
- ❑ Caret and selection management
- ❑ Text model
- ❑ And finally, how to put it all together

During the design phase, we decided to decouple the document model from the actual editor control, as this would give us more flexibility in implementing the editor and adapting it to specific needs. Being able to add to the SharpDevelop AddIn tree to extend the editor, and even use the editor control in the standalone configuration, exemplifies the flexibility of SharpDevelop.

Text Representation

Any text that we work with has to be represented in some manner in the memory, before it is edited. There are only a few alternative representations used in editors, which are divided into two categories:

- **Basic sequence data structures**
  These are the simplest possible data structures for representing text.

- **Composite sequence data structures**
  These are made from compositely nested or, more commonly, linked basic data structures. The terminology used here is introduced in C.S. Crowley's paper on data structures for text representation (refer to http://www.cs.unm.edu/~crowley/papers/sds/sds.html) – who, however, thinks that the composite data structures should be termed recursive. This is, of course, the more flexible approach. Yet for the time being, we have decided to go with a type of the basic sequence data structure named the **gap buffer**.

Let's look at basic sequence data structures in detail.

Basic Sequence Data Structures

To justify our choice of the gap buffer structure for the editor, first we will discuss all basic data structures used in editors and then discuss their pros and cons.

As we discussed in Chapter 2, choosing the appropriate data structure for text representation in the editor was a major issue in the history of SharpDevelop. First, we will look at the basic data structures that we use now.

Arrays

The simplest data structure capable of representing an editable text is an array or a string, which looks at memory as a single contiguous block containing the text to edit.

Obviously, this approach is not good from a performance point of view, as when we insert text, we increase the size of the buffer. If we consider a text buffer for a typical source code file with, for example, 500 to 1,000 lines and a maximum line length of 80 characters in one huge string, inserting or deleting even a single character requires moving every character to the right of the insertion point by one. If this happens at a point close to the beginning of the string, we have to move almost the entire string. If we type in a completely new sequence at this insertion point, this has to be repeated for every character typed.

Replacement might be a different matter though, as the string does not need to move. However, this would require a clever bit of code that tries to figure out whether we are first deleting and then inserting, or first inserting and then deleting – both of which are equivalent to a replace operation. Also, replacing a highlighted character would be a simple replace operation without any shifting.

You can experiment with this approach yourself with the following implementation that has been included for debugging and demonstration purposes in
`src\SharpDevelop\ICSharpCode.TextEditor\Document\TextBufferStrategy\StringText BufferStrategy.cs`:

```csharp
using System;
using ICSharpCode.Core.Properties;
using ICSharpCode.SharpDevelop.Internal.Undo;

namespace ICSharpCode.TextEditor.Document {

  // Simple implementation of the ITextBuffer interface implemented using a
  // string.
  // Only for fallback purposes.

  // Set up the StringTextBuffer using a string and an offset into it to
  // mark the caret position; then define basic operations
  public class StringTextBufferStrategy : ITextBufferStrategy
  {
    string storedText = "";

    public int Length {
      get { return storedText.Length; }
    }

    public void Insert(int offset, string text)
    {
      if (text != null) {
        storedText = storedText.Insert(offset, text);
      }
    }

    public void Remove(int offset, int length)
    {
      storedText = storedText.Remove(offset, length);
    }

    public void Replace(int offset, int length, string text)
    {
      Remove(offset, length);
      Insert(offset, text);
    }

    public string GetText(int offset, int length)
    {
      if (length == 0) {
        return "";
      }
      return storedText.
             Substring(offset, Math.Min(length,storedText.Length - offset));
    }

    public char GetCharAt(int offset)
    {
      if (offset == Length) {
        return '\0';
      }
      return storedText[offset];
```

```
      }

   public void SetContent(string text)
   {
      storedText = text;
   }
  }
 }
```

The text in the buffer consists of a single string manipulated using the .NET string functions. Replacement is done by the `Insert` and `Remove` methods at the corresponding position, implemented as an independent method instead of just calling the two methods, as these two methods can use different buffer strategies (implementing replacement in different ways). The position at which the manipulation takes place is given using an offset from the string's start.

Although the code is simple, the performance penalty is hidden. One may say that the .NET Framework handles moving characters around and we are not directly concerned with it; however, this isn't exactly true. .NET does not move characters around, as string objects are fixed once they have been created. Each editing action requires a new string object containing the new string to be created. The performance penalty due to this will be extremely high, as object creation uses precious resources. If you dare, you can try this out for yourself.

Linked Lists

Another of the basic sequence data structures is a linked list. This approach assigns an individual block to each character in the edit buffer and then links these blocks. Insert and delete operations, of course, are easy to implement with this approach as we just need to adjust links, and in the case of insert, assign a value to the new block.

Replacing is simpler still, done by just assigning a new value to the block. If this approach makes handling an edit buffer so easy, then why did we decide against using it in SharpDevelop? The key here is memory requirements, as on one hand, we need a lot of information about the sequence of characters in the buffer, and on the other, the buffer memory will become increasingly fragmented. This will degrade performance, as iterating to a given point takes increasingly longer times and the 'subjective speed' a user experiences is what makes an editor pleasant to work with.

The Gap Buffer Approach

For SharpDevelop, we decided to settle on the gap-buffer approach, as it is an efficient tradeoff between an array and a linked list. A gap buffer is a data structure where any two stretches of contiguous text in an array are separated by an empty stretch of array invisible to the user. This representation is also known as the buffer-gap, split-block, or two-span approach.

Theory of the Gap Buffer

The following figure illustrates the layout of a gap buffer containing the Formatting text with the caret sitting between the second t and the i:

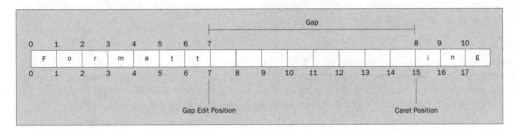

The numbers above the boxes are the user co-ordinates, as they represent the user's view of the edit buffer, and the ones below are the gap co-ordinates used internally in handling the buffer. Both co-ordinate systems refer to the locations between the characters in the buffer. The user and the caret see the user co-ordinates only, which are used in our implementation independent of the internal state of the gap.

Note that when an editing action occurs the gap is always to the left of the caret, but editing is done at the left end of the gap. Let's assume that we want to delete the t. The result is shown in the figure:

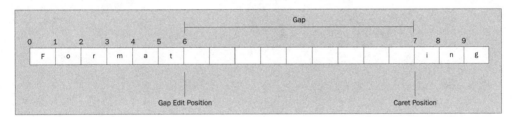

The gap has grown as a result of our deletion, with the total buffer size constant in memory. Both minimum and maximum sizes of the gap are usually given based on programmer's decisions. Only when the gap needs to be 'regrown' from minimum do we need to allocate additional memory and thus, increase the buffer size.

Next, we will try inserting characters, resulting in the string Formatstring being displayed:

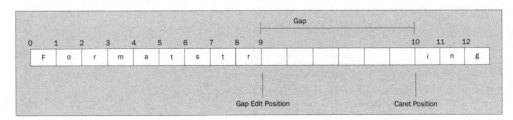

Now the gap has shrunk. A gap-buffer implementation always checks for the minimum and maximum sizes the gap can have and adjusts it accordingly if it violates the size constraint, while inserting more text than fits into the gap or deleting spans of text longer than the maximum gap size. The total buffer size will change in this case. As the minimum and maximum sizes of the gap are based on the programmer's decisions about the buffer's purpose and its expected size, fixing it is a matter of experience, so we will not give recommendations.

One of the advantages of the gap buffer representation is that the gap needs to be moved only when editing takes place in a position different from the current gap position. This means that caret movements from line to line or paging up and down can be performed without updating the internal representation of the edit buffer, since moving the buffer every time the caret position changes would be too expensive. This is why we use different co-ordinate systems internally and externally.

The Gap Buffer in Practice

The implementation of the gap buffer in SharpDevelop can be found in the `src\SharpDevelop\ICSharpCode.TextEditor\Document\TextBufferStrategy\GapTextBuf ferStrategy.cs` file:

```csharp
using System;
using System.Text;

namespace ICSharpCode.TextEditor.Document {

// Setting up the buffer and gap
  public class GapTextBufferStrategy : ITextBufferStrategy
  {
    char[] buffer = new char[0];

// Gap administration gets set up
    int gapBeginOffset = 0;
    int gapEndOffset   = 0;

    int minGapLength = 32;
    int maxGapLength = 256;

    public int Length {
      get { return buffer.Length - GapLength; }
    }

    int GapLength {
      get { return gapEndOffset - gapBeginOffset; }
    }

// Setting content for the buffer including handling of empty case
    public void SetContent(string text)
    {
      if (text == null) {
        text = String.Empty;
      }
      buffer = text.ToCharArray();
      gapBeginOffset = gapEndOffset = 0;
    }
```

```csharp
    public char GetCharAt(int offset)
    {
      return offset < gapBeginOffset ? buffer[offset] : buffer[offset +
        GapLength];
    }

    public string GetText(int offset, int length)
    {
      int end = offset + length;

      if (end < gapBeginOffset) {
        return new string(buffer, offset, length);
      }

      if (gapBeginOffset < offset) {
        return new string(buffer, offset + GapLength, length);
      }

      StringBuilder buf = new StringBuilder();
      buf.Append(buffer, offset,          gapBeginOffset - offset);
      buf.Append(buffer, gapEndOffset, end - gapBeginOffset);
      return buf.ToString();
    }

// Edit actions are done using calls of the Replace method defined below
    public void Insert(int offset, string text)
    {
      Replace(offset, 0, text);
    }

    public void Remove(int offset, int length)
    {
      Replace(offset, length, String.Empty);
    }

    public void Replace(int offset, int length, string text)
    {
      // The function body is discussed in detail later in this section
    }

    void PlaceGap(int offset, int length)
    {
      // The function body is discussed in detail later in this section
    }
  }
}
```

Initialization of the buffer is simple. We assign space for the text to be buffered plus the size of the gap. In this case, the size decisions are based on experience. The Insert and Remove routines are treated as special cases of replace operations – replacing 'nothing' when inserting and replacing the text with 'nothing' when deleting.

Things get interesting as soon as we get to the Replace part, which is not as simple as first deleting and then inserting, as in the StringTextBuffer code:

```
public void Replace(int offset, int length, string text)
    {
        if (text == null) {
            text = String.Empty;
        }

        PlaceGap(offset + length, Math.Max(0, text.Length - length));

        text.CopyTo(0, buffer, offset, Math.Min(text.Length, length));

        if (text.Length < length) {
            gapBeginOffset -= length - text.Length;
        } else if (text.Length > length) {
            int deltaLength = text.Length - length;
            gapBeginOffset += deltaLength;
            text.CopyTo(length, buffer, offset + length, text.Length - length);
        }
    }
```

After checking for an empty buffer, we place the gap where the edit action is to take place.
Then we work with the gap and text.copy, first copying the text into the gap, and then resizing the gap accordingly. We need to take into account the limitations on gap size to readjust it when necessary. This is done with the if statement at the end of the routine.

The movement of the buffer according to where it is supposed to go (before or after the current position), and whether the gap has to be resized, is the interesting part. All of this happens in the PlaceGap routine, which we called in the above code:

```
    void PlaceGap(int offset, int length)
    {

        int oldLength       = GapLength;

        int newLength       = maxGapLength + length;
        int newGapEndOffset = offset + newLength;
        char[] newBuffer    = new char[buffer.Length +
                                    newLength - oldLength];

        if (oldLength == 0) {
            Array.Copy(buffer, 0, newBuffer, 0, offset);
            Array.Copy(buffer, offset, newBuffer, newGapEndOffset,
                    newBuffer.Length - newGapEndOffset);
        } else if (offset < gapBeginOffset) {
            int delta = gapBeginOffset - offset;
            Array.Copy(buffer, 0, newBuffer, 0, offset);
            Array.Copy(buffer, offset, newBuffer, newGapEndOffset, delta);
            Array.Copy(buffer, gapEndOffset, newBuffer, newGapEndOffset + delta,
                    buffer.Length - gapEndOffset);
        } else {
```

```
            int delta = offset - gapBeginOffset;
            Array.Copy(buffer, 0, newBuffer, 0, gapBeginOffset);
            Array.Copy(buffer, gapEndOffset, newBuffer, gapBeginOffset, delta);
            Array.Copy(buffer, gapEndOffset + delta, newBuffer, newGapEndOffset,
                    newBuffer.Length - newGapEndOffset);
        }

        buffer          = newBuffer;
        gapBeginOffset  = offset;
        gapEndOffset    = newGapEndOffset;
    }
```

Dynamic resizing of arrays is handled by our code for the gap-buffer text representation. By using the `Array.Copy` method, performance is enhanced, when compared to moving buffer elements ourselves, as hand written movement of the buffer elements would incur a much higher number of memory operations at the lower level, with the corresponding overheads. This follows from a simple rule that every programmer should keep in mind – don't reinvent the wheel when it has been done and works well.

The interface for our text representation is defined in the `src\SharpDevelop\ICSharpCode.TextEditor\Document\TextBufferStrategy\ITextBufferStrategy.cs` file. Here is a short excerpt to give you an idea of this:

```
using ICSharpCode.Core.Properties;
using ICSharpCode.SharpDevelop.Internal.Undo;

namespace ICSharpCode.TextEditor.Document {

  // Interface to describe a sequence of characters that can be edited.
  public interface ITextBufferStrategy
  {
    // Returns the current length of the editable character sequence.
    int Length {
      get;
    }
    // Inserts a string of characters into the sequence.
    void Insert(int offset, string text);
  }
}
```

It is a good idea to name the pattern used in an interface so that the developers using this interface know what to expect. The implementation of the methods in the text buffer follow the Strategy pattern discussed in detail in Chapter 2.

The Future – The Piece Table

For the time being, this representation works well; however, it might become necessary to switch to a different text representation in the future. After discussing the various basic data sequences, we have the composite sequence data structures left to evaluate.

Composite Sequence Data Structures

There are three types of composite sequence data structures:

- ❑ The line span data structure
- ❑ Fixed size buffers
- ❑ The piece table

Now let's look at each of them.

Line Span Method

The line span data structure consists of a buffer holding a description of the blocks containing individual lines, which makes displaying the buffer content quite easy. However, editing operations can be cumbersome to handle, as operations concerning lines and characters in lines have to be handled separately. Avoiding problems with performance and memory with this approach requires extra implementation effort.

Fixed Size Buffers

The use of fixed size buffers avoids some of these problems, but it is inefficient in terms of memory usage, as most of the individual buffers (usually corresponding to lines of fixed length) are rarely fully used. Fortunately, fixed size buffers are more or less an obsolete approach, as dynamic memory management is no longer a problem in modern programming languages.

The Piece Table

Leaving aside possible new composite data representation structures, the most attractive of the composite approaches seems to be the piece table, which can be seen as a combination of the two approaches given. It has neither fixed size buffers nor buffers for individual lines. Instead, the buffer is split into pieces as needed, with a table giving the relationships between the pieces of the buffer – hence the name 'piece table'.

In this approach, we start with a single contiguous block containing the file read from the disk. While editing, the file is broken up into pieces, with the edited text set up in a new append-only block. Any appending is performed at its end, outside the read-only block, ensuring that the original text can always stay in read-only blocks. The offset and length information regarding the individual blocks is kept in the piece table. The individual blocks stay in place as long as the file is open, as any edit action only appends to the append-only block, turning the formerly active segment into a read-only one.

The main advantages a piece table provides are that other components of the software can easily access the buffers, as they always stay in place, and that unlimited undo and redo is easy to implement as all the necessary information resides in the translation table. Access to the buffer is done by looking up the piece table.

Implementing unlimited undo and redo operations directly in the text buffer is not an issue for the time being. We also implemented our own undo functionality, as undoing operations also occur outside the text editor.

Representing Lines

Text representation by a gap buffer implies that all lines are represented by the contents of two contiguous blocks of data, which we then have to divide into chunks representing lines. This task is handled by the Line Manager. Up to SharpDevelop release 0.88b, a Line Tracker Strategy handled this task. This pattern-based approach was abandoned because it proved to be too inflexible for the demands of the SharpDevelop editor. The Strategy pattern is discussed in Chapter 2.

Dividing the contents of the edit buffer into lines serves three purposes – housekeeping of lines, syntax highlighting, and folding administration (keeping a record of which lines are visible and which ones have been 'folded away' from sight). Syntax highlighting has been presented in Chapter 1 and will be discussed in Chapter 9. We will take a look at folding in Chapter 10 and Chapter 11. Beyond these tasks, events are raised when the number of lines changes, as it is important for the proper functioning of some other SharpDevelop features, such as bookmarking. This plethora of functions served by the Line Manager obviously goes far beyond the goals of a single Strategy pattern, as each function of the Line Manager might be represented by a strategy.

The task of breaking the edit buffer into discrete lines and keeping track of them is accomplished by the use of collections. The Line Manager is a complex piece of software, as we will see when we will look at the interfaces defined in the src\SharpDevelop\ICSharpCode.TextEditor\Document\LineManager\ILineManager.cs file:

```
namespace ICSharpCode.TextEditor.Document {

  // The line tracker keeps track of all lines in a document.
  public interface ILineManager
  {
    // Get a collection of all line segments
    LineSegmentCollection LineSegmentCollection {
      get;
    }

    // get LineSegmentCollection.Count
    int TotalNumberOfLines {
      get;
    }

    IHighlightingStrategy HighlightingStrategy {
      get;
      set;
    }

    int GetLineNumberForOffset(int offset);

    LineSegment GetLineSegmentForOffset(int offset);
    LineSegment GetLineSegment(int lineNumber);

    void Insert(int offset, string text);
    void Remove(int offset, int length);
    void Replace(int offset, int length, string text);
```

```
      void SetContent(string text);

      int GetLogicalLine(int lineNumber);
      int GetVisibleLine(int lineNumber);

      int GetNextVisibleLineAbove(int lineNumber, int lineCount);
      int GetNextVisibleLineBelow(int lineNumber, int lineCount);

      event LineManagerEventHandler LineCountChanged;
   }
}
```

We can see that there are interfaces for all the functionalities, like administration tasks, handling line-related events, and referring to the lines in the edit buffer. We can refer to the text either by offset or by line number. Furthermore, the terms logical line and visible line need to be explained. A logical line exists in the edit buffer but can be invisible. Visible lines are a subset of logical lines, as we need to distinguish between the total number of lines and the number of lines visible in a buffer for handling bookmarks and other features.

We will see in Chapter 9, that there is a Strategy pattern – HighlightingStrategy. As far as syntax highlighting goes, performing the actual highlighting is not the task of the Line Manager. It just informs the highlighting routines about which lines need to be updated.

Also, we find that there are functions for converting offset co-ordinates to lines or line segments. Offset co-ordinates are more natural for buffer-related operations, whereas the line co-ordinate system is better suited for preparing lines for display. The actual work of converting the edit buffer into lines is done in the src\SharpDevelop\ICSharpCode.TextEditor\Document\LineManager\LineSegment.cs file.

This class has a number of functions that go beyond the conversion from buffer to line, such as syntax highlighting:

```
using System;
using System.Collections;
using System.Text;

namespace ICSharpCode.TextEditor.Document {

  public class LineSegment : ISegment
  {
    int offset;
    int length;
    int delimiterLength;
    int foldLevel = 0;

    bool isVisible = true;

    ArrayList     words        = null;
    Stack highlightSpanStack = null;

    public bool IsVisible {
      get {return isVisible; }
```

```
      set {isVisible = value; }
    }

    public int Offset {
      get { return offset; }
      set { offset = value; }
    }

    public int Length {
      get  { return length - delimiterLength; }
    }

    public int TotalLength {
      get { return length; }
      set { length = value; }
    }

    public int DelimiterLength {
      get { return delimiterLength;}
      set { delimiterLength = value;}
    }

    public int FoldLevel {
      get { return foldLevel; }
      set { foldLevel = value;}
    }

    // highlighting information
    public ArrayList Words {
      get { return words;}
      set {words = value;}
    }

    public HighlightColor GetColorForPosition(int x)
    {
      int xPos = 0;
      foreach (TextWord word in Words) {
        if (x < xPos + word.Length) {
          return word.SyntaxColor;
        }
        xPos += word.Length;
      }
      return null;
    }

    public Stack HighlightSpanStack {
      get {
        return highlightSpanStack;
      }
      set {
        highlightSpanStack = value;
      }
    }
```

```
public LineSegment(int offset, int end, int delimiterLength)
{
   this.offset          = offset;
   this.length          = end - offset + 1;
   this.delimiterLength = delimiterLength;
}

public LineSegment(int offset, int length)
{
   this.offset          = offset;
   this.length          = length;
   this.delimiterLength = 0;
}

public override string ToString()
{
   return "[LineSegment: Offset = "+ offset +", Length = " + length + ",
           DelimiterLength = " + delimiterLength + ",
           FoldLevel = " + FoldLevel + "]";
}
```

This is mostly self-explanatory. The use of three variables to handle line length calls for some attention – Length, DelimiterLength, and TotalLength. Most of the code that uses the functionality supplied by the Line Manager references Length, which is the length of the line excluding the delimiting characters. However, for the work done inside the Line Manager, the total length of the lines must be known, as delimiters are also counted as characters in the offset view of the buffer. Now you may think a delimiter is a simple newline character, this may not necessarily be true.

In SharpDevelop, we are free to choose between Unix-style, DOS-style, and Macintosh-style line-end delimiters, which means that cr, lf, or both may be used, and each corresponds to one character in the buffer. Therefore, we need to take this variation of delimiter length into account, especially in the light of the fact that the user can choose which delimiters to use, and that SharpDevelop should handle all of these delimiter types, even when the user opens files imported from operating systems using delimiters that are not DOS-style. This happens while developing web-based applications (ASP.NET web services) and is the first small step in preparing SharpDevelop to port to other .NET-compatible platforms.

Another interesting element is FoldLevel, as SharpDevelop allows nested folding.

The one bit of code that you will have noticed as being a bit unusual is:

```
public override string ToString()
   {
      return "[LineSegment: Offset = "+ offset +", Length = " + length + ",
              DelimiterLength = " + delimiterLength + ",
              FoldLevel = " + FoldLevel + "]";
   }
```

This overload of the ToString method is used for writing the output to the console window for easy debugging, as SharpDevelop does not include a debugger, yet. This is not exactly elegant, but gets the job done. You will find such code in many places in SharpDevelop. Now you know what it is for.

For syntax highlighting, not only should the lines be provided but they must also be broken into segments corresponding to individual syntactical elements, for correct highlighting. We will discuss syntax highlighting in Chapter 9.

After the actual work of breaking the buffer into lines and line segments is done by `LineSegment.cs`, the `LineSegmentCollection.cs` file generates a collection of files. It can be found in the `src\SharpDevelop\ICSharpCode.TextEditor\Document\LineManager` directory.

This `LineSegmentCollection.cs` file is generated automatically by using the SharpDevelop's Typed C# Collection Wizard found under File | New | File | C#, as one of the available file types.

The resulting code looks like this excerpt:

```
using System;
using System.Collections;

namespace ICSharpCode.TextEditor.Document {

    // A collection that stores.Line objects.
    [Serializable()]
    public class LineSegmentCollection : CollectionBase {

        // Initializes a new instance of LineCollection
        public LineSegmentCollection() {
        }
        // Initializes a new instance of LineCollection based on another

        public LineSegmentCollection(LineSegmentCollection value) {
            this.AddRange(value);
        }

        // Initializes a new instance of LineCollection containing any array
        // of Line objects.
        public LineSegmentCollection(LineSegment[] value) {
            this.AddRange(value);
        }
        // Represents the entry at the specified index of the Line
        public LineSegment this[int index] {
            get {
                return ((LineSegment)(List[index]));
            }
            set {
                List[index] = value;
            }
        }
    }
```

We decided to use collections here and in the management of selections for two reasons – first, we can avoid casts, thus acquiring performance hits and making the code easier to read, secondly, collections are also checked at compile time to avoid errors due to adding inappropriate data. This collection is used by the `DefaultLineManager` and few other pieces of code (mostly in highlighting functions).

There is a minor quirk in this particular collection. We have an entry for every line, ending in a line delimiter, including the last line of the edit buffer. The quirk is that after a line end, a newline must follow, giving us an extra empty entry. If we forget to take this into consideration, we may have a problem in our new code. Therefore, it is strongly advised that accessing this collection should always go through the routines provided by the DefaultLineManager. These routines know about the empty entry and take care of it.

The file containing the code for the DefaultLineManager is located in src\SharpDevelop\ICSharpCode.TextEditor\Document\LineManager\ DefaultLineManager.cs. Here's a snippet from this file:

```
public int GetLineNumberForOffset(int offset)
{
  if (offset < 0 || offset > textLength) {
    throw new ArgumentOutOfRangeException("offset", offset,
                                 "should be between 0 and " +
                                 textLength);
  }
  if (offset == textLength) {
    if (lineCollection.Count == 0) {
      return 0;
    }
    // We need to substract 1 from the lineCollection.Count value to get
    // rid of the empty 'phantom'line. Especially when we are on the
    // last line.

    LineSegment lastLine = lineCollection[lineCollection.Count - 1];
    return lastLine.DelimiterLength > 0 ?
          lineCollection.Count : lineCollection.Count - 1;
  }

  return FindLineNumber(offset);
}
// This returns segments of lines for highlighting etc.

public LineSegment GetLineSegmentForOffset(int offset)
{
  if (offset < 0 || offset > textLength) {
    throw new ArgumentOutOfRangeException("offset", offset,
                                 "should be between 0 and " +
                                 textLength);
  }
  if (offset == textLength) {
    if (lineCollection.Count == 0) {
      return new LineSegment(0, 0);
    }
    LineSegment lastLine = lineCollection[lineCollection.Count - 1];
    return lastLine.DelimiterLength > 0 ?
          new LineSegment(textLength, 0): lastLine;
  }
  return GetLineSegment(FindLineNumber(offset));
}
```

The correct number of lines used is obtained by testing for the existence of that mysterious empty last line, as seen in the two methods listed.

We can also see that exception handling is important for staying within the buffer limits. In this listing, we just see the exception throwing code and the catching is handled the 'SharpDevelop way', which is, passing the exception up to the highest possible level before handling it. This gives a detailed trace of the dependencies in the code, so that bug fixes are made easier. Another important aspect of managing the lines in the buffer is handling events. Events are necessary for correctly handling line-related functionality outside the text management subsystem, for example, the bookmarks for a file must be adjusted automatically when the number of lines changes, otherwise they will point to the wrong place.

This is handled by the code in src\SharpDevelop\ICSharpCode.TextEditor\Document\LineManager\ LineManagerEventArgs.cs:

```csharp
using System;

namespace ICSharpCode.TextEditor.Document {

  public delegate void LineManagerEventHandler(object sender,
                                               LineManagerEventArgs e);
  public class LineManagerEventArgs : EventArgs
  {
    IDocumentAggregator document;
    int       start;
    int       moved;

    // Always a valid Document which is related to the Event.
    public IDocumentAggregator Document {
      get { return document; }
    }

    // -1 if no offset was specified for this event
    public int LineStart {
      get { return start; }
    }

    // -1 if no length was specified for this event
    public int LinesMoved {
      get { return moved; }
    }

    public LineManagerEventArgs(IDocumentAggregator document,
                                int lineStart, int linesMoved)
    {
      this.document = document;
      this.start    = lineStart;
      this.moved    = linesMoved;
    }
  }
}
```

The events occur when we either insert a newline (`lineStart` property), or move one or more lines (`linesMoved` property). This code illustrates the standard mechanism for event handling in C#.

Caret and Selection Management

We considered the administration of the buffer from the program's point of view. Now we will look at how the user's actions, like text and caret selections, are handled.

The caret is displayed as the cursor on screen. Selections are blocks of text marked by the user for some action to be performed on them. These interactions with the edit buffer are handled in the same way as the internal housekeeping.

The caret is handled through the interfaces defined in the `src\SharpDevelop\ICSharpCode.TextEditor\Document\Caret\ICaret.cs` file. They are listed below:

```csharp
using System;
using System.Drawing;
using System.Diagnostics;
using ICSharpCode.TextEditor.Document;
using System.Text;

namespace ICSharpCode.TextEditor.Document {

    // In this enumeration all caret modes are listed.
    public enum CaretMode {
        InsertMode,
        OverwriteMode
    }

    // The basic interface for the caret.
    public interface ICaret
    {
        // The current offset where the caret points to.
        int Offset {
            get;
            set;
        }

        // The 'preferred' column in which the caret moves, when it is moved
        // up/down.
        int DesiredColumn {
            get;
            set;
        }

        // The current caret mode.
        CaretMode CaretMode {
            get;
            set;
        }
```

```
      // Sets the caret visibility.
      bool Visible {
        get;
        set;
      }

      // Is called each time the caret is moved.
      event CaretEventHandler OffsetChanged;

      // Is called each time the CaretMode has changed.
      event CaretEventHandler CaretModeChanged;
    }
  }
```

The caret in SharpDevelop has two modes – insert and overwrite, and a Boolean value for visibility, which is responsible for the blinking of the caret. Events are raised when the caret moves to a new position.

The structure of the code for handling caret issues is quite similar to the code we looked at when we discussed line management. (Remember the offsets? They also point to a co-ordinate in the buffer, just as a caret does.) We will not go into details here to avoid tiresome repetitions.

The two files we need to handle the caret are
src\SharpDevelop\ICSharpCode.TextEditor\Document\Caret\DefaultCaret.cs and
src\SharpDevelop\ICSharpCode.TextEditor\Document\Caret\CaretEventArgs.cs.

Note that we have also overloaded the default ToString method for the same reason as in the Line Manager, which is debugging.

The handling of selections is done using the interface defined in the
src\SharpDevelop\ICSharpCode.TextEditor\Document\Selection\ISelection.cs file.
The following definitions are contained in this file:

```
using ICSharpCode.Core.Properties;
using ICSharpCode.SharpDevelop.Internal.Undo;

namespace ICSharpCode.TextEditor.Document {

  // An interface representing a portion of the current selection.
  public interface ISelection
  {
    // Returns the start offset of this selection.
    int Offset {
      get;
      set;
    }

    // Returns the length of this selection.
    int Length {
      get;
      set;
    }
```

```
   // Returns the starting line number of this selection.
   int StartLine {
     get;
   }

   // Returns the ending line number of this selection.
   int EndLine {
     get;
   }

   // Returns true, if the selection is rectangular.
   bool IsRectangularSelection {
     get;
   }

   // Returns the text which is selected by this selection.
   string SelectedText {
     get;
   }
  }
 }
```

The functionality provided is understandable, only the Boolean variable IsRectangularSelection, which is meant for future versions of SharpDevelop, may need some explanation. We have planned to include a feature allowing us to select rectangular screen sections regardless of line lengths, as in terminal emulator programs, which will be useful for quite a few purposes, for example, copying two columns of a table to some other location. However, currently this property isn't used.

The selection(s) is/are handled by a collection, using the code generated by the **Typed C# Collection Wizard**. As the code is very similar to that for the LineSegmentCollection that we saw earlier, we shall not list it again.

Note that we have included the possibility of selections on purpose, as the future of SharpDevelop might also support a multi-selection feature.

The code for the collection is contained in the src\SharpDevelop\ICSharpCode.TextEditor\Document\Selection\SelectionCollection .cs file.

The implementation of selection handling is to be found in the src\SharpDevelop\ICSharpCode.TextEditor\Document\Selection\DefaultSelection.cs file:

```
using System;

namespace ICSharpCode.TextEditor.Document {

   // Default implementation of ICSharpCode.TextEditor.Document.ISelection
   // interface.
   public class DefaultSelection : ISelection, ISegment
   {
     int offset   = -1;
```

```
    int length    = -1;
    IDocumentAggregator document = null;
    bool      isRectangularSelection = false;

// simple properties for Offset and Length omitted for brevity

    public int StartLine {
      get { return document.GetLineNumberForOffset(offset); }
    }

    public int EndLine {
      get { return document.GetLineNumberForOffset(offset + Length); }
    }

    public bool IsEmpty {
      get { return offset < 0 || length <= 0; }
    }

    // TODO Implement rectangular selections
    public bool IsRectangularSelection {
      get { return isRectangularSelection; }
      set { isRectangularSelection = value; }
    }

    public string SelectedText {
      get {
        if (document != null) {
          return document.GetText(offset, length);
        }
        return null;
      }
    }

    public DefaultSelection(IDocumentAggregator document,
                            int offset, int length)
    {
      this.document = document;
      this.offset   = offset;
      this.length   = length;
    }

    public override string ToString()
    {
      return "[Selection : Offset = " + Offset + ", Length = " +
             Length + "]";
    }
  }
}
```

We can see that, in this listing, the rectangular selections have been mentioned already, but commented out, for the future implementation of this feature. Also, note that, we have again overloaded the `ToString` method for debugging purposes. Selections are working on the line segment collection using the `LineSegment` interface that we discussed earlier in the *Representing Lines* section.

By now, we have a lot of functionality assembled for handling the document internally. Before we can assemble this, we need a way to hand over the buffer contents to the outside world, for use by display routines. As we will see, we need to abstract the representation of the data for this purpose. This will also facilitate an eventual transition to a piece table representation.

The Text Model

Before we explain the text model, we need to know a bit about co-ordinate systems. They refer either to positions of characters in a buffer or to the positions between characters in a buffer. Gap co-ordinates and user co-ordinates are based on the indices of the borders between characters and not on the indices of the characters themselves, since a line or selection begins and ends either before or after a character, never in it. Yet both are linear offset co-ordinates and are not fit for immediate display in the X-Y co-ordinate system of a screen. By linear offset, we refer to a co-ordinate system that uses only one co-ordinate. Simply put, we number the characters or the borders between characters, starting with zero at the start ('leftmost') position and count up. In X-Y systems, we address a character by the row and the column at which it is displayed.

The text model, which we will now discuss, is a mapping of the linear offset co-ordinates onto the X-Y co-ordinates.

The interface is defined in the src\SharpDevelop\ICSharpCode.TextEditor\Document\TextModel\ITextModel.cs file:

```
using System.Drawing;

using ICSharpCode.Core.Properties;
using ICSharpCode.SharpDevelop.Internal.Undo;

namespace ICSharpCode.TextEditor.Document {

  public interface ITextModel
  {
    int GetViewXPos(LineSegment line, int logicalXPos);
    int GetLogicalXPos(LineSegment line, int viewXPos);

    Point OffsetToView(int offset);
    int   ViewToOffset(Point p);
  }
}
```

Note that we deal only with X co-ordinates and since each line is one character high, we can use the line numbers as Y co-ordinates.

In this interface, we also encounter definitions for dealing with logical and view positions, when handling character-based screen co-ordinates (X-Y co-ordinates). For buffer co-ordinates, we provide offset handling.

The implementation of the text model, however, is more interesting than we would expect from the interface. The implementation is in the `src\SharpDevelop\ICSharpCode.TextEditor\Document\TextModel\DefaultTextModel.cs` file:

```csharp
using ICSharpCode.Core.Properties;
using ICSharpCode.SharpDevelop.Internal.Undo;

namespace ICSharpCode.TextEditor.Document {

  public class DefaultTextModel : ITextModel
  {
    static Encoding encoding = null;

    static DefaultTextModel()
    {
      try {
        encoding = Encoding.GetEncoding(Thread.CurrentThread.CurrentCulture.
                                   TextInfo.ANSICodePage);
      } catch (Exception) {
      }
    }

    IDocumentAggregator document;

    public DefaultTextModel(IDocumentAggregator document)
    {
      this.document = document;
    }

    public int GetLogicalXPos(LineSegment line, int viewXPos)
    {
      string text = "";
      if (line.Length > 0) {
        text = document.GetText(line.Offset, line.Length);
      }

      int max        = viewXPos;
      int xpos       = 0;
      int logicalPos = 0;

      while (logicalPos < text.Length) {
        if (xpos >= viewXPos) {
          break;
        }

        if (text[logicalPos] == '\t') {
          xpos += document.Properties.GetProperty("TabIndent", 4);
          xpos = (xpos / document.Properties.GetProperty("TabIndent", 4)) *
                 document.Properties.GetProperty("TabIndent", 4);
        } else {
          if (encoding != null) {
            xpos += encoding.GetByteCount(text[logicalPos].ToString());
          } else {
```

```
            ++xpos;
        }
    }
    ++logicalPos;
}
return logicalPos;
}
```

For successfully converting the document into a character-based co-ordinate system, we need to know about the widths of characters on screen. The most common example of a single character spanning several character widths on screen is the tabulator. This type of 'wide' characters is common in Asian languages.

The following code snippet, taken out of the above listing, shows us how this problem is solved:

```
if (encoding != null) {
        xpos += encoding.GetByteCount(text[logicalPos].ToString());
} else {
        ++xpos;
    }
```

Tabs are handled in a similar manner, but need special treatment as they may have different widths depending on the user's preference. Refer to the coding style guide (see Chapter 2) for our stance on tabs as an exclusive means of indenting. Tab width is a property we need to take into account:

```
if (text[logicalPos] == '\t') {
        xpos += document.Properties.GetProperty("TabIndent", 4);
        xpos = (xpos / document.Properties.GetProperty("TabIndent", 4)) *
            document.Properties.GetProperty("TabIndent", 4);
    }
```

Now, let's finally assemble all the pieces together.

Putting It All Together

Now we are finally done with all the pieces needed to put together a practical document management subsystem. They come together in the DocumentAggregator, which serves as a container for the functionality of the document management subsystem and provides this functionality to external code. It is made up along the usual lines with an interface definition file, a default implementation file, event code, and a factory.

The interface is defined in
src\SharpDevelop\ICSharpCode.TextEditor\Document\IDocumentAggregator.cs.

For easier understanding, we will split the file up:

```
using ICSharpCode.Core.Properties;
using ICSharpCode.SharpDevelop.Internal.Undo;

namespace ICSharpCode.TextEditor.Document {

  // This interface represents a container which holds a text sequence and
  // all necessary information about it. It is used as the base for a text
  // editor.
  public interface IDocumentAggregator
  {
    IProperties Properties {
      get;
      set;
    }

    UndoStack UndoStack {
      get;
    }

    bool ReadOnly {
      get;
      set;
    }

    bool UpdateDocumentRequested {
      get;
      set;
    }

    bool UpdateCaretLineRequested {
      get;
      set;
    }
```

The other properties defined in this file should look familiar by now. Skipping over a few more property definitions, we come to:

```
    // Caret Stuff
    void SetDesiredColumn();
    void SetCaretToDesiredColumn(LineSegment line);

    //LineManager stuff
    int TotalNumberOfLines {
      get;
    }

    int GetLineNumberForOffset(int offset);
    LineSegment GetLineSegmentForOffset(int offset);
    LineSegment GetLineSegment(int lineNumber);

    // functions that are used for folding
```

```
    // Get the logical line for a given visible line and visible line for a
    // given logical line.
    // example : lineNumber == 100 foldings are in the linetracker
    // between 0..1 (2 folded, invisible lines) this method returns 102
    // the 'logical' line number and 98 the 'visible' line number

    int GetLogicalLine(int lineNumber);
    int GetVisibleLine(int lineNumber);

    int GetNextVisibleLineAbove(int lineNumber, int lineCount);
    int GetNextVisibleLineBelow(int lineNumber, int lineCount);

    // TextStore Interface
    string TextContent {
      get;
      set;
    }

    int TextLength {
      get;
    }

    void Insert(int offset, string text);
    void Remove(int offset, int length);
    void Replace(int offset, int length, string text);
    char GetCharAt(int offset);
    string GetText(int offset, int length);

    // TextModel interface
    Point OffsetToView(int offset);
    int ViewToOffset(Point p);
    int GetViewXPos(LineSegment line, int logicalXPos);
    int GetLogicalXPos(LineSegment line, int viewXPos);

    event DocumentAggregatorEventHandler DocumentAboutToBeChanged;
    event DocumentAggregatorEventHandler DocumentChanged;
  }
}
```

Most of this code is simple, as we just interface with all the routines providing information about our document by using the DocumentAggregatorFactory, which is an implementation of the factory pattern discussed in Chapter 2 in the src\SharpDevelop\ICSharpCode.TextEditor\Document\DocumentAggregatorFactory.cs file. In this file, we find an interesting bit of code, which provides for building a standalone editor outside SharpDevelop:

```
using ICSharpCode.Core.Properties;
using ICSharpCode.Core.Services;
using ICSharpCode.SharpDevelop.Internal.Undo;

namespace ICSharpCode.TextEditor.Document {
```

```
   // This interface represents a container which holds a text sequence and
   // all necessary information about it.
   public class DocumentAggregatorFactory
   {
     public IDocumentAggregator CreateDocument()
     {
       DefaultDocumentAggregator doc = new DefaultDocumentAggregator();
#if !BuildAsStandalone
       PropertyService propertyService =
         (PropertyService)ServiceManager.Services.GetService
         (typeof(PropertyService));
       if (propertyService == null) {
         doc.Properties           = new DefaultProperties();
       } else {
         doc.Properties        =
           ((IProperties)propertyService.
           GetProperty("ICSharpCode.TextEditor.Document.Document.
                       DefaultDocumentAggregatorProperties",
                   new DefaultProperties()));
       }
#else
       doc.Properties           = new DefaultProperties();
#endif
       doc.UndoStack            = new UndoStack();
//       doc.TextBufferStrategy    = new StringTextBufferStrategy();
       doc.TextBufferStrategy    = new GapTextBufferStrategy();
       doc.Caret                = new DefaultCaret(doc);
       doc.FormattingStrategy    = new DefaultFormattingStrategy();
       doc.FoldingStrategy       = new IndentFoldingStrategy();
       doc.FormattingStrategy.Document = doc;

       doc.LineManager = new DefaultLineManager(doc, null);
       doc.BookmarkManager       = new BookmarkManager(doc.LineManager);
       doc.TextModel             = new DefaultTextModel(doc);
       return doc;
     }
```

The interesting part is contained in the #if – #else – #endif block. The properties have to be assigned values, which is no problem inside SharpDevelop, as internal defaults are provided for the case when no values are assigned. If no property value is returned by the SharpDevelop options, this default value comes into play. When we use the standalone version, this infrastructure does not exist, as it is part of SharpDevelop, which is why we have to use the #ifdef construct.

If you want to use the StringTextBufferStrategy for experimenting with the performance of this buffer model relative to the gap buffer model, you need only uncomment the line above GapTextBufferStrategy and comment out the GapTextBufferStrategy line instead.

Creating the DocumentAggregator for a file is easy:

```
   public IDocumentAggregator CreateFromFile(string fileName)
   {
     IDocumentAggregator document = CreateDocument();
     StreamReader stream = File.OpenText(fileName);
```

```
        document.TextContent = stream.ReadToEnd();
        stream.Close();
        return document;
    }
  }
}
```

That is all there is to it. Now the document is in an internal representation, fit for editing.

If you are interested in reading further about the issues involved in writing editors, we recommend that you visit http://www.finseth.com/~fin/craft/. This is the online version of the The Craft of Text Editing book, *which is currently out of print.*

Summary

In this chapter, we looked at all the components necessary for the internal representation and efficient handling of a document.

Presently, SharpDevelop uses the gap-buffer approach like most other modern editors, as it can be easily implemented, while a piece table might be an option for future versions of SharpDevelop.

We looked at how to break up a text buffer into lines and segments for purposes such as syntax highlighting and line folding, and examined the distinction between logical and visible lines. We also examined the pitfalls inherent in the possible variation of delimiter length and found that typed collections are a good way to handle line segments. Next, we looked at the handling of the caret and selections, which we found similar to handling line segments

Then we concerned ourselves with the transition from the internal model to a model suitable for handling an external system responsible for rendering the buffer contents on screen. We found that we have to adjust co-ordinates and have to take into account the varying width of certain characters when displayed on screen.

Lastly, we looked at how we can put these components together so that the actual editor can easily access the data buffer. For this purpose, we introduced the `DocumentAggregator`, which acts as a container for our components and can be used for building editors outside the SharpDevelop environment.

Now that we know how to manage text in an editor, we can examine syntax highlighting.

CHAPTER 9

9

Syntax Highlighting

When asked what features besides Code Completion and Solution Management we expect from an Integrated Development Environment (IDE), we will probably ask for syntax highlighting.

Sophisticated code listings can have hundreds, or even thousands of lines of code. Depending on the developer, source code varies in how well it is structured. Generally, source code displayed as simple black letters on white background, is more difficult to understand than code that is color-coded according to the function of each part.

This chapter provides guidelines for writing or extending existing syntax definition files for SharpDevelop and integrating them into the IDE. It has two major parts:

❑ **Syntax Highlighting Definitions**
In this section, we will examine the structure of SharpDevelop's syntax definition files and the underpinnings needed to create or extend a syntax definition file. We will also understand how to create definition files for our purposes, using the built-in definition file for the C# language.

❑ **Applying Syntax Highlighting**
Here, we will use the definition we create (in the *Syntax Highlighting Definitions* section), add it to SharpDevelop's repository and look into the highlighting process, and see how SharpDevelop validates the file and makes this feature available using the Highlighting Strategy.

Syntax Highlighting Definitions

Before we probe into source code, let us discuss the idea behind SharpDevelop's syntax highlighting functionality and why XML is used here. As we write our code, syntax highlighting displays recognized keywords in different colors, based on comparison of the user's code to 'predefined keywords'. These predefined keywords usually reside in a dictionary, or more precisely, in a resource file. We used the term 'dictionary' here, because the keywords should be hierarchically structured to accelerate the matching process, and hence we need a data format like XML, that offers such possibilities. Additionally, it is easy to validate and parse XML nodes, as the .NET Framework supports XML validation (XMLValidationReader class in the System.XML namespace).

Hence, SharpDevelop's syntax definition files are XML formatted, and have the .xshd (**XML s**yntax **h**ighlighting **d**efinition) extension. In addition, they are human-readable and can be created or extended easily using any editor. To handle validation, we may either use an XML validating editor for the creation of the definition file or decide to let SharpDevelop handle the process. The latter approach should be the last resort, as it is inconvenient to program.

Without further ado, we start with the structure of the .xshd files.

Increasing Ease of Use with XML

We can create our own syntax definition for any language. A simple .xshd file is shown in the listing (attribute values are just placeholders in this example):

```
<?XML version="1.0" ?>
<!--  barebone structure of a syntaxdefinition file-->
<SyntaxDefinition name="Name" extensions="Extension">
  <Environment>
    <!--  Refer to the next code listing for the body-->
  </Environment>
  <Digits name="Name" bold="true|false" italic=" true|false"
    color="Color" />
  <RuleSets>
    <!--  Body explained later in detail-->
  </RuleSets>
</SyntaxDefinition>
```

Do not worry about all these different node attributes, as they are explained in the next few lines.

Assume that, we use the C# language as an example. The root element of an .xshd file is <SyntaxDefinition> with two attributes – name and extensions. The name attribute represents the label of the entry, in the context menu. SharpDevelop allows users to switch syntax definitions (right-click in the code window and select **File mode**):

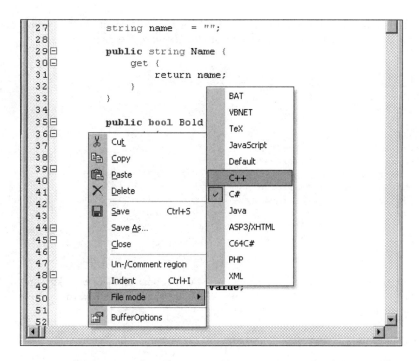

The `extensions` attribute assigns the appropriate file extensions to the definition file. Files with this attribute specified are automatically displayed using the appropriate definition file.

The next child element, called <Environment>, sets the appearance of the editor view (where we write the source code), with respect to colors of the line numbers, selections, bookmarks, and so on. Before looking at the elements contained in this node, let us see what happens if we choose the `C64C#` file mode, for example:

As mentioned before, we use the nodes of the `<Environment>` element to set the appearance of the editor view to our needs. This snippet is taken from the standard C# definition:

```
<Environment>
  <Default color = "Black" bgcolor="White"/>
  <VRuler color = "Blue"/>
  <Selection bgcolor = "LightBlue"/>
  <Cursor color = "DarkBlue"/>
  <LineNumbers color = "Black" bgcolor = "WhiteSmoke"/>
  <InvalidLines color = "Red"/>
  <EOLMarkers color = "DarkCyan"/>
  <SpaceMarkers color = "DarkCyan"/>
  <TabMarkers color = "DarkCyan"/>
  <CaretMarker color = "Yellow"/>
  <BookMarks color = "Black"  bgcolor = "#FF408080"/>
  <FoldLine color = "#808080" bgcolor="Black"/>
  <FoldMarker color = "#808080" bgcolor="White"/>
</Environment>
```

The setting of `<Default>` node causes the editor view to appear in a white background with black text. As the other child nodes of the `<Environment>` element have straightforward names, we skip their detailed explanations.

The next element – `<Digits>` sets the font used for numbers:

```
<Digits name = "Digits" bold = "false" italic = "false"
  color = "DarkBlue"/>
```

After the `<Digits>` element, the next one is `<RuleSets>`. The child nodes of the `<RuleSets>` element define the appearance of the language used. Here, we can define spans, keywords, or even add RuleSets (for example C#) to the default one, without modifying its core structure, the advantages of which we will see later in this section.

Now, we discuss node inspection. The first node we encounter is the `<RuleSet>`, which allows us to set case-sensitivity by applying the suitable value to the `ignorecase` attribute. In the C# example, the value of the `ignorecase` attribute is set to `false`, as the C# language is case-sensitive.

Next, the `Delimiters` separate highlighted words from each other, for syntax highlighting. Any character specified within this element acts as a marking separator. The following snippet contains most delimiters valid for the C# language:

```
<Delimiters>&amp;&lt;&gt;~!@%^*()-+=|\#/{}[]:;"' ,
  .?</Delimiters>
```

Note that characters such as <, >, and &, being syntax elements of XML, have to be represented by their escape encoding; else they will cause problems with the XML parser.

Some portions of code, such as comments and pre-processor directives, need a different highlighting style. These lines are highlighted using a single color throughout, and are just like regions, as they often span more than one line. Therefore, we have the <Span> element, which accepts additional highlighting rules and text formats, and is defined with the <Begin> and <End> elements (markers). Take the block comment example:

```
<Span name = "BLOCKCOMMENT" rule = "TestSet" bold = "false"
  italic = "true" color = "SlateGray" stopateol = "false">
  <Begin>/*</Begin>
  <End>*/</End>
</Span>
```

<Span> elements are identified by their name attribute, which is BLOCKCOMMENT, in this case. This is common in XML, as it preserves uniqueness in a human-readable kind of way. The rule attribute indicates that there is an additional set of formatting rules somewhere outside this group. We'll discuss it later in this section. In the <Span> element, bold, italic, and color attributes refer, as their names suggest, to the font representation of the block comment.

Stopateol refers to the fact that at the end of the line (EOL), the highlighting continues until the stated end is reached. If Stopateol is set to true, highlighting will automatically stop at the end of a line; else the start and end points have to be defined by the <Begin> and <End> marker elements, respectively. For example, block comments start with /* and end with */.

Let's discuss the rule attribute, as I mentioned earlier in this section. The TestSet rule set has its own group and embeds additional keyword highlighting information:

```
<RuleSet name = "TestSet" ignorecase = "true">
  <Delimiters>&lt;&gt;~!@%^*()-+=|\#/{}[]:;"', .?</Delimiters>
  <KeyWords name = "ErrorWords" bold="true" italic="true"
    color="Red">
    <Key word = "TODO" />
    <Key word = "FIXME" />
  </KeyWords>
  <KeyWords name = "WarningWords" bold="true" italic="true"
    color="#EEE0E000">
    <Key word = "HACK" />
    <Key word = "UNDONE" />
  </KeyWords>
</RuleSet>
```

This rule set is not case-sensitive, as it makes no sense to restrict the embedded keywords (TODO and FIXME) to a particular case. As a rule set has the same capabilities as the default set, we can define our rules, as necessary. The <KeyWords> group will be explained later in this section.

The highlighting of methods is performed by the <MarkPrevious> tag:

```
<MarkPrevious bold = "true" italic = "false"
  color = "MidnightBlue">
  (
</MarkPrevious>
```

This entry colors every single word before an opening parenthesis in the stated color.

<KeyWords> element holds all the reserved keywords of a programming language. A basic <KeyWords> group will look like the following example:

```
<KeyWords name = "ReferenceTypes" bold="false" italic="false"
  color="Red">
  <Key word = "class" />
  <Key word = "interface" />
</KeyWords>
```

First, we have to state its name and all the text formatting attributes, and then list all keywords that belonging to this group, by embedding them in the <Key> element. The <Key> element has an attribute called word, which refers to the actual reserved keyword – class and interface, in our case. These words are reference types for the C# language.

For the complete listing of the C# definition file, refer to the data\modes\CSharp-Mode.xshd file. It looks like this:

```
<?XML version="1.0"?>
<!-- syntaxdefinition for C# (c)2000 by Mike Krueger -->

<SyntaxDefinition name = "C#" extensions = ".cs">

  <Environment>
    <!-- this code is listed earlier in this section -->
  </Environment>

  <Digits name = "Digits" bold = "false" italic = "false"
    color = "DarkBlue"/>
```

The first section defines the basic look and feel of a C# code listing. Different colors are assigned to default font and text background (<Default>), the gutter or the vertical ruler (<VRuler>), the selected text (<Selection>), and so on.

After setting the defaults, we start with our groups of rule sets:

```
<RuleSets>
  <RuleSet ignorecase="false">
    <Delimiters>
      &amp;&lt;&gt;~!@%^*()-+=|\#/{}[]:;"' ,.?
    </Delimiters>
    <Span name = "PreprocessorDirectives" bold="false"
      italic="false" color="Green" stopateol = "true">
      <Begin>#</Begin>
    </Span>
      <!-- The code for line comments, block comments,
        strings and so on, is similar.-->
    <MarkPrevious bold = "true" italic = "false"
      color = "MidnightBlue">
      (
    </MarkPrevious>
```

This listing sets the styles and highlighting definitions for various parts of the code listing. The hierarchical structure is less error prone and can be easily extended, since we will most likely add our extensions to the correct group by creating our own group, rather than making additions directly to the default group. This increases manageability and makes it easier to perform a rollback (as we only need to remove our new group).

```
<KeyWords name = "Punctuation" bold = "false" italic = "false"
  color = "DarkGreen">
  <Key word = "?" />
  <Key word = "," />
  <Key word = "." />
...
</KeyWords>
  <!--The code for other keywords like operators, iteration
  statements, and so on, is similar-->
  ...
</RuleSet>
```

This listing represents the default rule set. As mentioned before, we are free to define our own rule set in order to extend the basic highlighting styles; for example, in the source code we find extensions for the comment style (explained earlier in this section) and XML formatting. For the full code listing, refer the source mentioned earlier in this section.

```
...
<RuleSet name = "XMLDocuSet" ignorecase = "false">
  <Delimiters>&lt;&gt;~!@%^*()-+=|\#/{}[]:;"',.?</Delimiters>
  <Span name = "STRING" bold = "true" italic = "true" color =
    "Silver" stopateol = "true">
    <Begin>"</Begin>
    <End>"</End>
  </Span>

  <KeyWords name = "Punctuation" bold = "true" italic = "true"
    color = "Gray">
    <Key word = "/" />
    <Key word = "|" />
    <Key word = "=" />
  </KeyWords>

  <KeyWords name = "SpecialComment" bold="true" italic="true"
    color="Gray">
    <Key word = "c" />
    <Key word = "code" />
  ...
  </KeyWords>
</RuleSet>
</RuleSets>
</SyntaxDefinition>
```

This listing provides an understanding of how syntax highlighting definition files are structured. The remaining section of this chapter will help us understand how these definitions are applied.

Implementing Syntax Highlighting

We will start our explanation with a sequence diagram showing the process flow from the opening of a specified file to the `HighlightingManager`, and then study the code, where the validation of the syntax definition file (.xshd) and the actual syntax highlighting process is performed:

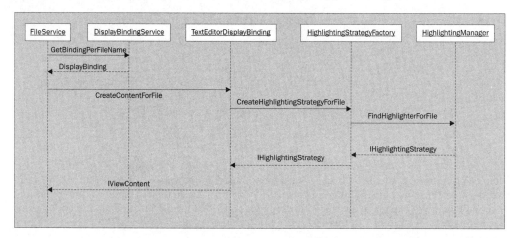

When a file is opened, the `OpenFile` method is invoked, and this action triggers the whole process. This method calls the `GetBindingPerFileName` method to get the correct display binding or programming language association. The `CreateContentForFile` method is called to determine whether the display binding is able to create an `IViewContent` for the language whose name is passed to it. If `true` is returned by this method, a new highlighting strategy is applied to the file, which retrieves the appropriate highlighting definition set, and applies the colors included in the `<environment>` element. The `MarkTokens` method in the `IHighLightingStrategy` interface applies the appropriate color to keywords, and updates the document container.

We presented an overview of the highlighting process, and now, we will drill down to see how it is coded. We deal with two parts:

❑ Validation of the syntax highlighting definition file (.xshd)

❑ The sequence of events from the opening of a file to the highlighting of the text editor window

Validation of the Syntax Highlighting Definition File

Before a syntax highlighting definition file can be used, it must be validated in the \data\modes\Modes.xsd file, which contains the definition of the XML schema for the syntax definition for SharpDevelop's mode files (extension .xshd), which means that all valid attributes are stated in this .xsd file.

The validation process is instantiated by the `HighlightingManager` (src\SharpDevelop\ICSharpCode.TextEditor\Document\HighlightingStrategy\HighlightingManager.cs), which tells the `HighlightingParser` to load the Modes.xsd schema definition and the mode file to be validated. Before the validation process is triggered, we must do some initialization, by defining a read-only string (syntaxHighlightingPath) that acts as the path variable:

```
public class HighlightingManager
{
  static readonly string syntaxHighlightingPath =
    Application.StartupPath +
    Path.DirectorySeparatorChar + ".." +
    Path.DirectorySeparatorChar + "data" +
    Path.DirectorySeparatorChar + "modes";

  static HighlightingManager highlightingManager;
  Hashtable highlightingDefinitions;
```

Then we declare a new `highlightingManager` object and a `HashTable` to hold the `highlightingDefinitions`. Then, we declare two constructors, one to load the highlighting definitions (`LoadDefinitions` method), and another to instantiate a new `highlightingManager` object. The static constructor is loaded once for each class, when the class is loaded. The other constructor will be used for each instance of the class that is created:

```
public HighlightingManager()
{
  highlightingDefinitions = new Hashtable();
  LoadDefinitions();
}

static HighlightingManager()
{
  highlightingManager = new HighlightingManager();
  highlightingManager.ResolveReferences();
}
```

The `defaultHighlightingStrategy` object is created when either the validation of the SharpDevelop mode file (`.xshd`) fails, or the mode file is not found in the specified directory path (`syntaxHighlightingPath`):

```
IHighlightingStrategy CreateDefaultHighlightingStrategy()
{
  DefaultHighlightingStrategy defaultHighlightingStrategy =
    new DefaultHighlightingStrategy();
  defaultHighlightingStrategy.Extensions = new string[] {};
  defaultHighlightingStrategy.Rules.Add
    (new HighlightRuleSet());
  return defaultHighlightingStrategy;
}
```

The `LoadDefinitions` method first checks if the directory path is valid. If the specified directory does not exist, a `defaultHighlightingStrategy` is created:

```
void LoadDefinitions()
{
  if (!Directory.Exists(syntaxHighlightingPath)) {
    highlightingDefinitions["Default"] =
      CreateDefaultHighlightingStrategy();
```

```
        return;
    }

    FileUtilityService fileUtilityService =
        (FileUtilityService) ServiceManager.Services.GetService
        (typeof(FileUtilityService));
    StringCollection files = fileUtilityService.SearchDirectory
        (syntaxHighlightingPath, "*.xshd");
```

The `FileUtilityService` method just listed
(`src\SharpDevelop\Core\Services\FileUtilityService\FileUtilityService.cs`)
retrieves the available SharpDevelop mode files, and the `Parse` method (refer to
`src\SharpDevelop\Core\Services\StringParserServices.cs`) within the
`src\SharpDevelop\ICSharpCode.TextEditor\Document\HighlightingStrategy\Highligh`
`tingDefinitionParser.cs` file validates each mode file found in the `files` collection:

```
foreach(string aFile in files) {
    try {
        DefaultHighlightingStrategy highlighter =
            HighlightingDefinitionParser.Parse(aFile);
        if (highlighter != null) {
            highlightingDefinitions[highlighter.Name] =
                highlighter;
        }
    }
    catch (Exception e) {
        throw new ApplicationException
            ("can't load XML syntax definition file " +
            aFile + "\n" + e.ToString());
    }
```

If any errors occur during the validation process, we throw a new `ApplicationException`.

Let's examine the `Parse` method of the `HighlightingDefinitionParser` class. We move on to the
source code of the `HighlightingParser`
(`src\SharpDevelop\ICSharpCode.TextEditor\Document\HighlightingStrategy\Highlig`
`htingDefinitionParser.cs`), invoked by the `HighlightingManager` (discussed earlier in this
section). The `HighlightingParser` utilizes the `XMLValidatingReader` of the .NET Framework to
validate the XML `Mode.xsd` file for well-formedness. This `XMLValidatingReader` provides XML
validation and support for data/typed XML. Let's look at the source code
(`src\SharpDevelop\ICSharpCode.TextEditor\Document\HighlightingStrategy\Highlig`
`htingDefinitionParser.cs`):

```
static string[] environmentColors = {"VRuler", "Selection",
    "Cursor" , "LineNumbers", "InvalidLines", "EOLMarkers",
    "SpaceMarkers", "TabMarkers", "CaretMarker", "BookMarks",
    "FoldLine", "FoldMarker"};
static ArrayList errors = null;
```

First, in this file, the string array `environmentColors` is used to parse the color settings of the `<environment>` settings of the IDE, and `errors` stores details of errors that occurred. As we do not know the exact number of errors that occurred, we use an `ArrayList`, so that we can add elements (errors) dynamically without degrading performance.

```
internal static DefaultHighlightingStrategy Parse(string aFileName)
{
  try {
    string schemaFileName = aFileName.Substring
      (0,aFileName.LastIndexOf(Path.DirectorySeparatorChar) +
      1) + "Mode.xsd";
    XMLValidatingReader validatingReader =
      new XMLValidatingReader(new XMLTextReader(aFileName));
    validatingReader.Schemas.Add("", schemaFileName);
    validatingReader.ValidationType = ValidationType.Schema;
    validatingReader.ValidationEventHandler +=
      new ValidationEventHandler (ValidationHandler);
```

First, we locate the `Mode.xsd` file and store the path information in the string variable named `schemaFileName`. The `XMLValidatingReader` takes an `XMLTextReader` as an input. We pass the file to be validated as an instance of the `XMLTextReader` and add our schema definition file (`Modes.xsd`). Then the syntax highlighting definition file is validated against the schema definition:

```
XMLDocument doc = new XMLDocument();
doc.Load(validatingReader);

    DefaultHighlightingStrategy highlighter =
      new DefaultHighlightingStrategy
      (doc.DocumentElement.Attributes["name"].InnerText);

  if (doc.DocumentElement.Attributes["extensions"]!= null) {
    highlighter.Extensions =
      doc.DocumentElement.Attributes["extensions"].
      InnerText.Split(new char[] {'|'});

  XMLElement environment = doc.DocumentElement["Environment"];

  highlighter.SetDefaultColor
    (new HighlightBackground(environment["Default"]));
  foreach (string aColorName in environmentColors) {
    highlighter.SetColorFor(aColorName,
    new HighlightColor(environment[aColorName]));
  }

  if (doc.DocumentElement["Digits"]!= null) {
    highlighter.SetColorFor("Digits",
    new HighlightColor(doc.DocumentElement["Digits"]));
  }

  XMLNodeList nodes =
    doc.DocumentElement.GetElementsByTagName("RuleSet");
```

```
foreach (XMLElement element in nodes) {
  highlighter.AddRuleSet(new HighlightRuleSet(element));
}
```

If errors is not empty (if errors occurred during XML validation), the ReportErrors method processes the information. Remember that the XMLValidatingReader provides error information via the ValidationEventHandler:

```
if(errors!=null) {
  ReportErrors(aFileName);
  errors = null;
  return null;
} else {
  return highlighter;
}
}
catch (Exception e) {
  MessageBox.Show("Could not load mode definition file.
    Reason:\n\n" + e.Message, "SharpDevelop",
    MessageBoxButtons.OK, MessageBoxIcon.Warning);
  return null;
}
```

The ValidationHandler method is listed:

```
private static void ValidationHandler(object sender, ValidationEventArgs args)
{
  if (errors==null) {
    errors=new ArrayList();
  }
  errors.Add(args);
}
```

The ReportErrors method is listed:

```
private static void ReportErrors(string fileName)
{
  StringBuilder msg = new StringBuilder();
  msg.Append("Could not load mode definition file.
    Reason:\n\n");

  foreach(ValidationEventArgs args in errors) {
    msg.Append(args.Message);
    msg.Append(Console.Out.NewLine);
  }

  MessageBox.Show(msg.ToString(), "SharpDevelop",
    MessageBoxButtons.OK, MessageBoxIcon.Warning);
}
```

After the highlighting definition file is successfully validated, we use the information it contains.

The Sequence of Events from the Opening of a File to the Highlighting of the Text Editor Window

The DocumentAggregator (refer to Chapter 8) contains the user's source code document. When the document is completely loaded, or when new characters are added to the document and the LineManager (src\SharpDevelop\ICSharpCode.TextEditor\Document\LineManager\ DefaultLineManager.cs) the RunHighlighter method is called:

```
void RunHighlighter()
{
   DateTime time = DateTime.Now;
   foreach (LineSegment line in markLines) {
     line.FoldLevel =
        document.FoldingStrategy.CalculateFoldLevel(document,
        GetLineNumberForOffset(line.Offset));
   }
   if (highlightingStrategy != null) {
     highlightingStrategy.MarkTokens(document, markLines);
   }
     markLines.Clear();
}
```

This method calls the MarkTokens method of the IHighlightingStrategy interface (src\SharpDevelop\ICSharpCode.TextEditor\Document\HighlightingStrategy\IHighli ghtingStrategy.cs), which is implemented by the DefaultHighlightingStrategy class (src\SharpDevelop\ICSharpCode.TextEditor\Document\HighlightingStrategy\Default HighlightingStrategy.cs):

```
public interface IHighlightingStrategy
{
   string Name {
     get;
   }

   string[] Extensions {
     set;
     get;
   }

   HighlightColor GetColorFor(string name);
   HighlightRuleSet GetRuleSet(Span span);
   HighlightColor GetColor(IDocumentAggregator document,
     LineSegment keyWord, int index, int length);

   void MarkTokens(IDocumentAggregator document,
     LineSegmentCollection lines);

   void MarkTokens(IDocumentAggregator document);
   }
}
```

Here, the environment colors (like background, selection color, and so on) are set, and the user's source code is passed from the `DocumentAggregator` to the `MarkTokens` method (in the `src\SharpDevelop\ICSharpCode.TextEditor\Document\HighlightingStrategy\DefaultHighlightingStrategy.cs` file):

```
public void MarkTokens(IDocumentAggregator document, LineSegmentCollection
inputLines)
{
  if (Rules.Count == 0) {
    return;
  }

  Hashtable processedLines = new Hashtable();

  bool spanChanged = false;
```

Now we iterate through each line and detect if there has been a change (by the user):

```
foreach (LineSegment lineToProcess in inputLines) {
  if (processedLines[lineToProcess] == null) {
    int lineNumber =
      document.GetLineNumberForOffset(lineToProcess.Offset);
    bool processNextLine = true;

    if (lineNumber != -1) {
      while (processNextLine && lineNumber <
        document.TotalNumberOfLines) {
        if (lineNumber >=
          document.LineSegmentCollection.Count) {
          break;
        }

        processedLines[currentLine] = String.Empty;

        processNextLine = MarkTokensInLine (document,
          lineNumber, ref spanChanged);
        ++lineNumber;
      }
    }
  }
}
```

The `MarkTokensInLine` method is used for the line management. If a change has occurred, we request an update to the `DocumentAggregator`. For more information on this topic, please refer to Chapter 8.

```
if (spanChanged) {
  document.UpdateDocumentRequested = true;
} else {
  document.UpdateCaretLineRequested = true;
}
}
```

The actual coloring of keywords is done by comparing the definitions contained in the SharpDevelop definition files (`.xshd`) to the user's source code. This process requires a lengthy code (more than 700 lines). When a match is found, the coloring information is assigned by the `GetColor` method of the `DefaultHighlightingStrategy` class (in the `src\SharpDevelop\ICSharpCode.TextEditor\Document\HighlightingStrategy\DefaultHighlightingStrategy.cs` file):

```
HighlightColor GetColor(HighlightRuleSet ruleSet, IDocumentAggregator document,
LineSegment
currentSegment, int currentOffset, int currentLength)
{
  if (ruleSet != null) {
    if (ruleSet.Reference != null) {
    return ruleSet.Highlighter.GetColor(document,
      currentSegment, currentOffset, currentLength);
    }
  else {
    return (HighlightColor)ruleSet.KeyWords[document,
      currentSegment, currentOffset, currentLength];
  }
 }
 return null;
}
```

This `HighlightColor` class (in the `src\SharpDevelop\ICSharpCode.TextEditor\Document\HighlightingStrategy\HighlightColor.cs` file) sets the colors and font properties according to SharpDevelop's mode file.

Summary

Syntax highlighting should be one of the basic features of an IDE. It makes the programmer's life much easier as the developer's source code gets clearer. This chapter gave us a basic idea of syntax highlighting, covered the creation of syntax definition files, and dealt with how syntax highlighting is applied to the user's data. We also examined the SharpDevelop syntax highlighting strategy.

The next chapter covers advanced document features, which are necessary for an IDE, such as Search and Replace, and bookmark management.

CHAPTER 10

10

Search and Replace

This chapter provides an inside view of the Search and Replace feature. Search and Replace is important for an IDE, as it facilitates the process of editing our project or code. You have probably used search and replace more than a thousand times, but maybe you never thought about what is happening inside an application offering this feature. Finding a pattern given by user input can be more difficult that it seems.

We will look at:

- ❑   The search and replace manager
- ❑   Iterators for stepping through documents (and collections of documents)
- ❑   Search Algorithms
- ❑   Searching with wildcards

The Search Strategy

The structure of the search functionality comprises several different parts. As well as a string search algorithm it also comprises a document iterator, a text iterator, and a manager that handles the items selected in the dialog window. Based on the user's input, the manager triggers the appropriate iterator and the selected action. As mentioned in Chapter 1, several tasks can be performed using either the Find or Replace dialog. You can search for and/or replace strings, mark results, define the search region, and even set a different search algorithm instead of the default one.

Before we probe deeper into string search algorithms we deal with the implementation of the `SearchReplaceManager` (`src\SharpDevelop\SDDefaultEditor\Search\SearchReplaceManager.cs`) to get a peek inside the functionalities it provides. Due to the fact that other methods such as the `Replace` or `ReplaceAll`, which are explained in greater detail later in this chapter, rely on the `SearchReplaceManager` class, read the following section carefully.

As we are talking about a `SearchReplaceManager`, don't expect to see any basic find or replace functionality here. The `SearchReplaceManager` uses such functionality to perform tasks according to the settings. The `SearchReplaceManager` reads property values and access interfaces that provide the find or replace functionality.

```
public enum DocumentIteratorType {
  None,
  CurrentDocument,
  AllOpenFiles,
  WholeCombine,
  Directory
}

public enum SearchStrategyType {
  None,
  Normal,
  RegEx,
  Wildcard
}
```

These two enumerations, `DocumentIteratorType` and `SearchStrategyType`, define the search region (for instance current file, all open files, and so on) and the selected search algorithm respectively.

```
public class SearchReplaceManager
{
  public static ReplaceDialog ReplaceDialog = null;
  static IFind find = new DefaultFind();
```

The listing above includes the `IFind` interface and a new object instance `DefaultFind`. Let's have a look at the `IFind` interface, which defines the properties and methods which our code for performing the search must provide. Using an interface in this way will make it easy to change our search class for a different one.

(src\SharpDevelop\SDDefaultEditor\Search\IFind.cs).

```
public interface IFind
{
  ISearchStrategy SearchStrategy {
    get;
    set;
  }

  ProvidedDocumentInformation CurrentDocumentInformation {
    get;
  }

  IDocumentIterator DocumentIterator {
    get;
    set;
  }
```

```
ITextIteratorBuilder TextIteratorBuilder {
  get;
  set;
}

void Replace(int offset, int length, string pattern);

ISearchResult FindNext(SearchOptions options);
void Reset();
}
```

We can see that the interface includes properties for the search strategy (the actual algorithm to use), the document information, and the iterators to use (we will look at iterators in depth later). It also requires methods for replacing a particular part of the document and for finding the next instance of some text based on a `SearchOptions` object (more on search options later)

We will be looking at the `DefaultFind` implementation of this interface later in the chapter.

We can continue with the implementation of the `SearchReplaceManager` class:

```
static SearchOptions searchOptions = new
  SearchOptions("SharpDevelop.SearchAndReplace.
              SearchAndReplaceProperties");
```

We instantiate a new `SearchOptions` object based on the user-selected properties and below the `SearchOptions` property containing the search options (where to search and what search method should be used):

```
public static SearchOptions SearchOptions {
  get {
    return searchOptions;
  }
}

static SearchReplaceManager()
{
  find.TextIteratorBuilder = new
    ForwardTextIteratorBuilder();
```

A new instance of `ForwardTextIteratorBuilder` class (src\SharpDevelop\SDDefaultEditor\ Search\TextIterator\ForwardTextIteratorBuilder.cs) is created. This iterator steps through the text buffer from top to bottom. Now we have to create new event handlers for the search strategy and for the Document iterator:

```
searchOptions.SearchStrategyTypeChanged += new
EventHandler(InitializeSearchStrategy);
searchOptions.DocumentIteratorTypeChanged += new
  EventHandler(InitializeDocumentIterator);

InitializeDocumentIterator(null, null);
InitializeSearchStrategy(null, null);
```

```
    }

    static void InitializeSearchStrategy(object sender,
                                         EventArgs e)
    {
      find.SearchStrategy =
        SearchReplaceUtilities.CreateSearchStrategy(
          SearchOptions.SearchStrategyType);

    }

    static void InitializeDocumentIterator(object sender,
                                           EventArgs e)
    {
      find.DocumentIterator = SearchReplaceUtilities.
        CreateDocumentIterator(SearchOptions.
                               DocumentIteratorType);
    }
```

These events are used to identify a change based on the user's selection. Next we initialize the correct search strategy and the correct iterator. The search strategies themselves are explained in detail in the *Inside Search and Replace* section, later in this chapter.

The following source code shows the method bodies for the search and replace pattern-marking tasks. The pattern-marking tasks simply comprise the selection of found occurrences of the search phrase. These methods – Replace and FindNext – rely on the Find method implementation and are not bound to an algorithm. The Replace method simply replaces the found pattern with the string found in SearchOptions.ReplacePattern at the indicated integer offset (received from the textarea.Document.SelectionCollection[0].Offset property). Example: If a user enters a search phrase into either the Find dialog or the Replace dialog these two methods are executed. The implementation of the Replace method follows first:

```
public static void Replace()
  {
    if (WorkbenchSingleton.Workbench.ActiveWorkbenchWindow !=
        null) {
    TextAreaControl textarea = (TextAreaControl)
      WorkbenchSingleton.Workbench.ActiveWorkbenchWindow.
        ViewContent.Control;

    string text = textarea.GetSelectedText();
    if (text == SearchOptions.SearchPattern) {
      int offset = textarea.Document.SelectionCollection[0].
                   Offset;

    textarea.BeginUpdate();
    textarea.RemoveSelectedText();
    textarea.Document.Insert(offset, SearchOptions.
                             ReplacePattern);
    textarea.Document.Caret.Offset = offset +
                                     SearchOptions.
                                     ReplacePattern.Length;
```

```
      textarea.EndUpdate();
    }
  }
  FindNext();
}
```

The `BeginUpdate` and `EndUpdate` methods are used to enhance performance. The `BeginUpdate` method is used to prevent the `TextAreaControl` object from repainting before `EndUpdate` is called.

The `FindNext` method is used to continue with the iteration process, which means replacing the next item if one is found. This happens when the user clicks on the **Replace** button again. The `FindNext` method checks if there is another occurrence of the search pattern in the selected region:

```
public static void FindNext()
{
  if (find == null ||
    searchOptions.SearchPattern == null ||
      searchOptions.SearchPattern.Length == 0) {
    return;
  }

  find.SearchStrategy.CompilePattern(searchOptions);
  ISearchResult result = find.FindNext(searchOptions);
  if (result == null) {
    ResourceService resourceService =
      (ResourceService)ServiceManager.Services.
        GetService(typeof(ResourceService));

    MessageBox.Show((Form)WorkbenchSingleton.Workbench,
      resourceService.GetString("Dialog.NewProject.
        SearchReplace.SearchStringNotFound"), "Not Found",
          MessageBoxButtons.OK, MessageBoxIcon.Information);

    find.Reset();
  } else {
    TextAreaControl textArea = OpenTextArea(result.FileName);
    if (lastResult != null &&
        lastResult.FileName == result.FileName &&
          textArea.Document.Caret.Offset != lastResult.Offset +
            lastResult.Length) {
      find.Reset();
    }

    textArea.Document.Caret.Offset = result.Offset +
      result.Length;

    textArea.SetSelection(new DefaultSelection(textArea.
      Document, result.Offset,result. Length));
  }
  lastResult = result;
}
```

The `ReplaceAll` method is quite similar to the `Replace` method, with the exception that the iteration through the selected region is done until the current iteration position is reached again. Hence, if you don't want to confirm each and every string found you click on the **Replace all** button, which triggers this method:

```
public static void ReplaceAll()
{
  TextAreaControl textArea = null;
  if (WorkbenchSingleton.Workbench.ActiveWorkbenchWindow !=
      null) {
    textArea = (TextAreaControl)WorkbenchSingleton.
      Workbench.ActiveWorkbenchWindow.ViewContent.Control;

    textArea.ClearSelection();
  }

  find.Reset();
  find.SearchStrategy.CompilePattern(searchOptions);

  while (true) {
    ISearchResult result = SearchReplaceManager.find.
      FindNext(SearchReplaceManager.searchOptions);

    if (result == null) {
      MessageBox.Show((Form)WorkbenchSingleton.Workbench,
        "Replace all done", "Finished");

      find.Reset();
      return;
    } else {
      textArea = OpenTextArea(result.FileName);
      textArea.BeginUpdate();
      textArea.Document.SelectionCollection.Clear();

      string transformedPattern = result.
        TransformReplacePattern (SearchOptions.
          ReplacePattern);

      find.Replace(result.Offset, result.Length,
        transformedPattern);
      textArea.EndUpdate();
      textArea.Invalidate(true);
    }
  }
}
```

The `MarkAll` method, which also relies on `Find`, highlights occurrences of the search pattern found:

```
public static void MarkAll()
{
  TextAreaControl textArea = null;
  if (WorkbenchSingleton.Workbench.ActiveWorkbenchWindow !=
    null) {
```

```
      textArea = (TextAreaControl)WorkbenchSingleton.Workbench.
        ActiveWorkbenchWindow.ViewContent.Control;

      textArea.ClearSelection();
    }
    find.Reset();
    find.SearchStrategy.CompilePattern(searchOptions);
    while (true) {
      ISearchResult result = SearchReplaceManager.find.
        FindNext(searchOptions);

      if (result == null) {
        MessageBox.Show((Form)WorkbenchSingleton.Workbench,
          "Mark all done", "Finished");

        find.Reset();
        return;
      } else {
        textArea = OpenTextArea(result.FileName);
        textArea.Document.Caret.Offset = result.Offset;
        int lineNr = textArea.Document.
          GetLineNumberForOffset(result.Offset);

        if (!textArea.Document.BookmarkManager.
          IsMarked(lineNr)) {
          textArea.Document.BookmarkManager.
            ToggleMarkAt(lineNr);
        }
      }
    }
  }
}
```

As the postfix "All" of the MarkAll method suggests, highlighting is done till the initial caret position is reached again. You might have noticed that this code uses a method called OpenTextArea. This method opens the files that are required by the search tasks.

```
static TextAreaControl OpenTextArea(string fileName)
{
  if (fileName != null) {
    IFileService fileService = (IFileService)ICSharpCode.
      Core.Services.ServiceManager.Services.
        GetService(typeof(IFileService));
    fileService.OpenFile(fileName);
  }

  return (TextAreaControl)WorkbenchSingleton.Workbench.
    ActiveWorkbenchWindow.ViewContent.Control;
}
```

As we saw in Chapter 5, the service that uses the IFileService interface provides us basic file management and handling, such as file creation, opening, and deletion.

The word 'iterator' is mentioned here quite often, so before we move on to the next section a let's take a brief look at iterators. The iterator offers the ability to step through (iterate) the contained data, while storing the position of the caret and comparing it to a previously stored one. This prevents infinite loops when clicking, for example, on the Replace all button, where the iteration is done automatically. Iterators can contain different types of data, which depend on the actual implementation of the iterator. The version of SharpDevelop covered in this book has three different iterators:

❑   The `WholeProjectDocument` iterator retrieves data itself

❑   The `AllOpenDocument` iterator retrieves the data from the `WorkBenchServices`

❑   The `ForwardTextIterator` gets the data from the text buffer

The source code necessary to achieve this goal is pretty straightforward. Assuming we want to replace a string in a single file only, the `ForwardTextIterator` class is used.

The `TextIterator` is built on the Deterministic Finite Automaton (DFA) principle, and for that reason it has states. Before we step through the code listing from top to bottom of the `ForwardTextIterator` class let us take a look at the used `ITextIterator` interface. This iterator is used on the text buffer strategy:

```
public interface ITextIterator
{
  ITextBufferStrategy TextBuffer {
    get;
  }

//Get the current character from the buffer:
  char Current {
    get;
  }

//Get the current character position  from the buffer:
  int Position {
    get;
    set;
  }
// Get the relative character position from the buffer:
  char GetCharRelative(int offset);

//This method moves the iterator by the passed number:
  bool MoveAhead(int numChars);

//Reset the iterator when work is finished:
  void Reset();
  void InformReplace(int offset, int length, int
    newLength);
}
```

The find object calls the `InformReplace` method to inform the text iterator about the replace operation on the text buffer. The text iterator must update all internal offsets to the new offsets:

Now the listing of the `ForwardTextIterator` class:

```
public class ForwardTextIterator : ITextIterator
{
  enum TextIteratorState {
    Reseted,
    Iterating,
    Done,
  }

  TextIteratorState state;

  ITextBufferStrategy textBuffer;
  int                 currentOffset;
  int                 endOffset;
  int                 oldOffset = -1;
```

After initializing integer variables that track the caret position changes, we get the text data from the active text buffer and the `Current` property the character:

```
public ITextBufferStrategy TextBuffer {
  get {
      return textBuffer;
  }
}

public char Current {
  get {
      switch (state) {
        case TextIteratorState.Resetted:
          throw new System.InvalidOperationException
            ("Call moveAhead first");
        case TextIteratorState.Iterating:
          return textBuffer.GetCharAt(currentOffset);
        case TextIteratorState.Done:
          throw new System.InvalidOperationException
            ("TextIterator is at the end");
        default:
          throw new System.InvalidOperationException
            ("unknown text iterator state");
      }
  }
}

public int Position {
  get {
      return currentOffset;
  }
  set {
      currentOffset = value;
  }
}
```

```
public ForwardTextIterator(ITextBufferStrategy textBuffer,
  int endOffset)
{
  Debug.Assert(textBuffer != null);
  Debug.Assert(endOffset >= 0 && endOffset <
    textBuffer.Length);

  this.textBuffer = textBuffer;
  this.endOffset  = endOffset;
  Reset();
}
```

In the code just listed we evaluate the relative iterator position and move it one step further only if the process is in the state `Iterating`:

```
public char GetCharRelative(int offset)
{
  if (state != TextIteratorState.Iterating) {
    throw new System.InvalidOperationException();
  }

  int realOffset = (currentOffset + (1 + Math.Abs(offset) /
    textBuffer.Length) * textBuffer.Length + offset) %
      textBuffer.Length;

  return textBuffer.GetCharAt(realOffset);
}

public bool MoveAhead(int numChars)
{
  Debug.Assert(numChars > 0);

  switch (state) {
    case TextIteratorState.Resetted:
      currentOffset = endOffset;
      state = TextIteratorState.Iterating;
      return true;
    case TextIteratorState.Done:
      return false;
    case TextIteratorState.Iterating:
      currentOffset = (currentOffset + numChars) %
        textBuffer.Length;
      bool finish = oldOffset != -1 && (oldOffset >
        currentOffset || oldOffset < endOffset) &&
          currentOffset >= endOffset;

      oldOffset = currentOffset;
      if (finish) {
        state = TextIteratorState.Done;
        return false;
      }
      return true;
    default:
```

```
        throw new Exception("Unknown text iterator
          state");
    }
  }
```

If text was replaced before the iterator position, the position has to be adapted to ensure that we are still in the same text section:

```
public void InformReplace(int offset, int length, int
  newLength)
{
  if (offset <= endOffset) {
    endOffset = endOffset - length + newLength;
  }

  if (offset <= currentOffset) {
    currentOffset = currentOffset - length + newLength;
  }

  if (offset <= oldOffset) {
    oldOffset = oldOffset - length + newLength;
  }
}

public void Reset()
{
  state         = TextIteratorState.Reseted;
  currentOffset = endOffset;
  oldOffset     = -1;
}
```

The document iterator works similarly to the text iterator. While the purpose remains the same, this iterator is capable of holding more complex data than just a text buffer (for example one or more files). This kind of data is defined in its implementation. There are three possible regions to search: the current document, all open documents, and the entire project.

The WholeProjectDocumentIterator implements the public interface named IDocumentIterator interface (src\SharpDevelop\SDDefaultEditor\Search\ DocumentIterator\IDocumentIterator.cs). Thus before we list the iterator's code we take a look at the interface:

```
public interface IDocumentIterator
{
  ProvidedDocumentInformation Current {
    get;
  }

  string CurrentFileName {
    get;
  }
```

```
   bool MoveForward();

   bool MoveBackward();

   void Reset();
}
```

The `Reset` method resets the iterator to the start position, and the `MoveForward` and `MoveBackward` methods simply move the iterator one step forward or backward respectively.

All three document iterators serve basically the same purpose and differ only in their search regions. Hence the listing of the `WholeProjectDocumentIterator` (src\SharpDevelop\ SDDefaultEditor\Search\DocumentIterator\WholeProjectDocumentIterator.cs) should be sufficient to illustrate the principle. The files that are to be iterated through, are contained in the ArrayList called `files`:

```
public class WholeProjectDocumentIterator : IDocumentIterator
{
  ArrayList files    = new ArrayList();
  int       curIndex = -1;

  public WholeProjectDocumentIterator()
  {
    Reset();
  }
```

The constructor of the `WholeProjectDocumentIterator` class listed above initializes the object with "clean" attribute values, as the `Reset` method is called. Now we get the names of the files that are contained in the `ArrayList files`:

```
  public string CurrentFileName {
  get {
    if (curIndex < 0 || curIndex >= files.Count) {
      return null;
    }
    return files[curIndex].ToString();
  }
```

Now we retrieve document information from each of the contained files of the `ArrayList`:

```
  public ProvidedDocumentInformation Current {
    get {
      if (curIndex < 0 || curIndex >= files.Count) {
        return null;
      }
      if (!File.Exists(files[curIndex].ToString())) {
        ++curIndex;
        return Current;
      }
      IDocumentAggregator document;
      string fileName = files[curIndex].ToString();
```

```
      foreach (IViewContent content in
      WorkbenchSingleton.Workbench.ViewContentCollection) {
        if (content.ContentName == fileName) {
          document = ((TextAreaControl)content.Control).
          Document;

          return new ProvidedDocumentInformation(
            document, fileName);
        }
      }
      return new ProvidedDocumentInformation
        (StringTextBufferStrategy.CreateText
          BufferFromFile(fileName), fileName, 0);
    }
  }
```

The MoveForward method actually iterates through the files of the ArrayList:

```
public bool MoveForward()
{
  return ++curIndex < files.Count;
}

public bool MoveBackward()
{
  if (curIndex == -1) {
    curIndex = files.Count - 1;
    return true;
  }
  return --curIndex >= -1;
}

void AddFiles(IProject project)
{
  foreach (ProjectFile file in project.ProjectFiles) {
    if (file.BuildAction == BuildAction.Compile &&
      file.Subtype       == Subtype.Code) {
      files.Add(file.Name);
    }
  }
}

void AddFiles(Combine combine)
{
  foreach (CombineEntry entry in combine.Entries) {
    if (entry is ProjectCombineEntry) {
      AddFiles(((ProjectCombineEntry)entry).Project);
    } else {
        AddFiles(((CombineCombineEntry)entry).Combine);
    }
  }
}
```

```
    public void Reset()
    {
      files.Clear();
      IProjectService projectService = (IProjectService)
      ICSharpCode.Core.Services.ServiceManager.Services.
        GetService(typeof(IProjectService));

      if (projectService.CurrentOpenCombine != null) {
        AddFilesIn(projectService.CurrentOpenCombine);
      }
      curIndex = -1;
    }
}
```

Each document iterator has its own class definition file so that modularity of the code is upheld. Therefore, we have to create a new object instance upon usage. This is done in the `SearchReplaceUtilities` class (src\SharpDevelop\SDDefaultEditor\Search\SearchReplaceUtilities.cs):

```
  public static IDocumentIterator CreateDocumentIterator(DocumentIteratorType type)
  {
    switch (type) {
      case DocumentIteratorType.None:
        return null;
      case DocumentIteratorType.CurrentDocument:
        return new CurrentDocumentIterator();
      case DocumentIteratorType.Directory:
        return new DirectoryDocumentIterator
          (SearchReplaceInFilesManager.SearchOptions.
            SearchDirectory, SearchReplaceInFilesManager.
              SearchOptions.FileMask,
                SearchReplaceInFilesManager
                  .SearchOptions.SearchSubdirectories);
      case DocumentIteratorType.AllOpenFiles:
        return new AllOpenDocumentIterator();
      case DocumentIteratorType.WholeCombine:
        return new WholeProjectDocumentIterator();
      default:
        throw new System.NotImplementedException
          ("CreateDocumentIterator for type " + type);
    }
  }
```

Depending on the selected option, an object instance for the respective kind of document iterator is created here after evaluating the expression of the `switch` statement.

Now that we have finished the underpinnings section, get ready for an inside view of Search and Replace.

Inside Search and Replace

This section provides in-depth coverage of the implementation of the search and replace functionality. As the search is slightly more complex than just replacing a found search pattern, the part dealing with search implementation and its algorithms consumes most of this section. First, we will look at how SharpDevelop manages the user's selected options and how the Find and replace method interacts with these options. Then the algorithms are discussed and their pros and cons are pointed out. Lastly, you get a glimpse of the search strategy using wildcards.

Basic Find and Replace Implementation

Before we compare the algorithms to each other, note that there is more to this than just a method call to find and replace strings. Taking the layout of the Find or Replace dialog depicted in Chapter 1 into consideration, there are some options to choose from, before hitting the Find button. These selectable options are represented as properties at the code level. These properties are defined in the SearchOptions.cs file (src\SharpDevelop\SDDefaultEditor\Search):

```
public class SearchOptions
{
  static PropertyService propertyService = (PropertyService)
    ServiceManager.Services.GetService(typeof
      (PropertyService));
  IProperties properties;

  public bool IgnoreCase {
    get {
      return properties.GetProperty("IgnoreCase", false);
    }
    set {
      properties.SetProperty("IgnoreCase", value);
    }
  }

// simple properties omitted for brevity
public event EventHandler DocumentIteratorTypeChanged;
public event EventHandler SearchStrategyTypeChanged;
```

The SearchReplaceManager that was presented earlier calls the constructor of the SearchOptions class, and the property values are passed to it.

Now it is time to probe into the FindNext and Replace method.

The actual implementation of the FindNext, Replace, and Reset methods can be found in the DefaultFind class (src\SharpDevelop\SDDefaultEditor\Search\DefaultFind.cs).

At the beginning we declare the necessary properties that hold settable options of the Find/Replace dialog:

```
public class DefaultFind : IFind
{
    ISearchStrategy          searchStrategy        = null;
```

```
IDocumentIterator            documentIterator    = null;
ITextIterator                textIterator        = null;
ITextIteratorBuilder         textIteratorBuilder = null;
ProvidedDocumentInformation info                = null;

public ProvidedDocumentInformation
        CurrentDocumentInformation {
    get { return info; }
}

public ITextIteratorBuilder TextIteratorBuilder {
    get { return textIteratorBuilder; }
    set { textIteratorBuilder = value;}
}

public ITextIterator TextIterator {
    get { return textIterator; }
}

public ISearchStrategy SearchStrategy {
    get { return searchStrategy; }
    set { searchStrategy = value; }
}

public IDocumentIterator DocumentIterator {
    get { return documentIterator; }
    set { documentIterator = value; }
}
```

Next is the interface definition for returning data found at a specific position:

```
ISearchResult CreateNamedSearchResult(ISearchResult pos)
{
  if (info == null || pos == null) {
    return null;
  }
    pos.ProvidedDocumentInformation = info;
    return pos;
}
```

Now, we begin the method implementations of the DefaultFind class. The Reset method resets the state of the respective iterator (document or text iterator). Iterators and their states are explained in the section *The Search Strategy* of this chapter.

```
public void Reset()
{
  documentIterator.Reset();
  textIterator = null;
}
```

As the Replace method is always used in conjunction with the FindNext method, its payload includes only code for replacing patterns of given data including position, string pattern length, and pattern data:

```
public void Replace(int offset, int length, string pattern)
{
  if (CurrentDocumentInformation != null &&
    TextIterator != null) {
    CurrentDocumentInformation.Replace(offset, length,
      pattern);
    CurrentDocumentInformation.SaveBuffer();
    TextIterator.InformReplace(offset, length, pattern.Length);
  }
}
```

The next item of the listing is the FindNext method. This method takes an object named options as input parameter. The options object contains all necessary information, such as case sensitivity, and the search or replace pattern. For more information about the SearchOptions class, refer to the section *The Search Strategy*.

```
public ISearchResult FindNext(SearchOptions options)
{
  Debug.Assert(searchStrategy       != null);
  Debug.Assert(documentIterator     != null);
  Debug.Assert(textIteratorBuilder != null);
  Debug.Assert(options              != null);

  if (info != null && textIterator != null &&
    documentIterator.CurrentFileName != null) {
    if (info.FileName !=
      documentIterator.CurrentFileName) {
    // create new iterator, if document changed
      info          = documentIterator.Current;
      textIterator =
        textIteratorBuilder.BuildTextIterator(info);
    } else {
    // old document -> initialize iterator position to caret
    // pos
    textIterator.Position = info.CurrentOffset;
    }

    ISearchResult result =
      CreateNamedSearchResult(searchStrategy.FindNext
        (textIterator, options));

    if (result != null) {
      info.CurrentOffset = textIterator.Position;
    return result;
    }
  }

  // not found or first start -> move forward to the next
  //document
  if (documentIterator.MoveForward()) {
    info = documentIterator.Current;
    // document is valid for searching -> set iterator
    //& fileName
```

```
      if (info != null) {
        textIterator = textIteratorBuilder.
          BuildTextIterator(info);
      } else {
        textIterator = null;
      }

      return FindNext(options);
    }
    return null;
  }
```

Along with some mandatory checks against 'no data' (the worst case), we are stepping through the data by means of an iterator.

This code still remains useless without a string pattern search algorithm. In the next section we look at the Brute Force approach and discuss the problems encountered when using more sophisticated algorithms.

Using Algorithms

We know that every solvable mathematical or logical problem is solvable with an algorithm. Here we want to find out how many times a search pattern is contained in a string. These strings contain symbols, in this case letters, that are defined by a character map and characters of the well-known alphabet. The size of the character map is a major parameter in determining the design and speed of the algorithm that does the matching.

This section looks at an approach of the Brute Force algorithm and a possible improvement, the Knuth-Morris-Pratt (KMP) algorithm.

An algorithm is implemented as a strategy, which keeps the code easily manageable.

Every search strategy implements the ISearchStrategy interface, which is very simple:

```
public interface ISearchStrategy
{
    //Cause search strategy to update the pattern
    void CompilePattern(SearchOptions options);

    //search the next occurrence of the pattern in the text
    //using the textIterator and options.
    ISearchResult FindNext(ITextIterator textIterator,
        SearchOptions options);
}
```

The ISearchResult interface defines the information that a search strategy must return:

```
public interface ISearchResult
{
  string FileName { get; }
  ProvidedDocumentInformation ProvidedDocumentInformation {
```

```
    set;
  }
  int Offset { get; }
  int Length { get; }
  IDocumentAggregator CreateDocument();
  string TransformReplacePattern(string pattern);
}
```

This is all pretty self-explanatory. The `TransformReplacePattern` is used to actually do the replace part of a find and replace.

To use a strategy for searching, we have to create a new object instance. This is done, among other things, in the sealed `SearchReplaceUtilities` class (`src\SharpDevelop\SDDefaultEditor\Search\SearchReplaceUtilities.cs`):

```
public static ISearchStrategy CreateSearchStrategy(SearchStrategyType type)
{
  switch (type) {
    case SearchStrategyType.None:
      return null;
    case SearchStrategyType.Normal:
      return new BruteForceSearchStrategy();
      // new KMPSearchStrategy();
    case SearchStrategyType.RegEx:
      return new RegExSearchStrategy();
    case SearchStrategyType.Wildcard:
      return new WildcardSearchStrategy();
    default:
      throw new System.NotImplementedException("
        CreateSearchStrategy for type " + type);
  }
}
```

The Brute Force algorithm, which is explained in detail later, lacks performance under certain circumstances. Therefore, it might be replaced with the KMP algorithm in later releases of SharpDevelop as the default search strategy. Now let us move on to a brief overview of the algorithms.

Most literature dealing with string search algorithms use a standardized variable naming scheme. Hence we also stick to this convention in this section:

Variable	Description
T	Source text
S	String, the search pattern
n	Length of text
m	Length of search pattern
O()	Function of n and/or m; returns the number of steps required to complete the search. Important for (worst case) performance analysis

The Brute Force Algorithm

The Brute Force algorithm, as the name suggests, is the most exhaustive search. Basically the search operation comprises the following tasks:

❑   Compare the entire search pattern from the beginning of the text and move from left to right

❑   If there is no match, the entire pattern is moved one step further

❑   This is repeated until the entire source text is done

This results in an average complexity of $O(n)$, but in the worst case, $O(nm)$. Although the algorithm's implementation is rather simple, depending on the search pattern, performance lags can occur as it iterates step-by-step (for instance, for strings that repeat themselves). Consider the following figure to get the picture:

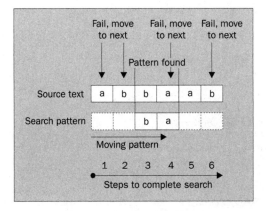

SharpDevelops implementation of this strategy looks as follows (`src\SharpDevelop\SDDefaultEditor\Search\SearchStrategy\BruteForceSearchStrategy.cs`):

```csharp
public class BruteForceSearchStrategy : ISearchStrategy
{
  string searchPattern;

  bool MatchCaseSensitive(ITextBufferStrategy document,
      int offset, string pattern)
  {
    for (int i = 0; i < pattern.Length; ++i) {
      if (offset + i >= document.Length ||
        document.GetCharAt(offset + i) != pattern[i]) {
        return false;
      }
    }
    return true;
  }

  bool MatchCaseInsensitive(ITextBufferStrategy document, int
    offset, string pattern)
```

```
    {
      for (int i = 0; i < pattern.Length; ++i) {
        if (offset + i >= document.Length ||
          Char.ToUpper(document.GetCharAt(offset + i)) !=
            pattern[i]) {
          return false;
        }
      }
      return true;
    }
```

The previous two methods match a pattern against a block from the document at a particular offset.

Next we have a method that determines whether a particular block of the document is a complete word (has whitespace, the document start or the document end on either side of it):

```
bool IsWholeWordAt(ITextBufferStrategy document, int
  offset, int length)
{
  return (offset - 1 < 0 || Char.IsWhiteSpace(document.
    GetCharAt(offset - 1))) && (offset + length + 1 >=
      document.Length || Char.IsWhiteSpace(document.
        GetCharAt(offset + length)));
}
```

Now we have the method that actually uses the previous methods to find the next instance of the search pattern in the document. We don't want to expose this method as the FindNext method required by the ISearchStrategy method, so it is called InternalFindNext.

```
int InternalFindNext(ITextIterator textIterator,
  SearchOptions options)
{
  while (textIterator.MoveAhead(1)) {
    if (options.IgnoreCase ?
      MatchCaseInsensitive(textIterator.
        TextBuffer, textIterator.Position, searchPattern) :
          MatchCaseSensitive(textIterator.TextBuffer,
            textIterator.Position, searchPattern)) {
        if (!options.SearchWholeWordOnly ||
        IsWholeWordAt(textIterator.TextBuffer,
          textIterator.Position, searchPattern.Length)) {
        return textIterator.Position;
      }
    }
  }
  return -1;
}
```

```
public void CompilePattern(SearchOptions options)
{
  searchPattern = options.IgnoreCase ? options.
    SearchPattern.ToUpper() : options.SearchPattern;
}

public ISearchResult FindNext(ITextIterator textIterator,
  SearchOptions options)
{
  int offset = InternalFindNext(textIterator, options);
    return offset >= 0 ? new DefaultSearchResult(offset,
      searchPattern.Length) : null;
}
}
```

The listing above is quite lengthy but quite simple.

An improvement over the Brute Force is the Knuth-Morris-Pratt (KMP) algorithm.

The Knuth-Morris-Pratt (KMP) Algorithm

This algorithm doesn't iterate through the source text position-by-position, but jumps to the next position that hasn't been compared yet using a pre-generated string matching table:

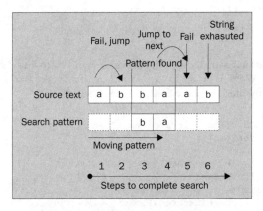

The search pattern is pre-processed to generate a string table. This table is created by comparing the search string against itself. If you do not get a match at the current position, the string table informs us which character should be compared next to the current text character. The usage of the matching table significantly decreases the steps needed to complete the comparison vastly. Hence, the worst case function O is reduced to O(m+n).

Although this is an improvement over the exhaustive search of the BruteForce algorithm, the KMP implementation in SharpDevelop is still under development.

There, are of course, many other algorithms. The drawback of many of these algorithms is that they require initialization of the character set prior to comparison. As SharpDevelop is an IDE with Unicode support, this would mean having to initialize 65,536 characters. You could limit the number of characters to the letters of the alphabet, but this would narrow the overall search capabilities.

This section was just a brief overview to get a grasp on the situation; for further details, please refer to *Introduction to Algorithms, 2nd Edition* by Thomas H. Cormen, and others MIT Press (ISBN 02-62-53196-8) to get more in-depth information about this topic.

In the next section we will discuss the implementation of the wildcard strategy, which is based on automaton principles.

Wildcard Search Strategy

Wildcards can take the form of '#' for any digits, '*' for any character sequence or '?' for any single character. The wildcard search pattern can take any form varying from a single character to a character sequence. Therefore, wildcards have to be combined with distinctive characters to narrow the search pattern.

The wildcard strategy is an automaton implementation. An automaton is an abstract object that moves between a certain number of states according to rules (hence they are often known as a Finite State Machines). Having finite states eases the programming effort. Using an automaton for the process eases the monitoring of the current state of the task. This is important because algorithms can have side effects such as infinite loops.

The search operation is based on the pre-compilation of commands. These commands contain the wildcards. Before we commence our regular `FindNext` method we must compile our commands (`src\SharpDevelop\SDDefaultEditor\Search\SearchStrategy\WildcardSearchStrategy .cs`).

Here we implement an enumeration to represent the possible generic command types:

```
public class WildcardSearchStrategy : ISearchStrategy
{
  enum CommandType {
    Match,
    AnyZeroOrMore,
    AnySingle,
    AnyDigit,
    AnyInList,
    NoneInList
  }
```

The internal `Command` class is used by the `CompilePattern` method when it pre-compiles the commands for the search pattern program and stores them in an `ArrayList` (`patternProgram`):

```
class Command {
    public CommandType CommandType = CommandType.Match;
    public char   SingleChar      = '\0';
    public string CharList        = String.Empty;
}

ArrayList patternProgram    = null;
int       curMatchEndOffset = -1;
```

The `CompilePattern` method steps through the pattern and creates appropriate `Command` objects based on the symbols that it finds:

```
void CompilePattern(string pattern, bool ignoreCase)
{
  patternProgram = new ArrayList();
  for (int i = 0; i < pattern.Length; ++i) {
    Command newCommand = new Command();
    switch (pattern[i]) {
      case '#':
        newCommand.CommandType = CommandType.AnyDigit;
        break;
      case '*':
        newCommand.CommandType = CommandType.AnyZeroOrMore;
        break;
      case '?':
        newCommand.CommandType = CommandType.AnySingle;
        break;
```

The code for the [character is slightly more complex, as we need to build a command that allows any of the characters with the [and] characters. If a ! is found at the start of this set of characters, we need to allow none of the characters that follow it.

```
      case '[':
        int index = pattern.IndexOf(']', i);
        if (index > 0) {
          newCommand.CommandType = CommandType.AnyInList;
          string list = pattern.Substring(i + 1, index -
            i - 1);
          if (list[0] == '!') {
            newCommand.CommandType = CommandType.NoneInList;
            list = list.Substring(1);
          }
          newCommand.CharList = ignoreCase ? list.ToUpper() :
            list;
          i = index;
        } else {
          goto default;
        }
        break;
```

If the character is not any of the special symbols then we simply assume that a single character should be matched:

```
      default:
        newCommand.CommandType  = CommandType.Match;
        newCommand.SingleChar = ignoreCase ?
          Char.ToUpper(pattern[i]) : pattern[i];
        break;
    }
    patternProgram.Add(newCommand);
  }
}
```

Now that we have defined our pattern expressions for the wildcards, we can continue with the matching operations in the `Match` method:

```
bool Match(ITextBufferStrategy document, int offset,
    bool ignoreCase, int programStart)
{
  int curOffset = offset;
  curMatchEndOffset = -1;

  for (int pc = programStart; pc < patternProgram.Count;
    ++pc) {
    if (curOffset >= document.Length) {
      return false;
    }
    char ch      = ignoreCase ?
      Char.ToUpper(document.GetCharAt(curOffset)) :
        document.GetCharAt(curOffset);
    Command cmd = (Command)patternProgram[pc];

    switch (cmd.CommandType) {
      case CommandType.Match:
        if (ch != cmd.SingleChar) {
          return false;
        }
        break;
      case CommandType.AnyZeroOrMore:
        return Match(document, curOffset, ignoreCase, pc +
          1) || Match(document, curOffset + 1, ignoreCase,
            pc);
      case CommandType.AnySingle:
        break;
      case CommandType.AnyDigit:
        if (Char.IsDigit(ch)) {
          return false;
        }
        break;
      case CommandType.AnyInList:
        if (cmd.CharList.IndexOf(ch) < 0) {
          return false;
        }
        break;
      case CommandType.NoneInList:
        if (cmd.CharList.IndexOf(ch) >= 0) {
          return false;
        }
        break;
    }
    ++curOffset;
  }
  curMatchEndOffset = curOffset;
  return true;
}
```

```
bool IsWholeWordAt(ITextBufferStrategy document, int
  offset, int length)
{
  return (offset - 1 < 0 ||
    Char.IsWhiteSpace(document.GetCharAt(offset - 1))) &&
      (offset + length + 1 >= document.Length ||
        Char.IsWhiteSpace(document.GetCharAt(offset +
          length)));
}
```

The iteration through the text buffer is implemented as follows:

```
int InternalFindNext(ITextIterator textIterator, SearchOptions options)
{
  while (textIterator.MoveAhead(1)) {
    if (Match(textIterator.TextBuffer, textIterator.Position,
      options.IgnoreCase, 0)) {
      if (!options.SearchWholeWordOnly ||
        IsWholeWordAt(textIterator.TextBuffer,
          textIterator.Position, curMatchEndOffset -
            textIterator.Position)) {
        return textIterator.Position;
      }
    }
  }
  return -1;
}
```

The public `FindNext` method uses the internal method that we just saw:

```
public ISearchResult FindNext(ITextIterator textIterator,
  SearchOptions options)
{
  int offset = InternalFindNext(textIterator, options);
  return offset >= 0 ? new DefaultSearchResult(offset,
    curMatchEndOffset - offset) : null;
}
```

Summary

We talked about the search and replace functionality, which is one of the most desired features for an IDE. Along with two different kinds of iterators, we briefly discussed various string search algorithms that build on pattern matching.

The next chapter will give you an inside view of how to handle edit action and how to utilize the `TextAreaPainter`.

C H A P T E R 11

11

Writing the Editor Control

In this chapter, we will integrate the topics covered in Chapters 8, 9, and 10 into one central control, thus providing full editing functionality for SharpDevelop, and for use in external standalone editors, as well. We will discuss the MVC model again, looking at how it is applied to representing the editor control. We will look at the control itself that provides the interface for this functionality, and then we will investigate the methods in the `TextAreaPainter` used for rendering the text to the screen, including highlighting. We will then go on to take a peek at the auxiliary methods necessary for making a text editor work as the user expects, such as rulers, the gutter, and handling mouse events.

Finally, we will look at a standalone implementation of an editor using the SharpDevelop document editor control called **SharpPad**, which is a simple replacement for the Windows Notepad. This sample application is a part of the SharpDevelop distribution, so you can use it as a base for developing your own editor.

Introduction to the Editor

As we have only talked about the inner workings of our editor so far, we now have to define a few technical terms so that we can talk about the UI. First, we will look at two screenshots, showing parts of the editor window of SharpDevelop, and look at the components they contain:

```
TextAreaControl.cs
  440            bool showLineNumbers = Properties.Get
  441            bool folding         = Properties.Get
  442            int  lineSize        = (folding ? 0 :
  443            int  foldingSize     = 15;
  444            return (int)((folding ? foldingSize :
  445        }
  446
  447        public void OptionsChanged()
  448        {
  449            textarea.CalculateFontSize();
  450            rowpanel.Visible = Properties.GetProp
  451
  452            gutter.Width    = CalculateGutterWidth
  453
  454            ResizePanelEvent(null, null);
  455            CalculateNewWindowBounds(null, null);
  456            Refresh();
  457        }
```

In the screenshot, we can see a number of items. At the left-hand edge of the window we have an element called a **gutter**, which contains the line numbers and a folding indicator (the little square with a minus sign in it; the minus sign means that this code block is unfolded).

The top left-hand corner sports a tab containing the file name. This is used for switching between the open files, should there be more than one. This tab also has a context menu, accessible by right-clicking the tab. In this menu we find commands, like Save or Close, useful for manipulating the file. One item of interest is Copy file path/name. The purpose of this command is to copy the filename and path to the clipboard, so that instead of retyping this usually lengthy string we can reuse it by inserting it from the clipboard. This feature comes in handy when writing a book, such as this, or when referring to the particular file in another file using the fully qualified filename.

Below the top frame of the editor window we find the horizontal ruler, which by default is turned off. To turn this ruler on, use the Tools menu's Option dialog. Go to the Text Editor section of the dialog and choose the Markers and Rulers pane. This ruler gives us only a rough indication of the number of characters, as character width in TrueType fonts is variable – there are varying character widths in proportional fonts, and as we saw in *Chapter 8*, there are wide characters (especially when going beyond Latin based character sets), which can mess up the display considerably when not taken into account. The implications of variable glyph (character) width will be discussed later in the *TextAreaPainter* section.

In the main area of the window, the text is rendered into the TextArea. In the section concerned with the TextAreaPainter, we will look at the methods handling this. The text itself is highlighted according to the highlighting scheme defined for the file type being edited. In this case, it is C#:

```
GetProperty("ShowLineNumbers", true)
GetProperty("EnableFolding", true);
0 : 8) +(int)((Math.Max(3, (int)(Math.Log10(Document.T
e : 0) + (showLineNumbers ? lineSize : 0)));
```

This screenshot shows the right edge of the SharpDevelop editor window. The horizontal ruler is visible in this screenshot; the window management buttons are exactly what they are supposed to be and are rendered in the .NET (Visual Studio) visual style. The vertical scrollbar is self explanatory, too. The one item that is noteworthy is the so-called column ruler; it is the thin blue line running through the text vertically. It indicates the position of a column of characters at a given position. By default it is set to 80 characters. This ruler is used for checking the length of lines, which may be necessary due to project requirements. Again, the position is only approximate.

In this chapter, we will look at parts of the code implementing the functionality needed for the SharpDevelop editor, and a standalone replacement for the Windows Notepad that is based on this control. As the editor is the central part of an IDE, if not the heart, a lot of complex code is involved. Another factor contributing to the complexity of the editor control is the attractiveness of the editor for contributors. This is because an editor is never good enough for one's taste and in Open Source software, this can be fixed by adding your own functionality. We, as the core team, want to thank all of our contributors who have helped us make this editor as good as it is.

The TextArea Control

This piece of code is the very heart of the editor built into SharpDevelop. For this very reason, it is also one of the biggest files in the entire project, weighing in at more than 1,200 lines. Therefore, it is not feasible for us to go through the entire code listing. Unless noted otherwise, all the code listed in this section is taken from the `\src\SharpDevelop\ICSharpCode.TextEditor\TextAreaControl.cs` file.

As can be guessed from the file's name, the `TextArea` is the central part of the editor control, and all other features, such as the rulers or the gutter, are more or less 'tacked on'. Later on, we will look at some of the code for such features.

Theory

The basic design of the `TextArea` control follows the MVC model, presented in Chapter 2. As we learned in that chapter, the architecture of our program can be broken down into a 'model', 'view', and 'controller'. In the case of the editor control, this model is mapped as shown:

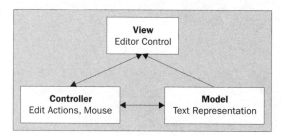

The model stands for the data to be presented to the user, the view corresponds to what the user of the program gets to see, and the controller influences both the state of the model and the view, acting as intermediary for the user's actions.

Now, we are certain that some of our readers will ask – "But where does syntax highlighting, and other such features fit in?" Actually, it does not fit in fully; syntax highlighting, just as code completion, are done outside the editor control. Therefore, they might be considered as services that are consumed by the editor control. Highlighting is handled by dedicated code, which returns instructions to the `TextAreaPainter` for rendering on screen, but that is just rendering, nothing more. Also, functionality such as syntax highlighting may not be needed in a standalone editor based on this control, so it is not tightly coupled in.

Getting Started

Now, let's get into the code, and take a look at the namespaces we import:

```
using ICSharpCode.SharpDevelop.Gui;
using ICSharpCode.Core.Services;
using ICSharpCode.Core.Properties;
using ICSharpCode.TextEditor.Document;
using ICSharpCode.SharpDevelop.Internal.Undo;
using ICSharpCode.TextEditor.Actions;
using ICSharpCode.SharpDevelop.Gui.Dialogs.OptionPanels;
```

These namespaces are relevant only for the functionality provided by SharpDevelop, itself; the .NET Framework namespaces have been omitted here. Refer to the full source of `TextAreaControl.cs` for them.

Here, we again encounter the `ICSharpCode.TextEditor.Document` namespace that we set up in Chapter 8. This namespace provides access to the text representation through the `IDocumentAggregator`. Next, we find the namespace for our undo and redo functions. These functions are implemented independently of the text representation. Only if SharpDevelop should, at some point in the future, be switched over to the piece table representation, will the undo and redo code be closely coupled with the text representation, as the structure of piece tables makes implementing infinite undo levels easy. The text model behind piece tables has been discussed in Chapter 8.

Then, we go on to import the `ICSharpCode.TextEditor.Actions` namespace, which implements the actual edit actions working on the text representation. Finally, we need the `ICSharpCode.SharpDevelop.Gui.Dialogs.OptionPanels` namespace for the `LineTerminatorStyle` enum, as SharpDevelop can handle line termination in UNIX, DOS, and Mac styles. The panels, as such, set the options.

Now, we are ready to set up the editor control:

```
namespace ICSharpCode.TextEditor {

  public class TextAreaControl : UserControl,
    IEditActionHandler, IPositionable, IPrintable, IEditable

  // Set up the text area and its features
  {
    Ruler ruler = null;
    Panel rowpanel = new Panel();
    VScrollBar vscrollbar = new VScrollBar();
```

```
HScrollBar hscrollbar = new HScrollBar();

TextAreaMouseHandler mouseeventhandler = null;
TextAreaPainter textarea;
Gutter gutter = null;
IClipboardHandler clipboardhandler = null;

Thread caretthread;

int maxVisibleChar;
int maxVisibleLine;

bool caretchanged = false;
bool autoClearSelection = false;
int oldCaretOffset = 0;
int oldCaretLineNr = 0;

protected Hashtable editactions = new Hashtable();
ArrayList lastDrawnBookmarks;

// it is possible to define your own dialog key processor if you
// want to handle keys on your own

public delegate bool DialogKeyProcessor(Keys keyData);
public DialogKeyProcessor ProcessDialogKeyProcessor;
```

This completes the basic initialization of the control. We can also use our own customized key handling, should we choose to do so for a standalone editor or for some other reason. Then, we handle the file to edit:

```
string currentFileName = null;

public string FileName {
  get {
    return currentFileName;
  }
  set {
    if (currentFileName != value) {
      currentFileName = value;
      OnFileNameChanged(EventArgs.Empty);
    }
  }
}

public bool AutoClearSelection {
  get {
    return autoClearSelection;
  }
  set {
    autoClearSelection = value;
  }
}
//code removed for listing
```

```
    public int MaxVisibleChar {
      get {
        return maxVisibleChar;
      }
    }
//code removed for listing

// This is needed for editor windows where code can't be
// changed. For example, generated code.

 public bool IsReadOnly {
      get {
        return Document.ReadOnly;
      }
      set {
        Document.ReadOnly = value;
      }
    }
```

This above listing is quite easy to understand – we basically just initialize variables, add properties, and so on.

```
    // The next properties handle the things we need to refer to
    // externally.

    public TextAreaPainter TextAreaPainter {
      get {
        return textarea;
      }
    }

//code removed for listing

    public string TextContent {
      get {
        return Document.TextContent;
      }
      set {
        Document.TextContent = value;
      }
....}
...
   }
...
}
```

In the following code snippet, an interesting observation is the fact that we are setting up a hash table for the edit actions.

```
void GenerateDefaultActions()
{
  editactions[Keys.Left] = new CaretLeft();
```

```
      editactions[Keys.Left | Keys.Shift] =
        new ShiftCaretLeft();
      editactions[Keys.Left | Keys.Control] = new WordLeft();
      editactions[Keys.Left | Keys.Control | Keys.Shift] =
        new ShiftWordLeft();
   //Code omitted for listing
   }
```

This goes on for quite a bit more and is pretty uninteresting. Much more interesting is the 'why' of this hash table. When we revert back to Chapter 3, we cannot help but think that this (initialization) is exactly what the AddIn tree was designed for. So why don't we use it in this case? The answer lies in the fact that we can also use this control in a standalone editor. In such a case, we will not have the SharpDevelop core at hand to provide an AddIn tree. Therefore, we must handle the initialization of the default edit actions inside the control itself. Besides, this is quite a good idea, as we can decouple the basic edit actions from the program we use the editor in.

The DefaultEditor used in SharpDevelop imports additional edit actions from the AddIn tree. In independent uses of the control, you may do something analogous for your own purposes. Another reason behind the use of a hash table is to speed up the key look-ups.

Speaking of building a standalone editor, such as SharpPad – which is provided with SharpDevelop – the inclusion of some additional code is necessary:

```
   public TextAreaControl() : this(new
     DocumentAggregatorFactory().CreateDocument())
   {
   }

   public TextAreaControl(IDocumentAggregator document)
   {
     textarea = new TextAreaPainter(this, document);
     gutter = new Gutter(textarea);

     clipboardhandler = new TextAreaClipboardHandler(this);
     mouseeventhandler = new TextAreaMouseHandler(this);

     Controls.Add(textarea);
     Controls.Add(rowpanel);
     Controls.Add(gutter);
     Controls.Add(vscrollbar);
     Controls.Add(hscrollbar);

     vscrollbar.ValueChanged +=
       new EventHandler(ScrollVScrollBar);
     hscrollbar.ValueChanged +=
       new EventHandler(ScrollHScrollBar);

     Resize += new System.EventHandler(ResizePanelEvent);
     gutter.Location = new Point(0, 0);
```

```
      textarea.Location = new Point(gutter.Width, 0);
      textarea.Resize +=
        new System.EventHandler(CalculateNewWindowBounds);

      Document.DocumentChanged +=
        new DocumentAggregatorEventHandler(BufferChange);
      Document.DocumentChanged +=
        new DocumentAggregatorEventHandler(DirtyChangedEvent);

      textarea.KeyPress += new KeyPressEventHandler(KeyPressed);
      document.Caret.OffsetChanged += new CaretEventHandler(NewCaretPos);

#if BuildAsStandalone
    //initialize the document properly
    document.HighlightingStrategy =
      HighlightingStrategyFactory.CreateHighlightingStrategy();
#endif
    ResizeRedraw = false;

    ruler = new Ruler(textarea);
    rowpanel.Controls.Add(ruler);

    Document.BookmarkManager.BeforeChanged +=
       new EventHandler(OnBeforeChangedBookMarks);
    Document.BookmarkManager.Changed += new EventHandler(OnChangedBookMarks);

    mouseeventhandler.Attach(this);
    caretthread = new Thread(new ThreadStart(CaretThreadMethod));
    caretthread.IsBackground = true;
    caretthread.Start();
    BufferChange(null, null);
    OptionsChanged();
    GenerateDefaultActions();
  }
```

Note that, in the editor, the caret is moved off into a separate thread because we cannot make it blink when it is inside the editor thread – the editor is busy looking at what we type. Having the caret in the same thread would slow down the editor in the user's subjective experience and prevent the caret from blinking regularly. The more the user typed, the slower the caret would blink – another factor in making the editor look slow.

The code for building a standalone editor is enclosed in the #if / #endif block. We also defined a number of properties of the editor earlier. We will only show a few of these here to give an idea of which properties are concerned. Again for the full code, refer to the SharpDevelop distribution.

```
// C# properties for some of the Editor Properties
// These allow someone to use the control and set some of
// the properties without knowing anything about SharpDevelop
public bool ShowSpaces
{
  get {
    return Properties.GetProperty("ShowSpaces", false);
  }
```

```
    set {
      Properties.SetProperty("ShowSpaces", value);
    }
  }

  public bool ShowTabs
  {
    get {
      return Properties.GetProperty("ShowTabs", false);
    }
    set {
      Properties.SetProperty("ShowTabs", value);
    }
  }

  public bool ShowEOLMarkers
  {
    get {
      return Properties.GetProperty("ShowEOLMarkers", false);
    }
    set {
      Properties.SetProperty("ShowEOLMarkers", value);
    }
  }
```

The listing above is quite essential for a standalone build. Now, let us look at the calculation of the width of the gutter to be displayed:

```
int CalculateGutterWidth()
{
  bool showLineNumbers = Properties.GetProperty("ShowLineNumbers", true);
  bool folding = Properties.GetProperty("EnableFolding", true);

  int lineSize = (folding ? 0 : 8) +
    (int) ((Math.Max(3, (int) (Math.Log10(Document.TotalNumberOfLines) +
    1))) * textarea.FontWidth);

  int foldingSize = 15;    // Arbitrary, but works for now
  return (int)((folding ? foldingSize : 0) +
    (showLineNumbers ? lineSize : 0));
  }
}
```

Calculating the width of the gutter is important, as it depends on how many digits we need in the line numbers. A gutter with a fixed width of, for example, three characters would probably be sufficient in most cases but provisions have to be made for longer files (having more than 999 lines). Here, we also see that we need to take folding into account when dealing with line numbers, as the numbers displayed should refer to lines in the file and not lines on the screen (remember the logical and visible of lines in Chapter 8?).

Folding the code block from the first figure of this chapter makes the display look like:

```
TextAreaControl.cs
|  |  |  |  |  |  |  |  |  |  |  |  |  |  |  |  |  |  |  |  |  |  |  |  |  |  |  |  |  |  |  |  |  |  |  |  |  |  |  |  |
440        bool showLineNumbers = Properties.GetProperty("Show
441        bool folding          = Properties.GetProperty("Enab
442        int  lineSize         = (folding ? 0 : 8) +(int)((Ma
443        int  foldingSize      = 15;
444        return (int)((folding ? foldingSize : 0) + (showLin
445    }
446
447    public void OptionsChanged()
448⊞   {
457    }
458
459    delegate void InvalidatePosDelegate(int offset);
460    delegate void UpdateDelegate();
461
462    /// <summary>
463    /// This method blinks the caret
464    /// </summary>
465    void CaretThreadMethod()
466⊟   {
467⊟       try {
468⊟           while (true) {
```

The square with the minus sign at line 448 has changed to a plus sign, indicating that the code block is folded away and the line numbers for the folded block are skipped.

A short historical note – up to and including version 0.89, the gutter was known as LineNumberView. It was renamed as the term 'view' has come to have a specific meaning in SharpDevelop. Refer to Chapter 6, for a definition of views in SharpDevelop.

Event Handling

Now, let's look at an example of event handling done in the editor – changing the options. The options are set by using three different panels, in the SharpDevelop options dialog. They are grouped into:

❑   **General**
     This contains the settings for code completion, folding, and screen font

❑   **Rulers and marker**
     For controlling the visibility of the rulers and markers

❑   **Behavior**
     For setting the tab width, indentation, and mouse wheel behavior

All these panels look quite similar:

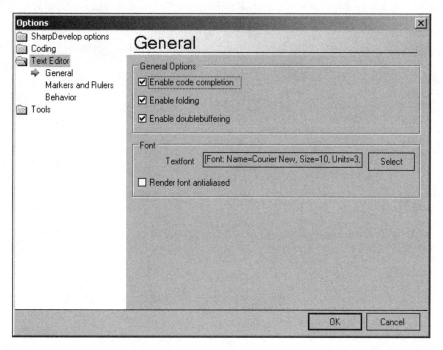

The settings from these dialogs are then passed on to our code by means of an event:

```
public void OptionsChanged()
{
  textarea.CalculateFontSize();
  rowpanel.Visible = Properties.GetProperty("ShowVRuler", false);

  gutter.Width = CalculateGutterWidth();

  ResizePanelEvent(null, null);
  CalculateNewWindowBounds(null, null);
  Refresh();
}
```

Here, we already get a hint that the font and font size selected for our editor window are important for correct rendering of the `TextArea`. Gutter width and column ruler also have to be updated, and then after resizing the panel, we can force a refresh.

Now, we have looked at quite a number of things that go on behind the scenes in our editor control. Next, we will consider how to handle editing. For this, we will use the task of inserting code. As we mentioned in Chapter 8, we have to differentiate between two different cases of insertion:

❑   Inserting a single character at the caret position

❑   Inserting a string at the caret position

These two cases are necessary, as sometimes entire strings need to be inserted into the code. A case when this occurs is when we perform a template insertion. The entire template string is inserted at once, instead of one character at a time:

```
public void InsertChar(char ch)
{
  BeginUpdate();
  if ((DocumentSelectionMode) Properties.GetProperty("SelectionMode",
    DocumentSelectionMode.Normal) == DocumentSelectionMode.Normal &&
    Document.SelectionCollection.Count > 0) {

    Document.Caret.Offset = Document.SelectionCollection[0].Offset;
    RemoveSelectedText();
  }

  Document.Insert(Document.Caret.Offset, ch.ToString());
  EndUpdate();

  int lineNr = Document.GetLineNumberForOffset(Document.Caret.Offset);
  UpdateLineToEnd(lineNr, Document.Caret.Offset -
    Document.GetLineSegment(lineNr).Offset);
  ++Document.Caret.Offset;

// Obsolete code below commented out - left in should we need a
// fall back
//   ++Document.Caret.DesiredColumn;
}

public void InsertString(string str)
{
  BeginUpdate();
  if ((DocumentSelectionMode)Properties.GetProperty(
    "SelectionMode", DocumentSelectionMode.Normal) ==
      DocumentSelectionMode.Normal &&
        Document.SelectionCollection.Count > 0) {

    Document.Caret.Offset = Document.SelectionCollection[0].Offset;
    RemoveSelectedText();
  }

  Document.Insert(Document.Caret.Offset, str);
  EndUpdate();

  int lineNr = Document.GetLineNumberForOffset(Document.Caret.Offset);
  UpdateLineToEnd(lineNr, Document.Caret.Offset -
    Document.GetLineSegment(lineNr).Offset);
  Document.Caret.Offset += str.Length;
// Obsolete code below, commented out - left in should we need
// a fallback.
//    Document.Caret.DesiredColumn += str.Length;
}
```

The main difference between these two methods is that for individual characters we use:

```
Document.Insert(Document.Caret.Offset, ch.ToString());
```

While, in case of string insertion we use:

```
Document.Insert(Document.Caret.Offset, str);
```

Please note that, both methods check for text selections made by the user, which are then deleted before inserting the input. After insertion, the line is updated and, when necessary, the line number will be adjusted. The caret position is updated last, so it will be redrawn in the appropriate position. This position is given in offset coordinates.

After inserting text, the number and length of lines may have changed, so we need to update the counts for these, as well as the size of the text buffer so that we know where we are in the buffer. For a single character insertion, we merely increase the offset by one:

```
++Document.Caret.Offset;
```

For a string, we add the string length to the caret offset:

```
Document.Caret.Offset += str.Length;
```

The other editing functions are similar in concept. Of course, all the editing actions depend on handling the keys pressed. This is done by the following code, for editing by insertion or replacement:

```
public void KeyPressed(object sender, KeyPressEventArgs e)
{
  if (Document.ReadOnly) {
    return;
  }

  char ch = e.KeyChar;
  if (ch < ' ') {
    return;
  }
  // This switch statement is here for later expansion. For now,
  // the default case is enough.
  switch (ch) {
    default:        // INSERT char
      if (!HandleKeyPress(ch)) {
        switch (Document.Caret.CaretMode) {
          case CaretMode.InsertMode:
          InsertChar(ch);
            break;
          case CaretMode.OverwriteMode:
            ReplaceChar(ch);
            break;
          default:
            Debug.Assert(false, "Unknown caret mode " +
```

```
                Document.Caret.CaretMode);
            break;
        }
    }
    break;
}
```

The behavior of the method is determined by looking at the caret mode. Next, we will look at handling dialog keys:

```
// This method executes a dialog key
public bool ExecuteDialogKey(Keys keyData)
{
  // Hack : two different '/' key codes !?!
  // really ugly stuff: two key codes for a slash depending on
  // where they come from. Possible .NET bug.
  if ((int)keyData == 131263) {
    keyData = Keys.Divide | Keys.Control;
  }

  // try, if a dialog key processor was set to use this
  if (ProcessDialogKeyProcessor != null &&
    ProcessDialogKeyProcessor(keyData)) {
    return true;
  }

  // if not (or the process was 'silent', use the standard
  // edit actions
  object action = editactions[keyData];
  autoClearSelection = true;
  if (action != null) {
    lock (Document) {
      ((IEditAction)action).Execute(this);
      if (HasSomethingSelected && autoClearSelection && caretchanged) {
        if ((DocumentSelectionMode)Properties. GetProperty(
          "SelectionMode", DocumentSelectionMode.Normal) ==
            DocumentSelectionMode.Normal) {
          ClearSelection();
        }
      }
    }
    return true;
  }
  return false;
}
```

Updating

Now that we have seen editing, we will look at the update methods. We need to distinguish between the different update types that are necessary for various update scenarios:

- ❑ UpdateLine
- ❑ UpdateLines
- ❑ UpdateToEnd
- ❑ UpdateLineToEnd
- ❑ BufferChange

It is quite clear what each of these updates does. The most important point to note is that BufferChange is of higher priority than the lesser updates concerning lines or line segments. It uses a separate document update flag for this purpose. The doUpdate flag for these minor updates is set using BeginUpdate and EndUpDate, so that the flag's status is always correct, considering what we just said about priority of updates:

```
bool doUpdate = false;
public void BeginUpdate()
{
  doUpdate = true;
}
public void EndUpdate()
{
  doUpdate = false;
  if (caretchanged) {
    NewCaretPos(null, null);
  }
}
```

If necessary, EndUpdate also readjusts the caret. Let's now look at one of the update methods:

```
public void UpdateLine(int line)
{
  UpdateLines(0, line, line);
}
public void UpdateLines(int xPos, int lineBegin, int lineEnd)
{
  //Do local copies of the vars, so we won't corrupt them.
  lineBegin = lineBegin;
  lineEnd = lineEnd;
  InvalidateLines((int)(xPos * textarea.FontWidth), lineBegin, lineEnd);
}
```

This code calls the InvalidateLines method, given below, which is overloaded; it marks the lines that are in need of being updated on the next redraw:

```
public void InvalidateLines(int xPos, int lineBegin, int lineEnd)
{
  if (doUpdate) {
```

```
      return;
    }
    int firstLine = vscrollbar.Value;
    lineBegin =
      Math.Max(Document.GetLogicalLine(lineBegin), vscrollbar.Value);

    lineEnd = Math.Min(lineEnd, vscrollbar.Value + maxVisibleLine);
    int y = Math.Max( 0, (int)(lineBegin * textarea.FontHeight));

    int height = Math.Min(textarea.Height,
      (int)((1 + lineEnd - lineBegin) * (textarea.FontHeight + 1)));
    int xScreen = xPos - textarea.ScreenVirtualLeft;

    textarea.Invalidate(new Rectangle(xScreen,
      y - 1 - textarea.ScreenVirtualTop, textarea.Width - xScreen,
      height + 3));
  }

  public void InvalidateLines(int from, int length, int lineBegin,
                              int lineEnd)
  {
    if (doUpdate) {
      return;
    }
    int firstLine = vscrollbar.Value;
    lineBegin = Math.Max(lineBegin, vscrollbar.Value);
    lineEnd = Math.Min(lineEnd, vscrollbar.Value + maxVisibleLine);
    int y = Math.Max( 0, (int)(lineBegin * textarea.FontHeight));
    int height = Math.Min(textarea.Height,
      (int) ((1 + lineEnd - lineBegin) * (textarea.FontHeight + 1)));

    textarea.Invalidate(new Rectangle((int)
      (textarea.FontWidth * from) - textarea.ScreenVirtualLeft,
      y - 1 - textarea.ScreenVirtualTop, (int)(textarea.FontWidth * length),
      height + 3));
  }
```

This code uses functionality from the TextAreaPainter, to display the contents of the text buffer on the screen.

Now, let's take a quick look at selections:

```
public void SetSelection(ISelection selection)
{
  autoClearSelection = false;
  ClearSelection();

  if (selection != null) {
    Document.SelectionCollection.Add(selection);
    UpdateLines(selection.StartLine, selection.EndLine);
  }
}
```

```
public void ClearSelection()
{
  while (Document.SelectionCollection.Count > 0) {
    ISelection s = Document.SelectionCollection[Document.
      SelectionCollection.Count - 1];

    Document.SelectionCollection.RemoveAt(Document.
      SelectionCollection.Count - 1);
    UpdateLines(s.StartLine, s.EndLine);
  }
}
public string GetSelectedText()
{
  StringBuilder builder = new StringBuilder();
  PriorityQueue queue = new PriorityQueue();
  foreach (ISelection s in Document.SelectionCollection) {
    queue.Insert(-s.Offset, s);
  }
  while (queue.Count > 0) {
    ISelection s = ((ISelection)queue.Remove());
    builder.Append(s.SelectedText);
  }
  return builder.ToString();
}
```

In this code segment, we add (or remove) the selection being made from a collection of selections, as multiple selections will be supported in the future. By planning ahead, we can minimize refactoring requirements in future. Next, we need to update the lines selected. Not so hard to do after all, isn't it?

The GetSelectedText method, in the above snippet, actually obtains the text selected and makes it available as a string. To this end, we build a queue into which we insert all the text contained in the collection made up from the line segments selected and then concatenate them into a string, removing the items concatenated from the queue.

Now let us move on to another central part of our editor control, the TextAreaPainter.

The TextAreaPainter

By now, we know almost everything that we need for implementing our editor in full. There's one exception – how do we get the text onto the screen? The user's perception about the responsiveness of an editor depends very much on the implementation of the screen rendering. What use are clever text models and efficient editing routines when the display of typed text lags noticeably behind typing speed?

Let's go back to the 'dark ages' of SharpDevelop – the earliest versions of the editor were integrated into SharpDevelop itself. This proved to be a bad idea, as it made maintenance of the code quite hard. We found that being able to implement different editors would be a better option. Later on, we decoupled the editor, but that was not the end of our problems. With our initial approach we encountered a massive problem. We used a painter control to display text, which in itself does not sound too bad, but the problem we encountered was quite interesting – the number of lines we could display was limited, and worse it varied with font and font size!

This was due to the fact that in vertical direction, the painter control can only handle a certain number of pixels, 32,768 pixels to be precise. As the pixel height of fonts varies with font size and type, the number of lines we could display varied as a function of these two parameters. Using the default font settings in SharpDevelop, this control could not display more than 2,100 lines. On the other hand, using the control was fast. It was faster than the approach we are using now, but the limit on the number of lines was annoying. Therefore, when we finally found a way to work around this limit we decided to use it, even though it involved a slight tradeoff in performance.

The `TextAreaPainter` contains the code responsible for the actual screen rendering of the text in our buffer, including all the trappings of formatting and highlighting. At more than 650 lines of code, this is also a substantial part of SharpDevelop. We cannot go into every single method contained in this file, so we will only discuss the important ones. Unless otherwise mentioned, the code given in this section is contained in the `\src\SharpDevelop\ICSharpCode.TextEditor\TextAreaPainter.cs` file.

We will now look at the trick applied to get around the limitations of the painter control:

```
// This class paints the textarea.
public class TextAreaPainter : Control
{
  // The TextAreaControl that owns this painter
  TextAreaControl textAreaControl = null;

  int screenVirtualTop  = 0;
  int screenVirtualLeft = 0;

  IDocumentAggregator document;
  PrintDocument printdocument;

  StringFormat measureStringFormat = StringFormat.GenericTypographic;

  ToolTip toolTip = new ToolTip();

  float fontWidth;
  float fontHeight;

  bool iHaveTheFocusLock = false;
  bool iHaveTheFocus = false;

  // internationalization support
  Ime ime = null;
  static Encoding encoding = null;

  public ToolTip ToolTip {
    get {
      return toolTip;
    }
    set {
      toolTip = value;
    }
  }

}
```

Did you spot the trick used in this code snippet? We are using virtual coordinates instead of the real x-y coordinates of the text buffer. To the painter control we show only a window into our buffer, always staying safely inside the limitations on size the control imposes, as discussed above. This makes response a little slower for the user, but then we don't have to limit the size of source code files that we can edit. Another point, central to correctly painting the `TextArea`, is the way strings are measured. To this end, we need to choose the correct measurement model:

```
StringFormat measureStringFormat = StringFormat.GenericTypographic;
```

We need to use `StringFormat` to avoid a problem inherent in TrueType fonts. At lower resolutions (not screen size, but the size of the pixels), TrueType fonts render badly because they are based on a vector design, which scales nicely with resolution. On a 600 dpi printer, such a font will be quite close in appearance to its design, but on a 96 dpi display screen a lot of details, such as serifs, will be lost and the letter may even be slightly shifted to the left or right. In some cases, the spacing between adjacent letters will also look irregular.

To some degree, these problems can be alleviated through **hinting** by the designer; this means that the designer will include instructions on how to best fit a glyph into given grid sizes. Until the arrival of .NET, the rendering was done by the GDI, which had problems in some cases. Now rendering is performed with the new GDI+. This has improved the rendering of fonts, and buffering which is also one of the background factors influencing perceived editor speed. This is yet another way in which .NET makes things better without extra effort on our part.

If you want to read more about the issues involved in resolution and font rendering, read the article at http://www.gotdotnet.com/team/windowsforms/gdiptext.aspx.

Now, we can finally solve the mystery of why we said that the horizontal ruler and the placing of the column ruler are only approximate. Fonts can use two different approaches for spacing between letters:

❑ **Monospaced Letters**
All monospaced letters have the same width – the letter 'X' has the same width as the letter 'l' – they are set into a rectangle of space, which is of the same size for any letter in the font. This is how older typewriter fonts usually work. A line written with such a font always contains the same number of letters.

❑ **Proportional Spacing**
Proportional spacing is aesthetically much more pleasing, as the distance between the letters is kept constant. In other words, the width of the rectangle into which the character is drawn varies with the character width. Or even worse, from our viewpoint for this section, they can overlap or intersect. Typographers call this **kerning**, and it makes for greater ease of reading but lots of headaches for us.

To see a rather extreme example of kerning, look at the figure overleaf and consider the XML comments starting with the three slashes, each in lines 472 to 475:

It shows the SharpDevelop editor with the Curlz MT font selected. Even the extreme spacing of such a font is handled gracefully. However, actually using such a font is not recommended from an ergonomic point of view.

Lines set in proportionally spaced fonts may contain varying numbers of characters in a given number of pixels. Furthermore, .NET does not always return proper character widths, even for monospaced fonts (in TrueType), which means that we can only set the rulers to averaged positions. You can see this for yourself in the second screenshot of this chapter; pay attention to how the column ruler sometimes cuts through characters.

Another thing we saw in the source code above, is that we have to handle focus changes. We need to do this so that we can make the caret invisible when the focus is away from the TextArea and we need to indicate that no editing can be done at this time. This is necessary, for example, when code completion is active and the user is supposed to select an item from the drop box.

Now let us get on with our code; here's another snippet:

```
static TextAreaPainter()
{
  try {
    encoding = Encoding.GetEncoding(Thread.CurrentThread.
      CurrentCulture.TextInfo.ANSICodePage);
  } catch (Exception) {
  }
}
```

When initializing our TextAreaPainter, we need to set the correct code page for the culture selected by the user, so that the text gets handled properly. The issues involved in internationalization were discussed in Chapter 7.

Now let's look at the code for painting a line:

```
// This Method paints the characters on the screen
void PaintTextLine(Graphics g, int lineNumber, RectangleF rect, PointF pos,
                   int virtualLeft, int virtualTop)
{
  int logicalXPosition = (int)(pos.X / fontWidth);
  bool lineIsBookmark = Document.BookmarkManager.IsMarked(lineNumber);

// Set up Syntax Highlighting and get the virtual code window ready.
  HighlightColor defaultColor =
    document.HighlightingStrategy.GetColorFor("DefaultColor");

  double drawingXPos = -virtualLeft;
  if (lineNumber >= Document.TotalNumberOfLines) {
    PaintInvalidTextLine(g, (int)(pos.X - virtualLeft),
      (int)(pos.Y - virtualTop));
    } else {
    LineSegment line = document.GetLineSegment(lineNumber);

    if (line.Words == null) {
      string text = document.GetText(line.Offset, line.Length);
      float xPos = 0;

      for (int i = 0; i < text.Length; ++i) {
      // Get tabs set. Hard coded for the moment, but see below.
        if (text[i] == '\t') {
          g.DrawString("    ", defaultColor.Font,
            new SolidBrush(defaultColor.Color), xPos - virtualLeft,
            pos.Y - virtualTop);

          xPos += g.MeasureString("    ", defaultColor.Font, 100,
            measureStringFormat).Width;
        } else {
          g.DrawString(text[i].ToString(), defaultColor.Font,
            new SolidBrush(defaultColor.Color), xPos - virtualLeft,
            pos.Y - virtualTop);

          xPos += g.MeasureString(text[i].ToString(),defaultColor.Font, 100,
            measureStringFormat).Width;
        }
      }
    }
```

After handling the default text case, we move on to special cases in highlighting, such as spaces, tabs, bookmarks, and so on:

```
    } else {
      HighlightColor spaceMarkerColor =
        document.HighlightingStrategy.GetColorFor("SpaceMarker");

      HighlightColor tabMarkerColor=
        document.HighlightingStrategy.GetColorFor("TabMarker");
      HighlightColor bookmarkColor =
        document.HighlightingStrategy. GetColorFor("Bookmark");
```

```
for (int i = 0; i < line.Words.Count; ++i) {
  switch (((TextWord)line.Words[i]).Type) {
    case TextWordType.Space:
      if (Properties.GetProperty("ShowSpaces", false) &&
        pos.X < rect.X + rect.Width) {
        g.DrawString("\u00B7", spaceMarkerColor.Font,
          new SolidBrush(spaceMarkerColor.Color),
          (int)drawingXPos, pos.Y - virtualTop);
      }
      drawingXPos += g.MeasureString(" ", defaultColor.Font, 2000,
        measureStringFormat).Width;
      ++logicalXPosition;
      break;

    // here tabs get done for real.
    case TextWordType.Tab:
      if (Properties.GetProperty("ShowTabs", false) &&
        pos.X < rect.X + rect.Width) {
        g.DrawString("\u00BB", tabMarkerColor.Font,
          new SolidBrush(tabMarkerColor.Color),
          (int)drawingXPos, pos.Y - virtualTop);
      }
      int oldLogicalXPosition = logicalXPosition;
      logicalXPosition += Properties.GetProperty("TabIndent", 4);
      logicalXPosition =
        (logicalXPosition /Properties.GetProperty("TabIndent", 4)) *
        Properties.GetProperty("TabIndent", 4);

      string measureMe = "";
      for (int j = 0; j < logicalXPosition - oldLogicalXPosition; ++j)
        {
        measureMe += " ";
      }
      drawingXPos += g.MeasureString(measureMe, defaultColor.Font,
        2000, measureStringFormat).Width;
      break;

    case TextWordType.Word:
      g.DrawString(((TextWord)line.Words[i]).Word,
        ((TextWord)line.Words[i]).Font, new SolidBrush(lineIsBookmark
        ? bookmarkColor.Color : ((TextWord)line. Words[i]).Color),
        (int)drawingXPos, pos.Y - virtualTop, measureStringFormat);

      drawingXPos += g.MeasureString(((TextWord)line.Words[i]).Word,
        ((TextWord)line.Words[i]). Font, 2000,
        measureStringFormat).Width;

      if (encoding != null) {
        logicalXPosition += encoding.GetByteCount(((TextWord)
            line.Words[i]).Word);
      } else {
        logicalXPosition += ((TextWord)line.Words[i]).Word.Length;
      }
      break;
```

```
        }
      }
    }

    // paint EOL markers, when they are set to visible
    if (Properties.GetProperty("ShowEOLMarkers", false) &&
        pos.X < rect.X + rect.Width) {
      HighlightColor EolMarkerColor =
        document.HighlightingStrategy.GetColorFor("EolMarker");
      g.DrawString("\u00B6", EolMarkerColor.Font,
        new SolidBrush(EolMarkerColor.Color),
        (int)drawingXPos, pos.Y - virtualTop);
    }
  }
}
```

This code demonstrates how we address the various problems, which we had discussed. We use proper string measurement for lines and handle our coordinates in the virtual x-y system. Characters of wider width, as already discussed in Chapter 8, are handled, as are tabs depending on the tab width the user has specified. To this end, we apply formatting dependent on the TextWordType, which can either be tab, space, or word. We also have code to handle the optional display of the end-of-line (EOL) markers.

Mouse Management

Mouse management is just a tedious matter of recalculating caret positions depending on the mouse's position on the screen, highlighting selections when the mouse button stays clicked, and so on. We will look at the interaction between the mouse and caret, but we won't go into too much of details. The code can be found in the \src\SharpDevelop\IcSharpCode.TextEditor\TextAreaMouseHandler.cs file.

We will just take a peek at how the caret is placed when the mouse is clicked inside the TextArea:

```
public void OnMouseClick(object sender, EventArgs e)
{
  if (dodragdrop) {
    return;
  }

  if (clickedOnSelectedText) {
  textarea.ClearSelection();
  Point realmousepos = new Point(0, 0);

  realmousepos.Y = Math.Min(textarea.Document.
    TotalNumberOfLines - 1, Math.Max(0, (
    (int)((mousepos.Y + textarea.TextAreaPainter.ScreenVirtualTop) /
    textarea.TextAreaPainter.FontHeight)))) ;

  LineSegment line = textarea.Document.GetLineSegment(realmousepos.Y);

  realmousepos.X = textarea.TextAreaPainter.GetVirtualPos(line,
    mousepos.X + extarea.TextAreaPainter.ScreenVirtualLeft);
```

```
      Point pos = new Point();
      pos.Y =
        Math.Min(textarea.Document.TotalNumberOfLines - 1, realmousepos.Y);
      pos.X = realmousepos.X;

      textarea.Document.Caret.Offset = textarea.Document.ViewToOffset(pos);
      textarea.Document.SetDesiredColumn();
    }
  }
```

Here, we see a nice example of the relationship between the real coordinates of the text buffer and the virtual coordinates of the painter control. We obtain our virtual coordinates for the position where the click happened and convert them to buffer coordinates, stored in realmousepos.Y and realmousepos.X, by adding appropriate offsets. Finally the caret position is updated.

Folding

Now for a quick look at folding. We will only consider the drawing of the fold marker in the gutter, as the internal representation of folding in the text has been discussed while looking at the text model in Chapter 8. Basically, the intention of this short section is to demonstrate drawing in the gutter of the editor.

The source code can be found in the \src\SharpDevelop\IcSharpCode.TextEditor\Gutter.cs file.

The function needed for drawing the folding indicator is:

```
void DrawFoldMarker(Graphics g, RectangleF rectangle, bool isClosed)
{
  HighlightColor foldMarkerColor =
    textarea.Document.HighlightingStrategy.GetColorFor("FoldMarker");

  HighlightColor foldLineColor = textarea.Document.HighlightingStrategy.
    GetColorFor("FoldLine");

  g.FillRectangle(new
    SolidBrush(foldMarkerColor.BackgroundColor), rectangle);

  g.DrawRectangle(new Pen(new SolidBrush(foldMarkerColor.Color)),
    new Rectangle(((int)rectangle.X,
    (int)rectangle.Y,(int)rectangle.Width,  (int)rectangle.Height));

  g.DrawLine(new Pen(new SolidBrush(foldLineColor.BackgroundColor)),
    rectangle.X + 2, rectangle.Y + rectangle.Height / 2,
    rectangle.X + rectangle.Width - 2, rectangle.Y + rectangle.Height / 2);

  if (isClosed) {
    g.DrawLine(new Pen(new SolidBrush(foldLineColor.BackgroundColor)),
      rectangle.X + rectangle.Width / 2, rectangle.Y + 2,
      rectangle.X + rectangle.Width / 2,
      rectangle.Y + rectangle.Height - 2);
  }
}
```

Most of this code just calls methods from the `System.Drawing` namespace. Colors for drawing are taken from the highlighting strategy applicable for the current file. The marker drawn depends on the Boolean state of `isClosed`; if `true`, the code is folded. We can see that the visualization of such status markers is quite easy to implement. Perhaps, you can think of other markers to implement, for example, flagging lines that had errors when the file was last built and so on.

SharpPad

As a freebie, you will find that SharpDevelop comes with a minimalist replacement for the Windows Notepad. The source code of SharpPad can be found in the `\samples\SharpPad\SharpPad.cs` file.

Bryan Livingston, one of our contributors, wrote this editor. Using a little over 400 lines of code, he implemented an editor by using the SharpDevelop editor control. Let us look at the namespaces that we need to import:

```
using System;
using System.Drawing;
using System.Collections;
using System.ComponentModel;
using System.Windows.Forms;
using System.Data;

using ICSharpCode.TextEditor;
```

Besides some namespaces from the .NET Framework, we only need to import our text editor! No other functionality has to be borrowed from SharpDevelop. Now you must have realized why the edit actions were put into the editor control itself and not into the AddIn tree, as would have be the proper approach had the control only been designed for use inside SharpDevelop. The editor Bryan wrote is really quite barebones, as you can see for yourself from the following screenshot. It shows SharpPad with the `authors.txt` file for SharpDevelop:

Most of the source code in SharpPad was auto-generated using Visual Studio .NET, so we will skip this part. We will concern ourselves only with the initializing and cleaning up components and the `Main` block.

First, we will look at the code for initialization and disposal:

```
private TextAreaControl FTextArea = new TextAreaControl();

public SharpPad()
{
  InitializeComponent();

  FTextArea.Dock = DockStyle.Fill;
  FTextArea.ShowInvalidLines = false;
  FTextArea.ShowLineNumbers = false;
  FTextArea.EnableFolding   = false;
  FTextArea.TabIndent = 3;

  Controls.Add(FTextArea);
}

// Clean up any resources being used.
protected override void Dispose( bool disposing )
{
  if( disposing )
  {
    if (components != null)
    {
      components.Dispose();
    }
  }
  base.Dispose( disposing );
}
```

It's quite what we would expect, except for some deviations from our coding style guide. But that is understandable; its author wasn't a member of the core team. The only item worth noting is that of all the functionality of the control only the tab indent is used; all others are set to `false`. After all, this is just to show standalone use of the control. Now let's move on to `Main`:

```
// The main entry point for the application.
 [STAThread]

static void Main()
{
  Application.Run(new SharpPad());
}

private void OpenMenuItem_Click(object sender, System.EventArgs e)
{
  if(OpenFileDialog.ShowDialog() == DialogResult.OK)
    FTextArea.LoadFile(OpenFileDialog.FileName);
}

private void SaveAsMenuItem_Click(object sender, System.EventArgs e)
{
  if(SaveFileDialog.ShowDialog() == DialogResult.OK)
    FTextArea.SaveFile(SaveFileDialog.FileName);
```

```
        }

    private void CloseMenuItem_Click(object sender, System.EventArgs e)
    {
      Close();
    }
    }
```

Apart from the Form code, we do not need more than these few lines to create our own editor by using the SharpDevelop editor control!

Summary

In this chapter, we looked at the editor control in SharpDevelop, how it fits in with the MVC model, and the components needed for it. We looked at the segments of code responsible for performing various tasks, like initialization, handling editing actions, updating the buffer, and selecting text.

We have dealt with the TextAreaPainter and the tradeoffs involved in making this kind of code work well. Next we concerned ourselves with mouse handling; then, we looked at drawing the folding markers in the gutter, as an example for working outside the TextArea.

Finally, we took a peek into the standalone implementation of editors, by using the SharpDevelop editor control. We used SharpPad, which is included with the SharpDevelop distribution, as an example.

CHAPTER 12

12

Writing the Parser

As the next step in moving SharpDevelop from editor to full-blown IDE, we will now look at writing a (partial) parser. A parser is an important component in such a piece of software, as it makes the IDE aware of the kind of text it is handling. Information provided by the parser (parse information) can be used by the IDE to offer a number of useful features, such as code completion – we will look at uses of parse information in the two subsequent chapters, 13 and 14.

In this chapter, we will examine the basic concepts behind programming language representation and the construction of parsers. Then, we will move on to discuss the design decisions regarding the actual implementation of a parser in SharpDevelop, including the reasons for not implementing a full (statement-level) parser, and the reasoning behind splitting the parser into an abstract layer and a language layer.

Finally, we will look at the implementation of our parser, examining how the parse tree is built and made accessible to the code relying on parser data.

Need for a Parser

At first glance, a parser may seem a strange thing to include in an IDE, as the code is handed over to the compiler for compilation (and then to the runtime for execution). Compilers include a parser, so you may well ask why we would need a separate parser at all; especially, because SharpDevelop handles compilation and execution of the programs by passing them to either the compiler or the runtime as required.

The answer is simple – a number of features in SharpDevelop need to be aware of the structure of the program at hand. These features are:

- ❑   Code Completion
- ❑   Method Insight
- ❑   The Class Scout

Note that syntax highlighting is not on this list, as it has its own, much simpler, mechanism for determining the nature of code elements (refer to Chapter 9). Syntax highlighting does not need a full parser, but rather only the lexical analyzer (also called a **lexer**).

In SharpDevelop, we first introduced syntax highlighting and then developed a mechanism to provide highlighting for arbitrary programming languages and styles. Only later in the life of our project, did we implement code completion and find that we needed a different approach, namely a parser.

In the next chapter, we will be looking at the inner workings of Code Completion and Method Insight; the Class Scout will be the topic of Chapter 14. In this chapter, we will look at how the parse information is made available, for the use of these features.

Parser and Language Theory

Before delving into the SharpDevelop parser, we need to get acquainted with the basic concepts behind parsing. Parsing is a huge topic however, we will be restricting our discussion to the most basic topics and some of the advanced topics, needed for understanding the parser at hand. If you want to obtain in-depth knowledge about parsing techniques and the issues involved, please refer to the book *Parsing Techniques – A Practical Guide* by Dick Grune and Ceriel J.H. Jacobs (ISBN 0-13-651431-6). As this book is out of print, you can try accessing its online version at http://www.cs.vu.nl/~dick/PTAPG.html.

Basic Definitions and Theory

First, we need to introduce a few definitions so that we have a common ground for our discussion. If you are familiar with the theory of parsers and the linguistics behind them, then you can safely skip ahead to the sections dealing with design decisions and implementation.

The text in an editor (or an IDE for that matter) is represented in a buffer (as we learned in Chapter 8). Even though the actual representation used in SharpDevelop is a gap buffer, we can consider the text as a contiguous string of characters. For our model, this is obvious when we look at the user coordinates, which disregard the buffer.

Parsing can be defined as structuring a linear representation of text in accordance with grammar. This means that we break up the text buffer into its elements according to rules, identifying the elements by their type. For example, English sentences can be broken up into nouns, verbs, adverbs, and so on. They may also be divided into different bigger entities called clauses. The types are identified by a lexer, which determines what type a word belongs to. The relationships between these elements are then established according to grammatical rules.

Now, let us discuss a bit about grammar. Again, if you know about parsing theory, you may safely skip this section.

Grammar

Grammar is a set of rules (we might also say a recipe) for producing valid sentences or expressions in a language. This sounds quite simple, but as we all know from practice, theory put to practice usually is not quite that simple. The complexity of language varies wildly. There are languages consisting of just a few letters, such as 'a', 'b', 'c', or even merely '1' and '0', but they are used in very formal contexts, such as linguistic theory or mathematics. On the other end of the spectrum, we have human languages with very complex rules, character sets that can include thousands of characters and exceptions to just about any rule.

Grammars can be classified into a number of types, called **Chomsky Grammars**. These types are derived from the top level, by applying restrictions on what can be done inside the scope of the grammar. We have listed these types in the following table, in descending order of complexity and power:

Type	Name	Restriction
Type 0	Phase structure grammar	Unrestricted
Type 1	Context-sensitive grammar	Only one 'left hand' symbol gets changed by a rule
Type 2	Context-free grammar	Only one symbol may be on the left side of the rule
Type 3	Regular grammar	On the right side, we may only have either a termination or a substitution followed by a termination
Type 4	Finite choice grammar	Only a termination can occur on the right side

For an in-depth discussion on grammars refer to Chapter 2 (Section 2.3) of the book by Grune and Jacobs.

Type 0 languages correspond to human languages with complete freedom and possible ambiguities inherent to them. As we go up, the types become more and more restrictive in what they can express; ending up with completely predictable statements of the nature '1 + 1 = 2'. Computer languages are found somewhere between the Type 1 and Type 2, depending on how we look at them.

Context sensitive, that is Type 1, might mean that a statement containing a variable assignment can only occur after the variable has been declared. If we are looking at the statement without looking at the entire program it is contained in, we can consider it to be of Type 2. Regular expressions can be seen as examples of a Type 3 language. Unless you really want to understand language theory fully, don't worry too much about these types.

In the previous table, we have talked quite a bit about 'left' and 'right' sides; we need some way to represent such rules, so that these terms will make sense. In the world of parser grammars (and linguistics), as per convention, the recipient is placed on the left side of the statement.

Now, consider this small fragment of a possible context-free (in short, CF) grammar:

```
variable -> foo|bar
statement -> (statement, variable)|variable
```

It means that the grammar element `variable` may be replaced by either `foo` or `bar`, and that the element `statement` may be replaced by `statement` appended with an element `variable` (either, `foo` or `bar`), or simply with a variable.

This trivial example doesn't do anything useful in itself, but it illustrates our idea of 'left side' and 'right side' in a grammar. Please keep in mind that, even though there is a superficial resemblance, such rules cannot be mapped onto assignment statements in programming languages. A sentence, in the grammatical sense, corresponds to any statement or construct in a programming language, be that an assignment or a conditional statement.

These rules work together to generate a potentially infinite set of sentences (from a grammatical point of view). However, not all programs that compile without error, according to the grammar, will do anything useful.

For the purposes of our discussion, we will only need to understand Type 2 grammars. From now on we will refer to them as **CF grammars**. Apart from a few exceptions, such as FORTRAN, most programming languages fall into this category. However, strictly speaking, almost all programming languages aren't purely CF, but for our purposes they are, as we look at the program from a low-level perspective where overall context does not matter. Later on in this chapter, we will look at the implications of this for our parser.

For CF grammars, we can find two meanings in one and the same word. For example, the sentence 'time flies' can be considered as grammatically correct, if one of the words is taken as a verb.

The statement that C# is a Type 2 grammar is not completely true. There are some context sensitivities hidden in the language, such as the requirement that variables must be declared before use. However, this only affects the compiler and is not of interest for our purpose. Since it doesn't concern our parser, we will not talk about this aspect. It also means that our parser is only a partial parser; whereas, the compiler's parser is a full parser, understanding the program code at all levels.

There are a number of representations available for representing grammatical expressions. Grammars are made up of **production rules** – recipes for creating valid sentences. As far as C# is concerned, the representation chosen for standardization was **eBNF** – the **extended Backus-Naur Form**. Basic BNF looks somewhat like this:

```
<statement>ₛ ::=  <value> | <line> + <value>
<value> ::= foo | bar | baz
<line>::= <value> - <line> | <value>
```

In this snippet, the angled brackets represent non-terminations (or placeholders) and the ::= means 'may be replaced by'. The components that go into a sentence are called tokens and are separated by whitespace. Rules and sentences are terminated by newlines. The subscript s indicates the starting statement of our rule set. Our example can produce outputs like these:

```
Foo

foo - baz

foo - baz + bar

foo + foo

bar - baz
```

We will admit that these outputs aren't really meaningful, but they do give us a fair idea of where CF grammars can lead us. Now, the remaining part is to introduce short-hand representations for repetitious bits of grammar. Spelling out things, such as 'one or more of the following', 'zero or more of something' is tedious work. Thus, abbreviations were invented, such as a superscript '+' for the former and a superscript '*' for the latter. The actual implementation of the parser was derived from grammar of this form.

Now let's move on to parsing.

Parsing

As we mentioned earlier, parsing is the structuring of a linear representation of a text according to a grammar, or as we will consider it now, the reconstruction of the production tree made up of a set of production rules applied sequentially to a starting input resulting in a given sentence.

A given grammar can produce an infinite number of valid sentences; not to mention the infinity of syntactically invalid sentences our parser may face, which were produced outside of its scope and just thrown at it. Our previous example hints at the fact that a tree can indeed represent the output produced by a grammar. In other words, when applying a rule we have a number of choices that we can branch into. For our example, starting with foo, we can obtain the following tree:

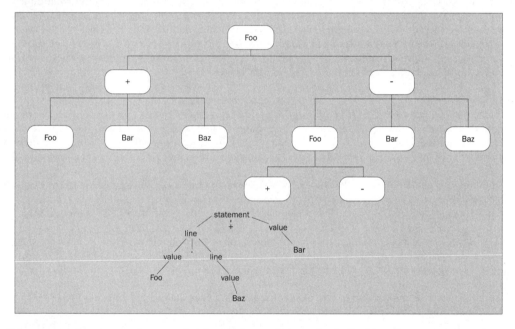

Of course, such a tree can be extended down to any arbitrary depth. Building the tree consists of two steps:

- ❏ **Identifying the tokens**
  This is called lexical analysis (or lexing), and

- ❏ **Identifying the rules that led to them**
  That is parsing proper

After creating the tree, we can examine such a tree in two distinct ways:

- ❏ Top-down, and

- ❏ Bottom-up

Any further subdivision of parsing techniques is a matter of the implementation of the approach chosen. 'Top-down' means that we start at the root, situated at the top of the tree representation, and work down through the branches, until we finally find the branch representing the statement we want to parse. In 'bottom-up' parsing, we look at the final sentence/output and try to work our way back to the root of the parse tree.

Next, we need to consider the searching technique for finding the correct sequence of operation to recreate our sentence. Again, we have two alternative approaches available to us:

- ❑   Depth-first, and
- ❑   Breadth-first

In the depth-first approach, our search follows each branch to its end and, if no correct solution is found, returns to the node and then proceeds on the next un-searched branch. This behavior is called **backtracking**. Breadth-first searching looks at all half-finished solutions at a given level of the tree, at the same time; when no valid solution is found at this level, it moves down to the next level. Obviously, combinations of approach and searching techniques are possible. However, discussing them and their possible implementations is beyond the scope of this book.

Another important factor to be taken into account, when choosing such a combination and its implementation, is the complexity of the algorithm. Here, complexity refers to the number of operations required to search the tree; this depends on the number of nodes. The number of operations determines the execution time. Unfortunately, for searching operations the complexity is exponential; this leaves the reduction of the exponent, as a way to minimizing execution times. Let's illustrate this with numbers.

Commonly, for general parsers (that is, for context-sensitive grammars) the known algorithms can only reach an exponent of 3; that is, the computational effort is given by a cubic equation. This means that 10 nodes would require 1,000 operations whereas 100 nodes would require 1,000,000 operations!

At first sight, this looks depressing – even a modest increase in the number of nodes increases the number of required operations by a large amount. Therefore, no such general parsers exist in practice. By specializing a parser for exactly one context-free language (grammar), we can do significantly better. Such parsers can reach linear time, which means the relation between the number of nodes and the operations merely is multiplicative, not exponential. This means that we can create a parser that will work in real time for SharpDevelop.

Technical Requirements

Before we can start designing our SharpDevelop parser, we have to consider the requirements for implementing a parser. A parser is made up of two parts – a control unit and an automaton performing the actual tedious work. The control unit reconstructs the tree from the output of the automaton, while the automaton corresponds to the lexer. The automaton bears a little further explanation.

This part of the parser is a non-deterministic automaton (NDA). It is an automaton because it performs its actions in response to encoded rules. As it can often make one of several possible choices, at any given point of its operation, it is considered to be non-deterministic.

Now, let's take a look at the information flow in a parser:

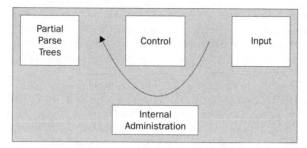

The general flow of information, in a parser, goes from the input to the partial parse trees, as output. It affects, and is affected by, the control and internal administration of the automaton. Usually, all the parts of a parser are affected by each step that is performed.

For example, the result of applying a rule to the input results in a decision being made by the control part, as to which rule should be used next. Internal administration has to handle the result, inserting it into the reconstructed statement and comparing it to the input to check whether the input is matched. The parse tree also changes according to the result of the applied rule.

The good thing about an NDA is that, as long as the input conforms to the grammar, the information in all parts is consistent. Of course, this cannot prevent the parser from getting stuck or moving in circles when trying to identify the rule sequence leading to the input at hand, but at least it guarantees that any parse tree eventually handed over to us is valid for our grammar. This is good to know, as we do not need to check the tree's validity externally.

We achieve a correct parse tree as soon as the state of the NDA's internal administration, which handles the reconstructed input, corresponds to the input string we copied for parsing. This is referred to as the reconstruction of the production tree resulting in a given sentence.

This background should be enough for you to understand how we designed and implemented the SharpDevelop parser.

The SharpDevelop Parser

We will now move on to discuss the implementation of the SharpDevelop parser.

We will begin by discussing the design decisions we made about the parser. After that, we will go on to look at the code for the parser and its working.

Design Decisions

When designing a parser, we have a number of important design decisions to make.

Do we need a parser, or will the features of the framework be enough to obtain the information we need? The answer is – we do, because while the powerful reflection feature of .NET can be used to extract information from (external) assemblies, it will not help us at all when extracting information from a text buffer.

What parsing technique should we use? As SharpDevelop provides extensible support for other programming languages, how should that be handled with regard to parsing? Should we use one general parser or a number of specific parsers? As experience in the field has shown, using a general parser, or rather a parser generator, is not practical for our purpose. The performance of general parsers is terrible, as their time dependency is exponential while language-specific parsers are time linear. Having a parser that takes four times as long for twice the file size is clearly out of the question.

At the outset, we just had a parser for C#, as that was – and is – the main focus of our development efforts. SharpDevelop itself is written in C#, so implementing a parser for it seemed natural. As SharpDevelop grew in popularity, other languages needed support too. So our choice was between implementing lots of different parsers and adapting the interfaces, with the features using the parsers for each parser separately, or doing something different. We settled for the latter.

We introduced the concept of an abstract parser. As we will see later on in this chapter, it is not the same as a general parser. For now, it is enough to say that this concept enables multi-language support, without changing the interfaces for each language.

Now, let's move on to the practical considerations.

Implementation

We will now deal with the implementation of the parser in SharpDevelop. As mentioned, we have introduced the concept of an abstract parser into our architecture. Before examining any code, we will look at it.

The Big Picture

The parser is based on an 'abstract' parser. In other words, all the information returned by the actual parser(s) is represented in an abstracted manner to the features using this output. At first glance, this may seem to be a daunting task, but it is not.

The .NET Framework is an example of an abstract architecture. It is based on the concept of compiling all languages to the same intermediate language (CIL – Common Intermediate Language) and having all languages use the same runtime (CLR – Common Language Runtime) for execution. This can only be done when the concepts underlying the implementation of all these languages use the same basic architecture –object orientation of the same flavor, identical data types, and so on.

This means that once we have identified a piece of code as being a variable, of say type int, we can be certain that all other languages using the .NET Famework will know the range of acceptable values and bit size for this variable.

Similarly, we can map any language for which we have a specific parser implementation, onto an abstract parse tree representation. For convenience, we call this an abstract parser. Its output will be a uniform internal representation of the code's structure. The users of this representation (like Code Completion, Method Insight, and Class Scout) won't even need to know what language the element was written in.

Now, let's move on to look at the general flow of data in our parser architecture. This is illustrated in the following diagram:

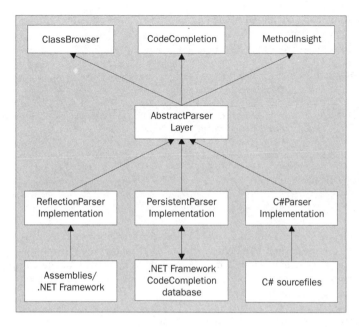

We can see that we have three consumers of data, as well as three providers of data; each with its own specific parser. This is necessary, as we need to know quite a lot for successful parsing of the code. Not all elements in our code are contained in the specific file that we edit; we use .NET reflection to handle references to assemblies and the .NET Famework.

Also, any .NET program that we can imagine of makes use of the framework functionality. So we need to provide parse information for the framework as well and since this is a large quantity of information, we do not want to repeat this process every time we start up SharpDevelop. Therefore, we make this information persistent by saving it to disk. Lastly, we will also need to look at our actual source code for the project, as new classes and members of classes will be added dynamically.

As all of the code is set in the same framework, we can use the same type of representation for the parsed information, in all three cases.

Now, we will look at the individual components that contribute to the parse tree, as shown in the previous diagram.

Reflection Parsing for Assemblies

In our programs, information about the referenced (external) assemblies also needs to be included for successful code completion. If we don't have the source code available, for these assemblies, how can we obtain this information? Without the source, we cannot parse and extract information – or can we?

We can extract information from assemblies. The .NET Famework provides reflection to do this job for us. It is as if this .NET feature was included just for our needs!

The source code for this reflection layer is found in the folder
`src\SharpDevelop\Base\Internal\Parser\ReflectionLayer`.

Now, let's look at the code contained in the `ReflectionClass.cs` file:

```
namespace SharpDevelop.Internal.Parser
{
  [Serializable]
  public class ReflectionClass : AbstractClass
  {
    BindingFlags flags = BindingFlags.Instance | BindingFlags.NonPublic |
      BindingFlags.Static | BindingFlags.Public;

    public override ICompilationUnit CompilationUnit {
      get {
        return null;
      }
    }
```

In the code snippet above, we refer to a `CompilationUnit` and `override` it with a `null`. Compilation units are used when parsing the editor buffer containing un-compiled source code, and are not needed here as we only have compiled code to deal with. We will look at compilation units when we deal with parsing files in the edit buffer. This override is necessary, as all three parser systems share a common interface that contains compilation units.

Using reflection we will extract the information that we want:

```
public static bool IsDelegate(Type type)
  {
    return type.IsSubclassOf(typeof(Delegate))
      && type != typeof(MulticastDelegate);
  }

public ReflectionClass(Type type, Hashtable xmlComments)
  {
    fullyQualifiedName = type.FullName;

    if (xmlComments != null) {
      XmlNode node = xmlComments["T:" + fullyQualifiedName] as XmlNode;
      if (node != null) {
        documentation = node.InnerXml;
      }
    }

    fullyQualifiedName = fullyQualifiedName.Replace("+", ".");

    // set classtype
    if (IsDelegate(type)) {
      classType = ClassType.Delegate;
      MethodInfo invoke = type.GetMethod("Invoke");
      ReflectionMethod newMethod = new ReflectionMethod(invoke, null);
      methods.Add(newMethod);
    } else if (type.IsInterface) {
      classType = ClassType.Interface;
    } else if (type.IsEnum) {
      classType = ClassType.Enum;
```

```
      } else if (type.IsValueType) {
        classType = ClassType.Struct;
      } else {
        classType = ClassType.Class;
      }

      modifiers = ModifierEnum.None;

      if (type.IsNestedAssembly) {
        modifiers |= ModifierEnum.Internal;
      }

      if (type.IsSealed) {
        modifiers |= ModifierEnum.Sealed;
      }

      if (type.IsNestedPrivate ) {

// We assume that private is the most frequently used one, and
// public the least.
```

As can be seen from the comment above, one little trick to speed up code containing a lot of conditions that need to be tested, is to sort them according to the expected frequency of each case. This ensures that evaluation of the conditions is broken off as soon as possible.

```
      modifiers |= ModifierEnum.Private;
      } else if (type.IsNestedFamily ) {
        modifiers |= ModifierEnum.Protected;
      } else if (type.IsNestedPublic || type.IsPublic) {
        modifiers |= ModifierEnum.Public;
      } else if (type.IsNestedFamORAssem) {
        modifiers |= ModifierEnum.ProtectedOrInternal;
      } else if (type.IsNestedFamANDAssem) {
        modifiers |= ModifierEnum.Protected;
        modifiers |= ModifierEnum.Internal;
      }

      // set base classes
      if (type.BaseType != null) { // it's null for System.Object ONLY !!!
        baseTypes.Add(type.BaseType.FullName);
      }

      if (classType != ClassType.Delegate) {
        // add members
        foreach (Type iface in type.GetInterfaces()) {
          baseTypes.Add(iface.FullName);
        }

        foreach (Type nestedType in type.GetNestedTypes(flags)) {
          innerClasses.Add(new ReflectionClass(nestedType, xmlComments));
        }

        foreach (FieldInfo field in type.GetFields(flags)) {
```

```
        if (!field.IsSpecialName) {
          IField newField = new ReflectionField(field, xmlComments);
          if (!newField.IsInternal) {
            fields.Add(newField);
          }
        }
      }

      foreach (PropertyInfo propertyInfo in type.GetProperties(flags)) {
        if (!propertyInfo.IsSpecialName) {
          ParameterInfo[] p = null;

          // we may not get the permission to access the index parameters
          try {
            p = propertyInfo.GetIndexParameters();
          } catch (Exception) {}
          if (p == null || p.Length == 0) {
            IProperty newProperty = new ReflectionProperty(propertyInfo,
              xmlComments);
            if (!newProperty.IsInternal) {
              properties.Add(newProperty);
            }
          } else {
            IIndexer newIndexer = new ReflectionIndexer(propertyInfo,
              xmlComments);
            if (!newIndexer.IsInternal) {
              indexer.Add(newIndexer);
            }
          }
        }
      }
    }
```

Note that the reflection layer does not have a compilation unit, as assemblies are already compiled code. Therefore, we have to overload the corresponding interface with a dummy. Then, we go on to extract the information for the class itself, taking care of the XML comments, which are stored in a hashtable when they are to be extracted.

The XML comments are used as documentation in tool-tips. All other elements of the class being processed are stored in individual objects derived from objects in the abstract parser, which will eventually make up a part of our parse tree. You can see a list of all the object collections in the first listing in the section about the abstract parser, as all three parser subsystems provide data to these collections. All objects derived this way are put into these collections of the respective types. Since we are using reflection for this we can access the information for all objects, independent of the language they were programmed in. For all members of the classes processed by this, we have code similar to the listing above.

As an example, of this, let us look at the code in the src\SharpDevelop\Base\Internal\Parser\ReflectionLayer\ReflectionMethod.cs file, which deals with information specific to methods:

```
namespace SharpDevelop.Internal.Parser
{
  [Serializable]
  public class ReflectionMethod : AbstractMethod
  {
    string GetParamList(MethodBase methodInfo)
    {
      StringBuilder propertyName = new StringBuilder("(");
      ParameterInfo[] p = methodInfo.GetParameters();
      if (p.Length == 0) {
        return String.Empty;
      }
      for (int i = 0; i < p.Length; ++i) {
        propertyName.Append(p[i].ParameterType.FullName);
        if (i + 1 < p.Length) {
          propertyName.Append(',');
        }
      }
      propertyName.Append(')');
      return propertyName.ToString();
    }
```

Here, we obtain the parameters for the method that we are currently handling and construct a string in parentheses, with parameters separated by commas. Next, we extract the XML comments and modifiers, again sorting the modifier cases for frequency and thus speed:

```
    public ReflectionMethod(MethodBase methodInfo, Hashtable xmlComments)
    {
      fullyQualifiedName = String.Concat(methodInfo.DeclaringType.FullName,
        ".", methodInfo.Name);

      XmlNode node = null;

      if (xmlComments != null) {
        node = xmlComments["M:" + fullyQualifiedName +
          GetParamList(methodInfo)] as XmlNode;
        if (node != null) {
          documentation = node.InnerXml;
        }
      }

      if (methodInfo.IsStatic) {
        modifiers |= ModifierEnum.Static;
      }

      if (methodInfo.IsAssembly) {
        modifiers |= ModifierEnum.Internal;
      }

      if (methodInfo.IsPrivate) {
      // We assume that private is the most frequently used one, and
      // public the least.
        modifiers |= ModifierEnum.Private;
```

```
      } else if (methodInfo.IsFamily) {
        modifiers |= ModifierEnum.Protected;
      } else if (methodInfo.IsPublic) {
        modifiers |= ModifierEnum.Public;
      } else if (methodInfo.IsFamilyOrAssembly) {
        modifiers |= ModifierEnum.ProtectedOrInternal;
      } else if (methodInfo.IsFamilyAndAssembly) {
        modifiers |= ModifierEnum.Protected;
        modifiers |= ModifierEnum.Internal;
      }

      foreach (ParameterInfo paramInfo in methodInfo.GetParameters()) {
        parameters.Add(new ReflectionParameter(paramInfo, node));
      }
      if (methodInfo is MethodInfo) {
        returnType =
          new ReflectionReturnType(((MethodInfo)methodInfo).ReturnType);
      } else {
        returnType = null;
      }
    }
  }
}
```

We see that, again we are creating objects for parameters. Other code elements contained in the assembly are treated in exactly the same way; therefore, we will not look at more of this code. By now, we have learned that reflection is one of the most powerful features the .NET Framework offers to ambitious programmers.

Let's move on to the persistent part of the parse tree.

Persistent Parsing for the Framework Class Library

The heart of all C# applications is the .NET Framework base class library (BCL). As the BCL does not change between SharpDevelop sessions (unless a new release of the .NET Framework has become available in the meantime), the information for these classes can be persisted between sessions. This saves a significant amount of overhead for performing parsing-dependent tasks. Of course, should you have a significant number – a thousand or more – of your own classes that will be included in all your projects, you may extend this feature to include them. In this section, we will look at making parse information persistent.

When we start SharpDevelop for the first time, after a clean install, a wizard with the SharpDevelop mascot, the clownfish Chloë, will pop up and guide us through the process of creating a code-completion database for the BCL.

The whole secret of creating persistent information for the parsing of the BCL is a persistent database. In fact, it is a binary file, in a format that we designed ourselves, as a full database wasn't necessary, besides it would have involved some penalty in overhead. The format of the binary file will be discussed when we look at the WriteTo method, later on in this section.

There are two modes available for creating the database. The original wizard only had the slower creation, which consumed a lot of memory, so we decided to implement the alternative faster one. The difference between the two methods is not in the information content but in the access method for some special cases. In fast creation mode, information about the parameters passed is omitted from the database. This has to be supplied at runtime, resulting in slower code completion.

We will begin by examining the code for classes contained in the `src\SharpDevelop\Base\ Internal\Parser\PersistanceLayer\PersistantClass.cs` file:

```
namespace SharpDevelop.Internal.Parser
{
  public sealed class PersistantClass : IClass
  {
    int classProxyIndex;
    ClassProxyCollection classProxyCollection;

    // an int arraylist of base types.
    ArrayList baseTypes = new ArrayList();

    // This collection is only used during creation, if for a basetype no
    // proxy index could be determined. It contains all those names as real
    // name. They should be read to baseTypesStringCollection when the
    // persistant class is read.
    StringCollection notFoundBaseTypes = new StringCollection();

    StringCollection baseTypesStringCollection = new StringCollection();

    ClassCollection innerClasses = new ClassCollection();
    FieldCollection fields = new FieldCollection();
    PropertyCollection properties = new PropertyCollection();
    MethodCollection methods = new MethodCollection();
    EventCollection events = new EventCollection();
    IndexerCollection indexer = new IndexerCollection();

    string fullyQualifiedName;
    string documentation;
    ClassType classType;
    ModifierEnum modifiers;

    public ICompilationUnit CompilationUnit {
      get {
        return null;
      }
    }
  }
```

Again, we overload the compilation unit with a dummy, as the BCL does not contain compilable code. Then, we go on to create a binary file to hold the proxy data, which we will need for generating the actual code-completion database. As we are using proxies, we will have to consider cases where the proxy will be unavailable, for example, inner classes. To this purpose, when no proxy is available we set `classProxyIndex` to `-1`. Then, we write the full information. In case of any unforeseen problems, this can also be considered to be a fallback:

```
    public PersistantClass(BinaryReader reader, ClassProxyCollection
                         classProxyCollection)
{
    this.classProxyCollection = classProxyCollection;
    classProxyIndex = reader.ReadInt32();

    if (classProxyIndex < 0) {
        fullyQualifiedName = reader.ReadString();
        documentation = reader.ReadString();
        modifiers = (ModifierEnum)reader.ReadUInt32();
        classType = (ClassType)reader.ReadInt16();
    }

    uint count = reader.ReadUInt32();
    for (uint i = 0; i < count; ++i) {
        int baseTypeIndex = reader.ReadInt32();
        if (baseTypeIndex < 0) {
            baseTypesStringCollection.Add(reader.ReadString());
        } else {
            baseTypes.Add(baseTypeIndex);
        }
    }
}
```

This snippet bears some resemblance to the code for the reflection layer, in the sense that we are creating objects for the abstract parser. Again, we do not have a compilation unit present, as the BCL is compiled code. One thing is significantly different here: proxy classes.

The idea behind using proxy classes is that we can be a lot more memory efficient when setting up the .NET Framework section of the parse tree. We merely need to provide a 'stand-in' for the real class and provide actual parse information only when the class is used in the code being edited. Proxy classes reduce the 20 megabytes of parse information needed for the full BCL parse information to a mere 600 kilobytes! This results in a significant reduction of the memory requirements for the parse information.

Now we continue with filling up the proxies:

```
    count = reader.ReadUInt32();
    for (uint i = 0; i < count; ++i) {
        innerClasses.Add(new PersistantClass(reader, classProxyCollection));
    }

    count = reader.ReadUInt32();
    for (uint i = 0; i < count; ++i) {
        fields.Add(new PersistantField(reader, classProxyCollection));
    }

//code omitted from listing
    }
```

Now that the proxies have been filled in, we can proceed to write the file. Again, we have to deal with classes, which don't have proxies. Checking for a value of -1 in the classProxyIndex does this. We simply write to a binary file, with the format being determined by the sequence of the elements we write to it. We go over each class and its members in the sequence in which they are found in the respective collections:

```
      public void WriteTo(BinaryWriter writer)
      {
        writer.Write(classProxyIndex);

        if (classProxyIndex < 0) {
          writer.Write(fullyQualifiedName);
          writer.Write(documentation);
          writer.Write((uint)modifiers);
          writer.Write((short)classType);
        }

        writer.Write((uint)(baseTypes.Count + notFoundBaseTypes.Count));
        foreach (int baseTypeIdx in baseTypes) {
          writer.Write(baseTypeIdx);
        }

        foreach (string baseType in notFoundBaseTypes) {
          writer.Write((int)-1);
          writer.Write(baseType);
        }


        writer.Write((uint)innerClasses.Count);
        foreach (PersistantClass innerClass in innerClasses) {
          innerClass.WriteTo(writer);
        }

        writer.Write((uint)fields.Count);
        foreach (PersistantField field in fields) {
          field.WriteTo(writer);
        }

        writer.Write((uint)properties.Count);
        foreach (PersistantProperty property in properties) {
          property.WriteTo(writer);
        }

//code omitted for listing
      }
```

After having seen how the data is written, we will look at obtaining the data. We build up a class proxy collection and fill in all the information we can obtain about the classes. If the class does not have a proxy, the index will be set to -1 by the following line:

```
classProxyIndex = classProxyCollection.IndexOf(c.FullyQualifiedName);
```

Now, let us look at the full routine, but keep in mind that we have omitted quite a lot of repetitive code. Basically, we just check each item for the existence of a proxy and return the full information if none is found, otherwise, the proxy information is returned. We just want to give you an idea of what we need to do:

```
    public PersistantClass(ClassProxyCollection classProxyCollection,
                           IClass c)
    {
      this.classProxyCollection = classProxyCollection;
      classProxyIndex = classProxyCollection.IndexOf(c.FullyQualifiedName);
      if (classProxyIndex < 0) {
        fullyQualifiedName = c.FullyQualifiedName;
        documentation = c.Documentation;
        modifiers = c.Modifiers;
        classType = c.ClassType;
      }

      foreach (string baseType in c.BaseTypes) {
        int idx = classProxyCollection.IndexOf(baseType);
        if (idx < 0) {
          notFoundBaseTypes.Add(baseType);
        } else {
          baseTypes.Add(idx);
        }
      }

      foreach (IClass innerClass in c.InnerClasses) {
        innerClasses.Add(new PersistantClass(classProxyCollection,
          innerClass));
      }

      foreach (IField field in c.Fields) {
        fields.Add(new PersistantField(classProxyCollection, field));
      }

//code omitted for listing
    }

    public ClassType ClassType {
      get {
        if (classProxyIndex < 0) {
          return classType;
        }
        return classProxyCollection[classProxyIndex].ClassType;
      }
    }
//code omitted for listing

    // regions are currently useless (only assembly classes are
    // made persistent)
    public IRegion Region {
      get {
        return null;
      }
    }

    public StringCollection BaseTypes {
      get {
        // convert base types first time they're requested
```

```
            if (baseTypes.Count > 0) {
              foreach (int index in baseTypes) {
               baseTypesStringCollection.Add
                 (classProxyCollection[index].FullyQualifiedName);
              }
              baseTypes.Clear();
            }
            return baseTypesStringCollection;
        }
     }

// code omitted for listing
   }
 }
```

Again, we have abbreviated the code so that it won't be too long. Still there is quite a lot left to look at, like how things varying from fully qualified names to access modifiers are handled. Refer to the source code for the complete listing.

The parse information that does not come from the code being edited is complete. Now, we can look at the actual C# parser that will deal with the code that the user is editing.

The C# Parser for the Editor

Now, we will finally get to the heart of the matter – the parser for the code being edited. For the time being, we can only parse C#, but a parser for VB.NET is in the works. Other parsers might also be implemented in our model; as long as they produce their parse information as objects, we can access them in the abstract parser layer.

Recursive Descent

For the SharpDevelop parser, we decided to use a parsing technique called **recursive descent**. As the name implies, it is a top-down method. It is well suited for customizing parsers for specific languages. Recursive descent is popular and well understood, not least due to its performance potential. Recursive descent is a depth-first search technique. A detailed explanation of this parsing technique can be found in the book by Grune and Jacobs.

The Parser Interface

We need to define a parser interface so that the C# parser and other future parsers have a common interface, which can be accessed by the abstract parser.

The parser interface is defined in the
src\SharpDevelop\Base\Internal\Parser\IParser.cs file:

```
   namespace SharpDevelop.Internal.Parser
   {

     [Flags]
     public enum ShowMembers {
       Public = 1,
       Protected = 2,
```

```
    Private = 4,
    Static = 8
}

public class ResolveResult
{
  object[] resolveContents;
  ShowMembers showMembers;

  public bool ShowPublic {
    get {
      return (showMembers & ShowMembers.Public) == ShowMembers.Public;
    }
  }

  public bool ShowProtected {
    get {
      return (showMembers & ShowMembers.Protected) ==
        ShowMembers.Protected;
    }
  }

  public bool ShowPrivate {
    get {
      return (showMembers & ShowMembers.Private) == ShowMembers.Private;
    }
  }

  public bool ShowStatic {
    get {
      return (showMembers & ShowMembers.Static) == ShowMembers.Static;
    }
  }

  public object[] ResolveContents {
    get {
      return resolveContents;
    }
  }

  public ShowMembers ShowMembers {
    get {
      return showMembers;
    }
  }

  public ResolveResult(object[] resolveContents, ShowMembers showMembers)
  {
    this.resolveContents = resolveContents;
    this.showMembers = showMembers;
  }
}

public interface IParser {
```

```
        string[] LexerTags {
          set;
        }

        ICompilationUnitBase Parse(string fileName);
        ICompilationUnitBase Parse(string fileName, string fileContent);

        // Resolves an expression.
        // The caretLineNumber and caretColumn are 1 based.
        ResolveResult Resolve(IParserService parserService,
                              string expression, int caretLineNumber,
                              int caretColumn, string fileName);
    }
}
```

One important notion in this interface is the compilation unit. A compilation unit represents the files of the project we are currently working on in the editor. We need it when resolving (as was already hinted at in Chapter 5). Resolving is necessary for each file that we parse, because we have two compilation units – a valid and a dirty one. By dirty we mean a compilation unit containing parse information obtained during an aborted parse run. This happens due to compile-time errors. A successful code completion can be performed only when the information from both units is merged together.

Now, let's look at the Class interface again. This can be found in src\SharpDevelop\Base\Internal\Parser\IClass.cs.

We will not reproduce it in full, but just enough to give us an idea of how it works:

```
namespace SharpDevelop.Internal.Parser
{
  public interface IClass : IDecoration
  {
    ICompilationUnit CompilationUnit {
      get;
    }

    string FullyQualifiedName {
      get;
    }

    string Name {
      get;
    }

    string Namespace {
      get;
    }

    ClassType ClassType {
      get;
    }

    IRegion Region {
```

```
      get;
   }

   StringCollection BaseTypes {
      get;
   }
// code removed for listing
   }
}
```

This looks exactly like the class interfaces we encountered earlier, and that is the way it should be, as information from all three parser parts has to fit together. Now, we will examine the Parser service, which will be discussed in more detail later on. For now, we just want to see how the parser is called.

The following code snippet can be found in the src\SharpDevelop\Base\Services\ParserService\DefaultParserService.cs file:

```
public IParseInformation ParseFile(string fileName, string fileContent)
{
   IParser parser = GetParser(fileName);
   if (parser == null) {
      return null;
   }

   parser.LexerTags = new string[] { "HACK", "TODO", "UNDONE", "FIXME" };
   ICompilationUnitBase parserOutput = parser.Parse(fileName,
      fileContent);

   ParseInformation parseInformation = parsings[fileName] as
      ParseInformation;

   if (parseInformation == null) {
      parseInformation = new ParseInformation();
   }

   if (parserOutput.ErrorsDuringCompile) {
      parseInformation.DirtyCompilationUnit = parserOutput;
   } else {
      parseInformation.ValidCompilationUnit = parserOutput;
      parseInformation.DirtyCompilationUnit = null;
   }

   parsings[fileName] = parseInformation;

   // TODO : move this into the compilation unit layer, it is closer to
   // resolver than to the parser.
   if (!parserOutput.ErrorsDuringCompile &&
      parseInformation.BestCompilationUnit is ICompilationUnit) {
      ICompilationUnit cu =
         (ICompilationUnit)parseInformation.BestCompilationUnit;
      foreach (IClass c in cu.Classes) {
         AddClassToNamespaceList(c);
         classes[c.FullyQualifiedName] =
```

```
            new ClasstableEntry(fileName, cu, c);
      }
    }

    OnParseInformationChanged(
      new ParseInformationEventArgs(fileName, parseInformation));
    return parseInformation;
  }
```

Here, we see how the parser is called; its output is routed either into the valid or dirty compilation unit, depending on the parser's status. One question still remains: how do we know what to parse? Up to now, we didn't see anything converting the edit buffer into parseable items. These items are technically called **tokens** and are produced by a subsystem called the **lexer**.

Now, we will have to switch back to a more theoretical discussion, but only for a short while. Before we can look at the code, we will have to look at the functions performed by a lexer:

- ❑ Match input characters to tokens by using rules
- ❑ Search through categories in patterns and return the matching patterns (examples of categories are literals, keywords, punctuation, and so on)
- ❑ Discard characters that are not part of tokens (for example, whitespace)
- ❑ Report lexical errors

The entirety of these actions is called 'lexical analysis', which gives the lexer its name. These tokens become the input for the parser. Now let's look at parts of the lexer code found in the src\CSharpParser\Lexer folder.

First, we will look at the lexer itself; it can be found in the Lexer.cs file:

```
namespace SharpDevelop.Internal.Parser {

  public class Lexer
  {
    public KeyWord keywords;
    IReader reader;
    int col = 1;
    int line = 1;

    CommentCollection miscComments = new CommentCollection();
    CommentCollection dokuComments = new CommentCollection();
    TagCollection tagComments = new TagCollection();
    string[] tags;

    public CommentCollection MiscComments {
      get {
        return miscComments;
      }
    }

    public CommentCollection DokuComments {
```

```
      get {
        return dokuComments;
      }
    }

    public TagCollection TagComments {
      get {
        return tagComments;
      }
    }
```

We start off by defining three different collections for comments, as C# provides comments for different purposes. Plain comments are preceded by two slashes, while XML comments are preceded by three slashes. Tag comments are something that we have come up with on our own; they are plain comments containing either HACK or TODO as a keyword, and are quite useful for coordinating development and bug fixes.

Now let's move on identifying other tokens (we have truncated this code):

```
    public string[] Tags {
      get {
        return tags;
      }
      set {
        tags = value;
      }
    }

// code removed for listing

    public Token Next()
    {
      while (!reader.Eos()) {
        char ch = reader.GetNext();
        if (Char.IsWhiteSpace(ch)) {
          ++col;
          if (ch == '\n') {
            ++line;
            col = 1;
          }
          continue;
        }
        if (Char.IsLetter(ch) || ch == '_') {
          int x = col;
          int y = line;
          string s = ReadIdent(ch);
          if (keywords.IsKeyWord(s)) {
            return new
              Token(TokenType.Keyword, keywords.GetKeyWord(s), x, y);
          }
          return new Token(TokenType.Identifier, s, x, y);
```

```
// code removed for listing
        }
        throw new ParserException("Error: Unknown char not read at (" +
            col + "/" + line + ") in Lexer.Next()\nIt was: " + ch, line, col);
    }

    return new Token(TokenType.EOF, null, col, line);
}
```

In the opening section of the file, we set up the data types needed for the various types of tokens, and then moved on to the code for creating tokens based on the chars we present to the lexer.

Next, we will look at distinguishing the identifiers from the keywords. The code for identifying keywords is found in the `KeyWords.cs` file:

```
namespace SharpDevelop.Internal.Parser {

  public enum KeyWordEnum {
      This,
      Base,
...
//code removed for listing
  }

  public class KeyWord
  {
    string[]  keywords = {
      "this",
      "base",
...
//Code removed for listing
    };

    Hashtable keyhash = new Hashtable();

    public KeyWord()
    {
      foreach (string keyword in keywords) {
        string newword = Char.ToUpper (keyword[0]) +
          keyword.Substring(1);
        keyhash[keyword] =
          (KeyWordEnum)Enum.Parse(typeof(KeyWordEnum), newword);
      }
    }

    public bool IsKeyWord(string word)
    {
      return keyhash[word] != null;
    }

    public KeyWordEnum GetKeyWord(string word)
    {
      return (KeyWordEnum)keyhash[word];
    }
```

In this snippet, the tokens identified as keywords are defined in an array of strings and are stored in a hashtable. Lexing, as we can see, is not one of the most glorious activities.

We will now move on to the next level of our parser – the abstract parser.

The Abstract Parser

In this part of the parser, all the components that we have discussed are joined to form a single unified structure – the parse tree. They produce objects, which are inherited from the objects defined in this central piece of code; thus here, we can address them in a coherent manner and make them available to the consumers of their information.

Let's now examine the code in the src\SharpDevelop\Base\Internal\Parser\Implementations\AbstractClass.cs file:

```
namespace SharpDevelop.Internal.Parser
{
  [Serializable]
  public abstract class AbstractClass : AbstractDecoration, IClass
  {
    protected string fullyQualifiedName;

    protected ClassType classType;
    protected IRegion region;

    protected StringCollection baseTypes = new StringCollection();

    protected ClassCollection innerClasses = new ClassCollection();
    protected FieldCollection fields = new FieldCollection();
    protected PropertyCollection properties = new PropertyCollection();
    protected MethodCollection methods = new MethodCollection();
    protected EventCollection events = new EventCollection();
    protected IndexerCollection indexer = new IndexerCollection();

    public abstract ICompilationUnit CompilationUnit {
      get;
    }
// Code omitted for listing

    public virtual string Name {
      get {
        string[] name = fullyQualifiedName.Split(new char[] {'.', '+'});
        return name[name.Length - 1];
      }
    }

    public virtual string Namespace {
      get {
        int index = fullyQualifiedName.LastIndexOf('.');
        return index < 0 ? String.Empty :
          fullyQualifiedName.Substring(0, index);
      }
    }
```

```
      // Code omitted for listing
```

In the code snippet, we set up the properties we need, as well as all the class and class member collections into which we collect the parse information provided by our parser subsystems. An interesting detail in the above code is:

```
public virtual string Name {
  get {
    string[] name = fullyQualifiedName.Split(new char[] {'.', '+'});
    return name[name.Length - 1];
  }
}
```

We need to split the fully qualified name into two different characters. For this, we use the '.', which we would expect, and the '+' sign, which is used for the inner classes returned by .NET reflection.

Now, we need a way to handle class inheritance:

```
public class ClassInheritanceEnumerator : IEnumerator, IEnumerable
{
  static IParserService parserService =
    (IParserService)ICSharpCode.Core.Services.
    ServiceManager.Services.GetService(typeof(IParserService));
  IClass topLevelClass;
  IClass currentClass  = null;
  Queue  baseTypeQueue = new Queue();

  public ClassInheritanceEnumerator(IClass topLevelClass)
  {
    this.topLevelClass = topLevelClass;
    baseTypeQueue.Enqueue(topLevelClass.FullyQualifiedName);
    PutBaseClassesOnStack(topLevelClass);
    baseTypeQueue.Enqueue("System.Object");
  }
  public IEnumerator GetEnumerator()
  {
    return this;
  }
```

We handle this by using enumerators, which rely on stacks. The stack operations are given below:

```
      void PutBaseClassesOnStack(IClass c)
      {
        foreach (string baseTypeName in c.BaseTypes) {
          baseTypeQueue.Enqueue(baseTypeName);
        }
      }

//code omitted for listing
      public bool MoveNext()
      {
```

```
            if (baseTypeQueue.Count == 0) {
              return false;
            }
            string baseTypeName = baseTypeQueue.Dequeue().ToString();

            IClass baseType = parserService.GetClass(baseTypeName);
            if (baseType == null) {
              ICompilationUnit unit = currentClass == null ? null :
                currentClass.CompilationUnit;
              if (unit != null) {
                foreach (IUsing u in unit.Usings) {
                  baseType = u.SearchType(baseTypeName);
                  if (baseType != null) {
                    break;
                  }
                }
              }
            }

            if (baseType != null) {
              currentClass = baseType;
              PutBaseClassesOnStack(currentClass);
            }

            return baseType != null;
          }

        public void Reset()
        {
          baseTypeQueue.Clear();
          baseTypeQueue.Enqueue(topLevelClass.FullyQualifiedName);
          PutBaseClassesOnStack(topLevelClass);
          baseTypeQueue.Enqueue("System.Object");
        }
      }
    }
  }
```

It is important to note that we declare the objects from which all the collections for the objects corresponding to syntactical units in the code are derived.

Finally, we make this parse information available to SharpDevelop.

Putting It All Together in the Parser Service

As mentioned in Chapter 5, the parser functionality is made available as a service. The definition of the interface for this service can be found in the `src\SharpDevelop\Base\Services\ParserService\IParserService.cs` file.

We will not look at it here, though. If you want to review the listing, please refer back to Chapter 5. What is important is that we must merge a dirty compilation unit with a valid compilation unit to provide a full set of parse information to our consumers.

Let's look at the code from the `src\SharpDevelop\Base\Services\ParserService\DefaultParserService.cs` file.

First we will examine the creation of the persistent database. You will remember that in the section on *Persistent Parsing for the Framework Class Library*, we said that there are two ways of creating the database. However, we will only look at creating the fast completing database, as the slow database is just a subset of it:

```
public void GenerateEfficientCodeCompletionDatabase(string createPath,
  IProgressMonitor progressMonitor)
{
  SetCodeCompletionFileLocation(createPath);

  AssemblyInformation frameworkAssemblyInformation =
    new AssemblyInformation();
  if (progressMonitor != null) {
    progressMonitor.BeginTask("generate code completion database",
      assemblyList.Length * 3);
  }

  // convert all assemblies
  for (int i = 0; i < assemblyList.Length; ++i) {
    try {
      string path =
        Environment.GetFolderPath(Environment.SpecialFolder.System) +
        @"\..\microsoft.net\framework\v1.0.3705\";
      frameworkAssemblyInformation.
        LoadAssembly(String.Concat(path, assemblyList[i], ".dll"));
      if (progressMonitor != null) {
        progressMonitor.Worked(i);
      }
    } catch (Exception e) {
      Console.WriteLine(e.ToString());
    }
    System.GC.Collect();
  }
```

Note that in the listing above the path is hard-coded. We have a good reason for this – when we install the .NET Framework SDK, our system path only includes the .NET Framework BCL. However, if we were to install the re-distributable .NET runtime or Visual Studio 7, it won't be included in the path. In future releases of SharpDevelop we will have to find a way around this.

Now let us move on to the creation of the class proxies and writing the database to disk:

```
// create all class proxies
for (int i = 0; i < frameworkAssemblyInformation.Classes.Count; ++i) {
  ClassProxy newProxy = new
    ClassProxy(frameworkAssemblyInformation.Classes[i]);
  classProxies.Add(newProxy);
  AddClassToNamespaceList(newProxy);

  if (progressMonitor != null) {
```

```
        progressMonitor.Worked(assemblyList.Length +
            (i * assemblyList.Length) /
            frameworkAssemblyInformation.Classes.Count);
    }
}

// write all classes and proxies to the disk
BinaryWriter classWriter =
    new BinaryWriter(new BufferedStream(new
    FileStream(codeCompletionMainFile, FileMode.Create,
    FileAccess.Write, FileShare.None)));
BinaryWriter proxyWriter =
    new BinaryWriter(new BufferedStream(new
    FileStream(codeCompletionProxyFile, FileMode.Create,
    FileAccess.Write, FileShare.None)));

for (int i = 0; i < frameworkAssemblyInformation.Classes.Count; ++i)
    {
    IClass newClass = frameworkAssemblyInformation.Classes[i];
    PersistantClass pc = new PersistantClass(classProxies, newClass);
    ClassProxy proxy = classProxies[i];
    proxy.Offset = (uint)classWriter.BaseStream.Position;
    proxy.WriteTo(proxyWriter);
    pc.WriteTo(classWriter);
    if (progressMonitor != null) {
        progressMonitor.Worked(2 * assemblyList.Length +
        (i * assemblyList.Length) /
        frameworkAssemblyInformation.Classes.Count);
    }
}
classWriter.Close();
proxyWriter.Close();
if (progressMonitor != null) {
    progressMonitor.Done();
}
}
```

This code snippet generates the actual database on the disk. It uses a separate binary writer for the classes and proxies. We know that not all classes have proxies, so this is necessary. We also calculate the status of the progress bar (denoted by `progressMonitor`) in this method, so that the user is informed of the progress.

Now we will look at setting the location of the completion file:

```
void SetCodeCompletionFileLocation(string path)
{
    FileUtilityService fileUtilityService =
        (FileUtilityService)ServiceManager.Services.
        GetService(typeof(FileUtilityService));
    string codeCompletionTemp =
        fileUtilityService.GetDirectoryNameWithSeparator(path);

    codeCompletionProxyFile = codeCompletionTemp +
```

```
      "CodeCompletionProxyData.bin";
    codeCompletionMainFile  = codeCompletionTemp +
      "CodeCompletionMainData.bin";
}

void SetDefaultCompletionFileLocation()
{
  PropertyService propertyService = (PropertyService)ServiceManager.
    Services.GetService(typeof(PropertyService));
  SetCodeCompletionFileLocation(propertyService.
    GetProperty("SharpDevelop.CodeCompletion.DataDirectory",
    String.Empty).ToString());
}
```

Note that, we have also provided a default location. Next, we will load the file containing the proxy data that we generated earlier (in the section on *Persistent Parsing for the Framework Class Library*):

```
void LoadProxyDataFile()
{
  if (!File.Exists(codeCompletionProxyFile)) {
    return;
  }
  BinaryReader reader =
    new BinaryReader(new BufferedStream(new FileStream
    (codeCompletionProxyFile, FileMode.Open,
    FileAccess.Read, FileShare.Read)));
  while (true) {
    try {
      ClassProxy newProxy = new ClassProxy(reader);
      classProxies.Add(newProxy);
      AddClassToNamespaceList(newProxy);
    } catch (Exception) {
      break;
    }
  }
  reader.Close();
}
```

This completes our discussion on database creation. Now, let's start with the parser:

```
public override void InitializeService()
{
  parser =
  (IParser[])(AddInTreeSingleton.AddInTree.GetTreeNode
  ("/Workspace/Parser").BuildChildItems(this)).ToArray(typeof(IParser));

  SetDefaultCompletionFileLocation();

  BinaryFormatter formatter = new BinaryFormatter();

  if (!File.Exists(codeCompletionProxyFile)) {
    RunWizard();
    SetDefaultCompletionFileLocation();
```

```
    }
    LoadProxyDataFile();
    IProjectService projectService =
        (IProjectService)ICSharpCode.Core.Services.
        ServiceManager.Services.GetService(typeof(IProjectService));
    projectService.CombineOpened += new CombineEventHandler(OpenCombine);
}
```

Every time we start up SharpDevelop, we need to check for the existence of the proxy file. If it's missing, we create it by using the code from the previous listing.

```
public void AddReferenceToCompletionLookup(IProject project,
                                           ProjectReference reference)
{
  if (reference.ReferenceType != ReferenceType.Project) {
    string fileName = reference.GetReferencedFileName(project);
    if (fileName == null || fileName.Length == 0 ||
      fileName.IndexOf("System") > 0) {
      return;
    }
    // HACK : Don't load references for non C# projects - can't be
    //parsed yet
    if (project.ProjectType != "C#") {
      return;
    }
    if (File.Exists(fileName)) {
      LoadAssemblyParseInformations(fileName);
    }
  }
}

void LoadAssemblyParseInformations(string assemblyFileName)
{
  if (loadedAssemblies[assemblyFileName] != null) {
    return;
  }
  loadedAssemblies[assemblyFileName] = true;

  AssemblyInformation assemblyInformation = new AssemblyInformation();
  assemblyInformation.LoadAssembly(assemblyFileName);
  foreach (IClass newClass in assemblyInformation.Classes) {
    AddClassToNamespaceList(newClass);
    classes[newClass.FullyQualifiedName] =
      new ClasstableEntry(null, null, newClass);
  }
}

public void OpenCombine(object sender, CombineEventArgs e)
{
  ArrayList projects = Combine.GetAllProjects(e.Combine);
  foreach (ProjectCombineEntry entry in projects) {
    foreach (ProjectReference r in entry.Project.ProjectReferences) {
      AddReferenceToCompletionLookup(entry.Project, r);
```

```
            }
        }
    }
```

Then, we can move on to starting the actual parser in a separate thread. Running the parser in the same thread would make SharpDevelop unusable.

```
public void StartParserThread()
{
  Thread t = new Thread(new ThreadStart(ParserUpdateThread));
  t.IsBackground = true;
  t.Priority    = ThreadPriority.Lowest;
  t.Start();
}

void ParserUpdateThread()
{
  while (true) {
    Thread.Sleep(1000);
    try {
      if (WorkbenchSingleton.Workbench.ActiveWorkbenchWindow.
        ViewContent != null) {
        IEditable editable = WorkbenchSingleton.Workbench.
          ActiveWorkbenchWindow.ViewContent.Control as IEditable;
        if (editable != null) {
          string fileName = WorkbenchSingleton.Workbench.
            ActiveWorkbenchWindow.ViewContent.ContentName;
          if (!(fileName == null || fileName.Length == 0)) {
            string content = null;
            content = editable.TextContent;
            Thread.Sleep(300);
            lock (parsings) {
              ParseFile(fileName, content);
            }
          }
        }
      }
    } catch (Exception) {}
  }
}
```

Now, let's examine the `Resolve` method, which deals with code resolution:

```
public ResolveResult Resolve(string expression, int caretLineNumber,
                             int caretColumn, string fileName)
{
  IParser parser = GetParser(fileName);
  if (parser != null) {
    return parser.Resolve(this, expression, caretLineNumber,
      caretColumn, fileName);
  }
  return null;
}
```

For now, we will content ourselves with looking at this call, as the resolving code does much more than just merge the two compilation units. The resolving process is a central part of the code completion mechanism, so we will look at it in detail in the next chapter. We included this topic here, as the merging part of the resolving process technically belongs to the parsing part of code completion.

Putting the parse information together into one 'big picture' is done by the following code:

```
Hashtable AddClassToNamespaceList(IClass addClass)
{
  string nSpace = addClass.Namespace;
  if (nSpace == null) {
    nSpace = String.Empty;
  }
  string[] path = nSpace.Split('.');
  Hashtable cur = namespaces;

  for (int i = 0; i < path.Length; ++i) {
    if (cur[path[i]] == null) {
      cur[path[i]] = new Hashtable();
    } else {
      if (!(cur[path[i]] is Hashtable)) {
        return null;
      }
    }
    cur = (Hashtable)cur[path[i]];
  }

  cur[addClass.Name] = new ClassProxy(addClass);

  return cur;
}
```

By using hashtables, we add the classes to the namespaces. We need to know which class resides in which namespace; otherwise, we won't be able to offer correct suggestions in code completion. Of course, to do this, we need to know the list of contents of the existing namespaces, too:

```
public ArrayList GetNamespaceContents(string subNameSpace)
{
  ArrayList namespaceList = new ArrayList();
  if (subNameSpace == null) {
    return namespaceList;
  }
  string[] path = subNameSpace.Split('.');
  Hashtable cur = namespaces;

  for (int i = 0; i < path.Length; ++i) {
    if (!(cur[path[i]] is Hashtable)) {
      return namespaceList;
    }
    cur = (Hashtable)cur[path[i]];
  }
```

```
      foreach (DictionaryEntry entry in cur)  {
        if (entry.Value is Hashtable) {
          namespaceList.Add(entry.Key);
        } else {
          namespaceList.Add(entry.Value);
        }
      }

      return namespaceList;
    }
```

Naturally, we need to know which namespaces actually exist in our project. How else could we add them to the list generated above? So we again use the same technique that we used above:

```
    public bool NamespaceExists(string name)
    {
      if (name == null) {
        return false;
      }
      string[] path = name.Split('.');
      Hashtable cur = namespaces;

      for (int i = 0; i < path.Length; ++i) {
        if (!(cur[path[i]] is Hashtable)) {
          return false;
        }
        cur = (Hashtable)cur[path[i]];
      }
      return true;
    }

    public string[]  GetNamespaceList(string subNameSpace)
    {
      Debug.Assert(subNameSpace != null);

      string[] path = subNameSpace.Split('.');
      Hashtable cur = namespaces;

      if (subNameSpace.Length > 0) {
        for (int i = 0; i < path.Length; ++i) {
          if (!(cur[path[i]] is Hashtable)) {
            return null;
          }
          cur = (Hashtable)cur[path[i]];
        }
      }

      ArrayList namespaceList = new ArrayList();
      foreach (DictionaryEntry entry in cur) {
        if (entry.Value is Hashtable && entry.Key.ToString().Length > 0) {
          namespaceList.Add(entry.Key);
        }
      }
```

```
        return (string[])namespaceList.ToArray(typeof(string));
    }
```

The classes are added to a list of namespaces used in the project, so that they are associated with the proper namespace. We need this for efficient code completion. The use of the various data structures, such as collections, dictionaries, hash tables, and arrays, provided by the .NET Framework makes this quite simple to implement.

The code for the collections used to hold the information was generated using the Typed C# Collection Wizard of SharpDevelop, so it is not particularly interesting to look at. We will just list a snippet from src\SharpDevelop\Base\Internal\Parser\Collections\ClassCollection.cs.

This should give us an idea of what the class collection generated by the wizard looks like:

```
namespace SharpDevelop.Internal.Parser
{
  [Serializable()]
  public class ClassCollection : CollectionBase {

    public ClassCollection() {
    }
    public ClassCollection(ClassCollection value) {
      this.AddRange(value);
    }

    public ClassCollection(IClass[] value) {
      this.AddRange(value);
    }
```

The information from the parser is now available to the features that need to use it.

Summary

In this chapter, we examined the theory of computer languages and their grammars. Then we moved on to the theoretical possibilities for parser implementations. With the understanding of the issues at hand, we went on to look at the SharpDevelop parser.

We discussed the design issues involved, and the architecture of the parser that we settled for. We learned about the advantages of implementing an abstract parser. Such a parser solves the problems of needing data residing outside the current file – in the assemblies referenced or from the framework – in an elegant manner. Besides, we can easily parse different languages, by using this abstract parser layer as a go-between between the code and parse tree users.

Then, we went on to look at the three components contributing to the parse information:

- ❑   Reflection for assemblies referenced

- ❑   Persistent parse information for the BCL

- ❑   Parser for code we work on

Then, we investigated the implementation of the abstract parser, and finally looked at tying all this information together, into a single service, for use by the SharpDevelop features that need parse information.

In the next chapter, we will look at two such features – code completion and method insight.

CHAPTER 13

13

Code Completion and Method Insight

In the last chapter, we looked at how the parse information is gathered. We will now look at how we can use it to help us with software development. In this chapter, we will be discussing Code Completion and Method Insight.

No programmer can be expected to remember all the classes, properties, and methods needed for the .NET Framework; let alone all the classes they have written. For example, SharpDevelop itself contains more than 1600 source files (each usually representing a class), and has over 86,000 lines of code. The .NET classes can be looked up by switching between the IDE and the .NET reference, while for the user-defined classes, we have to create documentation before they can be used. These aren't pleasant tasks; besides they're time consuming.

The solution is to offer interactive suggestions for appropriate completion possibilities of the statement at hand. Code Completion handles this. This also holds true for method parameters; they are suggested by our Method Insight feature.

In this chapter, we will look at how the parse information that we obtained using the parser discussed in Chapter 12 can be used to implement this kind of functionality.

Resolving Matters

In the previous chapter, we had a quick look at the Resolver but postponed the actual discussion until later. We did this because the Resolver is placed in the Parser project and may use parts of the Parser infrastructure. It is as language-dependant as the parser itself, even though the Resolver might be considered as a separate entity.

The Resolver not only reconciles the two compilation units that exist for any given file, but also performs additional tasks related to providing parse information for Code Completion. The Resolver attempts to identify the type of the expression coming before the dot, so that the type members to be displayed for completion can be properly selected.

To reiterate, the valid compilation unit represents the parse information obtained during the last run of the parser that was finished without errors, while the dirty compilation unit contains the parse information obtained during the last parser run that was aborted due to parser error. This can happen when a statement is not yet complete. The information in these two compilation units can vary and needs to be merged, so that Code Completion and Method Insight work properly.

The code implementing the Resolver is found in the `src\CSharpParser\Resolver.cs` file.

We will now look at the methods implemented in this file:

```
public ResolveResult Resolve(IParserService parserService,
                             string expression, int caretLineNumber,
                             int caretColumn, string fileName)
{
  this.parserService = parserService;
  this.caretLine    = caretLineNumber;
  this.caretColumn  = caretColumn;
  parseInformation  = parserService.GetParseInformation(fileName);

  if (parseInformation == null || expression == null) {
    return null;
  }
  this.type       = expression;
  this.expression = expression;

  ResolveResult res = null;
  cu = parseInformation.DirtyCompilationUnit as ICompilationUnit;
  if (cu != null) {
    callingClass = GetInnermostClass();
    res = Resolve();
    if (res != null && (res.Members != null && res.Members.Count > 0 ||
      res.Namespaces != null && res.Namespaces.Count > 0)) {
      return res;
    }
  }
  cu = parseInformation.ValidCompilationUnit as ICompilationUnit;
  if (cu != null) {
    callingClass = GetInnermostClass();
    res = Resolve();
  }
  return res;
}
```

As we can see, we rely on the Parser service of SharpDevelop since this is where all the parse information comes together. We also need to deal with coordinates for the caret, as this is where the dot-triggered completion happens. Depending on where we are in the code, we have to offer different things. For example, in `using` statements we should only offer namespaces.

First, we will handle the resolving process for dirty compilation unit, as this is most probably the compilation unit containing the recent parse information. Only then, we move on to the valid compilation unit. Both compilation units are resolved using the `Resolve` method. Now let's examine this method:

```
ResolveResult Resolve()
{
  expression = expression.TrimStart(null);

  // expression == null already checked
  System.Diagnostics.Debug.Assert(expression != null);
  if (expression == "") {
    return null;
  }

  int i;

  // the period that causes this Resolve() is not part of the expression
  if (expression[expression.Length - 1] == '.') {
    return null;
  }

  for (i = expression.Length - 1; i >= 0; --i) {
    if (!(Char.IsLetterOrDigit(expression[i]) || expression[i] == '.')) {
      break;
    }
  }
  // no Identifier before the period
  if (i == expression.Length - 1) {
    return null;
  }

  type = expression.Substring(i + 1);

  //hardcoded 'using' below, as this is c# specific
  if (expression.StartsWith("using ")) {
    string[] namespaces = parserService.GetNamespaceList(type);
    if (namespaces == null || namespaces.Length <= 0) {
      return null;
    }
    return new ResolveResult(namespaces);
  }

  bool showStatic = false;
  // try to find Class with name type
  IClass c = StaticLookup(type);
  if (c != null) {
    showStatic = true;
  } else {
    c = StepByStepLookup(type, callingClass);
  }
  if (c == null) {
    // Neither static nor dynamic class found, try if type is namespace
    ArrayList nsContents =
```

```
            parserService.GetNamespaceContents(SearchNamespace(type, cu));
        ArrayList classes    = new ArrayList();
        if (nsContents != null) {
            // Put the classes in another ArrayList (classes)
            // and remove them from nsContents so that
            // there are only the namespaces left
            for (int j = 0; j < nsContents.Count; ++j) {
                if (nsContents[j] is IClass) {
                    if (!((IClass)nsContents[j]).IsProtected ||
                      ((IClass)nsContents[j]).IsProtectedOrInternal) {
                        classes.Add(nsContents[j]);
                    }
                    nsContents.RemoveAt(j);
                    --j;
                }
            }
            return new
              ResolveResult((string[])nsContents.ToArray(typeof(string)),
              classes);
        }
        return null;
    }
    IClass returnClass = parserService.GetClass(c.FullyQualifiedName);
    if (returnClass == null) {
        returnClass = c;
    }

    return new ResolveResult(returnClass,
      ListMembers(new ArrayList(),returnClass, showStatic));
}
```

The snippet we just saw determines whether we are dealing with a namespace or a class, and if it's a class, whether it's static or dynamic. Then we look for class members. In the following code snippet, we will consider only static classes:

```
ArrayList ListMembers(ArrayList members, IClass curType,
                       bool showStatic)
{
    if (showStatic) {
        foreach (IClass c in curType.InnerClasses) {
            if (IsAccessible(curType, c)) {
                members.Add(c);
            }
        }
    }
    foreach (IProperty p in curType.Properties) {
        if (MustBeShown (curType, p, showStatic)) {
            members.Add(p);
        }
    }
    foreach (IMethod m in curType.Methods) {
        if (MustBeShown(curType, m, showStatic)) {
            members.Add(m);
```

```
      }
    }
    foreach (IEvent e in curType.Events) {
      if (MustBeShown(curType, e, showStatic)) {
        members.Add(e);
      }
    }
    foreach (IField f in curType.Fields) {
      if (MustBeShown(curType, f, showStatic)) {
        members.Add(f);
      }
    }
    if (curType.ClassType == ClassType.Class) {
      IClass baseClass = BaseClass(curType);
      if (baseClass != null) {
        ListMembers(members, baseClass, showStatic);
      }
    } else if (curType.ClassType == ClassType.Interface) {
      foreach (string s in curType.BaseTypes) {
        IClass baseClass = SearchType(s, curType.CompilationUnit);
        if (baseClass != null &&
          baseClass.ClassType == ClassType.Interface) {
          ListMembers(members, baseClass, showStatic);
        }
      }
    }
  }
  return members;
}
```

The foreach statements in the above snippet iterate through the collections of classes, methods, and so on, and determine which of these are to be displayed in code completion. Here, we have to take the scope (public, private, and so on) of the elements into consideration, as not all of them should be visible in our suggestions.

Now we will examine the part dealing with the step-by-step lookup of the class members. By step-by-step, we mean that we are splitting up the code segments and extracting the information contained in it (that is, determining the type that the expression or token belongs to):

```
IClass StepByStepLookup(string name, IClass curClass)
{
  if (curClass == null) {
    return null;
  }
  bool showStatic = false;
  string[] typename = name.Split('.');
  string current =
    SearchNamespace(typename[0], curClass.CompilationUnit);
  int i = 1;
  IClass curType = null;
  if (current != null) {
    for ( ; i < typename.Length; ++i) {
      current += "." + typename[i];
      if (!parserService.NamespaceExists(current)) {
```

```
          break;
        }
      }
      ++i;
      curType = parserService.GetClass(current);
      showStatic = true;
    } else if (typename[0] == "this") {
      if (InStatic()) {
        return null;
      }
      curType = curClass;
    } else if (typename[0] == "base") {
      if (InStatic()) {
        return null;
      }
      foreach (string baseClass in curClass.BaseTypes) {
        IClass c = SearchType(baseClass, curClass.CompilationUnit);
        if (c != null && c.ClassType == ClassType.Class) {
          curType = c;
          break;
        }
      }
    } else {
      current = typename[0];
      curType = SearchType(current, curClass.CompilationUnit);
      if (curType == null) {
        curType = DynamicLookup(current);
      } else {
        showStatic = true;
      }
    }
    if (curType == null) {
      return null;
    }
    for ( ; i < typename.Length; ++i) {
      curType = SearchMember(curType, typename[i], ref showStatic);
      if (curType == null) {
        return null;
      }
    }
    return curType;
}
```

Next, we have to determine the Boolean value indicating whether code completion is being used for a static member. IsAcessible decides whether the indicated member can be accessed from the current location. The MustBeShown method uses this information and the display state of static members to decide whether the specified member has to be shown, as a suggestion during code completion:

```
bool InStatic()
{
  IProperty property = GetProperty();
  if (property != null) {
    return property.IsStatic;
```

```
      }
      IMethod method = GetMethod();
      if (method != null) {
        return method.IsStatic;
      }
      return false;
    }

    bool IsAccessible(IClass c, IDecoration member)
    {
      if ((member.Modifiers & ModifierEnum.Public) == ModifierEnum.Public) {
        return true;
      }
      if ((member.Modifiers & ModifierEnum.Protected) ==
        ModifierEnum.Protected &&
        IsClassInInheritanceTree(c, callingClass)) {
        return true;
      }
      return c.FullyQualifiedName == callingClass.FullyQualifiedName;
    }

    bool MustBeShown(IClass c, IDecoration member, bool showStatic)
    {
      if ((!showStatic && ((member.Modifiers & ModifierEnum.Static) ==
        ModifierEnum.Static))||
        ( showStatic && !((member.Modifiers & ModifierEnum.Static) ==
        ModifierEnum.Static))) {
        return false;
      }
      return IsAccessible(c, member);
    }
```

Now let's examine the dynamic lookups that take care of the names depending on their environment, such as local variables, method parameters, etc.:

```
    IClass DynamicLookup(string typeName)
    {
      // check whether a variable named typeName exists
      foreach (Variable v in cu.LookUpTable) {
//    Console.WriteLine("Variable: " + v.Name + " Region = " + v.Region);
        if (v.Name == typeName && v.Region.IsInside(caretLine, caretColumn)) {
          if (v.ReturnType.ArrayDimensions != null &&
//        Console.WriteLine("variable found");
            v.ReturnType.ArrayDimensions.Length > 0) {
            return parserService.GetClass("System.Array");
          }
          return SearchType(v.ReturnType.FullyQualifiedName,
            callingClass.CompilationUnit);
        }
      }
```

```
      if (callingClass == null) {
        return null;
      }

      // try whether typeName is a method parameter
      IClass found = SearchMethodParameter(typeName);
      if (found != null) {
        return found;
      }

      // check if typeName == value in set method of a property
      if (typeName == "value") {
        found = SearchProperty();
        if (found != null) {
          return found;
        }
      }

      // try to determine whether a nonstatic member named typeName exits
      bool showStatic = false;
      found = SearchMember(callingClass, typeName, ref showStatic);
      if (found != null) {
        return found;
      }

      // try whether a static member named typeName exists
      showStatic = true;
      found = SearchMember(callingClass, typeName, ref showStatic);
      if (found != null) {
        return found;
      }

      // test for existence of a static member named typeName
      ClassCollection classes = GetOuterClasses();
      foreach (IClass c in GetOuterClasses()) {
        found = SearchMember(c, typeName, ref showStatic);
        if (found != null) {
          return found;
        }
      }

      return null;
    }
```

In this code snippet, the diagnostic `Console.Writeline()` statements (which were removed from the other snippets in this chapter) are left intact to demonstrate how easily complex code can be modified for testing purposes. Such a simple approach to code testing is often preferable to extensive debugging sessions, which should be performed only when serious problems arise.

Another reason we chose this approach to debugging lies in the fact that we do not have a debugger integrated into SharpDevelop. Switching between an external debugging session and the IDE is irritating. Of course, choosing this approach is ultimately a matter of personal preference.

Now we will look at static lookups:

```
IClass StaticLookup(string typeName)
{
  IClass c = parserService.GetClass(typeName);

  if (c == null) {
    c = SearchType(typeName, cu);
  }
  return c;
}

/// use the using statements to find the correct name of a namespace
string SearchNamespace(string name, ICompilationUnit unit)
{
  if (parserService.NamespaceExists(name)) {
    return name;
  }
  if (unit == null) {
    return null;
  }
  foreach (IUsing u in unit.Usings) {
    if (u.Region.IsInside(caretLine, caretColumn)) {
      string nameSpace = u.SearchNamespace(name);
      if (nameSpace != null) {
        return nameSpace;
      }
    }
  }
  return null;
}
```

We have used the `using` statements to identify the namespaces that we have to work on for obtaining the applicable code completion suggestions. Then we move on to identifying the classes, which can be suggested at the current completion point. This is handled in the `foreach` statement:

```
/// use the using statements to find a class
IClass SearchType(string name, ICompilationUnit unit)
{
  IClass c;
  c = parserService.GetClass(name);
  if (c != null) {
    return c;
  }
  if (unit == null) {
    return null;
  }
  foreach (IUsing u in unit.Usings) {
    if (u.Region.IsInside(caretLine, caretColumn)) {
      c = u.SearchType(name);
      if (c != null) {
        return c;
      }
```

```
      }
    }
    return null;
}
```

Finally, we have to decide whether a protected member should be displayed to the user or not. Remember that protected members are only accessible from within their own class and from sub-classes thereof:

```
bool IsClassInInheritanceTree(IClass possibleBaseClass, IClass c)
{
  if (possibleBaseClass == null || c == null) {
    return false;
  }
  if (possibleBaseClass.FullyQualifiedName == c.FullyQualifiedName) {
    return true;
  }
  foreach (string baseClass in c.BaseTypes) {
    if (IsClassInInheritanceTree(possibleBaseClass,
      parserService.GetClass(baseClass))) {
      return true;
    }
  }
  return false;
}
```

In order to determine the class code for which completion has occurred, we must discover the innermost class:

```
IClass GetInnermostClass()
{
  if (cu != null) {
    foreach (IClass c in cu.Classes) {
      if (c.Region.IsInside(caretLine, caretColumn)) {
        return GetInnermostClass(c);
      }
    }
  }
  return null;
}

IClass GetInnermostClass(IClass curClass)
{
  if (curClass == null) {
    return null;
  }
  if (curClass.InnerClasses == null) {
    return curClass;
  }
  foreach (IClass c in curClass.InnerClasses) {
    if (c.Region.IsInside(caretLine, caretColumn)) {
```

```
        return GetInnermostClass(c);
      }
    }
    return curClass;
  }

  ClassCollection GetOuterClasses()
  {
    ClassCollection classes = new ClassCollection();
    if (cu != null) {
      foreach (IClass c in cu.Classes) {
        if (c.Region.IsInside(caretLine, caretColumn)) {
          if (c != GetInnermostClass()) {
            classes.AddRange(GetOuterClasses(classes, c));
            classes.Add(c);
          }
          break;
        }
      }
    }
    return classes;
  }

  ClassCollection GetOuterClasses(ClassCollection classes,
    IClass curClass)
  {
    if (curClass != null) {
      foreach (IClass c in curClass.InnerClasses) {
        if (c.Region.IsInside(caretLine, caretColumn)) {
          if (c != GetInnermostClass()) {
            classes.AddRange(GetOuterClasses(classes, c));
            classes.Add(c);
          }
          break;
        }
      }
    }
    return classes;
  }
}
}
```

Note that in this code snippet we are concerned with the caret position, as the resolution process is geared towards providing information for code completion.

We will now move on to look at the implementation of Code Completion in SharpDevelop.

Code Completion

As we mentioned in Chapter 1, Code Completion is one of the central features distinguishing a modern IDE, from a mere plain text editor. Code completion offers us a list of type members that may be used in the context of the current line. For the completion string currently selected, a tool-tip will offer additional information.

The diagram given below shows the flow of information needed for Code Completion:

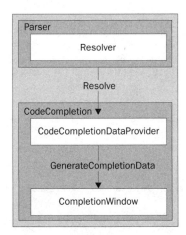

This diagram shows why the Resolver can be considered as being outside the scope of the Parser. The Resolver is elementary for code completion; it provides the base for actually using the parse information for the file in the edit buffer.

The files implementing code completion are part of the SDDefaultEditor and reside in the src\SharpDevelop\SDDefaultEditor\Gui\Editor\CompletionWindow directory.

First, let's look at the interface of the CompletionDataProvider that is found in the ICompletionDataProvider.cs file.

The interface code is:

```
namespace ICSharpCode.SharpDevelop.DefaultEditor.Gui.Editor
{
  public interface ICompletionDataProvider
  {
    ImageList ImageList {
      get;
    }

    ICompletionData[] GenerateCompletionData(string fileName,
      IDocumentAggregator document, char charTyped);
  }
}
```

We only need an `ImageList` containing the icons, representing the different member types of the items, for the completion suggestions, and the completion data itself.

The `CompletionDataProvider` is implemented in `CodeCompletionDataProvider.cs`:

```csharp
namespace ICSharpCode.SharpDevelop.DefaultEditor.Gui.Editor
{
  public class CodeCompletionDataProvider : ICompletionDataProvider
  {
    static ClassBrowserIconsService classBrowserIconService =
      (ClassBrowserIconsService)ServiceManager.Services.
      GetService(typeof(ClassBrowserIconsService));

    static IParserService parserService =
      (IParserService) ICSharpCode.Core.Services.ServiceManager.Services.
      GetService(typeof(IParserService));

    Hashtable insertedElements = new Hashtable();

    public ImageList ImageList {
      get {
        return classBrowserIconService.ImageList;
      }
    }

    int caretLineNumber;
    int caretColumn;
    string fileName;

    ArrayList completionData = null;

    public ICompletionData[] GenerateCompletionData(string fileName,
      IDocumentAggregator document, char charTyped)
    {
      completionData = new ArrayList();
      this.fileName = fileName;

      // the parser works with 1 based coordinates, so we add 1 to the
      //values
      caretLineNumber =
        document.GetLineNumberForOffset(document.Caret.Offset) + 1;
      caretColumn = document.Caret.Offset -
        document.GetLineSegment(caretLineNumber - 1).Offset + 1;
      string expression = TextUtilities.
        GetExpressionBeforeOffset(document, document.Caret.Offset);
      ResolveResult results;

      if (expression.Length == 0) {
        return null;
      }
      if (charTyped == ' ') {
        if (expression == "using" || expression.EndsWith(" using") ||
          expression.EndsWith("\tusing")|| expression.EndsWith("\nusing")||
          expression.EndsWith("\rusing")) {
```

```
                string[] namespaces = parserService.GetNamespaceList("");
                AddResolveResults(new ResolveResult(namespaces));
                }
            }
        } else {

            results = parserService.Resolve(expression, caretLineNumber,
                caretColumn, fileName);

            AddResolveResults(results);
        }
        return
            (ICompletionData[])completionData.ToArray(typeof(ICompletionData));
    }

    void AddResolveResults(ResolveResult results)
    {
        if (results != null) {
            if (results.Namespaces != null && results.Namespaces.Count > 0) {
                foreach (string s in results.Namespaces) {
                    completionData.Add(new CodeCompletionData(s,
                        classBrowserIconService.NamespaceIndex));
                }
            }
            if (results.Members != null && results.Members.Count > 0) {
                foreach (Object o in results.Members) {
                    if (o is IClass) {
                        completionData.Add(new CodeCompletionData((IClass)o));
                    } else if (o is IProperty) {
                        completionData.Add(new CodeCompletionData((IProperty)o));
                    } else if (o is IMethod) {
                        IMethod method = (IMethod)o;
                        if (insertedElements[method.Name] == null &&
                            !method.IsConstructor) {
                            completionData.Add(new CodeCompletionData(method));
                            insertedElements[method.Name] = method;
                        }
                    } else if (o is IField) {
                        completionData.Add(new CodeCompletionData((IField)o));
                    } else if (o is IEvent) {
                        completionData.Add(new CodeCompletionData((IEvent)o));
                    }
                }
            }
        }
    }
}
```

Here, we set up the `ImageList` for the icons. The appearance of the icons depends on the ambience (visual style) selected by the user for the Class Browser.

We then move on to assemble the completion data for the file currently being edited. Note that we have to be aware of the current caret position, as this controls the completion suggestions that are displayed. The caret position is counted from position 1 and not 0, as might be expected when considering the index base of arrays. A parser always starts at line 1, character 1.

We then provide namespace information obtained earlier in the step-by-step lookup to enable completion of using statements, and then we provide the results of the Resolver for code completion. The completion information is added after removing duplicates, due to overloading of methods, removal of constructors, and assigning icons to the various members.

The file CodeCompletionData.cs handles this task:

```
namespace ICSharpCode.SharpDevelop.DefaultEditor.Gui.Editor
{
  class CodeCompletionData : ICompletionData
  {
    static ClassBrowserIconsService classBrowserIconService =
      (ClassBrowserIconsService)ServiceManager.Services.
      GetService(typeof(ClassBrowserIconsService));

    static IParserService parserService = (IParserService)ICSharpCode.Core.
      Services.ServiceManager.Services.GetService(typeof(IParserService));
    static AmbienceService ambienceService = (AmbienceService)
      ServiceManager.Services.GetService(typeof(AmbienceService));

    int       imageIndex;
    int       overloads;
    string    text;
    string    description;
    string    documentation;
    string    completionString;
    IClass    c;
    bool      convertedDocumentation = false;

    public int Overloads {
      get {
        return overloads;
      }
      set {
        overloads = value;
      }
    }

    public int ImageIndex {
      get {
        return imageIndex;
      }
      set {
        imageIndex = value;
      }
    }
```

```
public string[] Text {
  get {
    return new string[] { text };
  }
  set {
    text = value[0];
  }
}
```

In this snippet, we define the variables. The variable `convertedDocumentation` is intended for using the documentation that can be automatically generated from XML comments, as a source of descriptive information to be displayed in tool-tips.

Then we generate description texts:

```
public string Description {
  get {
    // get correct delegate description (when description is requested).
    // in the classproxies methods aren't saved, therefore delegate
    // methods must be got through the real class
    if (c is ClassProxy && c.ClassType == ClassType.Delegate) {
      description = ambienceService.CurrentAmbience.Convert
        (parserService.GetClass(c.FullyQualifiedName));
      c = null;
    }

    // don't give a description string, if no documentation or
    //description is provided
    if (description.Length + documentation.Length == 0) {
      return null;
    }
    if (!convertedDocumentation) {
      convertedDocumentation = true;
      try {
        XmlDocument doc = new XmlDocument();
        doc.LoadXml("<doc>" + documentation + "</doc>");
        XmlNode root    = doc.DocumentElement;
        XmlNode paramDocu = root.SelectSingleNode("summary");
        documentation = paramDocu.InnerXml;
      } catch (Exception e) {
        Console.WriteLine(e.ToString());
      }
    }
    return description +
      (overloads > 0 ? " (+" + overloads + " overloads)" : String.Empty)
      + "\n" + documentation;
  }
  set {
    description = value;
  }
}
```

Now, we are all set to put together the code completion data that we have generated:

```
public CodeCompletionData(string s, int imageIndex)
{
  description = documentation = String.Empty;
  text = s;
  completionString = s;
  this.imageIndex = imageIndex;
}

public CodeCompletionData(IClass c)
{
  // save class (for the delegate description shortcut
  this.c = c;
  imageIndex = classBrowserIconService.GetIcon(c);
  text = c.Name;
  completionString = c.Name;
  description = ambienceService.CurrentAmbience.Convert(c);
  documentation = c.Documentation;
}

public CodeCompletionData(IMethod method)
{
  imageIndex  = classBrowserIconService.GetIcon(method);
  text        = method.Name;
  description = ambienceService.CurrentAmbience.Convert(method);
  completionString = method.Name;
  documentation = method.Documentation;
}

public CodeCompletionData(IField field)
{
  imageIndex  = classBrowserIconService.GetIcon(field);
  text        = field.Name;
  description = ambienceService.CurrentAmbience.Convert(field);
  completionString = field.Name;
  documentation = field.Documentation;
}

public CodeCompletionData(IProperty property)
{
  imageIndex  = classBrowserIconService.GetIcon(property);
  text        = property.Name;
  description = ambienceService.CurrentAmbience.Convert(property);
  completionString = property.Name;
  documentation = property.Documentation;
}

public CodeCompletionData(IEvent e)
{
  imageIndex  = classBrowserIconService.GetIcon(e);
  text        = e.Name;
  description = ambienceService.CurrentAmbience.Convert(e);
  completionString = e.Name;
```

```
        documentation = e.Documentation;
      }

    public void InsertAction(TextAreaControl control)
    {
      ((SharpDevelopTextAreaControl)control).InsertString(completionString);
    }
  }
}
```

In this code snippet, we populate the completion data, and add the appropriate icons. We also add the description strings, where available. They are used later on for the tool-tips. The information for these descriptions cannot be obtained from the proxy classes, which we use to save memory when building the code completion database (refer to Chapter 12). Therefore, we have to obtain this data from the real classes represented by the proxies. At of the time of writing, the XML tags contained in the description strings haven't been removed. This will change in the next release.

Finally, we define `InsertAction` for inserting the `completionString` into the edit buffer.

A special case of Code Completion is Template Completion. Templates are used when a code snippet is to be inserted by using shorthand, for example, typing `cwrl` and then `ctrl-j` will insert `Console.WriteLine` at the caret position. This is coded in the `TemplateCompletionDataProvider.cs` file:

```
namespace ICSharpCode.SharpDevelop.DefaultEditor.Gui.Editor
{
  public class TemplateCompletionDataProvider : ICompletionDataProvider
  {
    public ImageList ImageList {
      get {
        return null;
      }
    }

    public ICompletionData[] GenerateCompletionData(string fileName,
      IDocumentAggregator document, char charTyped)
    {
      ArrayList completionData = new ArrayList();

      foreach (CodeTemplate template in CodeTemplateLoader.Template) {
        completionData.Add(new TemplateCompletionData(template));
      }

      return
        (ICompletionData[])completionData.ToArray(typeof(ICompletionData));
    }

    class TemplateCompletionData : ICompletionData
    {
      CodeTemplate template;
```

```
        public int ImageIndex {
          get {
            return 0;
          }
        }

        public string[] Text {
          get {
            return new string[] { template.Shortcut, template.Description };
          }
        }

        public string Description {
          get {
            return template.Text;
          }
        }

        public void InsertAction(TextAreaControl control)
        {
          ((SharpDevelopTextAreaControl)control).InsertTemplate(template);
        }

        public TemplateCompletionData(CodeTemplate template)
        {
          this.template = template;
        }
      }
    }
  }
```

Another case where completion comes handy is comments. One of the features of the C# language is the XML comment system, which greatly simplifies the task of documenting the interfaces of the code. These comments consist of specialized XML tags inserted into a special style of single line comment.

Whenever we type an opening pointed bracket (<) in a comment line starting with three slashes, a list of XML comment tags is displayed. These tags are paired, so that a closing tag can be automatically inserted when the opening tag is typed in. Comment completion uses data generated by the code in CommentCompletionDataProvider.cs:

```
namespace ICSharpCode.SharpDevelop.DefaultEditor.Gui.Editor
{
  public class CommentCompletionDataProvider : ICompletionDataProvider
  {
    static ClassBrowserIconsService classBrowserIconService =
      (ClassBrowserIconsService)ServiceManager.Services.
      GetService(typeof(ClassBrowserIconsService));

    static IParserService parserService = (IParserService)
      ICSharpCode.Core.Services.ServiceManager.Services.
      GetService(typeof(IParserService));
```

```
ICompilationUnit cu;

int caretLineNumber;
int caretColumn;

string[][] commentTags = new string[][] {
  new string[] {"c", "marks text as code"},
  new string[] {"code", "marks text as code"},
  new string[] {"example", "A description of the code example\n
    (must have a <code> tag inside)"},
  new string[]
    {"exception cref=\"\"", "description to an exception thrown"},
  new string[] {"list type=\"\"", "A list"},
  new string[] {"listheader", "The header from the list"},
  new string[] {"item", "A list item"},
  new string[] {"term", "A term in a list"},
  new string[] {"description", "A description to a term in a list"},
  new string[] {"param name=\"\"", "A description for a parameter"},
  new string[] {"paramref name\"\"", "A reference to a parameter"},
  new string[] {"permission cref=\"\"", ""},
  new string[] {"remarks", "Gives description for a member"},
  new string[] {"returns", "Gives description for a return value"},
  new string[] {"see cref=\"\"", "A reference to a member"},
  new string[] {"seealso cref=\"\"",
    "A reference to a member in the seealso section"},
  new string[] {"summary", "A summary of the object"},
  new string[] {"value", "A description of a property"}
};

public ImageList ImageList {
  get {
    return classBrowserIconService.ImageList;
  }
}

// Returns true, if the given coordinates are in the region.
bool IsBetween(int row, int column, IRegion region)
{
  return row >= region.BeginLine &&
    (row <= region.EndLine || region.EndLine == -1);
}

// Returns the class in which the caret currently is, returns null
// if the caret is outside the class boundaries.
IClass GetCurrentClass(IDocumentAggregator document, string fileName)
{
  if (cu != null) {
    foreach (IClass c in cu.Classes) {
      if (IsBetween(caretLineNumber, caretColumn, c.Region)) {
        return c;
      }
    }
  }
```

```
    return null;
  }

public ICompletionData[] GenerateCompletionData(string fileName,
  IDocumentAggregator document, char charTyped)
{
  caretLineNumber =
    document.GetLineNumberForOffset(document.Caret.Offset) + 1;
  caretColumn = document.Caret.Offset -
    document.GetLineSegment(caretLineNumber - 1).Offset + 1;
  IParseInformation parseInformation =
    parserService.GetParseInformation(fileName);

  if (parseInformation == null) {
    return null;
  }

  cu = parseInformation.MostRecentCompilationUnit as ICompilationUnit;
  if (cu == null) {
    return null;
  }

  IClass callingClass = GetCurrentClass(document, fileName);
  bool inComment = false;
  foreach (Comment comment in cu.DokuComments) {
    if (IsBetween(caretLineNumber, caretColumn, comment.Region)) {
      inComment = true;
      break;
    }
  }

  ArrayList completionData = new ArrayList();

  if (inComment) {
    foreach (string[] tag in commentTags) {
      completionData.Add(new CommentCompletionData(tag[0], tag[1]));
    }
  }

  return (ICompletionData[])
    completionData.ToArray(typeof(ICompletionData));
}

class CommentCompletionData : ICompletionData
{
  string text;
  string description;

  public int ImageIndex {
    get {
      return classBrowserIconService.MethodIndex;
    }
  }
```

```
        public string[] Text {
          get {
            return new string[] { text };
          }
        }

        public string Description {
          get {
            return description;
          }
        }

        public void InsertAction(TextAreaControl control)
        {
          ((SharpDevelopTextAreaControl)control).InsertString(text);
        }

        public CommentCompletionData(string text, string description)
        {
          this.text        = text;
          this.description = description;
        }
      }
    }
  }
```

Now that we have a full set of code completion data, we will move on to look at Code Completion itself. The UML diagram, opposite, shows the implementation of Code Completion and Method Insight:

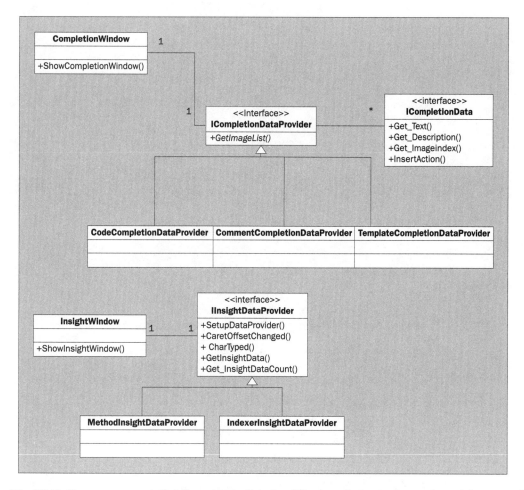

The UML diagrams are superficially quite similar, the differences being in the number of data providers and the additional CompletionData interface for code completion.

Let's see how Code Completion is displayed using the data providers we examined above. The source code is located in the CompletionWindow.cs file. The first segment looks like this:

```
namespace ICSharpCode.SharpDevelop.DefaultEditor.Gui.Editor
{
  public class CompletionWindow : Form
  {
    ICompletionDataProvider completionDataProvider;
    TextAreaControl control;
    ListView listView = new MyListView();
    DeclarationViewWindow declarationviewwindow =
      new DeclarationViewWindow();
```

```csharp
int insertLength = 0;

class MyListView : ListView
{
  protected override bool ProcessDialogKey(Keys keyData)
  {
    if (keyData == Keys.Tab) {
      OnItemActivate(null);
    }
    return base.ProcessDialogKey(keyData);
  }
}

string GetTypedString()
{
  return control.Document.
    GetText(control.Document.Caret.Offset - insertLength, insertLength);
}

void DeleteInsertion()
{
  if (insertLength > 0) {
    control.Document.Remove
      (control.Document.Caret.Offset - insertLength, insertLength);
    control.UpdateLine(control.Document.
      GetLineNumberForOffset(control.Document.Caret.Offset), 0, 0);
  }
}

void ListKeypressEvent(object sender, KeyPressEventArgs ex)
{
  switch (ex.KeyChar) {
    case (char)27: // Escape
      LostFocusListView(null, null);
      return;
    case '\b': //Backspace
      new ICSharpCode.TextEditor.Actions.Backspace().Execute(control);
      if (insertLength > 0) {
        --insertLength;
      } else {
        // no need to delete here (insertLength <= 0)
        LostFocusListView(null, null);
      }
      break;
    default:
      if (ex.KeyChar != '_' && !Char.IsLetterOrDigit(ex.KeyChar)) {
        if (listView.SelectedItems.Count > 0) {
          ActivateItem(null, null);
        } else {
          LostFocusListView(null, null);
        }
        control.KeyPressed(this, ex);
        return;
      } else {
```

```
        control.InsertChar(ex.KeyChar);
        ++insertLength;
      }
      break;
  }

  // select the current typed word
  int lastSelected = -1;
  int capitalizationIndex = -1;

  string typedString = GetTypedString();
  for (int i = 0; i < listView.Items.Count; ++i) {

    if (listView.Items[i].Text.ToUpper().
      StartsWith(typedString.ToUpper())) {
      int currentCapitalizationIndex = 0;
      for (int j = 0; j < typedString.Length &&
        j < listView.Items[i].Text.Length; ++j) {
        if (typedString[j] == listView.Items[i].Text[j]) {
          ++currentCapitalizationIndex;
        }
      }

      if (currentCapitalizationIndex > capitalizationIndex) {
        lastSelected = i;
        capitalizationIndex = currentCapitalizationIndex;
      }
    }
  }

  listView.SelectedItems.Clear();
  if (lastSelected != -1) {
    listView.Items[lastSelected].Focused  = true;
    listView.Items[lastSelected].Selected = true;
    listView.EnsureVisible(lastSelected);
  }
  ex.Handled = true;
}
```

Here, we set up things, prior to initializing code completion itself.

Then we create a form, containing a listView, to display the completion strings and their icons, and set up key handling. Next, we select the currently typed word, as we need to determine what suggestions for completion to display. Then we go on to initialize the listView and display it:

```
void InitializeControls()
{
  Width = 340;
  Height = 210 - 85;
```

```
    StartPosition = FormStartPosition.Manual;
    FormBorderStyle = FormBorderStyle.None;
    TopMost = true;
    ShowInTaskbar = false;

    listView.Dock = DockStyle.Fill;
    listView.View = View.Details;
    listView.AutoArrange = true;
    listView.Alignment = ListViewAlignment.Left;
    listView.HeaderStyle = ColumnHeaderStyle.None;
    listView.Sorting = SortOrder.Ascending;
    listView.MultiSelect = false;
    listView.FullRowSelect = true;
    listView.HideSelection = false;
    listView.SmallImageList = completionDataProvider.ImageList;
    listView.KeyPress += new KeyPressEventHandler(ListKeypressEvent);

    listView.LostFocus += new EventHandler(LostFocusListView);
    listView.ItemActivate += new EventHandler(ActivateItem);
    listView.SelectedIndexChanged +=
      new EventHandler(SelectedIndexChanged);
    this.Controls.Add(listView);
}

// Shows the filled completion window; if it has no items it isn't shown
public void ShowCompletionWindow(char firstChar)
{
  FillList(true, firstChar);

  if (listView.Items.Count > 0) {
    Rectangle size =
      listView.Items[0].GetBounds(ItemBoundsPortion.Entire);

    ClientSize = new Size(size.Width +
      SystemInformation.VerticalScrollBarWidth + 4,
      size.Height * Math.Min(10, listView.Items.Count));

    declarationviewwindow.Show();
    Show();

    listView.Select();
    listView.Focus();

    listView.Items[0].Focused = listView.Items[0].Selected = true;
    control.TextAreaPainter.IHaveTheFocus = true;
  } else {
    control.Focus();
  }
}
```

We also need to determine the position where the completion window will be drawn – for this there are two possible scenarios:

- at the caret position
- at a predetermined position

The former is used when we would expect it: when we are typing the code. The latter when we have completion triggered programmatically. For example, this would be the case when the Code Completion dropdown would extend beyond the SharpDevelop window, like when editing in the last line of the editor. Then, we will have to open its offset from the caret position. This is done by the following code snippet:

```
string fileName;

public CompletionWindow(TextAreaControl control, string fileName,
                        ICompletionDataProvider completionDataProvider)
{
  this.fileName = fileName;
  this.completionDataProvider = completionDataProvider;
  this.control = control;

  Point caretPos =
    control.Document.OffsetToView(control.Document.Caret.Offset);

  Point visualPos = new
    Point(control.TextAreaPainter.GetVirtualPos(control.Document.
    GetLineSegmentForOffset(control.Document.Caret.Offset), caretPos.X),
    (int)((1 + caretPos.Y) * control.TextAreaPainter.FontHeight) -
    control.TextAreaPainter.ScreenVirtualTop);

   Location = control.TextAreaPainter.PointToScreen(visualPos);
   InitializeControls();
}

// Creates a new Completion window at a given location
CompletionWindow(TextAreaControl control, Point location,
  ICompletionDataProvider completionDataProvider)
{
  this.completionDataProvider = completionDataProvider;
  this.control              = control;
  Location = location;
  InitializeControls();
}
```

We have to handle the selection of a completion suggestion made by the user:

```
void SelectedIndexChanged(object sender, EventArgs e)
{
  if (listView.SelectedItems.Count > 0) {
    ICompletionData data =
      (ICompletionData)listView.SelectedItems[0].Tag;
```

```
      if (data.Description != null) {
        listView.EnsureVisible(listView.SelectedIndices[0]);
        Point pos = new Point(Bounds.Right,Bounds.Top +
          listView.GetItemRect(listView.SelectedIndices[0]).Y);
        declarationviewwindow.Location    = pos;
        declarationviewwindow.Description = data.Description;
      } else {
        declarationviewwindow.Size = new Size(0, 0);
      }
    }
  }
}

void ActivateItem(object sender, EventArgs e)
{
  control.TextAreaPainter.IHaveTheFocusLock = true;
  if (listView.SelectedItems.Count > 0) {
    ICompletionData data =
      (ICompletionData)listView.SelectedItems[0].Tag;
    DeleteInsertion();
    data.InsertAction(control);
    LostFocusListView(sender, e);
  }
  control.TextAreaPainter.IHaveTheFocusLock = false;
}
```

Here, the Boolean `control.TextAreaPainter.IHaveTheFocusLock` needs special attention. We need to take care of it, as the caret in the editor window should not be visible when the completion window, or any other window, takes the focus away from the editor window.

Finally, we have to close the completion window when it loses the focus in its turn, and with implementing the list called in `ShowCompletionWindow`:

```
void LostFocusListView(object sender, EventArgs e)
{
  control.Focus();
  declarationviewwindow.Close();
  Close();
}

void FillList(bool firstTime, char ch)
{
  ICompletionData[] completionData = completionDataProvider.
    GenerateCompletionData(fileName, control.Document, ch);
  if (completionData == null || completionData.Length == 0) {
    return;
  }
  if (firstTime && completionData.Length > 0) {
    int columnHeaders = completionData[0].Text.Length;
    for (int i = 0; i < columnHeaders; ++i) {
      ColumnHeader header = new ColumnHeader();
      header.Width = -1;
      listView.Columns.Add(header);
    }
```

```
        }
      listView.BeginUpdate();
      foreach (ICompletionData data in completionData) {
        ListViewItem newItem = new ListViewItem(data.Text, data.ImageIndex);
        newItem.Tag = data;
        listView.Items.Add(newItem);
      }
      listView.EndUpdate();
    }
```

That's all we need for Code Completion. Using parse information is quite simple, isn't it? Now let's examine the implementation of Method Insight in SharpDevelop.

Method Insight

In principle, Method Insight is similar to Code Completion. It offers a tool-tip containing the parameters required by the method we just typed in. From our UML diagram (refer to the *Code Completion* section), we can see that it is similar in basic structure but simpler, as we only have to deal with one data provider. Also, we don't need an interface to the data, like we had for Code Completion.

The source code is contained in the directory src\SharpDevelop\SDDefaultEditor\Gui\Editor\InsightWindow.

Let's first look at the data provider. It is implemented in the file InsightDataProvider.cs:

```
namespace ICSharpCode.SharpDevelop.DefaultEditor.Gui.Editor
{
  public class MethodInsightDataProvider : IInsightDataProvider
  {
    ClassBrowserIconsService classBrowserIconService =
      (ClassBrowserIconsService) ServiceManager.Services.
      GetService(typeof(ClassBrowserIconsService));
    IParserService parserService = (IParserService)ServiceManager.
      Services.GetService(typeof(IParserService));
    AmbienceService ambienceService = (AmbienceService)
      ServiceManager.Services.GetService(typeof(AmbienceService));

    string fileName = null;
    IDocumentAggregator document = null;
    MethodCollection methods  = new MethodCollection();

    int caretLineNumber;
    int caretColumn;

    public int InsightDataCount {
      get {
        return methods.Count;
      }
    }
  }
```

```
public string GetInsightData(int number)
{
  IMethod method = methods[number];
  IAmbience conv = ambienceService.CurrentAmbience;
  conv.ConversionFlags = ConversionFlags.StandardConversionFlags;
  return conv.Convert(method) + "\n" + method.Documentation;
}
```

Note that, to obtain the method insight data, we have used some of the services discussed in Chapter 5.

Now, we can move on to see where we are in the document, and then retrieve the information for the method at hand:

```
int initialOffset;
public void SetupDataProvider(string fileName,
                             IDocumentAggregator document)
{
  this.fileName = fileName;
  this.document = document;
  initialOffset = document.Caret.Offset;

  string word = TextUtilities.
    GetExpressionBeforeOffset(document, document.Caret.Offset);
  string methodObject = word;
  string methodName   = null;
  int idx = methodObject.LastIndexOf('.');
  if (idx >= 0) {
    methodName   = methodObject.Substring(idx + 1);
    methodObject = methodObject.Substring(0, idx);
  } else {
    methodObject = "this";
    methodName   = word;
  }

  if (methodName.Length == 0 || methodObject.Length == 0) {
    return;
  }
```

If the methods are unknown to Method Insight they need to be retrieved and stored; should they be known but have changed (for example, we have overloaded a method), they need to be updated. The following code snippet handles this:

```
// the parser works with 1 based coordinates,
//so we add 1 to the indices
caretLineNumber =
  document.GetLineNumberForOffset(document.Caret.Offset) + 1;
caretColumn = document.Caret.Offset -
  document.GetLineSegment(caretLineNumber).Offset + 1;

bool contructorInsight = word.StartsWith("new ");
if (contructorInsight) {
  methodObject = word.Substring(word.LastIndexOf("new ") + 4);
```

```
      }

      ResolveResult results = parserService.
        Resolve(methodObject, caretLineNumber, caretColumn, fileName);

      if (results != null && results.Type != null) {
        if (contructorInsight) {
          AddConstructors(results.Type);
        } else {
          foreach (IClass c in results.Type.ClassInheritanceTree) {
            AddMethods(c, methodName, false);
          }
        }
      }
    }

    bool IsAlreadyIncluded(IMethod newMethod)
    {
      foreach (IMethod method in methods) {
        if (method.Name == newMethod.Name) {
          if (newMethod.Parameters.Count != method.Parameters.Count) {
            return false;
          }

          for (int i = 0; i < newMethod.Parameters.Count; ++i) {
            if (newMethod.Parameters[i].ReturnType !=
              method.Parameters[i].ReturnType) {
              return false;
            }
          }

          // take out old method, when it isn't documented.
          if (method.Documentation == null ||
            method.Documentation.Length == 0) {
            methods.Remove(method);
            return false;
          }
          return true;
        }
      }
      return false;
    }

    void AddConstructors(IClass c)
    {
      foreach (IMethod method in c.Methods) {
        if (method.IsConstructor && !method.IsStatic) {
          methods.Add(method);
        }
      }
    }

    void AddMethods(IClass c, string methodName, bool discardPrivate)
```

```
    {
      foreach (IMethod method in c.Methods) {
        if (!(method.IsPrivate && discardPrivate) &&
            method.Name == methodName &&
            !IsAlreadyIncluded(method)) {
          methods.Add(method);
        }
      }
    }
  }
```

Of course, we also have to check for changes in the caret position, to find out whether we need Method Insight at the new position. After all, we trigger Method Insight only under specific circumstances (when we find ourselves at the end a method name). The case statement is used to keep track of the paired and nested elements in our text buffer, such as bracketing:

```
public bool CaretOffsetChanged()
{
  bool closeDataProvider = document.Caret.Offset <= initialOffset;
  int brackets = 0;
  int curlyBrackets = 0;
  if (!closeDataProvider) {
    bool insideChar   = false;
    bool insideString = false;
    for (int offset = initialOffset; offset <
      Math.Min(document.Caret.Offset, document.TextLength); ++offset) {
      char ch = document.GetCharAt(offset);
      switch (ch) {
        case '\'':
          insideChar = !insideChar;
          break;
        case '(':
          if (!(insideChar || insideString)) {
            ++brackets;
          }
          break;
        case ')':
          if (!(insideChar || insideString)) {
            --brackets;
          }
          if (brackets <= 0) {
            return true;
          }
          break;
        case '"':
          insideString = !insideString;
          break;
        case '}':
          if (!(insideChar || insideString)) {
            --curlyBrackets;
          }
          if (curlyBrackets < 0) {
            return true;
          }
```

```
                break;
            case '{':
                if (!(insideChar || insideString)) {
                   ++curlyBrackets;
                }
                break;
            case ';':
                if (!(insideChar || insideString)) {
                  return true;
                }
                break;
            }
          }
        }

        return closeDataProvider;
      }

    }
  }
```

While comparing Method Insight to Code Completion, a few additional issues need to be addressed. Constructors must have their own code in order to be handled properly. We also need to count the curly brackets to ensure they are properly balanced.

As an additional case of our insight provider, we also have a data provider for indexers in the `IndexerInsightDataProvider.cs` file. Accessing them is done through a slightly different API, so we have this separate piece of code:

```
namespace ICSharpCode.SharpDevelop.DefaultEditor.Gui.Editor
{
  public class IndexerInsightDataProvider : IInsightDataProvider
  {
    ClassBrowserIconsService classBrowserIconService =
      (ClassBrowserIconsService) ServiceManager.Services.
      GetService(typeof(ClassBrowserIconsService));
    IParserService parserService = (IParserService)ServiceManager.
      Services.GetService(typeof(IParserService));
    AmbienceService ambienceService = (AmbienceService)ServiceManager.
      Services.GetService(typeof(AmbienceService));

    string fileName = null;
    IDocumentAggregator document = null;
    IndexerCollection methods  = new IndexerCollection();

    public int InsightDataCount {
      get {
        return methods.Count;
      }
    }

    public string GetInsightData(int number)
    {
```

```
        IIndexer method = methods[number];
        IAmbience conv = ambienceService.CurrentAmbience;
        conv.ConversionFlags = ConversionFlags.StandardConversionFlags;
        return conv.Convert(method) + "\n" + method.Documentation;
    }

    int initialOffset;
    public void SetupDataProvider(string fileName,
                                  IDocumentAggregator document)
    {
        this.fileName = fileName;
        this.document = document;
        initialOffset = document.Caret.Offset;

        string word = TextUtilities.
          GetExpressionBeforeOffset(document, document.Caret.Offset);
        string methodObject = word;

        // the parser works with 1 based coordinates
        //   so we add 1 to the values
        int caretLineNumber =
          document.GetLineNumberForOffset(document.Caret.Offset) + 1;
        int caretColumn = document.Caret.Offset -
          document.GetLineSegment(caretLineNumber - 1).Offset + 1;
        ResolveResult results = parserService.Resolve(methodObject,
          caretLineNumber, caretColumn, fileName);
        if (results != null && results.Type != null) {
          foreach (IClass c in results.Type.ClassInheritanceTree) {
            foreach (IIndexer indexer in c.Indexer) {
              methods.Add(indexer);
            }
          }
        }
    }


      // caret offset handling omitted for listing
      return closeDataProvider;
    }

    public bool CharTyped()
    {
      int offset = document.Caret.Offset - 1;
      if (offset >= 0) {
        return document.GetCharAt(offset) == ']';
      }
      return false;
    }
  }
}
```

Comparing this to our earlier code snippet (the one we saw while looking at methods), we can see that the big case statement, which we needed with methods, is omitted. Indexers exist only inside square brackets, so we need not handle other cases. The code is simpler, as we do not need to look for arbitrary methods. We know what we are looking for and where.

Finally, we have everything needed for displaying the method insight information. The code for this is given in the `InsightWindow.cs` file.

Again, we will look at the setup first. Here, we setup a new form containing the method insight suggestions and get our data providers ready:

```
namespace ICSharpCode.SharpDevelop.DefaultEditor.Gui.Editor
{
  public class InsightWindow : Form
  {
    TextAreaControl control;
    Stack insightDataProviderStack = new Stack();
    CaretEventHandler caretOffsetChangedEventHandler;
    EventHandler focusEventHandler;
    KeyPressEventHandler keyPressEventHandler;
    TextAreaControl.DialogKeyProcessor dialogKeyProcessor;

    class InsightDataProviderStackElement
    {
      public int currentData;
      public IInsightDataProvider dataProvider;

      public InsightDataProviderStackElement(IInsightDataProvider
        dataProvider)
      {
        this.currentData  = 0;
        this.dataProvider = dataProvider;
      }
    }

    public void AddInsightDataProvider(IInsightDataProvider provider)
    {
      provider.SetupDataProvider(fileName, control.Document);
      if (provider.InsightDataCount > 0) {
        insightDataProviderStack.
          Push(new InsightDataProviderStackElement(provider));
      }
    }

    int CurrentData {
      get {
        return ((InsightDataProviderStackElement)
          insightDataProviderStack.Peek()).currentData;
      }
      set {
        ((InsightDataProviderStackElement)
          insightDataProviderStack.Peek()).currentData = value;
      }
    }

    IInsightDataProvider DataProvider {
      get {
        if (insightDataProviderStack.Count == 0) {
```

```
        return null;
      }
      return ((InsightDataProviderStackElement)
        insightDataProviderStack.Peek()).dataProvider;
  }
}

void CloseCurrentDataProvider()
{
  insightDataProviderStack.Pop();
  if (insightDataProviderStack.Count == 0) {
    Close();
  } else {
    resized = false;
    Refresh();
  }
}
```

Then, we will display our method insight information:

```
public void ShowInsightWindow()
{
  if (!Visible) {
    if (insightDataProviderStack.Count > 0) {
      control.TextAreaPainter.IHaveTheFocusLock = true;
      Show();
      dialogKeyProcessor =
        new TextAreaControl.DialogKeyProcessor(ProcessTextAreaKey);
      control.ProcessDialogKeyProcessor += dialogKeyProcessor;
      control.Focus();
      control.TextAreaPainter.IHaveTheFocus     = true;
      control.TextAreaPainter.IHaveTheFocusLock = false;
    }
  } else {
    resized = false;
    Refresh();
  }
}
string fileName;

public InsightWindow(TextAreaControl control, string fileName)
{
  this.control = control;
  this.fileName = fileName;
  Point caretPos =
    control.Document.OffsetToView(control.Document.Caret.Offset);
  Point visualPos = new
    Point(control.TextAreaPainter.GetVirtualPos(control.Document.
    GetLineSegmentForOffset(control.Document.Caret.Offset), caretPos.X),
    (int)((1 + caretPos.Y) * control.TextAreaPainter.FontHeight) -
    control.TextAreaPainter.ScreenVirtualTop);
```

```
        focusEventHandler = new EventHandler(TextEditorLostFocus);
        caretOffsetChangedEventHandler =
          new CaretEventHandler(CaretOffsetChanged);

        control.TextAreaPainter.IHaveTheFocusChanged += focusEventHandler;
        control.Document.Caret.OffsetChanged +=
          caretOffsetChangedEventHandler;
        keyPressEventHandler = new KeyPressEventHandler(KeyPressEvent);
        control.TextAreaPainter.KeyPress += keyPressEventHandler;

        Location = control.TextAreaPainter.PointToScreen(visualPos);

        StartPosition   = FormStartPosition.Manual;
        FormBorderStyle = FormBorderStyle.None;
        TopMost         = true;
        ShowInTaskbar   = false;
        Size            = new Size(0, 0);

        SetStyle(ControlStyles.UserPaint, true);
        SetStyle(ControlStyles.DoubleBuffer, true);
    }

    // Methods that are inserted into the TextArea :
    bool ProcessTextAreaKey(Keys keyData)
    {
      switch (keyData) {
        case Keys.Escape:
          Close();
          return true;
        case Keys.Down:
          if (DataProvider != null && DataProvider.InsightDataCount > 0) {
            CurrentData = (CurrentData + 1) % DataProvider.InsightDataCount;
            resized = false;
            Refresh();
          }
          return true;
        case Keys.Up:
          if (DataProvider != null && DataProvider.InsightDataCount > 0) {
            CurrentData = (CurrentData + DataProvider.InsightDataCount - 1)
              % DataProvider.InsightDataCount;
            resized = false;
            Refresh();
          }
          return true;
      }
      return false;
    }
```

In the case of Method Insight, we use a `TextArea` control for display. The rest of the code is similar to what we discussed earlier for handling user actions and caret changes, so we won't discuss it.

In this chapter, we have seen two powerful uses of the parse information; in the next chapter we will move on to another very interesting use – code navigation using the Class Scout.

Summary

In this chapter, we discussed the issues involved in helping the user to rapidly write the code without having to refer to external documentation of classes and their members. We then examined how we can harness the information provided by SharpDevelop's Parser service to this end.

We learned about the role of the Resolver in providing parse information and looked at how this information is made available for Code Completion and Method Insight.

We then looked at providing the data needed to the Code Completion system and discussed data provision for general Code Completion and for Template Completion. We also examined the implementation of Code Completion, including handling the focus changes between windows.

Finally, we looked at Method Insight, and the differences in its implementation as compared to Code Completion.

CHAPTER 14

14

Navigating Code with the Class Scout and the Assembly Scout

The source code for SharpDevelop contains more than 1,600 files, most of them containing a class each. In such a huge project, is there a way to quickly find the implementation of an individual class and its members? Besides, what about the references to external assemblies, what do they contain? How can we access them?

Agreed, files are named according to the class they contain, directories and paths correspond to the namespaces, but wouldn't it be nice to have a way to see all the classes in a project and open the source file for that class just by clicking? Even for smaller projects, this sounds like a good idea.

In this chapter, we will look at a way of using the parse information to answer these questions. We will be examining the Class Scout and Assembly Scout, which make it possible for us to navigate through the various classes and assemblies involved in our project.

Let's begin our discussion with the Class Scout.

The Class Scout

In programming, finding the source code for a given class in a project is a frequent task, be it for reference or be it for working on the code of the class. In case of big projects, the task of finding the appropriate file can be tiresome, if performed manually.

To address this problem, we have implemented a Class Scout in SharpDevelop that allows us to browse all the classes available to us in our project. As we learned in Chapter 12, the information needed to identify the classes used by our code is easily available.

Implementing the Class Scout

Let's look at a simplified UML diagram showing the implementation of the Class Scout:

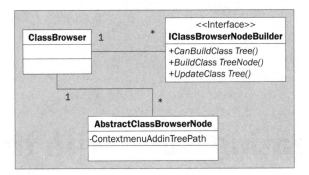

The Class Scout provides an interface and defines an Addin tree node for its context menu. It's no big deal, but the code behind it is quite interesting.

Let's start our discussion by examining the code in `ClassScout.cs` file, which is located in the `src\SharpDevelop\Base\Gui\Pads\ClassScout` directory:

```
namespace ICSharpCode.SharpDevelop.Gui.Pads
{
  public class ClassScoutTag
  {
    int    line;
    string filename;

    public int Line {
      get {
        return line;
      }
    }

    public string FileName {
      get {
        return filename;
      }
    }

    public ClassScout (int line, string filename)
    {
      this.line = line;
      this.filename = filename;
    }
  }

  // This class is the project scout tree view
  public class ClassScout : TreeView, IPadContent
  {
```

```
Panel contentPanel = new Panel();
int imageIndexOffset = -1;
ResourceService resourceService = (ResourceService)
  ServiceManager.Services.GetService(typeof(ResourceService));

IClassScoutScoutNodeBuilder[] classScoutScoutNodeBuilders =
  new IClassScoutNodeBuilder[] {
  new DefaultDotNetClassScoutNodeBuilder()
};

public string Title {
  get {
    return
      resourceService.GetString("MainWindow.Windows.ClassScoutLabel");
  }
}

public Bitmap Icon {
  get {
    return resourceService.GetBitmap("Icons.16x16.Class");
  }
}

public Control Control {
  get {
    return contentPanel;
  }
}
```

In this code snippet, we set up a couple of things:

❏   **Class Scout tags** These tags are necessary for providing the jump points necessary when
   clicking on a class in the class scout. For this functionality, each class member in the tree must
   be provided with the filename and line number.

❏   **The Class Scout,** as a tree view. The tree view of the classes and their members is displayed in
   a SharpDevelop pad.

Now, we will move on to the code responsible for setting up the class scout:

```
public ClassScout()
{
  ClassScoutIconsService classScoutIconService =
    (ClassScoutIconsService)ServiceManager.Services.
    GetService(typeof(ClassScoutIconsService));

  this.ImageList  = classScoutIconService.ImageList;

  imageIndexOffset = ImageList.Images.Count;
  FileUtilityService fileUtilityService = (FileUtilityService)
    ServiceManager.Services.GetService(typeof(FileUtilityService));
```

```
      foreach (Image img in fileUtilityService.ImageList.Images) {
        ImageList.Images.Add(img);
      }

      LabelEdit = false;
      HotTracking = false;
      AllowDrop = true;
      HideSelection = false;
      Dock = DockStyle.Fill;

      IProjectService projectService = (IProjectService)
        ICSharpCode.Core.Services.ServiceManager.Services.
        GetService(typeof(IProjectService));

      projectService.CombineOpened +=
        new CombineEventHandler(OnCombineOpen);
      projectService.CombineClosed +=
        new CombineEventHandler(OnCombineClosed);

      IParserService parserService = (IParserService)ICSharpCode.Core.
        Services.ServiceManager.Services.GetService(typeof(IParserService));

      contentPanel.Controls.Add(this);
      AmbienceService ambienceService = (AmbienceService)
        ServiceManager.Services.GetService(typeof(AmbienceService));
      ambienceService.AmbienceChanged +=
        new EventHandler(AmbienceChangedEvent);
    }
```

This snippet sets options for the display (of the scout), and the various services and event handlers that can be connected to the events of other classes, we are interested in.

The next snippet deals with updating the display:

```
    void AmbienceChangedEvent(object sender, EventArgs e)
    {
      if (parseCombine != null) {
        DoPopulate();
      }
    }
```

By changing the ambience, the display of classes information can be adapted to the user's preference; C#, Visual Basic, and .NET styles are available. The Ambience service was discussed in Chapter 5.

Then comes the code for updating the parse information in the tree:

```
    void UpdateParseInformation(TreeNodeCollection nodes,
                               ParseInformationEventArgs e)
    {
      foreach (TreeNode node in nodes) {
        if (node.Tag is IProject) {
          IProject p = (IProject)node.Tag;
```

```
        if (p.IsFileInProject(e.FileName)) {
          foreach (IClassScoutNodeBuilder classScoutNodeBuilder in
            classScoutNodeBuilders) {
            if (classScoutNodeBuilder.CanBuildClassTree(p)) {
              classScoutNodeBuilder.UpdateClassTree(node, e);
            }
          }
        }
      }
    }
  }
```

Next, we will examine the code needed for opening the file containing the class selected by the user:

```
protected override void OnDoubleClick(EventArgs e)
  {
    base.OnDoubleClick(e);
    TreeNode node = SelectedNode;
    ClassScoutTag tag = node.Tag as ClassScoutTag;
    if (tag != null) {
      IFileService fileService =
        (IFileService)ICSharpCode.Core.Services.ServiceManager.Services.
        GetService(typeof(IFileService));
      fileService.OpenFile(tag.FileName);

      IViewContent content =
        fileService.GetOpenFile(tag.FileName).ViewContent;
      if (content is IPositionable) {
        if (tag.Line > 0) {
          ((IPositionable)content).JumpTo(new Point(0, tag.Line - 1));
          content.Control.Focus();
        }
      }
    }
  }
```

Here, we use the `ClassScoutTag` to retrieve the name of the required file, open it as a content of the editor window, and finally jump to the appropriate line where the desired class is defined.

The following snippet populates the tree view by making a call to the `Populate` method (it is explained later in this section):

```
void DoPopulate()
{
  BeginUpdate();
  Nodes.Clear();
  try {
    Populate(parseCombine, Nodes);
  } catch (Exception e) {
    MessageBox.Show(e.ToString(), "Parse Error", MessageBoxButtons.OK,
      MessageBoxIcon.Error);
  }
```

```
      EndUpdate();
   }
```

If an error occurs while parsing the file, we need to handle it. Such errors can occur when the parser runs into syntactically incorrect code, or when the file is damaged. The code snippet that we just examined handles these types of errors.

Parsing is started in a new thread; otherwise, SharpDevelop would be 'blocked' while the file was being parsed. As Combines in SharpDevelop are made up of Projects, we need to parse the files contained in both the Projects and sub-projects:

```
Combine parseCombine;

delegate void MyD();

void StartPopulating()
{
  StartParser();
  Invoke(new MyD(DoPopulate));
}

void StartParser()
{
  ParseCombine(parseCombine);
}

void StartCombineparse(Combine combine)
{
  parseCombine = combine;

  System.Threading.Thread t =
    new Thread(new ThreadStart(StartPopulating));
  t.IsBackground = true;
  t.Priority = ThreadPriority.Lowest;
  t.Start();
}

public void ParseCombine(Combine combine)
{
  foreach (CombineEntry entry in combine.Entries) {
    if (entry is ProjectCombineEntry) {
      ParseProject(((ProjectCombineEntry)entry).Project);
    } else {
      ParseCombine(((CombineCombineEntry)entry).Combine);
    }
  }
}

void ParseProject(IProject p)
{
  if (p.ProjectType == "C#") {
    foreach (ProjectFile finfo in p.ProjectFiles) {
      if (finfo.BuildAction == BuildAction.Compile) {
```

```
          IParserService parserService =
            (IParserService)ICSharpCode.Core.Services.
            ServiceManager.Services.GetService(typeof(IParserService));
          parserService.ParseFile(finfo.Name);
        }
      }
    }
  }
```

Currently parsing of C# is supported; there are plans to add support for Visual Basic. NET.

Now that we have successfully parsed our Combine, let's look at the `Populate` method that populates the tree:

```
void Populate(IProject p, TreeNodeCollection nodes)
{
  // only C# is currently supported.
  bool builderFound = false;
  foreach (IClassScoutNodeBuilder classScoutNodeBuilder in
    classScoutNodeBuilders) {
    if (classScoutNodeBuilder.CanBuildClassTree(p)) {
      TreeNode prjNode =
        classScoutNodeBuilder.BuildClassTreeNode(p, imageIndexOffset);
      nodes.Add(prjNode);
      prjNode.Tag = p;
      builderFound = true;
      break;
    }
  }

  // no builder found -> create 'dummy' node
  if (!builderFound) {
    TreeNode prjNode = new TreeNode(p.Name);
    FileUtilityService fileUtilityService = (FileUtilityService)
      ServiceManager.Services.GetService(typeof(FileUtilityService));
    prjNode.SelectedImageIndex = prjNode.ImageIndex = imageIndexOffset +
      fileUtilityService.GetImageIndexForProjectType(p.ProjectType);
    prjNode.Nodes.Add(new TreeNode("No class builder found"));
    prjNode.Tag = p;
    nodes.Add(prjNode);

  }
}

public void Populate(Combine combine, TreeNodeCollection nodes)
{
  ClassScoutIconsService classScoutIconService =
    (ClassScoutIconsService)ServiceManager.
    Services.GetService(typeof(ClassScoutIconsService));
  TreeNode combineNode = new TreeNode(combine.Name);
  combineNode.SelectedImageIndex = combineNode.ImageIndex =
    classScoutIconService.CombineIndex;
  foreach (CombineEntry entry in combine.Entries) {
```

```
        if (entry is ProjectCombineEntry) {
          Populate(((ProjectCombineEntry)entry).Project, combineNode.Nodes);
        } else {
          Populate(((CombineCombineEntry)entry).Combine, combineNode.Nodes);
        }
      }
      nodes.Add(combineNode);
    }
```

For populating the tree, we add entries for each class and its members containing the name, an image corresponding to the type, and the tag. As shown in the code snippet, the `Populate` method is recursive, thereby allowing us to handle nestled Combines. In SharpDevelop, for projects beyond a minimal size nested combines make sense, as this will make the development process more modular, so nestled Combines are common.

To complete our Class Scout, we have to provide the code for opening and closing the combines, and also, for navigating the tree view by using the mouse:

```
void OnCombineOpen(object sender, CombineEventArgs e)
{
  Nodes.Clear();
  Nodes.Add(new TreeNode("Loading..."));
  StartCombineparse(e.Combine);
}
```

In the above code snippet, we begin to build the tree. We set a temporary node to indicate the process has begun and then start the real work of parsing the Combine.

Now, we will move on to the other end of the process – closing combines. This is simple, but we also need to examine the handling of mouse clicks, so that a tree made up of several combines expands and collapses properly:

```
void OnCombineClosed(object sender, CombineEventArgs e)
{
  Nodes.Clear();
}

protected override void OnMouseDown(MouseEventArgs e)
{
  TreeNode node = (TreeNode)GetNodeAt(e.X, e.Y);

  if (node != null) {
    SelectedNode = node;
  }
  base.OnMouseDown(e);
}
```

This snippet sets a node as active when we click on it.

Next, we need to open up the sub-tree and populate it in case of a left click; if it's a right click then we have to pop up a context menu:

```
protected override void OnMouseUp(MouseEventArgs e)
{
  if (e.Button == MouseButtons.Right && SelectedNode != null &&
    SelectedNode is AbstractClassScoutNode) {
      AbstractClassScoutNode selectedScoutNode =
        (AbstractClassScoutNode)SelectedNode;
    if (selectedScoutNode.ContextmenuAddinTreePath != null &&
      selectedScoutNode.ContextmenuAddinTreePath.Length > 0) {
      MenuCommand[] contextMenu =
        (MenuCommand[])(AddInTreeSingleton.AddInTree.GetTreeNode
        (selectedScoutNode.ContextmenuAddinTreePath).
        BuildChildItems(this)).ToArray(typeof(MenuCommand));
      if (contextMenu.Length > 0) {
        PopupMenu popup = new PopupMenu();
        PropertyService propertyService = (PropertyService)
          ServiceManager.Services.GetService(typeof(PropertyService));
        popup.Style = (Crownwood.Magic.Common.VisualStyle)
          propertyService.GetProperty
          ("ICSharpCode.SharpDevelop.Gui.VisualStyle",
          Crownwood.Magic.Common.VisualStyle.IDE);
        popup.MenuCommands.AddRange(contextMenu);
        popup.TrackPopup(PointToScreen(new Point(e.X, e.Y)));
        return;
      }
    }
  }
  base.OnMouseUp(e);
}
```

If the type of the class member changes, we need to handle display-related events, like changing the name of the title and associated icon:

```
protected virtual void OnTitleChanged(EventArgs e)
{
  if (TitleChanged != null) {
    TitleChanged(this, e);
  }
}

protected virtual void OnIconChanged(EventArgs e)
{
  if (IconChanged != null) {
    IconChanged(this, e);
  }
}

public event EventHandler TitleChanged;
public event EventHandler IconChanged;
}
```

This part of the code is simple, except for one item – the pop up menu. This menu for the Class Scout is a new feature of SharpDevelop, and provides further functionality by using the class information.

At the time of writing, this menu contains only one item – **ExportSignature**. This option exports the signature of a class, interface, or method to the clipboard, from where it can be easily pasted into other places. This is extremely useful while making the documentation for our classes. One of our motivations behind this was to make our lives as authors of this book easier.

We have plans to add other features, such as sorting the tree by name or type, exporting the class tree to XML (for easier documentation), and so on; if you have some good ideas feel free to contact us or even better, you can contribute them!

Now, let's move on to the actual building of the tree and its nodes. This is done by the code contained in the file src\SharpDevelop\Base\Gui\Pads\ClassScout\NodeBuilder\DefaultDotNetClassScoutNodeBuilder.cs:

```
namespace ICSharpCode.SharpDevelop.Gui.Pads
{
  public class DefaultDotNetClassScoutNodeBuilder : IClassScoutNodeBuilder
  {
    int imageIndexOffset;
    IAmbience languageConversion;

    public DefaultDotNetClassScoutNodeBuilder()
    {
    }

    public bool CanBuildClassTree(IProject project)
    {
      return true;
    }

    void GetCurrentAmbience ()
    {
      ClassScoutIconsService classScoutIconService =
        (ClassScoutIconsService)ServiceManager.Services.
        GetService(typeof(ClassScoutIconsService));
      AmbienceService ambienceService = (AmbienceService)ServiceManager.
        Services.GetService(typeof(AmbienceService));

      languageConversion = ambienceService.CurrentAmbience;
      languageConversion.ConversionFlags = ConversionFlags.None;
    }

    public TreeNode BuildClassTreeNode(IProject p, int imageIndexOffset)
    {
      GetCurrentAmbience();
      this.imageIndexOffset = imageIndexOffset;
      TreeNode prjNode = new AbstractClassScoutNode(p.Name);
      FileUtilityService fileUtilityService = (FileUtilityService)
        ServiceManager.Services.GetService(typeof(FileUtilityService));
      prjNode.SelectedImageIndex = prjNode.ImageIndex = imageIndexOffset +
```

```
        fileUtilityService.GetImageIndexForProjectType(p.ProjectType);

    foreach (ProjectFile finfo in p.ProjectFiles) {
      if (finfo.BuildAction == BuildAction.Compile) {
        int i = 0;
        IParserService parserService =
          (IParserService)ICSharpCode.Core.Services.ServiceManager.
          Services.GetService(typeof(IParserService));
        if (parserService.GetParser(finfo.Name) == null) {
          continue;
        }
        while (parserService.GetParseInformation(finfo.Name) == null) {
          Thread.Sleep(100);
          if (i++ > 5) {
            break;
          }
        }
        if (parserService.GetParseInformation(finfo.Name) == null) {
          continue;
        }
        IParseInformation parseInformation =
          parserService.GetParseInformation(finfo.Name);
        if (parseInformation != null) {
          ICompilationUnit unit = parseInformation.BestCompilationUnit as
            ICompilationUnit;
          if (unit != null) {
            foreach (IClass c in unit.Classes) {
              TreeNode node = GetPath(c.Namespace, prjNode.Nodes, true);
              if (node == null) {
                node = prjNode;
              }
              Insert(node.Nodes, finfo.Name, c);
            }
          }
        }
      }
    }
  }
  return prjNode;
}

TreeNode GetNodeFromCollectionTreeByName(TreeNodeCollection collection,
                                         string name)
{
  foreach (TreeNode node in collection) {
    if (node.Text == name) {
      return node;
    }
  }
  return null;
}
```

This code snippet sets up the requirements, such as the ambience to be used for the tree, for the build process and then proceeds to build the nodes. While building, we have to check whether the parser thread has returned the necessary information, if not, we have to wait until it does so. The following code snippet handles this (it is a part of the code snippet given above):

```
while (parserService.GetParseInformation(finfo.Name) == null) {
        Thread.Sleep(100);
        if (i++ > 5) {
           break;
        }
      }
      if (parserService.GetParseInformation(finfo.Name) == null) {
        continue;
      }
      IParseInformation parseInformation =
        parserService.GetParseInformation(finfo.Name);
      if (parseInformation != null) {
        ICompilationUnit unit = parseInformation.BestCompilationUnit as
          ICompilationUnit;
        if (unit != null) {
          foreach (IClass c in unit.Classes) {
            TreeNode node = GetPath(c.Namespace, prjNode.Nodes, true);
            if (node == null) {
              node = prjNode;
            }
            Insert(node.Nodes, finfo.Name, c);
          }
        }
      }
```

On finding no valid parse information, we either sleep for a predetermined time or try to determine the compilation unit to be used for populating the tree. Compilation units were discussed in Chapter 8. The tree nodes are then added to a collection.

```
        public TreeNode GetPath(string directory, TreeNodeCollection root,
                bool create)
    {
      ClassScoutIconsService classScoutIconService =
        (ClassScoutIconsService) ServiceManager.
        Services.GetService(typeof(ClassScoutIconsService));

      string[] treepath  = directory.Split(new char[] { '.' });
      TreeNodeCollection curcollection = root;
      TreeNode curnode = null;

      foreach (string path in treepath) {

        if (path.Length == 0 || path[0] == '.') {
          continue;
        }

        TreeNode node =
          GetNodeFromCollectionTreeByName(curcollection, path);
        if (node == null) {
```

```
         if (create) {
             TreeNode newnode = new AbstractClassScoutNode(path);
             newnode.ImageIndex = newnode.SelectedImageIndex =
                 classScoutIconService.NamespaceIndex;

             curcollection.Add(newnode);
             curnode = newnode;
             curcollection = curnode.Nodes;
             continue;
         } else {
             return null;
         }
     }
     curnode = node;
     curcollection = curnode.Nodes;
 }
 return curnode;
}
```

Now, all that is left for building the tree is to insert the nodes of the collection into the tree proper:

```
void Insert(TreeNodeCollection nodes, string filename, IClass c)
{
    ClassScoutIconsService classScoutIconService =
        (ClassScoutIconsService)ServiceManager.Services.
        GetService(typeof(ClassScoutIconsService));
    AbstractClassScoutNode cNode = new AbstractClassScoutNode(c.Name);
    cNode.SelectedImageIndex = cNode.ImageIndex =
        classScoutIconService.GetIcon(c);
    cNode.ContextmenuAddinTreePath =
        "/SharpDevelop/Views/ClassScout/ContextMenu/ClassNode";

    cNode.Tag = new ClassScoutTag(c.Region.BeginLine, filename);

    nodes.Add(cNode);
    // don't insert delegate 'members'
    if (c.ClassType == ClassType.Delegate) {
        return;
    }

    TreeNode cbNode;

    foreach (IClass innerClass in c.InnerClasses) {
        if (innerClass.ClassType == ClassType.Delegate) {
            cbNode = new
                AbstractClassScoutNode(languageConversion.Convert(innerClass));
            cbNode.Tag =
                new ClassScoutTag(innerClass.Region.BeginLine, filename);
            cbNode.SelectedImageIndex = cbNode.ImageIndex =
                classScoutIconService.GetIcon(innerClass);
            cNode.Nodes.Add(cbNode);
        } else {
            Insert(cNode.Nodes, filename, innerClass);
```

```
          }
      }

      foreach (IMethod method in c.Methods) {
         cbNode =
         new AbstractClassScoutNode(languageConversion.Convert(method));
         cbNode.Tag = new ClassScoutTag(method.Region.BeginLine, filename);
         cbNode.SelectedImageIndex = cbNode.ImageIndex =
            classScoutIconService.GetIcon(method);
         cNode.Nodes.Add(cbNode);
      }

      foreach (IProperty property in c.Properties) {
         cbNode =
            new AbstractClassScoutNode(languageConversion.Convert(property));
         cbNode.Tag = new ClassScoutTag(property.Region.BeginLine, filename);
         cbNode.SelectedImageIndex = cbNode.ImageIndex =
            classScoutIconService.GetIcon(property);
         cNode.Nodes.Add(cbNode);
      }

      foreach (IField field in c.Fields) {
         cbNode =
            new AbstractClassScoutNode(languageConversion.Convert(field));
         cbNode.Tag = new ClassScoutTag(field.Region.BeginLine, filename);

         cbNode.SelectedImageIndex = cbNode.ImageIndex =
            classScoutIconService.GetIcon(field);
         cNode.Nodes.Add(cbNode);
      }

      foreach (IEvent e in c.Events) {
         cbNode = new AbstractClassScoutNode(languageConversion.Convert(e));
         cbNode.Tag = new ClassScoutTag(e.Region.BeginLine, filename);
         cbNode.SelectedImageIndex = cbNode.ImageIndex =
            classScoutIconService.GetIcon(e);
         cNode.Nodes.Add(cbNode);
      }
   }
```

Here, the images associated with the tree nodes are obtained using `classScoutIconService`; we have discussed this service in Chapter 5.

Now, we need a class for displaying the nodes in the Class Scout and we need to make the tree nodes aware of the context menu. These tasks are handled by the code in `src\SharpDevelop\Base\Gui\Pads\ClassScout\ScoutNode\AbstractClassScoutNode.cs`:

```
namespace ICSharpCode.SharpDevelop.Gui.Pads
{
   public class AbstractClassScoutNode : TreeNode
   {
      protected string contextmenuAddinTreePath = String.Empty;
```

```
    // We choose to return the add-in tree path instead of a popup menu
    // or a menuitem collection, because we don't want to add a
    // Magic library or Windows.Forms dependency.
    public virtual string ContextmenuAddinTreePath {
      get {
        return contextmenuAddinTreePath;
      }
      set {
        contextmenuAddinTreePath = value;
      }
    }

    public AbstractClassScoutNode(string name) : base(name)
    {
    }
  }
}
```

Note that, this is not really an abstract base class; we call it abstract because we plan to make it abstract in future, just as we plan to do with `BuildClassTreeNode`.

We didn't use a popup or menu item collection as we wanted to minimize the number of dependencies on features specific to a given platform. Furthermore, this makes it easier to switch platforms, should we need to do so. A possible case where this would be necessary is in porting SharpDevelop to other .Net implementations, such as DotGNU or Mono on Linux systems. This completes our discussion about the Class Scout.

Displaying classes and their members is quite useful, but what about references? Assemblies and DLLs, also, contain information that we might want to look at. The next section will provide us with a solution for this problem.

The Assembly Scout

The Assembly Scout allows us to investigate assemblies and DLLs that we want to reference in our projects, or which contain functionality we want to implement ourselves. We will first look at the features of the scout and then discuss its implementation.

Markus Palme has contributed most of the code for this section.

Browsing References with an Assembly Scout

The Assembly Scout can be accessed in two ways, either by using the File | Open | File menu item to open an assembly or a DLL, or by navigating to a reference in the current project using the Project Scout and then double-clicking on the reference. Now, let's take a short tour of the Assembly Scout:

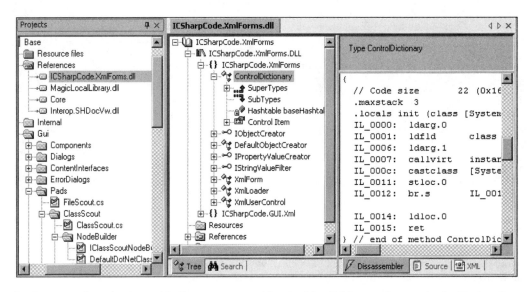

In the screenshot, the Assembly Scout was started by double-clicking a reference in the Project Scout. It consists of two panels. The first one is a tree view representing classes and members, similar to the Class Scout, grouped with a Search tab in the left hand pane. The right-hand pane contains information about the tree node that is highlighted in the left-hand pane. This pane offers three tabs for displaying information.

Currently, the disassembly information is shown, as this is always available for any reference. Now, we will switch the tabs to display the source code, as shown:

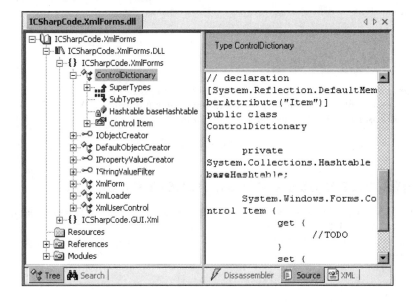

Here, we can see the source code for the same DLL file. If the source code isn't available then the pane will simply display **Source view not available**. Since we do not have a decompiler available, we can only see the skeleton of the code. Clicking the **XML** tab will display the following:

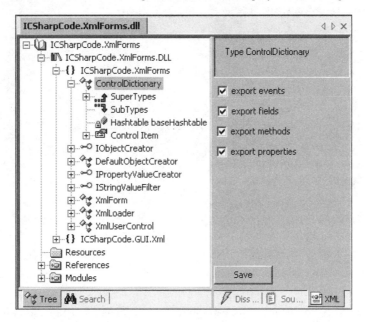

To make documentation tasks easier, the Assembly Scout allows us to export XML data describing the reference. This way, references can be easily incorporated with other XML documents, to generate other forms of documentation using XSLT.

Now that we have seen what the Assembly Scout is, let's move on to look at how this is achieved.

Writing the Assembly Scout

The Assembly Scout resides in the `src\BackendBindings\ObjectBrowser\src` directory.

At first this might seem a little illogical, since most of the back-end bindings that we discussed up to now were concerned with programming languages and compilers. However, the display bindings (including the Assembly Scout) are also back-end bindings, as they are not a part of SharpDevelop's Core, but may be exchanged when necessary.

We will begin by looking at how the Assembly Scout displays its information and then will work our way down through the code. We will start our discussion with the `DisplayInformation.cs` file, which implements the Assembly Scout as a view (that is, as a Display Binding):

```
namespace AssemblyScout
{
    public class DisplayInformation : IDisplayBinding
    {
```

```
  public bool CanCreateContentForFile(string fileName)
  {
    return Path.GetExtension(fileName) == ".dll" ||
      Path.GetExtension(fileName) == ".exe";
  }

  public bool CanCreateContentForLanguage(string language)
  {
    return false;
  }


  public IViewContent CreateContentForFile(string fileName)
  {
    DisplayInformationWrapper wrapper = new DisplayInformationWrapper();
    wrapper.LoadFile(fileName);
    return wrapper;
  }

  public IViewContent CreateContentForLanguage(string language,
                                               string content)
  {
    return null;
  }
}
```

We first check whether we can actually create content for the Scout, depending on whether the assembly file (a DLL) can be accessed, and whether we can handle the language. If both checks are successful, we can create the content. Then, we create the view containing our content:

```
public class DisplayInformationWrapper : IViewContent
{
  string filename = "";
  public MagicControls.TabControl tctrl;

  Control control = null;
  ReflectionTree tree = null;
  public Control Control {
    get {
      return control;
    }
  }

  string untitledName = "";
  public string UntitledName {
    get {
      return untitledName;
    }
    set {
      untitledName = value;
    }
  }
```

```
public string ContentName {
  get {
    return filename;
  }
  set {
    filename = value;
    OnContentNameChanged(null);
  }
}

public bool IsUntitled {
  get {
    return ContentName == null;
  }
}

public bool IsDirty {
  get {
    return false;
  }
  set {
  }
}

public bool IsReadOnly {
  get {
    return false;
  }
}
public bool IsViewOnly {
  get {
    return true;
  }
}

IWorkbenchWindow workbenchWindow;

public IWorkbenchWindow WorkbenchWindow {
  get {
    return workbenchWindow;
  }
  set {
    workbenchWindow = value;
    workbenchWindow.Title = filename;
  }
}
```

Then, we set up our view by using the tab controls of the Magic Library for navigating the tabs in the Scout and create a window for the Reflection tree view. Finally, we set up a Workbench window for displaying the Assembly Scout. We then create the content:

```
public bool CanCreateContentForFile(string fileName)
  {
```

```
    return Path.GetExtension(fileName) == ".dll" ||
      Path.GetExtension(fileName) == ".exe";
}

public bool CanCreateContentForLanguage(string language)
{
  return false;
}


public IViewContent CreateContentForFile(string fileName)
{
  LoadFile(fileName);
  return this;
}
public void Undo()
{
}
public void Redo()
{
}

public IViewContent CreateContentForLanguage(string language,
                                             string content)
{
  return null;
}

public void LoadFile(string filename)
{
  tree.LoadFile(filename);
  this.filename = filename;
  OnContentNameChanged(null);
}

public void SaveFile(string filename)
{
}

public void OnContentNameChanged(EventArgs e)
{
  if (ContentNameChanged != null) {
    ContentNameChanged(this, e);
  }
}
public void OnDirtyChanged(EventArgs e)
{
  if (DirtyChanged != null) {
    DirtyChanged(this, e);
  }
}
public event EventHandler ContentNameChanged;
public event EventHandler DirtyChanged;
```

We can create the content only for a `.dll` or `.exe` file. Loading the files is delegated. We also set up event handling for changes to the information displayed. Now we get to the central routine for setting up the display:

```
public DisplayInformationWrapper()
{
  Panel panel = new Panel();
  panel.Dock = DockStyle.Fill;

  tctrl = new MagicControls.TabControl();
  tctrl.Dock      = DockStyle.Fill;
  tctrl.Dock      = DockStyle.Left;
  tctrl.Width     = 350;

  MagicControls.TabPage treeviewpage =
    new MagicControls.TabPage("Tree");
  treeviewpage.Icon = resourceService.GetIcon("Icons.16x16.Class");
  ReflectionTree reflectiontree = new ReflectionTree();
  this.tree = reflectiontree;
  treeviewpage.Controls.Add(reflectiontree);
  tctrl.TabPages.Add(treeviewpage);

  MagicControls.TabPage indexviewpage =
    new MagicControls.TabPage("Search");
  indexviewpage.Icon = resourceService.GetIcon("Icons.16x16.FindIcon");
  ReflectionSearchPanel SearchPanel =
    new ReflectionSearchPanel(reflectiontree);
  SearchPanel.ParentDisplayInfo = this;
  indexviewpage.Controls.Add(SearchPanel);
  tctrl.TabPages.Add(indexviewpage);

  Splitter vsplitter = new Splitter();
  vsplitter.BorderStyle = System.Windows.Forms.BorderStyle.Fixed3D;

  vsplitter.Location = new System.Drawing.Point(0, 200);
  vsplitter.TabIndex = 5;
  vsplitter.TabStop = false;
  vsplitter.Size = new System.Drawing.Size(3, 273);
  vsplitter.Dock = DockStyle.Left;


  Splitter hsplitter = new Splitter();
//code omitted from listing

  MagicControls.TabControl tctrl2 = new MagicControls.TabControl();
  tctrl2.Dock = DockStyle.Fill;


  MagicControls.TabPage ildasmviewpage =
    new MagicControls.TabPage("Dissassembler");
  ildasmviewpage.Icon = resourceService.GetIcon("Icons.16x16.ILDasm");
  ildasmviewpage.Controls.Add(new ReflectionILDasmView(reflectiontree));
  tctrl2.TabPages.Add(ildasmviewpage);
```

```
// code omitted from listing

    panel.Controls.Add(hsplitter);
    panel.Controls.Add(tctrl2);
    panel.Controls.Add(new ReflectionInfoView(reflectiontree));

    panel.Controls.Add(vsplitter);
    panel.Controls.Add(tctrl);

    this.control = panel;
  }
}
```

Note that, for the sake of brevity we have omitted repetitive pieces of code. The code segment makes use of the controls provided by the Magic Library (http://www.dotnetmagic.com) to draw the Assembly Scout containing the tabbed views that we have seen in the above screenshots. Creating such a complex form without using a library like Magic would be quite hard.

We will move on to the individual parts of the Scout, starting with the tree view that is at the heart of the Assembly Scout. The code can be found in `ReflectionTree.cs`.

As usual, we will start by going through the setup and then load the assembly we are interested in:

```
namespace SharpDevelop.Gui.Edit.Reflection
{
  public class ReflectionTree : TreeView
  {
    ArrayList  assemblies = new ArrayList();

    public event EventHandler Changed;

    public ArrayList Assemblies {
      get {
        return assemblies;
      }
    }

    public PrintDocument PrintDocument {
      get {
        return null;
      }
    }

    public bool WriteProtected {
      get {
        return false;
      }
      set {
      }
    }
```

```
public void LoadFile(string filename)
{
  try {
    AddAssembly(Assembly.LoadFrom(filename));
  } catch (Exception e) {
    MessageBox.Show("can't load " + filename+ " invalid format.\n(you
      can only view .NET assemblies)\n " + e.ToString());
  }
}

public void SaveFile(string filename)
{
}

public void AddAssembly(Assembly assembly)
{
  assemblies.Add(assembly);
  TreeNode node =
    new ReflectionFolderNode(Path.GetFileNameWithoutExtension
    (assembly.CodeBase), assembly, ReflectionNodeType.Assembly, 0, 1);
  Nodes.Add(node);
  PopulateTreeView();
  Thread t = new Thread(new ThreadStart(PopulateTreeView));

  t.IsBackground = true;
  t.Start();
}
```

While loading the assembly, we have to handle possible exceptions arising from attempts at loading
.NET-incompatible `.dll` and `.exe` files. While adding the assembly, we have to insert it into the tree at
a new node and start populating the tree view. This is done in a new thread, so that the user is not
blocked from working in SharpDevelop, till it is completed.

Populating the tree view is done by the following piece of code, which uses recursion to navigate the
tree. Recursion is a very popular technique for such situations:

```
public void PopulateTreeView(ReflectionNode parentnode)
{
  foreach (ReflectionNode node in parentnode.Nodes) {
    if (!node.Populated) {
      node.Populate();
    }
    PopulateTreeView(node);
  }
}

public void PopulateTreeView()
{
  foreach (ReflectionNode node in Nodes) {
    if (!node.Populated)
      node.Populate();
    PopulateTreeView(node);
  }
```

```
  }

  internal static AmbienceReflectionDecorator languageConversion;

  public ReflectionTree()
  {
    if (Changed != null) {} // to prevent these pesky compiler warnings

    Dock = DockStyle.Fill;

    ClassScoutIconsService classScoutIconService =
      (ClassScoutIconsService)ServiceManager.Services.
      GetService(typeof(ClassScoutIconsService));
    AmbienceService ambienceService = (AmbienceService)ServiceManager.
      Services.GetService(typeof(AmbienceService));

    languageConversion = ambienceService.CurrentAmbience;
    languageConversion.ConversionFlags =
      languageConversion.ConversionFlags &
      ~(ConversionFlags.UseFullyQualifiedNames |
      ConversionFlags.ShowModifiers |
      ConversionFlags.ShowParameterNames);

    this.ImageList = classScoutIconService.ImageList;

    LabelEdit = false;
    HotTracking = false;
    AllowDrop = true;
    HideSelection = false;
  }
```

In this code snippet, we set up the appearance of the Reflection tree, as the way tree nodes' text is written depends on the selected ambience.

Now, we will handle the individual members and type, generating the actual nodes; we also handle language conversion:

```
  public void GoToMember(MemberInfo member, Assembly MemberAssembly)
  {
    foreach (ReflectionNode node in Nodes) {

      Assembly assembly = (Assembly)node.Attribute;
      string pathname = member.DeclaringType.Name;
      string paramtext = "";

      if (member is MethodInfo) {
        paramtext = languageConversion.Convert(member as MethodInfo);
      } else if (member is PropertyInfo) {
        paramtext = " : " +
          languageConversion.Convert(member as PropertyInfo);
      } else if (member is FieldInfo) {
        paramtext = " : " +
          languageConversion.Convert(member as FieldInfo);
```

```
      }

      if (assembly.FullName == MemberAssembly.FullName) {
        ReflectionNode curnode =
          (ReflectionNode)node.GetNodeFromCollection(node.Nodes,
          Path.GetFileName(assembly.CodeBase));
        if (member.DeclaringType.Namespace != null) {
          curnode =
            (ReflectionNode)curnode.GetNodeFromCollection(curnode.Nodes,
            member.DeclaringType.Namespace);
        }

        TreeNode path = curnode;
        TreeNode foundnode =
          node.GetNodeFromCollection(path.Nodes, pathname);

        ReflectionNode classnode = (ReflectionNode)foundnode;

        TreeNode membernode = classnode.GetNodeFromCollection
          (classnode.Nodes, member.Name + paramtext);
        membernode.EnsureVisible();
        SelectedNode = membernode;
      }
    }
}

public void GoToType(Type type)
{
  foreach (ReflectionNode node in Nodes) {
    Assembly assembly = (Assembly)node.Attribute;
    if (type.Assembly.FullName == assembly.FullName) {

      ReflectionNode curnode =
        (ReflectionNode)node.GetNodeFromCollection(node.Nodes,
        Path.GetFileName(assembly.CodeBase));

      //curnode = (ReflectionNode)curnode.GetNodeFromCollection
        (curnode.Nodes, Path.GetFileName(assembly.CodeBase));

      string typename = type.ToString();
      int lastindex = typename.LastIndexOf('.');
      TreeNode path = curnode;
      string nodename = typename;
      if (lastindex != -1) {
        string pathname = typename.Substring(0, lastindex);
        TreeNode tnode =
          node.GetNodeFromCollection(node.Nodes, pathname);
        if (tnode == null) {
          return; // TODO : returns, if the tree isn't up to date.
        } else
          path = tnode;
        nodename = typename.Substring(lastindex + 1);
      }
```

```
            TreeNode foundnode =
                node.GetNodeFromCollection(path.Nodes, nodename);
            foundnode.EnsureVisible();
            SelectedNode = foundnode;
            return;
        }
    }
    AddAssembly(type.Assembly);
    GoToType(type);
}
```

Again, we use the `classBroserIconService` and the `ambienceService` to give the tree nodes their proper appearance. Then, we add the members of the assembly. In doing so, we need to take care of language conversion so that the members are properly displayed.

The information for the type is obtained through the use of .NET reflection, which is performed in the file `ReflectionNode.cs` (we will discuss it later in this section). Next, we provide a routine for jumping to a type the user is interested in.

To complete the tree, we have to handle double-clicks and folding:

```
protected override void OnDoubleClick(EventArgs e)
{
  ReflectionNode rn = (ReflectionNode)SelectedNode;
  if (rn == null)
    return;
  switch (rn.Type) {

    case ReflectionNodeType.Link: // clicked on link, jump to link.
      if (rn.Attribute is Type) {
        GoToType((Type)rn.Attribute);
      }
      break;

    case ReflectionNodeType.Reference:
        // clicked on assembly reference, open assembly
        // check if the assembly is open
        AssemblyName name = (AssemblyName)rn.Attribute;
        foreach (ReflectionNode node in Nodes) {
          if (node.Type == ReflectionNodeType.Assembly) {
            if (name.FullName == ((Assembly)node.Attribute).FullName)
              // if yes, return
              return;
          }
        }
        AddAssembly(Assembly.Load(name));
        break;
    }
}

protected override void OnBeforeCollapse(TreeViewCancelEventArgs e)
{
  base.OnBeforeCollapse(e);
```

```
      ((ReflectionNode)e.Node).OnCollapse();
   }

   protected override void OnBeforeExpand(TreeViewCancelEventArgs e)
   {
      base.OnBeforeExpand(e);

      // populate node
      ReflectionNode rn = (ReflectionNode)e.Node;
      if (!rn.Populated)
         rn.Populate();

      ((ReflectionNode)e.Node).OnExpand();
   }
}
```

The type of the node determines the double-click's result. In the case of a type, we use the `GoToType` method that we defined above, while for a reference we add the assembly in question, if it is not yet open.

Next, we will look at the code for the right-hand panels. We will start with the code in `ReflectionSourceView.cs` file.

This code lists the source code of the assembly (if it is available). First we set up the view:

```
namespace SharpDevelop.Gui.Edit.Reflection
{
   public class ReflectionSourceView : UserControl
   {
      RichTextBox    rtb;
      ReflectionTree tree;


      void CopyEvent(object sender, EventArgs e)
      {
         Clipboard.SetDataObject(new DataObject(DataFormats.Text, rtb.Text));
      }
      public ReflectionSourceView(ReflectionTree tree)
      {
         rtb = new RichTextBox();
         rtb.ReadOnly = true;

         ResourceService resourceService = (ResourceService)ServiceManager.
            Services.GetService(typeof(ResourceService));
         rtb.Font = resourceService.LoadFont("Courier New", 10);

         this.tree = tree;

         Dock = DockStyle.Fill;

         tree.AfterSelect += new TreeViewEventHandler(SelectNode);
```

```
      Controls.Add(rtb);
      rtb.Dock = DockStyle.Fill;
      rtb.ContextMenu = new ContextMenu(new MenuItem[] {
        new MenuItem("Copy", new EventHandler(CopyEvent))
      });
    }
```

We have added handling of events in the tree view, as we have to react to the user selecting the member to be displayed. Further, we add a new menu item to the context menu. This done, we move on to populate the source view. As this is a long piece of code, containing sizeable blocks of very similar conditional statements or enumerations, to avoid repetition we have omitted a great part of these. The omissions are marked in the listing:

```
    static string GetTypeString(string type)
    {
      string[,] types = new string[,] {
        {"System.Void",    "void"},
        {"System.Object", "object"},
        {"System.Boolean", "bool"},
        {"System.Byte", "byte"},
        {"System.SByte", "sbyte"},
//code omitted from listing
        {"System.Decimal", "decimal"},
        {"System.String", "string"}
      };

      for (int i = 0; i < types.GetLength(0); ++i) {
        type = type.Replace(types[i, 0], types[i, 1]);
      }
      return type;
    }
```

First, the type is obtained, and then we move on to get the attributes of the objects. The latter part is tricky, as we can't easily look them up. Instead, we have to assemble the actual string piece-by-piece, taking care of possible exceptions arising from non-existent items:

```
    string GetAttributes(int indent, object[] attributes)
    {
      string back = "";
      if (attributes.Length > 0) {
        foreach (object o in attributes) {
          for (int i = 0; i < indent; ++i)
            back += "\t";
          back += "[";
          Type attrtype = o.GetType();
          back += attrtype.FullName + "(";
          try {
            object result = attrtype.InvokeMember ("Value",
              BindingFlags.Default | BindingFlags.GetField |
              BindingFlags.GetProperty, null, o, new object [] {});
            if (result is string) {
```

```
                    back += '"' + result.ToString() + '"';
                } else {
                    string resultstring = result.ToString();
                    if (result.GetType().IsEnum &&
                        !Char.IsDigit(resultstring[0]))
                        back += result.GetType().FullName + ".";
                    back += resultstring;
                }
            } catch (Exception) {
                try {
                    object result = attrtype.InvokeMember ("MemberName",
                        BindingFlags.Default |BindingFlags.GetField |
                        BindingFlags.GetProperty, null, o, new object [] {});
                    back += '"' + result.ToString() + '"';
                } catch (Exception) {

                }
            }
            back += ")]\n";
        }
    }
    return back;
}
```

Now that the objects have been taken care of, we will do the same for members:

```
string GetAttributes(int indent, MemberInfo type)
{
  return GetAttributes(indent, type.GetCustomAttributes(true));
}
void ShowTypeInfo(Type type)
{
  rtb.Text = "";
  {
    string attr2 =
      GetAttributes(0, type.Assembly.GetCustomAttributes(true));
    rtb.Text += "// assembly attributes\n" + attr2 +
      "\n// declaration\n";
  }
  string attr = GetAttributes(0, type);
  rtb.Text += attr;

  if (type.IsSealed && !type.IsEnum)
    rtb.Text += "sealed ";

  if (type.IsAbstract && !type.IsInterface)
    rtb.Text += "abstract ";
```

This segment checks for attributes such as `public`, `private`, and so on, so we can safely skip these conditional statements from our listing:

```
//code omitted for listing
    rtb.Text += type.Name;

    if (!type.IsEnum) {
      Type[] interfaces = type.GetInterfaces();
      if (interfaces.Length > 0) {
        rtb.Text += " : ";
        for (int i = 0; i < interfaces.Length; ++i) {
          rtb.Text += interfaces[i].FullName;
          if (i + 1 <interfaces.Length)
            rtb.Text += ", ";
        }
      }
    }

    rtb.Text += "\n{\n";
```

Then, we have to figure out the constructor:

```
    if (!type.IsEnum) {

      ConstructorInfo[] constructorinfos =
      type.GetConstructors(BindingFlags.Public | BindingFlags.NonPublic);
      MethodInfo[] methodinfos = type.GetMethods(BindingFlags.Instance |
        BindingFlags.Static | BindingFlags.Public |
        BindingFlags.NonPublic | BindingFlags.DeclaredOnly);

      FieldInfo[] fieldinfos = type.GetFields(BindingFlags.Instance |
        BindingFlags.Static | BindingFlags.Public |
        BindingFlags.NonPublic);

      PropertyInfo[] propertyinfos = type.GetProperties
        (BindingFlags.Instance | BindingFlags.Static | BindingFlags.Public
        | BindingFlags.NonPublic | BindingFlags.DeclaredOnly);
      EventInfo[] eventinfos  = type.GetEvents(BindingFlags.Instance |
        BindingFlags.Static | BindingFlags.Public |
        BindingFlags.NonPublic | BindingFlags.DeclaredOnly);
```

In the above code snippet, we look for all the field information that we can get on the constructor.

```
      foreach (FieldInfo fieldinfo  in fieldinfos) {
        if (fieldinfo.DeclaringType.Equals(type)) {
          rtb.Text += "\t";

          if (fieldinfo.IsPrivate) { // private
            rtb.Text += "private ";
          } else
          if (fieldinfo.IsFamily) { // protected
```

```
                rtb.Text += "protected ";
//code omitted from listing
            }

            rtb.Text += GetTypeString(fieldinfo.FieldType.ToString()) + " "
                + fieldinfo.Name + ";\n\n";
        }
    }
```

Now, we have to construct the strings for the code to be displayed:

```
        foreach (ConstructorInfo constructorinfo in constructorinfos) {
          if (constructorinfo.DeclaringType.Equals(type))
          if ((constructorinfo.Attributes & MethodAttributes.SpecialName) ==
          0) {
          attr = GetAttributes(1, constructorinfo);
          rtb.Text += attr;
          rtb.Text += "\t";

          if (!type.IsInterface) {
            if (constructorinfo.IsPrivate) { // private
              rtb.Text += "private ";
            } else
            if (constructorinfo.IsFamily ) { // protected
              rtb.Text += "protected ";
//code omitted from listing
          }

          rtb.Text += " " + type.Name +"(";
          ParameterInfo[] pinfo = constructorinfo.GetParameters();
          for (int i = 0; i < pinfo.Length; ++i) {
            string typetxt = pinfo[i].ParameterType.ToString();
            if (typetxt[typetxt.Length-1] == '&') {
              typetxt = "ref " + typetxt.Substring(0, typetxt.Length-1);
            }
            rtb.Text += GetTypeString(typetxt) + " " + pinfo[i].Name +
              ((i < pinfo.Length - 1) ? ", " : "");
          }
          if (type.IsInterface)
            rtb.Text += ");\n\n";
          else {
            rtb.Text += ")\n\t{\n\t\t//TODO\n\t}\n\n";
          }
        }
      }
    }
```

Even though we can't get all the information for a complete reconstruction of the constructor, at least now we have a skeleton that we can display.

Let us now move on to examining the methods:

```
foreach (MethodInfo methodinfo in methodinfos) {
  if (methodinfo.DeclaringType.Equals(type))
  if ((methodinfo.Attributes & MethodAttributes.SpecialName) == 0) {
    attr = GetAttributes(1, methodinfo);
    rtb.Text += attr;
    rtb.Text += "\t";

    if (!type.IsInterface) {
      if (methodinfo.IsPrivate) { // private
        rtb.Text += "private ";
      } else
      if (methodinfo.IsFamily ) { // protected
        rtb.Text += "protected ";
//code omitted from listing
      }
    rtb.Text += GetTypeString(methodinfo.ReturnType.ToString()) +
      " " + methodinfo.Name +"(";
    ParameterInfo[] pinfo = methodinfo.GetParameters();
    for (int i = 0; i < pinfo.Length; ++i) {
      string typetxt = pinfo[i].ParameterType.ToString();
      if (typetxt[typetxt.Length-1] == '&') {
        typetxt = "ref " + typetxt.Substring(0, typetxt.Length-1);
      }
      rtb.Text += GetTypeString(typetxt) + " " + pinfo[i].Name +
        ((i < pinfo.Length - 1) ? ", " : "");
    }
```

If we are dealing with an interface we will fill the string with a blank; otherwise, it's filled with the string TODO, which shows that there is no code to display:

```
    if (type.IsInterface)
      rtb.Text += ");\n\n";
    else {
      rtb.Text += ")\n\t{\n\t\t//TODO\n\t}\n\n";
    }
  }
}
```

Then we iterate through the property information, constructing the code to be output in a manner similar to the previous case:

```
foreach (PropertyInfo propertyinfo in propertyinfos) {
  if (propertyinfo.DeclaringType.Equals(type)) {
    attr = GetAttributes(1, propertyinfo);
    rtb.Text += attr;
    rtb.Text += "\t";

    rtb.Text += GetTypeString(propertyinfo.PropertyType.ToString())
      + " " + propertyinfo.Name + " {\n";
```

```
if (propertyinfo.CanRead) {
        rtb.Text += "\t\tget";
        if (type.IsInterface)
          rtb.Text += ";\n";
        else {
          rtb.Text += " {\n\t\t\t//TODO\n\t\t}\n";
        }
      }
      if (propertyinfo.CanWrite) {
        rtb.Text += "\t\tset";
        if (type.IsInterface)
          rtb.Text += ";\n";
        else {
          rtb.Text += " {\n\t\t\t//TODO\n\t\t}\n";
        }
      }
      rtb.Text += "\t}\n\n";
    }
  }
```

We insert TODO as a placeholder for non-interface properties.

Now, let's move on to events and enumerations:

```
    foreach (EventInfo eventinfo in eventinfos) {
      if (eventinfo.DeclaringType.Equals(type)) {
        rtb.Text += "\tevent " + eventinfo.EventHandlerType + " " +
          eventinfo.Name + ";\n";
      }
    }
  }

  if (type.IsEnum) {
    FieldInfo[] fieldinfos = type.GetFields();
    object enumobj = type.Assembly.CreateInstance(type.FullName);
    foreach (FieldInfo fieldinfo in fieldinfos) {
      if (fieldinfo.IsLiteral) {
        attr = GetAttributes(1, fieldinfo);
        rtb.Text += attr;
        rtb.Text += "\t" + fieldinfo.Name + " = " +
          (int)fieldinfo.GetValue(enumobj) + ",\n";
      }
    }
  }

  rtb.Text += "}";
  rtb.Refresh();
}
```

The code to be displayed is obtained by using the GetTypeString and GetAttributes methods. As the code is mostly made up of tests for attributes, such as public, private, etc., we have removed some parts for brevity. The GetAttributes method performs the task of converting the attributes to attribute definitions. Here, we also try to reconstruct the constructor parameters from the reflection information.

Although, we are not sure that this approach works all the time, nonetheless, we use it, leaving property settings out, as they can't be done this way. It seems that we will have to live with this limitation.

To remind the programmer about missing code snippets, we insert TODO into empty sets of curly braces. This is not a full source code disassembler, as it is not needed to investigate the structure of an assembly. For our purpose, a code skeleton is good enough. You can see the skeleton with the TODOs in the screenshot of the source view that we looked at in the beginning of this section.

We also need to decide whether we have some code to display or alternatively display the No source view available message:

```
void SelectNode(object sender, TreeViewEventArgs e)
{
  ReflectionNode node = (ReflectionNode)e.Node;

  rtb.Text = "";
  if (node is ReflectionTypeNode)
    ShowTypeInfo((Type)node.Attribute);
  else
    switch (node.Type) {
      case ReflectionNodeType.Namespace:
        rtb.Text = "namespace " + node.Text + " {\n}";
        break;
      default:
        rtb.Text = "No source view available";
        break;
    }


}
}
```

Now, we move on to the disassembler view. It uses the Microsoft .NET IL Disassembler tool (ildasm.exe), supplied with the .NET Framework SDK to decompile the intermediate language code contained in the assembly to a human readable form. This is done in the ReflectionILDasmView.cs file.

The code is shown below:

```
namespace SharpDevelop.Gui.Edit.Reflection
{
  public class ReflectionILDasmView : UserControl
  {
    RichTextBox tb = new RichTextBox();
    ReflectionTree tree;
```

```
public ReflectionILDasmView(ReflectionTree tree)
{
  this.tree = tree;

  Dock = DockStyle.Fill;
  tb.Font = new System.Drawing.Font("Courier New", 10);
  tb.Dock = DockStyle.Fill;
  tb.ScrollBars = RichTextBoxScrollBars.Both;

  tb.WordWrap  = false;
  tb.ReadOnly  = true;
  Controls.Add(tb);

  tree.AfterSelect += new TreeViewEventHandler(SelectNode);
}
```

Again, we carry out the setup; this time we use a rich textbox. We also listen to the tree view events.

Then, we select the node that we want to disassemble and work on it:

```
void SelectNode(object sender, TreeViewEventArgs e)
{
  ReflectionNode node = (ReflectionNode)e.Node;

  Assembly assembly = null;
  string item = " /item=";

  if (node.Attribute is Assembly) {
    assembly = (Assembly)node.Attribute;
  } else if (node.Attribute is Type) {
    Type type = (Type)node.Attribute;
    item += type.FullName;
    assembly = type.Module.Assembly;
  } else if (node.Attribute is MethodBase) {
    MethodBase method = (MethodBase) node.Attribute;
    item += method.DeclaringType.FullName + "::" + method.Name;
    assembly = method.DeclaringType.Module.Assembly;
  } else {
    tb.Text = "<NO ILDASM VIEW AVAIBLE>";
    return;
  }
  tb.Text = GetILDASMOutput(assembly, item).Replace("\n", "\r\n");
}

private string GetILDASMOutput(Assembly assembly, string item)
{
  try {
    string args = '"' + assembly.Location + '"' + item +
      " /NOBAR /TEXT";
    ProcessStartInfo psi = new ProcessStartInfo("ildasm.exe", args);

    psi.RedirectStandardError  = true;
    psi.RedirectStandardOutput = true;
```

```
            psi.RedirectStandardInput   = true;
            psi.UseShellExecute = false;
            psi.CreateNoWindow = true;

            Process process = Process.Start(psi);
            string output = process.StandardOutput.ReadToEnd();
            process.WaitForExit();

            int cutpos = output.IndexOf(".namespace");

            if (cutpos != -1) {
              return output.Substring(cutpos);
            }

            cutpos = output.IndexOf(".class");
            if (cutpos != -1) {
              return output.Substring(cutpos);
            }

            cutpos = output.IndexOf(".method");
            if (cutpos != -1) {
              return output.Substring(cutpos);
            }

            return output;
        } catch (Exception) {
            return "ildasm.exe is not installed\n(works only with the SDK)";
        }
      }
    }
  }
```

In this part also, we have to provide for the possibility of not finding the appropriate content. However, the really interesting bit of code is the one dealing with starting ildasm.exe and catching its output. In doing so, we have to handle the following issues:

❑ ildasm.exe may not be installed

❑ Capturing the output of ILDasm

The first issue is handled through exception handling, the second by starting ILDasm in a separate process with redirected input and output. This output is read using:

```
    string output = process.StandardOutput.ReadToEnd();
```

Note that, for proper formatting we need to convert the line terminators of ILDasm's output from LF to the CR/LF format, which is the standard line termination format in the SelectNode routine:

```
    tb.Text = GetILDASMOutput(assembly, item).Replace("\n", "\r\n");
```

Now let's step down one more level and look at building the nodes of the Reflection tree. The code can be found in the
`src\BackendBindings\AssemblyScout\src\Nodes` directory.

Here, we can find the code for the different types of nodes:

- General
- Type
- Member
- Folder

We will be examining only two of these, the general nodes and type nodes. The code for the general nodes can be found in the file `ReflectionNode.cs`.

We will look at some code snippets taken from this file:

```
namespace SharpDevelop.Gui.Edit.Reflection
{
  public enum ReflectionNodeType {
    Folder,
    Resource,
    Assembly,
    Library,
    Namespace,
    Type,
    Constructor,
    Method,
    Field,
    Property,
    SubTypes,
    SuperTypes,
    Reference,
    Event,
    Link,
    Module,
  }

  public class ReflectionNode : TreeNode
  {
    protected const int CLASSINDEX     = 14;
    protected const int STRUCTINDEX    = CLASSINDEX + 1 * 4;
    protected const int INTERFACEINDEX = CLASSINDEX + 2 * 4;
    protected const int ENUMINDEX      = CLASSINDEX + 3 * 4;
    protected const int METHODINDEX    = CLASSINDEX + 4 * 4;
    protected const int PROPERTYINDEX  = CLASSINDEX + 5 * 4;
    protected const int FIELDINDEX     = CLASSINDEX + 6 * 4;
    protected const int DELEGATEINDEX  = CLASSINDEX + 7 * 4;

    protected ReflectionNodeType type;
    protected string             name;
    protected object             attribute;
```

```
           protected bool  populated = false;

       public ReflectionNodeType Type {
         get {
           return type;
         }
         set {
           type = value;
         }
       }

       public object Attribute {
         get {
           return attribute;
         }
       }

       public bool Populated {
         get {
           return populated;
         }
       }

       public string Name {
         get {
           return name;
         }
         set {
           name = value;
         }
       }
```

We start off by calculating uniquely distinguishable numerical indexes for the node types.

We then move on to actual nodes:

```
       public ReflectionNode(string name, object attribute,
                           ReflectionNodeType type) : base(name)
       {
         this.attribute = attribute;
         this.type = type;
         this.name = name;
         if (type == ReflectionNodeType.Namespace ||
           type == ReflectionNodeType.Assembly  ||
           type == ReflectionNodeType.Library   ||
           type == ReflectionNodeType.Type) {
           Nodes.Add(new TreeNode(""));
         }
         if (type == ReflectionNodeType.Field) {
           Text =
             ReflectionTree.languageConversion.Convert((FieldInfo)attribute);
         } else
         if (type == ReflectionNodeType.Property) {
```

```
        Text = ReflectionTree.
            languageConversion.Convert((PropertyInfo)attribute);
    }
    SetIcon();
}


protected virtual void SetIcon()
{
    ClassScoutIconsService classScoutIconService =
        (ClassScoutIconsService)ServiceManager.Services.
        GetService(typeof(ClassScoutIconsService));

    switch (type) {
        case ReflectionNodeType.Link:
            break;
        case ReflectionNodeType.Resource:
            ImageIndex  = SelectedImageIndex = 11;
            break;

//code omitted from listing

        case ReflectionNodeType.SuperTypes:
            ImageIndex  = SelectedImageIndex = 5;
            break;

        case ReflectionNodeType.Event:
            EventInfo eventinfo = (EventInfo)attribute;
            ImageIndex  = SelectedImageIndex =
                classScoutIconService.GetIcon(eventinfo);
            MethodInfo add    = eventinfo.GetAddMethod();
            MethodInfo raise  = eventinfo.GetRaiseMethod();
            MethodInfo remove = eventinfo.GetRemoveMethod();

            if (add != null)
                Nodes.Add(new ReflectionMethodNode(add));
            if (raise != null)
                Nodes.Add(new ReflectionMethodNode(raise));
            if (remove != null)
                Nodes.Add(new ReflectionMethodNode(remove));
            break;

        case ReflectionNodeType.Property:
            PropertyInfo propertyinfo = (PropertyInfo)attribute;
            ImageIndex  = SelectedImageIndex =
                classScoutIconService.GetIcon(propertyinfo);

            if (propertyinfo.CanRead) {
                Nodes.Add(new ReflectionMethodNode
                    (propertyinfo.GetGetMethod()));
            }
            if (propertyinfo.CanWrite) {
                Nodes.Add(new ReflectionMethodNode
                    (propertyinfo.GetSetMethod()));
```

```
            }
          break;

      case ReflectionNodeType.Field:
        FieldInfo fieldinfo = (FieldInfo)attribute;
        ImageIndex = SelectedImageIndex =
          classScoutIconService.GetIcon(fieldinfo);
        break;
      default:
        throw new Exception("ReflectionFolderNode.SetIcon : unknown
          ReflectionNodeType " + type.ToString());
    }
  }
}
```

In this snippet, we create nodes and assign the appropriate icons. With these nodes, we can now populate the tree:

```
public virtual void Populate()
{
  switch (type) {
    case ReflectionNodeType.Assembly:
      PopulateAssembly((Assembly)attribute, this);
      break;
    case ReflectionNodeType.Library:
      PopulateLibrary((Assembly)attribute, this);
      break;
  }
  populated = true;
}

public TreeNode GetNodeFromCollection(TreeNodeCollection collection,
                                      string title)
{
  foreach (TreeNode node in collection)
    if (node.Text == title) {
      return node;
    }
  return null;
}

void PopulateLibrary(Assembly assembly, TreeNode parentnode)
{
  parentnode.Nodes.Clear();
  string[] manifestresourcenames = assembly.GetManifestResourceNames();
  Type[] types = assembly.GetTypes();
  foreach (Type type in types) {
    if(type.ToString().IndexOf("PrivateImplementationDetails") == -1) {
      string typename = type.ToString();
      int lastindex = typename.LastIndexOf('.');
      TreeNode path = parentnode;
      string nodename = typename;

      if (lastindex != -1) {
```

```
        string pathname = typename.Substring(0, lastindex);
        TreeNode node = GetNodeFromCollection(parentnode.Nodes,
          pathname);
        if (node == null) {
          TreeNode newnode = new ReflectionFolderNode(pathname, null,
            ReflectionNodeType.Namespace, 3, 3);
          newnode.Nodes.Clear();
          parentnode.Nodes.Add(newnode);
          path = newnode;
        } else
          path = node;
        nodename = typename.Substring(lastindex + 1);
      }
      path.Nodes.Add(new ReflectionTypeNode(nodename, type));
    }
  }
}

void PopulateAssembly(Assembly assembly, TreeNode parentnode)
{
  parentnode.Nodes.Clear();

  TreeNode node = new ReflectionFolderNode(Path.GetFileName
    (assembly.CodeBase), assembly, ReflectionNodeType.Library, 2, 2);
  parentnode.Nodes.Add(node);

  ReflectionFolderNode resourcefolder = new ReflectionFolderNode
    ("Resources", assembly, ReflectionNodeType.Folder, 6, 7);
  string[] resources = assembly.GetManifestResourceNames();
  foreach (string resource in resources) {
    resourcefolder.Nodes.Add(new
      ReflectionNode(resource, null, ReflectionNodeType.Resource));
  }
  parentnode.Nodes.Add(resourcefolder);

  ReflectionFolderNode referencefolder = new ReflectionFolderNode
    ("References", assembly, ReflectionNodeType.Folder, 9, 10);
  AssemblyName[] references = assembly.GetReferencedAssemblies();
  foreach (AssemblyName name in references) {
    referencefolder.Nodes.Add(new
      ReflectionNode(name.Name, name, ReflectionNodeType.Reference));
  }
  parentnode.Nodes.Add(referencefolder);

  ReflectionFolderNode modulefolder = new ReflectionFolderNode
    ("Modules", assembly, ReflectionNodeType.Folder, 9, 10);
  parentnode.Nodes.Add(modulefolder);
  Module[] modules = assembly.GetModules(true);
  foreach(Module module in modules) {
    modulefolder.Nodes.Add(new ReflectionNode
      (module.Name, null, ReflectionNodeType.Module));
  }
}
```

The `PopulateLibrary` method makes the information from the manifest of the assembly available to us. This information is then used together with the reflection information, obtained from the assembly, to populate the tree. Both assembly metadata and reflection information are powerful features of .NET.

Let's look at type nodes, as a representative example of the other node types. The code can be found in the file `ReflectionTypeNode.cs`

We will be looking at a shortened version of the code:

```csharp
namespace SharpDevelop.Gui.Edit.Reflection
{
  public class ReflectionTypeNode : ReflectionNode
  {
    public ReflectionTypeNode(string name, Type type) :
      base (name, type, ReflectionNodeType.Type)
    {
    }

    protected override void SetIcon()
    {
      ClassScoutIconsService classScoutIconService =
        (ClassScoutIconsService)ServiceManager.Services.
        GetService(typeof(ClassScoutIconsService));
      ImageIndex  = SelectedImageIndex =
        classScoutIconService.GetIcon((Type)attribute);
    }

    public override void Populate()
    {
      Type type = (Type)attribute;
      Nodes.Clear();

      ConstructorInfo[] constructorinfos = type.GetConstructors
        (BindingFlags.Public | BindingFlags.NonPublic);
      MethodInfo[] methodinfos = type.GetMethods(BindingFlags.Instance |
        BindingFlags.Static | BindingFlags.Public | BindingFlags.NonPublic |
        BindingFlags.DeclaredOnly);
      FieldInfo[] fieldinfos = type.GetFields(BindingFlags.Instance |
        BindingFlags.Static | BindingFlags.Public | BindingFlags.NonPublic);
//code omitted from listing

      Nodes.Add(supertype);
      if (type.BaseType !- null) {
        ReflectionNode basetype = new ReflectionNode(type.BaseType.Name,
          type.BaseType, ReflectionNodeType.Link);
        basetype.ImageIndex = basetype.SelectedImageIndex =
          classScoutIconService.GetIcon(type.BaseType);
        supertype.Nodes.Add(basetype);
      }

      foreach (Type baseinterface in  type.GetInterfaces()) {
        ReflectionNode inode = new ReflectionNode(baseinterface.Name,
          baseinterface, ReflectionNodeType.Link);
```

```
        inode.ImageIndex = inode.SelectedImageIndex =
            classScoutIconService.GetIcon(baseinterface);
        supertype.Nodes.Add(inode);
    }

    Nodes.Add(new ReflectionNode("SubTypes", type,
        ReflectionNodeType.SubTypes));

    foreach (ConstructorInfo constructorinfo in constructorinfos) {
        Nodes.Add(new ReflectionMethodNode(constructorinfo));
    }

    foreach (MethodInfo methodinfo in methodinfos) {
        if (methodinfo.DeclaringType.Equals(type))
        if ((methodinfo.Attributes & MethodAttributes.SpecialName) == 0)
            Nodes.Add(new ReflectionMethodNode(methodinfo));
    }
//code omitted from listing
        populated = true;
    }
  }
}
```

Here, we use the information provided through reflection to sort types in our assemblies into the appropriate nodes in the tree.

Summary

In this chapter, we have discussed how parse information obtained from the SharpDevelop parser can be used in facilitating navigation through code by implementing a Class Scout.

We looked at using the Class Scout and how a tree representing classes in a project can be implemented. We then went on to learn how such a tree can be used to navigate the source code of a project.

We examined how information contained in the assemblies referenced by our project, can be used to our advantage. For this purpose, we implemented an Assembly Scout that allows us to look at the source code, wherever possible, and in other cases at the disassembled code. While implementing the assembly scout, we discussed another use of the powerful reflection feature of .NET and how ILDasm can be used to investigate references that come without source code.

Now, we have completed our discussion of the source code for writing an IDE, and we are ready to move on to the visual side of programming – implementing a Forms Designer.

CHAPTER 15

15

The Designer Infrastructure

In this chapter, we will introduce the Forms Designer infrastructure. We will look at implementing a forms designer from scratch. We will get acquainted with the .NET component model, and learn about services in the .NET forms designer infrastructure. Services in the .NET forms designer infrastructure don't have much to do with services in SharpDevelop, except for their purpose. The services in the designer infrastructure act as helper classes, providing different functionalities that build the whole system.

In this chapter we will look at:

- ❑ **The forms designer overview** – We will learn about the components of the designer that we have to implement and the support provided by the .NET Framework

- ❑ **The .NET component model** – To understand the working of the designer infrastructure we need to have some insight into the .NET component model

- ❑ **Designer Host Implementation** – We will see how to start to write our own forms designer

Forms Designer Overview

The SharpDevelop Forms Designer consists of three main components:

- ❑ **A Toolbox containing controls** – From the Toolbox, the user can select the component that is to be inserted into the Designer area.

- ❑ **The Designer area** – In this area the layout can be changed visually by using drag and drop.

- ❑ **A Property grid** – The Property grid shows the properties of the currently selected component. These can be altered and the changes are reflected in the Designer area (given that the changes pertain to the visible properties).

Let's take a look at the following screenshot, to get an idea of what the components look like:

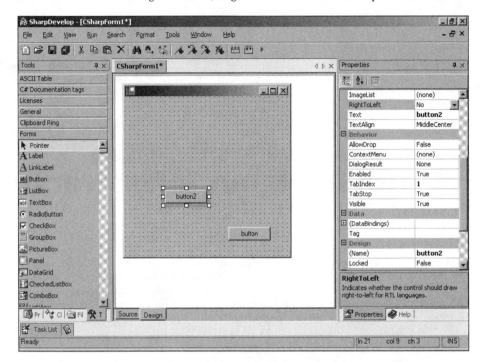

On the left, we can see the Toolbox containing the Windows Forms components, which are identified by the component name and an icon. At the center of the screen we can find the Designer area, where the user can design the layout of the form. To the right is the property grid, where properties of the currently selected component can be altered.

The first item in the Toolbox is the Pointer item. This item is not a Windows Forms component; instead, it is used to deselect the current item. If another item is selected and then clicked in the Designer area then the selected item will get added to the Designer area. When the Pointer item is selected, nothing is added to the Designer area; it gets automatically selected after a component is inserted, to indicate that the insertion has been completed.

Now we will examine the implementation of such a designer.

Implementation Considerations

Our first few attempts at creating a forms designer failed, as we tried to implement it in .NET. It was extremely difficult because in .NET it is difficult to program a control to just display, without reacting to events. This is called **design-time** behavior; during design time the control should be inactive. The opposite is called **run-time** behavior, which is the normal behavior.

For example, when we press a button in the Designer area it should not fire the click event; instead, it should draw a selection border (this is design-time behavior). Drawing the border isn't a problem but turning off the control's event handler is hard, we couldn't find a good way of doing it.

Fortunately, we didn't have to implement the Forms Designer completely from ground up. The .NET Framework has its own built-in designer. As far as we know, Eddie Sheffield was the first programmer, outside Microsoft, who figured out how to turn on the internal forms designer in the .NET Framework. He announced his efforts in the SharpDevelop forum and soon after released the first version of his designer. SharpDevelop took the forms designer from Eddie Sheffield and extended it to generate code and to read code changes back.

.NET's built-in designer is poorly documented and Microsoft has never released a designer example to work with. However, we assume that we can safely rely on it, as it's a part of the .NET Framework. But, we doubt whether this approach will work in Mono (as it lacks Forms, and I don't think they will have a root designer for their GTK# components soon) or any other .NET Framework implementation. This makes the forms designer highly platform dependent.

Design Overview

As mentioned in the last section, only a part of the forms designer needs to be implemented:

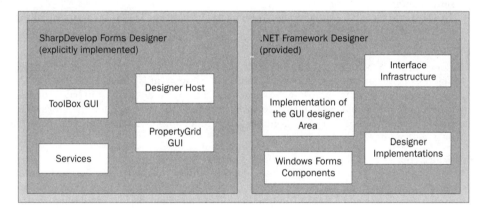

In the figure, to the left are the parts we have to implement, and to the right is what the .NET Framework provides us. The .NET Framework requires the implementation of services. We will look at the service system later on, in this chapter; we will examine the service implementation in the next chapter. We have already discussed SharpDevelop's services in Chapter 5. The services discussed here have a similar purpose. The Designer is build on top of these services, just as SharpDevelop is built on top of the SharpDevelop services, but the implementation of the service infrastructure is a bit different.

Services are mostly used in the Designer for:

❑ Managing the Toolbox

❑ Keeping track of the currently selected components

❑ Displaying the context menu and managing menu commands

Now let's look at the Designer Host:

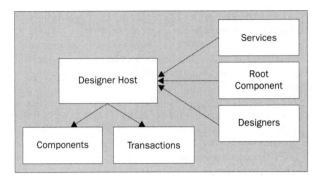

The Designer Host acts as the service container and service provider. A service container contains services and the provider gives access to services stored in a container. Besides service management, the designer performs the following tasks:

❑ **Initialization**
The host must be activated and deactivated when necessary. The host has an initialization mechanism that allows host implementations to signal the initialization. This prevents the host from being used before the initialization is complete.

❑ **Components**
The host manages components (the definition of component is given in the next section, for now think of it as an instance); it can create and destroy components and has a special component called **root component**. This root component is a component in a forms designer, which is usually a `Form` or `UserControl`. This root component represents the class that will be generated during code generation.

❑ **Transactions**
The host manages transactions. Transactions are similar to actions (like add/remove/move components; anything that would alter the output file created by the designer). The host has a property indicating whether it is in transaction and another property providing a description of the current transaction. These are useful for displaying the status of the Designer Host. Transactions are created for almost all operations, like create, move, or remove.

❑ **Designer**
The host manages the so-called designers. Each component has a designer attached to it. A designer inserts menu actions into the context menu of a component at design time. Later on, in this chapter, we will see how designers are implemented.

We can think of the Designer Host, as a service container and a component creation service. To understand the Designer Host we need to look at the .NET components.

The .NET Component Model

A component in .NET is a class that implements the `System.ComponentModel.IComponent` interface. The idea behind the component model is simple. A component is an object that can be modified in a visual designer. Now, let's examine the `IComponent` interface. The interface code was constructed by referring to the .NET SDK documentation:

```
public interface IComponent : IDisposable
{
  ISite Site {
    get;
    set;
  }
  event EventHandler Disposed;
}
```

All components have the `Dispose` method defined in the `IDisposable` interface. The only functionality added to a component, besides `Dispose`, is the `Site` property.

The `Site` property is set when the component is added to a container. It is reset when the component is removed from the container. In the SharpDevelop implementation, the container does this setting and resetting.

The `ISite` object has three main functions:

❑   By using the `DesignMode` property, it tells the component that it is in design mode.

❑   It binds the component to a container. Therefore, it is possible to access the container in which the component is stored, through the component itself.

❑   It holds the name of the component stored in the container. All components in the container have a unique name identifying them.

Any object of a class implementing `ISite` is a service provider. All services in the Designer Host are available to the components that are created by the host, through the `ISite` property. In addition, the `ISite` object is the bridge between the component and the container.
The `ISite` object has a reference to the container and to the component that is attached to `Site`.

Now, we will look at the `ISite` interface definition:

```
public interface ISite : IServiceProvider
{
  IComponent Component {
    get;
  }
  IContainer Container {
    get;
  }

  bool DesignMode {
    get;
  }

  string Name {
    get;
    set;
  }
}
```

Given the earlier explanation, the interface does not hold any surprises for us. One thing that is interesting, though, is the base interface ISserviceProvider; we'll dissect it next.

The Service Interfaces

We have seen the ServiceManager class in Chapter 5. It had a GetService method, which accepted a type and returned the services, in the ServiceManager, having the requested type. The IServiceProvider interface in the System namespace does exactly this. It has only one method:

```
public interface IServiceProvider
{
   object GetService(Type serviceType);
}
```

This interface is the base interface for the ISite interface (as we have seen in the last section) and the designer host implements it too. Note that, this is similar to SharpDevelop's service system, as a service is identified through its type rather than through a name or an identification number. The idea behind these 'types' of services is a bit like that of the singleton model – only one service of each type exists for a specific task.

Unlike SharpDevelop, each designer host has its own service provider (and service container, which contains the service). This means that more than one object of a specific type may exist during run time. The SharpDevelop services are more like singleton objects, as only one service of each type exists at run time. However, this is due to design decisions. SharpDevelop needs only one instance of 'SharpDevelop' during run time (in the same process), but it might have more than one Designer (we can have two design areas open) and the designer services should not interfere with each other.

We have looked at the service provider, but there's one big question still left – where are the services stored? This is answered by the System.ComponentModel.Design.IServiceContainer interface.

The IServiceContainer extends the IServiceProvider with AddService and RemoveService methods, in different versions:

```
public interface IServiceContainer : IServiceProvider
{
   void AddService(Type serviceType, object serviceInstance);
   void AddService(Type serviceType, ServiceCallback callback);
   void AddService(Type serviceType, object serviceInstance, bool promote);
   void AddService(Type serviceType, ServiceCallback callback, bool promote);
   void RemoveService(Type serviceType);
   void RemoveService(Type serviceType, bool promote);
}
```

Service containers may be contained by other service containers, thereby forming a tree. The root of the tree is the service container of the designer host. With the promote flag set to false, the request is handled at the current service container in the tree. If the promote flag is set to true, it indicates that the add or remove operation (that is, adding/removing from the topmost service container in the tree) should be handed over to the base container. This allows for a service to be added or removed globally.

If a service is added to the service container from the component, it is not accessible at the host level (it is not in the root container; instead, it is in the component container). With the `promote` flag it can be made accessible at the host level. The way it is handled depends on the implementation; under the SharpDevelop Forms Designer implementation, there is only one service container for the host and for all components.

Some methods do not take the service object directly; instead, they get a `ServiceCreatorCallback` object. The `ServiceCreatorCallback` is a delegate and has the following signature:

```
public delegate object ServiceCreatorCallback(
    IServiceContainer container,
    Type serviceType
);
```

The `callback` method is used to delay the creation of the services object, until the service is requested. This makes sense for services, which may never be used, to optimize memory consumption and performance. It exists as a default implementation of this service container. The class is called `System.ComponentModel.Design.ServiceContainer`.

Now, we have looked at how services are managed. We have already studied designers and we know the term Designer Host. Now, we will look at the concept of designers in the .NET component model.

.NET Designers

Generally, a designer for .NET is not a GUI component. When we speak about designers, we refer to an object that has the following properties:

- ❑ It is attached to a component at design time. A designer can change the component's behavior at design time. Each designer has an `Initialize` method that associates the component with the designer. In the `Initialize` method the object can be configured for design time, if required.

- ❑ A designer can provide custom services or access the host services for performing various tasks, like changing the toolbar.

- ❑ Designers can add menu commands to the context menu of a component at design time.

- ❑ A designer can implement an action for components that are added to the tray. The tray is the place for non-visible components and the designer can add an action that is performed when the user double-clicks on that component.

Now, let's go back to the designer functionality. All functionality is defined in the `System.ComponentModel.Design.IDesigner` interface:

```
public interface IDesigner : IDisposable
{
  IComponent Component {get;}
  DesignerVerbCollection Verbs {get;}

  void DoDefaultAction();
  void Initialize(IComponent component);
}
```

The `DesignerVerbCollection` contains objects of the type
`System.ComponentModel.Design.DesignerVerb`. These are simply menu commands, which are
added to the context menu at design time. The `DoDefaultAction` method is called for component-tray
components.

The Designer Host instantiates the components that it contains, and in this creation process the
designers for the components are instantiated, too. The designer for a component is available through
the Designer Host.

Now, we know what a designer is, but there are some questions yet to be answered:

❑   How to tell the Designer Host which designer to instantiate for a component

❑   How to implement the designer itself

Telling the designer host which designer to instantiate for a component is easy. Just use the
`System.ComponentModel.DesignerAttribute` to mark which designer should be used.
For example:

```
[Designer(typeof(System.Windows.Forms.Design.DocumentDesigner),
    typeof(IRootDesigner))]
public class MyControl : UserControl {
}
```

Implementation of custom designers is outside the scope of this book (there is plenty of online
documentation available, for example, you can refer to http://www.gotdotnet.com). In our discussion,
we will concentrate on instantiating designers.

We can write a routine that checks for the `DesignerAttribute` attribute, through the inheritance tree
and then instantiate the specified designer. However, this is easily done with the
`System.ComponentModel.TypeDescriptor` utility class. This class has a method defined:

```
public static IDesigner CreateDesigner(IComponent component,
                                       Type designerBaseType);
```

This method allows us to instantiate a designer for a given component. It returns `null` if the designer is
missing (note that Windows Forms controls always have a default designer inherited from `Control`).
The Designer Host implemented in SharpDevelop uses this method to create designers for each
created component.

Now that we have a clue about the general working of the system, let's see how to display it on the screen.

The Root Designer

The root designer is the designer for the root component (a root component is the component that
contains all other components). But what makes a root designer special is that it provides a view for the
design area. From a root designer, a view (that is, a Windows Forms control) can be requested to display
the Designer area. For example, the root designer of `Form` and `UserControl` is the
`System.Windows.Forms.Design.DocumentDesigner` class, which provides the familiar Designer
area of SharpDevelop (and Visual Studio .NET).

The `IRootDesigner` interface looks like this:

```
public interface IRootDesigner : IDesigner, IDisposable
{
  ViewTechnology[] SupportedTechnologies {
    get;
  }

  object GetView(ViewTechnology technology);
}
```

The root designer may provide more than one view technology (`ViewTechnology` is an enumeration).
It is implemented for future extensibility of the designer infrastructure. In time a successor to Windows
Forms may appear, but apparently Microsoft has the option to reuse the current designer infrastructure
when the GUI framework is switched.

Currently there are two view technologies:

❏ `ViewTechnology.WindowsForms`
    If this view technology is supported, the `GetView` call returns a `Control`. If a requested view
    technology is not supported, the method will throw a `System.ArgumentException`.

❏ `ViewTechnology.Passthrough`
    If this view technology is supported, the `GetView` call returns an object, which is passed
    through to the development environment. This is used for custom view technologies defined
    by the IDE. SharpDevelop currently does not support view technologies other than Windows
    Forms. Visual Studio accepts this view technology and the `GetView` call may return an object
    from type `IVsWindowPane`. Further information about this is available in the Visual Studio
    Integration Program (http://msdn.microsoft.com/vstudio/vsip).

Now let's look at the implementation of the Designer Host.

Designer Host Implementation

In this section we will be examining the Designer Host. We will be discussing the various aspects
involved, like:

❏ Setting up the designer host

❏ Implementing component management

❏ Implementing transaction management

The designer host is implemented in
`src\SharpDevelop\FormDesigner\FormDesigner\Hosts\DefaultDesignerHost.cs`.

First, we will look at the basic designer host implementation. The designer host class starts with:

```
public class DefaultDesignerHost : DefaultServiceContainer,
                                   IDesignerLoaderHost
{
  DesignComponentContainer container = null;
  Stack transactions = new Stack();
  DesignerLoader myLoader = new DefaultDesignerLoader();

  public DefaultDesignerHost ()
  {
    container = new DesignComponentContainer(this);
    Reload();
  }
```

We will see the purpose of the `DesignComponentContainer` and `Stack` in the next sections. For now, we will study the `DesignerLoader`. The `DesignerLoader` is used to load a serialized designer document (document is the root component that may contain other components; this is what is displayed in the designer area).

The Designer Host inherits from the `DefaultServiceContainer` class that implements the `ServiceContainer`. This class uses the .NET default implementation of the service container. Inserting a class around the .NET implementation of this container allows us to listen to `GetService` requests. We found this useful for figuring out the services requested by the framework and which we, therefore, needed to implement.

The next part in the class definition is the implementation of the `IDesignerLoaderHost` and the `IDesignerHost` members, which deal with loading and activation:

```
public bool Loading {
  get { return myLoader.Loading; }
}

public void Activate()
{
  OnActivated(EventArgs.Empty);
}

public void Deactivate()
{
  OnDeactivated(EventArgs.Empty);
}

public void EndLoad(string baseClassName, bool successful,
                    ICollection errorCollection)
{
  OnLoadComplete(EventArgs.Empty);
}

public void Reload()
{
  myLoader.BeginLoad(this);
```

```
      OnLoadComplete(EventArgs.Empty);
   }

   protected virtual void OnActivated(EventArgs e);
   protected virtual void OnDeactivated(EventArgs e);
   protected virtual void OnLoadComplete(EventArgs e);

   public event EventHandler Activated;
   public event EventHandler Deactivated;
   public event EventHandler LoadComplete;
```

The `IDesignerLoaderHost` extends the `IDesignerHost` with two methods – `Reload` and `EndLoad`. As we can see in the code snippet, the `EndLoad` method does not recognize the parameters it receives. But again, this code is currently not used; however, we have to implement it, as it's an interface. Only `Activate` and `Deactivate` get called and they trigger the corresponding events; but the Forms Designer structure also works without calling them. Currently, the Designer Host does nothing during activation and deactivation.

Now, we look at the component management part of the designer host:

```
public IContainer Container {
   get { return container; }
}

public IComponent RootComponent {
   get { return container.RootComponent; }
}

public string RootComponentClassName {
   get {
      return RootComponent == null ? null :
        RootComponent.GetType().Name;
   }
}

public IComponent CreateComponent(Type componentClass)
{
   INameCreationService nameCreationService =
     (INameCreationService)GetService(typeof(INameCreationService));
   return this.CreateComponent(componentClass,
     nameCreationService.CreateName(container, componentClass));
}

public IComponent CreateComponent(Type componentClass, string name)
{
   IComponent component = Activator.CreateInstance(componentClass) as
     IComponent;
   if (component == null) {
      throw new ArgumentException("The specified Type id not an IComponent",
        "componentClass");
   }
```

```
    INameCreationService nameCreationService =
      (INameCreationService)GetService(typeof(INameCreationService));

    if (!nameCreationService.IsValidName(name)) {
      name = nameCreationService.CreateName(container, componentClass);
    }
    container.Add(component, name);

    return component;
  }

  public void DestroyComponent(IComponent component)
  {
    component.Dispose();
  }

  public IDesigner GetDesigner(IComponent component)
  {
    if (component == null) {
      return null;
    }
    return (IDesigner)container.Designers[component];
  }

  public Type GetType(string typeName)
  {
    return Type.GetType(typeName);
  }
```

The component management part of the designer host delegates most of the functionality to the
DesignComponentContainer class. For creating a valid component name it uses the
INameCreationService. This service (like other services) must be implemented and put into the
Designer Host, for making the above code work.

Note that the Designer Host creates and destroys components. All components that are added to the
Designer area must be created with the CreateComponent of the Designer Host. DestroyComponent
gets called when a component is removed from the Forms Designer area. This is done with a simple
Dispose call. The GetType method just delegates to the Type class.

Now, we will look at the DesignComponentContainer class, which performs the component
handling. It can be found under src\SharpDevelop\FormDesigner\FormDesigner\Hosts\
DesignComponentContainer.cs:

```
public class DesignComponentContainer : IContainer
{
  DefaultDesignerHost host = null;

  HybridDictionary components = new HybridDictionary();
  HybridDictionary designers = new HybridDictionary();

  IComponent rootComponent = null;
```

```
int unnamedCount = 0;

public DesignComponentContainer(DefaultDesignerHost host)
{
  this.host = host;

  ComponentChangeService componentChangeService = componentChangeService =
    host.GetService(typeof(IComponentChangeService)) as
    ComponentChangeService;
  if (componentChangeService != null) {
    componentChangeService.ComponentRename +=
      new ComponentRenameEventHandler(OnComponentRename);
  }
}
```

The ComponentChangeService is the service, which has events indicating component operations, like adding, removing, or renaming a component. We will examine the ComponentChangeService in this chapter, after we have finished discussing the Designer Host.

Then, we have some basic properties listed:

```
public IDictionary Designers {
  get { return designers; }
}

public IComponent RootComponent {
  get { return rootComponent; }
}

public ComponentCollection Components {
  get {
    IComponent[] datalist = new IComponent[components.Count];
    components.Values.CopyTo(datalist, 0);
    return new ComponentCollection(datalist);
  }
}
```

Note that, instead of merely returning a collection, the Components property generates the ComponentCollection out of the dictionaries.

The Dispose method calls Dispose on all components in the container:

```
public void Dispose()
{
  foreach (IComponent component in components.Values) {
    component.Dispose();
  }
  components.Clear();
}
public bool ContainsName(string name)
{
  return components.Contains(name);
}
```

The ContainsName method just delegates the call to the dictionary.

Now, we will see the Add method, which attaches the Site property to the component and creates the designer:

```
public void Add(IComponent component, string name)
{
  if (name == null) {
    name = unnamedCount + "_unnamed";
    ++unnamedCount;
  }

  if (ContainsName(name)) {
    throw new ArgumentException("name", "A component named " + name +
      " already exists in this container");
  }

  ISite site = new ComponentSite(this, component);
  site.Name = name;
  component.Site = site;

  ComponentChangeService componentChangeService = host.GetService
    (typeof(IComponentChangeService)) as ComponentChangeService;

  if (componentChangeService != null) {
    componentChangeService.OnComponentAdding(component);
  }

  IDesigner designer = null;

  if (components.Count == 0) {
    // This is the first component. It must be the
    // "root" component and therefore it must offer
    // a root designer
    designer =
      TypeDescriptor.CreateDesigner(component, typeof(IRootDesigner));
    rootComponent = component;
  } else {
    designer =
      TypeDescriptor.CreateDesigner(component, typeof(IDesigner));
  }

  // If we got a designer, initialize it
  if (designer != null) {
    designer.Initialize(component);
    designers[component] = designer;
  }

  components.Add(component.Site.Name, component);
  if (componentChangeService != null) {
    componentChangeService.OnComponentAdded(component);
  }
}
```

```
public void Add(IComponent component)
{
  this.Add(component, null);
}
```

Note that the designers are stored in a separate dictionary, and that the `componentChangeService` gets informed about the component `Add` operation.

Now we will examine the `Remove` method, which does the exact opposite – it removes a `Site` from the component. After that, it removes the component from the dictionary, sets the `site` property to `null`, and finally removes the designer attached to the component:

```
public void Remove(IComponent component)
{
  string name = null;
  ISite site  = component.Site;

  if (site != null) {
    name = site.Name;
  } else { // if no site is attached search for the name manually
    foreach (string k in components.Keys) {
      IComponent c = components[k] as IComponent;
      if (c == component) {
        name = k;
        break;
      }
    }
  }

  if (name == null || !components.Contains(name)) {
    return;
  }

  components.Remove(name);
  component.Site = null;

  IDesigner designer = designers[component] as IDesigner;

  if (designer != null) {
    designer.Dispose();
    designers.Remove(component);
  }
}
```

When a component is renamed, the component is first removed from the dictionary and then re-inserted with the new name:

```
void OnComponentRename(object sender, ComponentRenameEventArgs e)
{
  components.Remove(e.OldName);
  components.Add(e.NewName, e.Component);
}
```

Now we will look at the `ISite` implementation. Note that, instead, of having a child container for each component, all `GetService` calls are delegated to the Designer Host:

```
// ISite implementation
class ComponentSite : ISite
{
  IComponent component;
  DesignComponentContainer designComponentContainer;
  bool isInDesignMode;
  string name;

  public ComponentSite(DesignComponentContainer designComponentContainer,
                       IComponent component)
  {
    this.component = component;
    this.designComponentContainer = designComponentContainer;
    this.isInDesignMode = true;
  }

  public IComponent Component {
    get { return component; }
  }

  public IContainer Container {
    get { return designComponentContainer; }
  }

  public bool DesignMode {
    get { return isInDesignMode; }
  }

  public string Name {
    get {
      return name;
    }
    set {
      Control nameable = component as Control;
      if (nameable != null) {
        nameable.Name = value;
      }
      name = value;
    }
  }

  public object GetService(Type serviceType)
  {
    return designComponentContainer.DesignerHost.GetService(serviceType);
  }
}
```

The last part of the designer host deals with transaction management. A transaction is an action that alters the components stored in the service container.

```csharp
public bool InTransaction {
  get { return transactions.Count > 0; }
}

public string TransactionDescription {
  get {
    if (InTransaction) {
      DesignerTransaction trans =
        (DesignerTransaction)transactions.Peek();
      return trans.Description;
    }
    return null;
  }
}

public DesignerTransaction CreateTransaction()
{
  return this.CreateTransaction(null);
}

public DesignerTransaction CreateTransaction(string description)
{
  OnTransactionOpening(EventArgs.Empty);

  DesignerTransaction transaction = null;

  if (description == null) {
    transaction = new DefaultDesignerTransaction(this);
  } else {
    transaction = new DefaultDesignerTransaction(this, description);
  }

  transactions.Push(transaction);

  OnTransactionOpened(EventArgs.Empty);

  return transaction;
}

internal void FireTransactionClosing(bool commit)
{
  OnTransactionClosing(new DesignerTransactionCloseEventArgs(commit));
}

internal void FireTransactionClosed(bool commit)
{
  OnTransactionClosed(new DesignerTransactionCloseEventArgs(commit));
  transactions.Pop();
}

// canonical event methods
protected virtual void OnTransactionOpened(EventArgs e);
protected virtual void OnTransactionOpening (EventArgs e);
protected virtual void
```

```
      OnTransactionClosing(DesignerTransactionCloseEventArgs e);
   protected virtual void
      OnTransactionClosed(DesignerTransactionCloseEventArgs e);

   public event EventHandler TransactionOpened;
   public event EventHandler TransactionOpening;
   public event DesignerTransactionCloseEventHandler TransactionClosed;
   public event DesignerTransactionCloseEventHandler TransactionClosing;
}
```

Note that transactions are stored on a stack. The transaction that is on top of the stack is the current transaction (and the first transaction that will be closed).

The designer transaction implementation is defined under src\SharpDevelop\FormDesigner\
FormDesigner\Hosts\DefaultDesignerTransaction.cs:

```
public class DefaultDesignerTransaction : DesignerTransaction
{
   DefaultDesignerHost host = null;

   public DefaultDesignerTransaction(DefaultDesignerHost host) : base()
   {
      this.host = host;
   }
   public DefaultDesignerTransaction(DefaultDesignerHost host, string desc) :
      base(desc)
   {
      this.host = host;
   }

   protected override void OnCancel()
   {
      host.FireTransactionClosing(false);
      host.FireTransactionClosed(false);
   }

   protected override void OnCommit()
   {
      host.FireTransactionClosing(true);
      host.FireTransactionClosed(true);
   }
}
```

The Designer Host gets informed about transactions, but the host does not know anything about the type of the transaction. The transaction has a description, which identifies it but nothing more.

Even the 'requester' of the transaction is unknown. The description may be displayed in the status bar or something similar. Currently, it not used anywhere inside SharpDevelop but it is implemented because it was easy and we might use the transactions in a future version. Even parsing the description does not really make sense, as the description strings are localized to the language of the installed .NET Framework.

Now let's look at the implementation of the two services that we discussed in this section; the Component Change Service and the Name Creation Service

Designer Host Services

In this section, we will look at the first few services that we encountered in the Designer Host implementation. A full list of services, their purpose and implementation will be given in the next chapter.

The ComponentChangeService

The Component Change service is just a container for events that indicate component change operations. These operations include altering a component property, and adding, removing, or renaming a component. It is currently not used for anything special, but the implementation of undo and redo needs to be informed about the add/remove and change events (but it can be used for more than that).

An undo/redo manager must listen to the `ComponentChangeService` to create the undo for the operation that was last executed. The `ComponentChangeService` interface declares events only. The implementation defines methods that make it easier for the forms designer to fire the events.

The `ComponentChangeService` is defined under `src\SharpDevelop\FormDesigner\FormDesigner\Services\ComponentChangeService.cs`:

```
public class ComponentChangeService : IComponentChangeService
{
  public void OnComponentChanged(object component, MemberDescriptor member,
                                 object oldValue, object newValue)
  {
    if (ComponentChanged != null) {
      ComponentChanged(this, new ComponentChangedEventArgs(component,
        member, oldValue, newValue));
    }
  }
}
```

Note that, the `MemberDescriptor` is a framework class, in the `System.ComponentModel` namespace, which is used to specify what has changed (for example, which property). We have removed the bodies from the following `OnXYZ` operations, as they are similar:

```
  public void OnComponentChanging(object component, MemberDescriptor member)
  public void OnComponentAdded(IComponent component);
  public void OnComponentAdding(IComponent component);
  public void OnComponentRemoved(IComponent component);
  public void OnComponentRemoving(IComponent component);
  public void OnComponentRename(object component, string oldName,
                                string newName)
  public event ComponentEventHandler          ComponentAdded;
  public event ComponentEventHandler          ComponentAdding;
  public event ComponentChangedEventHandler   ComponentChanged;
  public event ComponentChangingEventHandler  ComponentChanging;
  public event ComponentEventHandler          ComponentRemoved;
  public event ComponentEventHandler          ComponentRemoving;
  public event ComponentRenameEventHandler    ComponentRename;
}
```

The `ComponentChangeService` is easy to understand. Any service that is interested in one of the events it defines, can listen to the `ComponentChangeService` to perform this task. For example, we had mentioned that the component container listens to the `ComponentRename` event for renaming the component inside the container component representation.

Now we will look at the service, which is used in the designer host for creating a default name for a component.

The Name Creation Service

The Name Creation service is not required for making the designer work, but it is part of the .NET infrastructure and has a use in the Designer Host. Alternatively, the Designer Host may have created the name on its own. As far as we know, the Framework Designer infrastructure doesn't request this service but this service is often used inside our structure (think of any name checking operation, adding a new component, renaming, etc.). Other services also get requested from the infrastructure to perform specific tasks, but this is an issue addressed in the next chapter.

The Name Creation service is defined under `src\SharpDevelop\FormDesigner\FormDesigner\Services\NameCreationService.cs`:

```
public class NameCreationService : INameCreationService
{
  IDesignerHost host;

  public NameCreationService(IDesignerHost host)
  {
    this.host = host;
  }

  public string CreateName(IContainer container, Type dataType)
  {
    string name = Char.ToLower (dataType.Name[0]) +
      dataType.Name.Substring(1);

    if (container.Components[name] == null) {
      return name;
    }

    int number = 2;
    while (container.Components[name + number.ToString()] != null) {
      ++number;
    }
    return name + number.ToString();
  }

  public bool IsValidName(string name)
  {
    if (name == null || name.Length == 0 || !(Char.IsLetter(name[0]) ||
      name[0] == '_')) {
      return false;
    }
```

```
      foreach (char ch in name) {
        if (!Char.IsLetterOrDigit(ch) && ch != '_') {
          return false;
        }
      }
      return !((DesignComponentContainer)host.Container).ContainsName(name);
    }

    public void ValidateName(string name)
    {
      if (!IsValidName(name)) {
        throw new System.Exception("Invalid name " + name);
      }
    }
  }
```

This class creates a name and validates a given name to determine whether the name can be used. The name creation is simple. The type of the object is taken as the name (with a lowercase start letter). If it exists, it tries to find a name that has the form typeName + number. The first free number is used as valid name.

The IsValidName method checks the name for any invalid characters and whether it's a duplicate name. The ValidateName method does the same, but it throws an exception on an invalid name instead of returning a specific value, which is the specified behavior of this method, (as mentioned in the framework documentation). All methods in this class are defined in the INameCreationService interface.

In the last section of this chapter, we will look at the Design Panel that is used inside the Forms Designer as the Design area.

The Design Panel

The Design Panel represents the Design area in the SharpDevelop Forms Designer. It gets a Designer Host as constructor argument. The panel handles the Windows.Forms issues on its own:

```
class DesignPanel : Panel
{
  public DesignPanel(IDesignerHost host)
  {
    Debug.Assert(host != null);

    IRootDesigner rootDesigner = host.GetDesigner(host.RootComponent) as
      IRootDesigner;
    if (rootDesigner == null) {
      MessageBox.Show("Can't create root designer for " +
        host.RootComponent, "Error", MessageBoxButtons.OK,
        MessageBoxIcon.Error);
      return;
    }
```

```
  if (!TechnologySupported(rootDesigner.SupportedTechnologies,
    ViewTechnology.WindowsForms)) {
    MessageBox.Show("Root designer does not support Windows Forms view
      technology.", "Error", MessageBoxButtons.OK, MessageBoxIcon.Error);
    return;
  }

  BackColor = Color.White;
  Control view =
    (Control)rootDesigner.GetView(ViewTechnology.WindowsForms);
  view.Dock = DockStyle.Fill;
  this.Controls.Add(view);
}

bool TechnologySupported(ViewTechnology[] technologies,
  ViewTechnology requiredTechnology)
{
  foreach (ViewTechnology technology in
    rootDesigner.SupportedTechnologies) {
    if (technology == requiredTechnology) {
      return true;
    }
  }
  return false;
}
}
```

This class performs some security checks. It is always good to check for as many error cases as possible. First it gets the root designer for the root component and checks whether it has a root designer attached to it and if the root designer is able to generate a Windows Forms Control (with the check if the ViewTechnology.WindowsForms is supported). Finally, the view is generated and placed as a control on the panel that fills the whole panel.

Summary

In this chapter, we examined the Designer Host. It is the component where all services come together to form the underlying Forms Designer. We learned that the host stores services and we looked at two of them, used in the Designer Host implementation itself.

Now, we know that designers are not GUI components; instead they are objects that can change the GUI behavior. We have looked at how designers are created but not where they get used; we will see this in the next chapter. We have learned about a special designer called root designer. We have examined the part of the forms designer code that interacts with this root designer to create the Design area panel.

In the next chapter, we will look at the services implemented in the SharpDevelop Forms Designer and their purpose. We will discuss how they interact with the rest of the forms designer infrastructure to make up a fully functional forms designer.

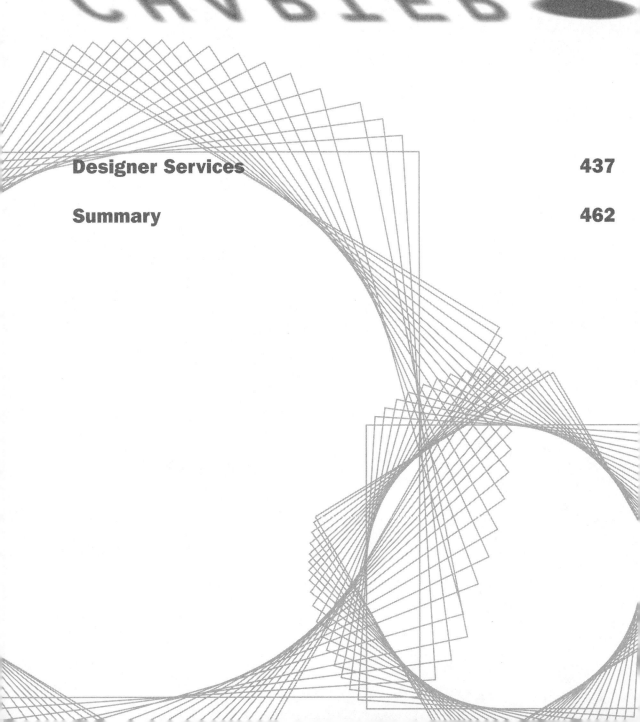

CHAPTER 16

16

Implementing a Windows Forms Designer

In this chapter, we will examine all the services that are necessary for implementing a Windows Forms designer. We will look at how they are implemented in SharpDevelop, and how they interact with each other and the designer framework to support common uses.

We will be looking at:

❑ The services that are required for making the basic forms designer work

❑ Some designer services of minor importance, which are implemented but not required for a basic forms designer; these provide some useful functionalities.

Designer Services

In this section, we will look at the basic services required for making the Forms designer work, which are:

❑ **Toolbox Service**
This wraps some toolbox functionality for the designer infrastructure

❑ **Menu Command Service**
This service displays context menus and is used for calling commands, which affect the components in the design area

❑ **Selection Service**
This handles the selection of components and keeps track of the selected components

Toolbox Service

The Toolbox service represents the Toolbox in the IDE. The Toolbox contains components that we can place onto our forms. The interface implemented by this service is the `System.Drawing.Design.IToolboxService` interface, which is a part of the .NET Framework.

The main purpose of the Toolbox service is to store `ToolBoxItem` objects. Toolbox items simply contain a type, bitmap, and text. The Design area uses the Toolbox service to create new components. When the Design area is clicked, the type of the component is stored in the `ToolBoxItem` object.

The following screenshot shows the SharpDevelop Toolbox:

In this Toolbox, the **Forms** category is active and it contains various components. These items represent the Toolbox items in the service. Toolbox items have their individual images, which are defined by the component implementer.

How does the designer know which Toolbox item should be used for creating a component?

The Toolbox service contains the functionality for selecting a component. After a Toolbox item is selected, clicking on the Design area will create a component of the Toolbox type in the Design area. The Design area does this automatically and there is not much code to understand.

The service is implemented in the `src\SharpDevelop\FormDesigner\FormDesigner\Services\ToolboxService.cs` file.

We will look at the interface to get an understanding of what the service does. We won't go through the full implementation. As the interface mainly wraps containers, the implementation won't provide us with any valuable insights. The interface describes just a container for Toolbox items:

```
public interface IToolboxService
{
   void AddToolboxItem(ToolboxItem toolboxItem, string category);
   void AddToolboxItem(ToolboxItem toolboxItem);
```

```
void AddLinkedToolboxItem(ToolboxItem toolboxItem, string category,
                          IDesignerHost host);
void AddLinkedToolboxItem(ToolboxItem toolboxItem, IDesignerHost host);

void RemoveToolboxItem(ToolboxItem toolboxItem, string category);
void RemoveToolboxItem(ToolboxItem toolboxItem);

ToolboxItemCollection GetToolboxItems(string category,
                                      IDesignerHost host);
ToolboxItemCollection GetToolboxItems(string category);
ToolboxItemCollection GetToolboxItems(IDesignerHost host);
ToolboxItemCollection GetToolboxItems();
```

A `category` is a group of Toolbox items. In the current implementation, there is only one global category, which contains all Toolbox items (it is represented under the Forms group inside the SharpDevelop Toolbox implementation).

The first part of the interface manages the Toolbox items. Toolbox items may be linked to a designer host. Currently this functionality is not used in SharpDevelop; when we use it the designer host will contain the selected item and there will only be one Global Selection service, which handles all designer areas; however, currently we have a Toolbox service for each designer host.

Now we will look at how to select a Toolbox item:

```
void SetSelectedToolboxItem(ToolboxItem toolboxItem);

ToolboxItem GetSelectedToolboxItem(IDesignerHost host);
ToolboxItem GetSelectedToolboxItem();

void SelectedToolboxItemUsed();
```

The Toolbox implementation of SharpDevelop calls `SetSelectedToolboxItem`, and the Designer area calls `SelectedToolboxItemUsed` when the item is used (when it's placed into the Design area). After that, we set the selected item to `null`, otherwise, the Toolbox item remains selected.

The service has functionality to serialize and deserialize Toolbox items:

```
object SerializeToolboxItem(ToolboxItem toolboxItem);

ToolboxItem DeserializeToolboxItem(object serializedObject,
                                   IDesignerHost host);
ToolboxItem DeserializeToolboxItem(object serializedObject);
```

Currently the implementation doesn't make use of serializing Toolbox items; therefore, it is unimplemented.

But how are the items serialized and deserialized? We can put (and remove) custom Toolbox item creators into the service with these four functions:

```
void AddCreator(ToolboxItemCreatorCallback creator, string format,
                IDesignerHost host);
void AddCreator(ToolboxItemCreatorCallback creator, string format);
void RemoveCreator(string format, IDesignerHost host);
void RemoveCreator(string format);
```

A `ToolboxItemCreatorCallback` delegate has the following signature:

```
public delegate ToolboxItem ToolboxItemCreatorCallback(
    object serializedObject,
    string format
);
```

How are items serialized using a custom method? The answer is that they won't be serialized by this service, but rather through a registered callback. A user-defined method, which is not part of this service, serializes them. But, the deserialization can be customized using the `ToolboxItemCreatorCallback`.

The SharpDevelop `IToolboxService` implementation does not implement the serialization functionality, as currently it is not needed. There are some more helper functions for the serialization parts (which are not implemented either):

```
bool IsToolboxItem(object serializedObject, IDesignerHost host);
bool IsToolboxItem(object serializedObject);

bool IsSupported(object serializedObject, ICollection filterAttributes);
bool IsSupported(object serializedObject, IDesignerHost host);
```

The `SetCursor` method changes the current application mouse cursor to a cursor that represents the selected toolbox item:

```
bool SetCursor();
```

It returns `true` when the cursor is set to a cursor representing the current selected Toolbox item. It returns `false` when no item is selected and the cursor is set to the standard cursor.

The `Refresh` method redraws the toolbox:

```
void Refresh();
```

In the current implementation, this method does nothing because the service only wraps the real SharpDevelop toolbar to this interface! Refreshing is done by a mechanism different from this service.

Finally properties that represent the Toolbox categories are listed:

```
CategoryNameCollection CategoryNames {
    get;
}

string SelectedCategory {
    get;
    set;
}
}
```

We have finished looking at the entire interface, but we still do not know how the Toolbox is filled with Toolbox items. For this very purpose there is a method defined in `src\SharpDevelop\` `FormDesigner\FormDesigner\FormDesignerDisplayBindingBase.cs`:

```
ArrayList BuildToolboxFromAssembly(Assembly assembly)
{
  ArrayList toolBoxItems = new ArrayList();

  Hashtable images = new Hashtable();

  // try to load resource icons
  foreach (string name in assembly.GetManifestResourceNames()) {
    try {
      Bitmap bitmap = newBitmap(Image.
        FromStream(assembly.GetManifestResourceStream(name)));
      images[name] = bitmap;
    } catch {}
  }

  foreach (Module module in assembly.GetModules(false)) {
    foreach (Type type in module.GetTypes()) {
      if (type.IsDefined(typeof(ToolboxItemFilterAttribute), true)) {
        object[] attributes = type.
          GetCustomAttributes(typeof(ToolboxItemFilterAttribute), true);

        // here we should enumerate all attributes ...
        ToolboxItemFilterAttribute attr =
          (ToolboxItemFilterAttribute) attributes[0];

        // get only the components
        //that require 'Windows Forms' toolbox filter
        if (attr.FilterType == ToolboxItemFilterType.Allow &&
          attr.FilterString == "System.Windows.Forms") {
          if (images[type.FullName + ".bmp"] != null) {
            ToolboxItem item = new ToolboxItem(type);
            // filter out UserControl manually
            if (item.DisplayName != "UserControl") {
              toolBoxItems.Add(item);
  } } } } } } //closing braces collapsed for brevity

  toolBoxItems.Sort(new ToolboxItemSorter());
  return toolBoxItems;
}
```

This method iterates through all types in the assembly and inserts all types having their `ToolboxItemFilterAttribute` set to `System.Windows.Forms`, and an icon defined in the assembly resources.

With the toolbox filled, we will move on to context menus, which are an important feature in a modern-day application.

Menu Command Service

The Menu Command service is used to display all context menus in the Design area. When the user right-clicks in the Design area (which is defined in the .NET Framework), a method from the Menu Command service is called. Therefore, this service must be implemented to make all context menus work.

Besides displaying menus, the Menu Command service also acts as a command execution service. The Designer Framework puts `MenuCommands` into the service. A client can execute the commands using a `CommandID` object that identifies a specific command, which is used for making the menu commands in the IDE. The menu commands simply call the Menu Command service.

There are many commands defined and implemented in the framework infrastructure. We will look at them at the end of this section.

The service is defined in the `src\SharpDevelop\FormDesigner\FormDesigner\Services\MenuCommandService.cs` file:

```
class MenuCommandService : IMenuCommandService
{
  IDesignerHost host;
  ArrayList     commands = new ArrayList();
  ArrayList     verbs    = new ArrayList();

  public DesignerVerbCollection Verbs {
    get {
      DesignerVerbCollection verbCollection =
        CreateDesignerVerbCollection();
      verbCollection.AddRange((DesignerVerb[])verbs.
        ToArray(typeof(DesignerVerb)));
      return verbCollection;
    }
  }

  public MenuCommandService(IDesignerHost host)
  {
    this.host = host;
  }

  public void AddCommand(MenuCommand command)
  {

    Debug.Assert(command != null);
    Debug.Assert(command.CommandID != null);
    Debug.Assert(!commands.Contains(command));
    this.commands.Add(command);
  }

  public void AddVerb(DesignerVerb verb)
  {
    Debug.Assert(verb != null);
    this.verbs.Add(verb);
  }
```

The Menu Command service contains commands and verbs. The commands are provided by the framework. verbs are like commands but they are user-defined. Verbs can be added by anyone but usually the designers of the components define verbs for their components.

The `CreateDesignerVerbCollection` method creates a verb collection that contains all verbs defined by the designers that are attached to the selected components (for more information about designers, refer to Chapter 15). It gets the selected component, and uses the verb collection of its attached designer to create a verb collection that is specific for this component.

If the selected component is the root component, the default verbs that are stored in the menu command are attached to the returned collection also. One framework component that has verbs attached to is the Tab control, which allows us to add or remove Tab pages in the context menu.

```
public DesignerVerbCollection CreateDesignerVerbCollection()
{
  DesignerVerbCollection designerVerbCollection = new
    DesignerVerbCollection();

  ISelectionService selectionService = (ISelectionService)
    host.GetService(typeof(ISelectionService));

  if (selectionService != null && selectionService.SelectionCount == 1) {
    IComponent selectedComponent =
      selectionService.PrimarySelection as Component;
    if (selectedComponent != null) {
      IDesigner designer = host.GetDesigner
        ((IComponent)selectedComponent);
      if (designer != null) {
        designerVerbCollection.AddRange(designer.Verbs);
      }
    }

    if (selectedComponent == host.RootComponent) {
      designerVerbCollection.AddRange(this.verbs);
    }
  }
  return designerVerbCollection;
}
```

Also the service allows commands and verbs to be removed:

```
public void RemoveCommand(MenuCommand command)
{
  Debug.Assert(command != null);
  commands.Remove(command.CommandID);

}

public void RemoveVerb(DesignerVerb verb)
{
  Debug.Assert(verb != null);
  verbs.Remove(verb);

}
```

Now we will look at the methods used to invoke and find a command:

```
public bool GlobalInvoke(CommandID commandID)
{
  MenuCommand menuCommand = FindCommand(commandID);
  if (menuCommand == null) {
    MessageBox.Show("Can't find command " + commandID, "Error");
    return false;
  }

  menuCommand.Invoke();
  return true;
}

public MenuCommand FindCommand(CommandID commandID)
{
  foreach (MenuCommand menuCommand in commands) {
    if (menuCommand.CommandID == commandID) {
      return menuCommand;
    }
  }

  foreach (DesignerVerb verb in Verbs) {
    if (verb.CommandID == commandID) {
      return verb;
    }
  }
  return null;
}
```

Before any kind of invocation can happen, we have to display the menu that contains the commands. The ShowContextMenu method takes the menu command and verbs and constructs a context menu using the Magic library, and displays it. It has a CommandID, which specifies the menu ID to be displayed. The menu ID is different, according to what the user had clicked (for example, the Component tray has a different menu ID as compared to a button in the root component). The menu ID is used for displaying context-sensitive menus. It gets the screen position, which determines where to show the context menu:

```
public void ShowContextMenu(CommandID menuID, int x, int y)
{
  Crownwood.Magic.Menus.PopupMenu popup =
    new Crownwood.Magic.Menus.PopupMenu();

  PropertyService propertyService =
    (PropertyService) ICSharpCode.Core.Services.ServiceManager.Services.
                      GetService(typeof(PropertyService));

  popup.Style =
    (Crownwood.Magic.Common.VisualStyle) propertyService.
    GetProperty("ICSharpCode.SharpDevelop.Gui.VisualStyle",
    Crownwood.Magic.Common.VisualStyle.IDE);
  ArrayList menuCommands = new ArrayList();
```

```
        foreach (MenuCommand command in commands) {
          if (command.Visible && command.Enabled) {
            if (ContextMenuCommand.GetStandardCommandName(command.CommandID) !=
            null) {
              menuCommands.Add(new ContextMenuCommand(command));
            }
          }
        }

        foreach (DesignerVerb verb in Verbs) {
          if (verb.CommandID.Guid  == menuID.Guid ) {
            menuCommands.Add(new ContextMenuCommand(verb));
          }
        }

      popup.MenuCommands.AddRange((Crownwood.Magic.Menus.MenuCommand[])
        menuCommands.ToArray(typeof(Crownwood.Magic.Menus.MenuCommand)));
      popup.TrackPopup(new Point(x, y));
    }
```

The `ContextMenuCommand` class is a wrapper class for the `Crownwood.Magic.Menus.MenuCommand` class. We don't look at it here because the implementation of this class will not bring us any new insights. It just wraps a name (which is displayed) to the menu command using the field name from the `System.ComponentModel.Design.StandardCommands` class.

The `StandardCommands` class contains public static `CommandID` fields and a method that converts the `CommandID` to a screen name. This will be replaced in future versions with SharpDevelop standard menus, which allow localization and real customization of these menus.

The commands defined by the standard commands class are:

```
AlignBottom, AlignHorizontalCenters, AlignLeft, AlignRight,
AlignToGrid, AlignTop, AlignVerticalCenters,

ArrangeBottom, ArrangeIcons, ArrangeRight, LineupIcons,

BringForward, BringToFront, SendBackward, SendToBack,

CenterHorizontally, CenterVertically,
SizeToControl, SizeToControlHeight, SizeToControlWidth, SizeToFit,
SizeToGrid, SnapToGrid,

Copy, Cut, Delete, Paste, Replace, SelectAll,

F1Help, Properties, PropertiesWindow, TabOrder, VerbFirst, VerbLast,

Group, Ungroup,

HorizSpaceConcatenate, HorizSpaceDecrease, HorizSpaceIncrease,
HorizSpaceMakeEqual,
VertSpaceConcatenate, VertSpaceDecrease, VertSpaceIncrease, VertSpaceMakeEqual,
```

```
MultiLevelRedo, MultiLevelUndo, Redo, Undo,

LockControls, ShowGrid, ShowLargeIcons, ViewGrid
```

Additional commands are defined in the `System.Windows.Forms.Design.MenuCommands` class:

```
DesignerProperties,

KeyCancel, KeyDefaultAction,
KeyMoveDown, KeyMoveLeft, KeyMoveRight, KeyMoveUp,
KeyNudgeDown,  KeyNudgeLeft, KeyNudgeRight, KeyNudgeUp,
KeyNudgeHeightDecrease, KeyNudgeHeightIncrease, KeyNudgeWidthDecrease,
KeyNudgeWidthIncrease,

KeyReverseCancel, KeySelectNext, KeySelectPrevious,
KeySizeHeightDecrease, KeySizeHeightIncrease,
KeySizeWidthDecrease, KeySizeWidthIncrease,
KeyTabOrderSelect
```

The class is called `MenuCommands` but most commands shown are key actions (they start with the prefix Key). So why is this class called `MenuCommands` and not `KeyboardCommands`?

The `MenuCommands` class contains IDs for menus. Remember the `ShowContextMenu` method from the Menu Command service has a `CommandID` as a parameter. The correct menu to display can be determined by comparing the given ID with the IDs from the `MenuCommands` class.
The `MenuCommands` class defines the following menus by `CommandID`:

```
ComponentTrayMenu, ContainerMenu, SelectionMenu, TraySelectionMenu,
```

Armed with this knowledge about available commands, let's look at how to execute those stock commands.

Executing the Standard Commands

Executing the standard commands is really simple. All commands that are used inside SharpDevelop are defined inside the
`src\SharpDevelop\FormDesigner\Commands\FormCommands.cs` file.

The commands extend this class:

```
public abstract class AbstractFormDesignerCommand : AbstractMenuCommand
{
  public abstract CommandID CommandID {
    get;
  }

  public override void Run()
  {
    IWorkbenchWindow window =
      WorkbenchSingleton.Workbench.ActiveWorkbenchWindow;
    if (window == null) {
```

```
      return;
    }

  FormDesignerDisplayBindingBase formDesigner =
    window.ViewContent as FormDesignerDisplayBindingBase;

  if (formDesigner != null) {
    IMenuCommandService menuCommandService =
      (IMenuCommandService)formDesigner.DesignerHost.
      GetService(typeof(IMenuCommandService));
    menuCommandService.GlobalInvoke(CommandID);
  }
} }
```

The `AbstractFormDesignerCommand` just gets the Menu Command service and executes the `CommandID`, which must be given by a subclass. For example, the bring-to-front command looks like:

```
public class BringToFront : AbstractFormDesignerCommand
{
  public override CommandID CommandID {
    get {
      return StandardCommands.BringToFront;
    }
  }
}
```

Many standard commands are used inside the Format menu of SharpDevelop to execute specific tasks.

Now we will look at something a bit more difficult – the execution of keyboard commands.

Implementing a Key Event Handler

The problem with the key handler was that no existing service could be found that can take a key and perform the appropriate action. Instead, a class was implemented that extended the `System.Windows.Forms.IMessageFilter` interface. `IMessageFilter` objects can be used in Windows Forms to filter a specific window event.

This interface declares only one method:

```
bool PreFilterMessage(ref Message m);
```

If this method returns `true`, the message will be filtered out and not passed any further in the event filter chain.

An object of the `IMessageFilter` class must be put into the message filter queue. This is done with a call to the `System.Windows.Forms.Application.AddMessageFilter` method.

The class that is used for the key events, in the forms designer, is implemented in `src\SharpDevelop\ FormDesigner\FormDesigner\FormKeyHandler.cs`:

```
public class FormKeyHandler : IMessageFilter
{
  const int keyPressedMessage = 0x100; // WM_KEYDOWN

  Hashtable keyTable = new Hashtable();
```

The `keyPressedMessage` is a magic number, which is rooted in the native Windows message system. It just says that the message, which is sent, is of type 'key pressed'.

A hash table is used for providing a fast, clean, and easy way to map a key to a command. The table is initialized in the constructor:

```
  public FormKeyHandler ()
  {
    // normal keys
    keyTable[Keys.Left]  = new CommandWrapper(MenuCommands.KeyMoveLeft);
//code omitted for listing

    // shift modified keys
    keyTable[Keys.Left | Keys.Shift]  =
      new CommandWrapper(MenuCommands.KeySizeWidthDecrease);
//code omitted for listing

    // ctrl modified keys
    keyTable[Keys.Left | Keys.Control]  =
      new CommandWrapper(MenuCommands.KeyNudgeLeft);
//code omitted for listing

    // ctrl + shift modified keys
    keyTable[Keys.Left | Keys.Control | Keys.Shift]  =
      new CommandWrapper(MenuCommands.KeyNudgeWidthDecrease);
//code omitted for listing
  }
```

Now we will look at the filter method, which filters the keyboard events. This method gets all Windows messages but we only care about the keyboard pressed events; therefore, we use the `keyPressedMessage` value that we defined earlier (in this section) to check whether the message refers to a key being pressed.

```
  public bool PreFilterMessage(ref Message m)
  {
    if (m.Msg != keyPressedMessage) {
      return false;
    }

    if (WorkbenchSingleton.Workbench.ActiveWorkbenchWindow == null) {
      return false;
    }

    FormDesignerDisplayBindingBase formDesigner =
      WorkbenchSingleton.Workbench.ActiveWorkbenchWindow.ViewContent as
```

```
      FormDesignerDisplayBindingBase;
  if (formDesigner == null || !formDesigner.IsFormDesignerVisible) {
    return false;
  }

  Keys keyPressed = (Keys)m.WParam.ToInt32() | Control.ModifierKeys;
  CommandWrapper commandWrapper = (CommandWrapper)keyTable[keyPressed];

  if (commandWrapper != null) {
    IMenuCommandService menuCommandService =
      (IMenuCommandService)formDesigner.DesignerHost.
      GetService(typeof(IMenuCommandService));
    ISelectionService   selectionService =
      (ISelectionService)formDesigner.DesignerHost.
      GetService(typeof(ISelectionService));
    ICollection components = selectionService.GetSelectedComponents();
    menuCommandService.GlobalInvoke(commandWrapper.CommandID);

    if (commandWrapper.RestoreSelection) {
      selectionService.SetSelectedComponents(components);
    }
    return true;
  }
  return false;
}
```

Some commands remove the selection when they are executed when, in fact, they should not, for example, some resizing commands (remember that we haven't implemented these commands, as we can't access their source code). For this reason, the selection from the selection manager is saved before the command is called, and restored after it is executed. This is done for all commands, except the commands that alter the selection (for example, when the Tab key selects the next component).

A CommandWrapper class is used instead of putting the CommandID object directly into the hash table. The CommandWrapper provides a RestoreSelection field; if this is set to false it won't restore the selection afterwards. The CommandWrapper is an internal class.

```
class CommandWrapper
{
  CommandID commandID;
  bool      restoreSelection;

  public CommandID CommandID {
    get {
      return commandID;
    }
  }

  public bool RestoreSelection {
    get {
      return restoreSelection;
    }
  }
```

```
      public CommandWrapper(CommandID commandID) : this(commandID, true)
      {
      }
      public CommandWrapper(CommandID commandID, bool restoreSelection)
      {
        this.commandID        = commandID;
        this.restoreSelection = restoreSelection;
      }
    }
```

So far we have seen a bit of the Selection service usage; now we will look at it in more detail.

Selection Service

The Selection service holds all selected components. The following screenshot shows what selections
can look like:

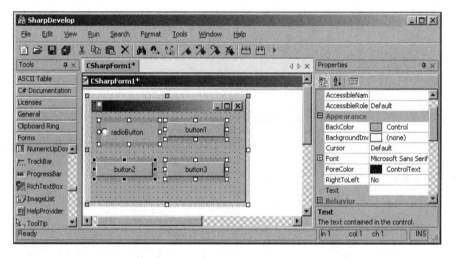

Note that the button2 component is surrounded by small black squares, whereas for the other selected
components they are white. This indicates that button2 is a special component, or the primary selection. The
Selection service must have a way to handle the primary selection, as well as the other selected components.

In the Properties window, the common properties are displayed. Common properties are those
properties that all selected components share. For example, you can change the font of all the selected
components throught the Properties window.

How is this implemented? We can find the code in src\SharpDevelop\FormDesigner\
FormDesigner\Services\SelectionService.cs:

```
  public class SelectionService : ISelectionService
  {
    IDesignerHost host;
    ArrayList selectedComponents = new ArrayList();
```

The Selection service stores all selected components in an `ArrayList`. The primary selection is the first element in this list:

```
public object PrimarySelection {
  get {
    if (selectedComponents.Count > 0) {
      return selectedComponents[0];
    }
    return null;
  }
}
public int SelectionCount {
  get {
    return selectedComponents.Count;
  }
}

public SelectionService(IDesignerHost host)
{
  Debug.Assert(host != null);
  this.host = host;
  ((IComponentChangeService)host.
    GetService(typeof(IComponentChangeService))).ComponentRemoved +=
      new ComponentEventHandler(ComponentRemovedHandler);
}
```

The next listing shows the `get` methods for the components:

```
public bool GetComponentSelected(object component)
{
  return selectedComponents.Contains(component);
}

public ICollection GetSelectedComponents()
{
  return selectedComponents.ToArray();
}
```

The `set` method is special because it needs to take care of modifier key states. The expected behavior is:

❑ **Shift pressed** – When more than one component is passed to the method, they should replace the selection (this is done by other designers; therefore, this behavior is standard). When one component is passed, it should be added to the selection as a new primary selection. If the component is already selected it should be removed from the selection.

❑ **Control pressed** – If one component is passed to the method, the control key behaves like the shift key. Otherwise the components should be added to the current selection and the new root component is one of the added components.

❑ **No Modifier key** – If a selected component is passed to the method, the selected component should become the new root component. Otherwise, the new component(s) should replace the current selection.

Now, let's look at the method that handles this behavior:

```
public void SetSelectedComponents(ICollection components,
                                  SelectionTypes selectionType)
{
  OnSelectionChanging(EventArgs.Empty);
  if (components == null || components.Count == 0) {
    selectedComponents.Clear();
    FireSelectionChange();
    return;
  }

  bool controlPressed = (Control.ModifierKeys & Keys.Control) ==
    Keys.Control;
  bool shiftPressed  = (Control.ModifierKeys & Keys.Shift)   ==
    Keys.Shift;
  switch (selectionType) {
    case SelectionTypes.Replace:
      ReplaceSelection(components);
      break;
    default:
      if (components.Count == 1 && (controlPressed || shiftPressed)) {
        ToggleSelection(components);
      } else if (controlPressed) {
        AddSelection(components);
      } else if (shiftPressed) {
        ReplaceSelection(components);
      } else {
        NormalSelection(components);
      }
      break;
  }
  selectedComponents.TrimToSize();
  FireSelectionChange();
}

public void SetSelectedComponents(ICollection components)
{
  SetSelectedComponents(components, SelectionTypes.MouseDown);
}

#region SetSelection helper methods
  void ToggleSelection(ICollection components)
  {
    foreach (object component in components) {
      if (GetComponentSelected(component)) {
        selectedComponents.Remove(component);
      } else {
        selectedComponents.Insert(0, component);
      }
    }
  }
```

```
  void AddSelection(ICollection components)
  {
    foreach (object component in components) {
      if (!GetComponentSelected(component)) {
        selectedComponents.Insert(0, component);
      }
    }
  }

  void ReplaceSelection(ICollection components)
  {
    selectedComponents.Clear();
    AddSelection(components);
  }

  void NormalSelection(ICollection components)
  {
    if (components.Count == 1) {
      // just getting the first == last element in the components
      object componentToAdd = null;
      foreach (object component in components) {
        componentToAdd = component;
      }

      if (GetComponentSelected(componentToAdd)) {
        selectedComponents.Remove(componentToAdd);
        selectedComponents.Insert(0, componentToAdd);
        return;
      }
    }
    ReplaceSelection(components);
  }
#endregion
```

As always, there might be someone interested in knowing when a selection changes. Therefore, we have some events that inform about selection change:

```
#region Event methods
  void ComponentRemovedHandler(object sender, ComponentEventArgs e)
  {
    if (selectedComponents.Contains(e.Component)) {
      OnSelectionChanging(EventArgs.Empty);
      selectedComponents.Remove(e.Component);
      if (selectedComponents.Count == 0) {
        selectedComponents.Add(host.RootComponent);
      }
      FireSelectionChange();
    }
  }

  void FireSelectionChange()
  {
    OnSelectionChanged(EventArgs.Empty);
```

```
      ((DesignerEventService)host.RootComponent.Site.
        GetService(typeof(IDesignerEventService))).FileSelectionChanged();
    }

    protected virtual void OnSelectionChanging(EventArgs e)
    {
      if (SelectionChanging != null) {
        SelectionChanging(this, e);
      }
    }

    protected virtual void OnSelectionChanged(EventArgs e)
    {
      if (SelectionChanged != null) {
        SelectionChanged(this, e);
      }
    }
#endregion
    public event EventHandler SelectionChanging;
    public event EventHandler SelectionChanged;
}
```

This completes the entire Selection service.

There is one important service left – the IDesignerSerializationService. This service is used for serializing components. Without it, the Cut, Copy, and Paste commands won't work correctly. It is discussed in the next chapter as it builds on the XML persistence format, which we will be studying in that chapter.

The services we have looked at so far are the bare minimum requirement, which must be implemented to make the .NET Forms Designer work. Now we will look at some of the services that help us with the Forms Designer.

Additional Important Services

In this section, we will look at some services that are less important but nonetheless worth examing:

- ❑ **Designer Option Service**
  This service is used for grid options

- ❑ **Dictionary Service**
  This wraps a HashTable as a service

- ❑ **UI Service**
  This is used to display message boxes and has some UI properties

- ❑ **Type Descriptor Filter Service**
  This filters attributes, events, and properties

Designer Option Service

The Designer Option service is able to handle specified designer options. Currently, it holds only three options: `GridSize`, `ShowGrid`, and `SnapToGrid`.

The service is defined under
`src\SharpDevelop\FormDesigner\FormDesigner\Services\DesignerOptionService.cs`:

```
public class DesignerOptionService : IDesignerOptionService
{
  public const string GridSize   = "GridSize";
  public const string ShowGrid   = "ShowGrid";
  public const string SnapToGrid = "SnapToGrid";

  const string GridSizeWidth  = "GridSize.Width";
  const string GridSizeHeight = "GridSize.Height";
```

These constants are the option names, which are pre-defined by the framework infrastructure. Note that the last two values are not public, as the service is referenced through the interface and the interface doesn't have these values.

These options are stored into pages. Each page has its own set of options:

```
public const string FormsDesignerPageName =
  "SharpDevelop Forms Designer\\General";

Hashtable pageOptionTable = new Hashtable();

public DesignerOptionService()
{
  Hashtable defaultTable = new Hashtable();

  defaultTable[GridSize]   = new Size(8, 8);
  defaultTable[ShowGrid]   = false;
  defaultTable[SnapToGrid] = false;

  pageOptionTable[FormsDesignerPageName] = defaultTable;
}

public object GetOptionValue(string pageName, string valueName)
{
  Hashtable pageTable = (Hashtable)pageOptionTable[pageName];

  if (pageTable == null) {
    return null;
  }

  switch (valueName) {
    case GridSizeWidth:
      return ((Size)pageTable[GridSize]).Width;
    case GridSizeHeight:
      return ((Size)pageTable[GridSize]).Height;
    default:
```

```
            return pageTable[valueName];
        }
    }

    public void SetOptionValue(string pageName, string valueName, object val)
    {
        Hashtable pageTable = (Hashtable)pageOptionTable[pageName];

        if (pageTable == null) {
            pageOptionTable[pageName] = pageTable = new Hashtable();
        }

        switch (valueName) {
            case GridSizeWidth:
                Size size      = ((Size)pageTable[GridSize]);
                size.Width     = (int)val;
                pageTable[GridSize] = size;
                break;
            case GridSizeHeight:
                size           = ((Size)pageTable[GridSize]);
                size.Height    = (int)val;
                pageTable[GridSize] = size;
                break;
            default:
                pageTable[valueName] = val;
                break;
        }
    }
}
```

One thing that we can learn from this service is how to handle structures. Instead of getting the size, setting the Width size value, and writing the size back in the hash table, we could have done:

```
size = ((Size)pageTable[GridSize]);
size.Width = (int)val;
pageTable[GridSize] = size;
```

You may ask, why can't we simply use:

```
((Size)pageTable[GridSize]).Width = (int)val;
```

The reason is simple but can easily be forgotten. Size is not a class; it is a structure. This means that when it is unboxed with (Size)pageTable[GridSize], a copy is given back, and if the Width property is updated in the copy, the original structure is not affected.

Therefore, we create a copy, alter the property in the copy, and then write the copy back; thereby, overwriting the original structure. Unfortunately, just from viewing the source code we can't tell if we are handling structures or classes. We can only say this if we know about the type that we are using.

Dictionary Service

The Dictionary service just wraps a hash table data structure as a service. It is the smallest (and simplest) of all services. Currently, we aren't sure where it gets used inside the Designer Framework but we have implemented it, as it is defined and easy to implement according to the framework specification.

The service is implemented under `src\SharpDevelop\FormDesigner\FormDesigner\Services\DictionaryService.cs`:

```
public class DictionaryService : IDictionaryService
{
  Hashtable table = new Hashtable();

  public object GetKey(object val)
  {

    foreach (DictionaryEntry entry in table) {
      if (entry.Value == val) {
        return entry.Key;
      }
    }
    return null;
  }

  public object GetValue(object key)
  {
    return key == null ? null : table[key];
  }

  public void SetValue(object key, object val)
  {
    if (key != null) {
      table[key] = val;
    }
  }
} }
```

Now we will move on to the UI service.

UI Service

The UI service has several purposes:

- ❑ It displays messages (error messages and standard messages).

- ❑ It gives access to the Dialog Owner window. This window is used to set the owner property correctly for dialogs that pop up.

- ❑ It defines a dictionary that stores UI styles. Currently two styles are defined: HighlightColor and DialogFont. The HighlightColor is used as background color of the Component tray and the DialogFont property specifies the font that is used in the tray for displaying the component name.

The UI Service is implemented under `src\SharpDevelop\FormDesigner\FormDesigner\Services\UIService.cs`:

```csharp
public class UIService : IUIService
{
  IDictionary styles = new Hashtable();

  public IDictionary Styles {
    get {
      return styles;
    }
  }

  public UIService()
  {
    ResourceService resourceService = (ResourceService)
      ServiceManager.Services.GetService(typeof(ResourceService));
    styles["DialogFont"]     = resourceService.LoadFont("Tahoma", 10);
    styles["HighlightColor"] = Color.White;
  }

  public void SetUIDirty()
  {
    // TODO: Fixme!
  }
```

The `SetUIDirty` method works a bit like the `Redraw` methods, inside the SharpDevelop abstract GUI system. The `SetUIDirty` method gets called when a component is selected, and then the implementation may choose to alter the enable state of some menu commands. However, currently, SharpDevelop has no use for this method.

The UI service is able to show a component editor but this functionality is currently not implemented:

```csharp
public bool CanShowComponentEditor(object component)
{
  return false;
}

public bool ShowComponentEditor(object component, IWin32Window parent)
{
  throw new System.NotImplementedException
    ("Cannot display component editor for " + component);
}
```

Now we will look at the method that gets the main window, and the method that shows a dialog:

```csharp
public IWin32Window GetDialogOwnerWindow()
{
  return (IWin32Window)WorkbenchSingleton.Workbench;
}

public DialogResult ShowDialog(Form form)
```

```
  {
    return form.ShowDialog(GetDialogOwnerWindow());
  }
```

The following methods are used for displaying error messages:

```
public void ShowError(Exception ex)
{
  ShowError(ex, null);
}

public void ShowError(string message)
{
  ShowError(null, message);
}

public void ShowError(Exception ex, string message)
{
  string msg = String.Empty;

  if (ex != null) {
    msg = "Exception occurred: " + ex.ToString() + "\n";
  }

  if (message != null) {
    msg += message;
  }
  ResourceService resourceService = (ResourceService)
    ServiceManager.Services.GetService(typeof(ResourceService));

  MessageBox.Show(GetDialogOwnerWindow(), msg,
                  resourceService.GetString("Global.ErrorText"),
                  MessageBoxButtons.OK, MessageBoxIcon.Error);
}
```

The following three methods show standard messages:

```
public void ShowMessage(string message)
{
  ShowMessage(message, "", MessageBoxButtons.OK);
}

public void ShowMessage(string message, string caption)
{
  ShowMessage(message, caption, MessageBoxButtons.OK);
}

public DialogResult ShowMessage(string message, string caption,
                                MessageBoxButtons buttons)
{
  return MessageBox.Show(GetDialogOwnerWindow(), message, caption,
                         buttons);
}
```

The `ShowToolWindow` function is currently not implemented. It gets a `Guid` and displays the specified Tool window. The Tool window's `Guid` values are defined in the `System.ComponentModel.Design.StandardToolWindows` class.

Tool windows are the pads inside SharpDevelop (for details, refer to the *Pads* section in Chapter 6), and this function may be added later during the development process.

However, the designer infrastructure doesn't use this function and the show pad functionality is implemented differently in SharpDevelop. Therefore, it doesn't really make sense to implement all functions in the services when they are not used by the designer infrastructure.

```
public bool ShowToolWindow(Guid toolWindow)
{
  return false;
}
}
```

Now we will move on to the Type Descriptor Filter service.

Type Descriptor Filter Service

The Type Descriptor Filter service is used for filtering attributes, events, and properties of components. The designer of a component may implement the `IDesignerFilter` interface, which allows the designer implementation to filter unused or unnecessary properties and events.

The service just passes the request it receives over to the `IDesignerFilter` object. The service is defined under `src\SharpDevelop\FormDesigner\FormDesigner\Services\TypeDescriptorFilterService.cs`:

```
public class TypeDescriptorFilterService : ITypeDescriptorFilterService
{
```

The `GetDesignerFilter` method gets the designer of the component using the `Site` property. It gets the designer host, which returns the designer of a component. The designer is cast to `IDesignerFilter` and if the designer implements this interface, the object is returned. If it does not implement this interface, `null` is returned. Therefore, it is up to the designer implementer to make sense of filtering attributes, events, or properties.

This method is used internally:

```
IDesignerFilter GetDesignerFilter(IComponent component)
{
  ISite site = component.Site;

  if (site == null) {
    return null;
  }

  IDesignerHost host = site.GetService(typeof(IDesignerHost)) as
    IDesignerHost;
```

```
      if (host == null) {
        return null;
      }

      IDesigner designer = host.GetDesigner(component);

      return designer as IDesignerFilter;
    }
```

Now we will look at the filter methods, which just delegate their calls over to the IDesignerFilter object.

We aren't sure this is the right way of implementing it but it seems to make sense, as the designer filter has two methods of filtering attributes, events, and properties. These methods are PreFilterXYZ and PostFilterXYZ (where XYZ stands for attributes, events, or properties). We just call these methods to get the filtering done:

```
    public bool FilterAttributes(IComponent component, IDictionary attributes)
    {
      IDesignerFilter designerFilter = GetDesignerFilter(component);
      if (designerFilter != null) {
        designerFilter.PreFilterAttributes(attributes);
        designerFilter.PostFilterAttributes(attributes);
      }
      return false;
    }

    public bool FilterEvents(IComponent component, IDictionary events)
    {
      IDesignerFilter designerFilter = GetDesignerFilter(component);
      if (designerFilter != null) {
        designerFilter.PreFilterEvents(events);
        designerFilter.PostFilterEvents(events);
      }
      return false;
    }

    public bool FilterProperties(IComponent component, IDictionary properties)
    {
      IDesignerFilter designerFilter = GetDesignerFilter(component);
      if (designerFilter != null) {
        designerFilter.PreFilterProperties(properties);
        designerFilter.PostFilterProperties(properties);
      }
      return false;
    }
  }
```

Now let's look at the unimplemented services.

Unimplemented Services

So far, we have looked at the services that are implemented, and have discussed at least the basic functions that make them work. Some of these services are more important than others, but there are still some services left that have only skeleton implementations, which do nothing.

These services are not required to make a forms designer work but they will be implemented in the future. Many of the services that we examined in this chapter began their life as skeleton implementations that grew useful over time. The skeleton implementations that are currently present are:

- ❑   IExtenderProviderService
    This service adds extender providers, which extend the properties shown in the property grid of a component.

- ❑   IEventBindingService
    This service exposes events as property objects, and is used to show the events of a method in a property grid (to make the events 'designable').

- ❑   ITypeResolutionService
    This service should be used to load types at design time. It provides GetAssembly/GetType methods. Currently all types inside the SharpDevelop designer are loaded from the standard assemblies. This service will become important when custom controls are supported.

Summary

In this chapter, we have looked at all of the services required to make the Forms Designer work.

We have examined how to handle the Toolbox and notifying that a component is selected for insertion in the Design area. We now know how Toolbox items are constructed and we have looked at the service that represents the Toolbox.

We have gone through how the context menu is displayed in the Design area and how the standard commands work. We examined how to call a pre-defined command and handle keyboard actions inside the Design area.

We looked at the Selection service, which handles the selected components. We discussed how the modifier keys change the selection behavior and we looked at how the primary selection is implemented.

In the next chapter, we will learn about making components persistent, by using XML. We will look at how code is generated and learn how to implement roundtripping.

CHAPTER 17

17

Code Generation

In this chapter, we will learn about making forms persistent (being able to store them to disk and restore them), and how code is generated (a forms designer should be able to generate executable code from the graphical representation of a form). We will look at:

❑ **The XML form's persistence format** – This will give us an idea of how the components are stored on the disk

❑ **The code that generates the XML format** – Here we will see how properties are read and stored as XML

❑ **The class that reads the XML format back** – We will see what happens when the forms designer can't read the XML format back

❑ **Generating C#/VB.NET code** – We will see how to use CodeDOM to produce source code from of the XML format

❑ **Round trip** – This deals with reading the code back in the designer

Making Components Persistent

This is important because the form designer is useless unless it can store (and retrieve) files. Here, we will discuss:

❑ The XML form's persistence

❑ Generating the XML

❑ Loading the XML

❑ Designer Serialization

The XML Forms Persistence Format

To introduce the form format, it's best to start with an example form. Take a look at this screenshot of the form designer:

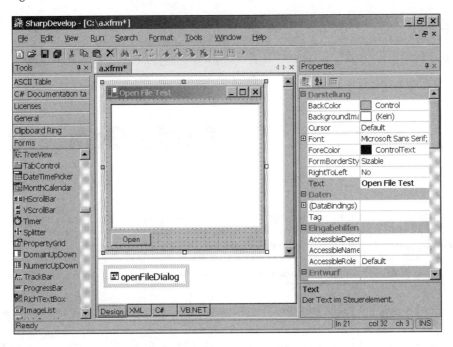

This Designer area contains four components: the form, textbox, and button, which are the visible ones, and the openFileDialog (invisible). We need a format that can describe all the properties of the components, and can recognize the location of the components. For example, the button and textbox are child controls of the form.

The XML representation of the previous example is:

```
<Components version="1.0">
  <System.Windows.Forms.Form>
    <Name value="CreatedObject0" />
    <Controls>
      <System.Windows.Forms.RichTextBox>
        <Name value="richTextBox" />
        <TabIndex value="1" />
        <Text value="" />
        <Location value="{X=8,Y=8}" />
        <Size value="{Width=280, Height=224}" />
      </System.Windows.Forms.RichTextBox>
      <System.Windows.Forms.Button>
        <Name value="button" />
        <TabIndex value="0" />
        <Text value="Open" />
```

```
        <Location value="{X=8,Y=240}" />
      </System.Windows.Forms.Button>
    </Controls>
    <Text value="Open File Test" />
    <DockPadding value="" />
    <SnapToGrid value="True" />
    <DrawGrid value="True" />
    <GridSize value="{Width=8, Height=8}" />
  </System.Windows.Forms.Form>
  <System.Windows.Forms.OpenFileDialog>
    <Name value="openFileDialog" />
  </System.Windows.Forms.OpenFileDialog>
</Components>
```

The root node of the XML is called <Components>. It is has a mandatory child component, which is the form or user control (currently supported by SharpDevelop), followed by zero or more invisible components (for example, tray controls). In the previous example, the OpenFileDialog is outside our System.Windows.Forms.Form declaration – our XML format specifies that components not contained within either Windows Forms or user controls go in the Tray. The <Components> XML format is just a property name and value pair, where the property name is the XML node name and the value is stored in the value attribute. Collections are an exception (look at the <Controls> node); instead of having attributes assigned to them, they contain a list of XML components.

With the previous format, we can now store and load XML forms. Let's look at the XML generation.

Generating the XML

To generate the XML for the components we have to solve a couple of problems:

❑ **Which properties should be saved to XML** – Not all properties need to be stored, for example, those containing default values can be skipped in the XML file.

❑ **How to access the tray components?** – The Tray is below the Designer area. We don't have a Tray service (or something similar) that will provide an easy answer to this question, and cannot access the component tray directly (as this restriction is imposed by Microsoft in the .NET architecture).

To answer these questions, let's look at the source code of the XmlFormGenerator given in src\SharpDevelop\FormDesigner\FormDesigner\Xml\XmlFormGenerator.cs file:

```
public class XmlFormGenerator
{
  public XmlElement GetElementFor(XmlDocument doc, object o)
  {
    if (doc == null) {
      throw new ArgumentNullException("doc");
    }

    if (o == null) {
```

```
        throw new ArgumentNullException("o");
    }

    try {
        XmlElement el = doc.CreateElement(o.GetType().FullName);
```

After the initial checks, the call to GetType and the creation of the XmlElement from the object type, we get a PropertyDescriptorCollection using the System.ComponentModel.TypeDescriptor class. This collection contains PropertyDescriptor objects that tell us whether the property should be serialized (actual serialization is shown later in this section) or not:

```
        PropertyDescriptorCollection properties =
            TypeDescriptor.GetProperties(o);

        Control ctrl = o as Control;
        bool nameInserted = false;
        if (ctrl != null) {
            XmlElement childEl = doc.CreateElement("Name");
            XmlAttribute valueAttribute = doc.CreateAttribute("value");
            valueAttribute.InnerText = ctrl.Name;
            childEl.Attributes.Append(valueAttribute);
            el.AppendChild(childEl);
            nameInserted = true;
        }

        // the Controls collection should be generated as the last
        // element because properties like 'anchor' in the child elements
        // must be applied after the size has been set.
        foreach (PropertyDescriptor pd in properties) {
            if (pd.Name == "Name" && nameInserted) {
                continue;
            }
            if (pd.Name == "DataBindings" ||
                // TabControl duplicate TabPages Workaround (TabPages got
                // inserted twice : In Controls and in TabPages)
                (o.GetType().FullName == "System.Windows.Forms.TabControl" &&
                    pd.Name == "Controls")) {
                continue;
            }
```

Here, we get the property value by using the PropertyDescriptor object:

```
        XmlElement childEl = doc.CreateElement(pd.Name);
        object propertyValue = null;
        try {
            propertyValue = pd.GetValue(o);
        } catch (Exception) {
            continue;
        }
```

We handle collections differently from normal properties. As mentioned earlier, list nodes have elements as child nodes and all other properties have a `value` attribute assigned to them:

```
    // lists are other than normal properties
    if (propertyValue is IList) {
      foreach (object listObject in (IList)propertyValue) {
        XmlElement newEl = GetElementFor(doc, listObject);
        if (newEl != null) {
          childEl.AppendChild(newEl);
        }
      }

      // only insert lists that contain elements (no empty lists!)
      if (childEl.ChildNodes.Count > 0) {
        el.AppendChild(childEl);
      }
    } else if (pd.ShouldSerializeValue(o) && pd.IsBrowsable) {
      XmlAttribute valueAttribute = doc.CreateAttribute("value");
      valueAttribute.InnerText = propertyValue == null ?
        null : propertyValue.ToString();
      childEl.Attributes.Append(valueAttribute);
      el.AppendChild(childEl);
    }
  }
```

The previous source code answers our first question. The `PropertyDescriptor` is used for this. It contains a `ShouldSerializeValue` method and an `IsBrowsable` property; both values are used to determine whether the property should be stored in the XML file or not. In this implementation, only properties changed by the user (`IsBrowsable=changeable`) in the property window are stored.

Next, we will handle the special case of collections containing value types. We need to get the value type to set the values of the collection properties. However, we can't do this normally because most value types don't have properties that can be read to set the value type. For example, the `String` is a basic type and there is no property inside the `String` type that sets the value of the string.

Currently, these types get a `value` attribute assigned and the `value` is used to restore the type. In the code generation part, we examine whether the element has any child nodes assigned (in this case, it isn't a `value` type) and if not, we store the object value in the `valueAttribute` (using the `ToString` method):

```
    // fallback to ToString, if no members can be generated (for example
    // handling System.String)
    if (el.ChildNodes.Count == 0) {
      XmlAttribute valueAttribute = doc.CreateAttribute("value");
      valueAttribute.InnerText = o.ToString();
      el.Attributes.Append(valueAttribute);
    }

  return el;
  } catch (Exception e) {
    Console.WriteLine(e.ToString());
  }
  return null;
}
```

Now, let's look at the method used for serializing the components inside a designer host:

```
public XmlElement GetElementFor(XmlDocument doc, IDesignerHost host)
{
  XmlElement componentsElement   = doc.CreateElement("Components");

  XmlAttribute versionAttribute = doc.CreateAttribute("version");
  versionAttribute.InnerText = "1.0";
  componentsElement.Attributes.Append(versionAttribute);

  // insert root element
  componentsElement.AppendChild(GetElementFor(doc, host.RootComponent));

  // insert any non QUI (=tray components)
  foreach (IComponent component in host.Container.Components) {
    if (!(component is Control)) {
      componentsElement.AppendChild(GetElementFor(doc, component));
    }
  }
  return componentsElement;
}
}
```

This method tells us how tray components are found; we go through the whole component container and store all components that do not inherit from `Control`. These components are displayed inside the component tray because they cannot be added to the `Controls` collection of a GUI component.

With the saving implemented, we will now turn to loading persisted form definitions.

Loading the XML

Loading the XML file is more difficult than generating it, because many objects are easily transformed (they transform themselves) to a string by using the `ToString` method. For example, `Color`, `Size`, or `Enumeration` objects do this on the fly. But unfortunately, the transformation back is not as easy.

For example, if we want to transform a string to an enumeration, we use:

```
EnumType enumConverted = (EnumType)Enum.Parse(typeof(EnumType),
  stringToParse);
```

This makes the implementation more complicated because the transformation back depends on the type. Therefore, we will look at it in more detail. The `XmlFormReader` class, which reads back the XML file, is defined under `src\SharpDevelop\FormDesigner\FormDesigner\Xml\XmlFormReader.cs`:

```
public class XmlFormReader
{
  IDesignerHost host;

  public XmlFormReader(IDesignerHost host)
  {
    this.host = host;
  }
```

The `CreateObject` method just transforms the XML back to an object. This method is used in the `DesignerSerializationService` to deserialize an object:

```
public object CreateObject(string xmlContent)
{
  XmlDocument doc = new XmlDocument();
  doc.LoadXml(xmlContent);

  return CreateObject(doc.DocumentElement);
}
```

The `SetUpDesignerHost` method sets up a designer host with the components of an XML file:

```
public void SetUpDesignerHost(string xmlContent)
{
  XmlDocument doc = new XmlDocument();
  doc.LoadXml(xmlContent);
  Console.WriteLine(xmlContent);
  if (doc.DocumentElement.Attributes["version"] == null) {
    CreateObject(xmlContent);
  } else {
    foreach (XmlElement el in doc.DocumentElement.ChildNodes) {
      CreateObject(el);
    }
  }
}
```

The `SetUpObject` method sets the properties of an object to the contents of an `XmlElement`:

```
void SetUpObject(object currentObject, XmlElement element)
{
  foreach (XmlNode subNode in element.ChildNodes) {
    if (subNode is XmlElement){
      XmlElement subElement = (XmlElement)subNode;
      SetAttributes(currentObject, subElement);
    }
  }
}
```

Now we will look at the `SetAttributes` method that sets a single attribute (to `property`) of an object to the contents in a XML element, which is either a key and value pair or a collection name with sub-items:

```
// Sets all properties in the object o to the xml element el.
void SetAttributes(object o, XmlElement el)
{
  if (el.Attributes["value"] != null) {
    string val = el.Attributes["value"].InnerText;
    try {
      SetValue(o, el.Name, val);
    } catch (Exception) {}
  } else {
```

```
         PropertyInfo propertyInfo = o.GetType().GetProperty(el.Name);
      object pv = propertyInfo.GetValue(o, null);
      if (pv is IList) {
        foreach (XmlNode subNode in el.ChildNodes) {
          if (subNode is XmlElement){
            XmlElement subElement = (XmlElement)subNode;
            object collectionObject = CreateObject(subElement);

            if (collectionObject != null) {
              try {
                ((IList)pv).Add(collectionObject);
              } catch (Exception e) {
                Console.WriteLine("Exception while adding to a collection:"
                  + e.ToString());
              }
  } } } } }   } //closing braces collapsed for brevity
```

The next method sets a single property to a specific value. This method converts the string to the property type:

```
void SetValue(object o, string propertyName, string val)
{
  Console.WriteLine("Set Property " + propertyName + " to " + val);
  try {
    PropertyInfo propertyInfo = o.GetType().GetProperty(propertyName);
    if (val.StartsWith("{") && val.EndsWith("}")){
      val = val.Substring(1, val.Length - 2);
      object propertyObject = null;
      if (propertyInfo.CanWrite) {
        Type type = host.GetType(propertyInfo.PropertyType.FullName);
        propertyObject = type.Assembly.CreateInstance
          (propertyInfo.PropertyType.FullName);
      } else {
        propertyObject = propertyInfo.GetValue(o, null);
      }

      Regex propertySet  =
        new Regex(@"(?<Property>[\w]+)\s*=\s*(?<Value>[\w\d]+)",
          RegexOptions.Compiled);
      Match match = propertySet.Match(val);
      while (true) {
        if (!match.Success) {
          break;
        }
        SetValue(propertyObject, match.Result("${Property}"),
          match.Result("${Value}"));
        match = match.NextMatch();
      }

      if (propertyInfo.CanWrite) {
        propertyInfo.SetValue(o, propertyObject, null);
      }
    } else if (propertyInfo.PropertyType.IsEnum) {
```

```
        propertyInfo.SetValue(o, Enum.Parse(propertyInfo.PropertyType, val),
          null);
    } else if (propertyInfo.PropertyType == typeof(Color)) {
      string color = val.Substring(val.IndexOf('[') + 1).Replace("]", "");
      string[] argb = color.Split(',', '=');
      if (argb.Length > 1) {
        propertyInfo.SetValue(o, Color.FromArgb(Int32.Parse(argb[1]),
          Int32.Parse(argb[3]), Int32.Parse(argb[5]), Int32.Parse(argb[7])),
          null);
      } else {
        propertyInfo.SetValue(o, Color.FromName(color), null);
      }
    } else if (propertyInfo.PropertyType == typeof(Font)) {
      string[] font = val.Split(',', '=');
      propertyInfo.SetValue(o, new Font(font[1], Int32.Parse(font[3])),
        null);
    } else if (propertyInfo.PropertyType ==
        typeof(System.Windows.Forms.Cursor)) {
      string[] cursor = val.Split('[', ']', ' ', ':');
      PropertyInfo cursorProperty =
        typeof(System.Windows.Forms.Cursors).GetProperty(cursor[3]);
      if (cursorProperty != null) {
        propertyInfo.SetValue(o, cursorProperty.GetValue(null, null), null);
      }

    } else {
      propertyInfo.SetValue(o, Convert.ChangeType
        (val, propertyInfo.PropertyType), null);
    }
  } catch (Exception e) {
    Console.WriteLine(e.ToString());
    throw new ApplicationException("error while setting property " +
      propertyName + " of object "+ o.ToString() + " to value '" + val+
      "'");
  }
}
```

The last method in this class creates an object based on `value` property of the XML element details. It uses the host's `GetType` method to try to create an object of this type:

```
// Creates a new instance of object name. It tries to resolve name in
// System.Windows.Forms, System.Drawing and System namespace.
object CreateObject(XmlElement objectElement)
{
  Type type = host.GetType(objectElement.Name);
  if (type == null) {
    return null;
  }
```

Now if the XML element has a `value` attribute assigned, we try to convert the value to the type of the XML element and the object is given back:

```
    if (objectElement.Attributes["value"] != null) {
      return System.Convert.ChangeType(objectElement.Attributes["value"].
        InnerText, type);
    }
```

Otherwise, we try to create an instance and set the name of the object (if the XML element has a name property assigned). If the type implements IComponent, we have to use the CreateComponent method from the host to make it designable inside the Design area:

```
    object newObject = type.Assembly.CreateInstance(type.FullName);

    string componentName = null;
    if (objectElement["Name"] != null &&
        objectElement["Name"].Attributes["value"] != null) {
      componentName = objectElement["Name"].Attributes["value"].InnerText;
    }

    if (newObject is IComponent) {
      newObject = host.CreateComponent(newObject.GetType(), componentName);
    }

    SetUpObject(newObject, objectElement);

    return newObject;
  }
}
```

Next, we are going to look at the usage of XML serialization and deserialization. SharpDevelop allows us to load and store the values into the XML format directly, but the XML format gets used in a service too (which is Cut and Paste), which we will look at it, in the next section.

The Designer Serialization Service

We can now implement the designer serialization service. This service is used by the Cut, Copy, and Paste actions to store the components on the clipboard.

The service is relatively simple, with only two methods:

❑   Serialize - This method stores components into a collection

❑   Deserialize - This retrieves stored elements out of a collection

This service is defined under src\SharpDevelop\FormDesigner\FormDesigner\Services\DesignerSerializationService.cs:

```
public class DesignerSerializationService : IDesignerSerializationService
{
  IDesignerHost host = null;
```

```
  public DesignerSerializationService(IDesignerHost host)
  {
    this.host = host;
  }

  public ICollection Deserialize(object serializationData)
  {
    ArrayList elements = new ArrayList();
    foreach (string xmlContent in (ArrayList)serializationData) {
      elements.Add
        (new XmlFormReader(host).LoadContentDefinition(xmlContent));
    }
    return elements;
  }

  public object Serialize(ICollection objectCollection)
  {
    ArrayList elements = new ArrayList();
    foreach (object o in objectCollection) {
      StringWriter writer = new StringWriter();
      XmlDocument doc = new XmlDocument();
      doc.LoadXml("<" + o.GetType().FullName + "/>");
      XmlElement el = new XmlFormGenerator().GetElementFor(new
        XmlDocument(), o);
      foreach (XmlNode node in el.ChildNodes) {
        doc.DocumentElement.AppendChild(doc.ImportNode(node, true));
      }
      doc.Save(writer);
      elements.Add(writer.ToString());
    }
    return elements;
  }
}
```

This snippet shows that the XML persistence layer is more important than just storing the form on disk. We need a method to store the details of an object copied in the clipboard, in XML format, because it is serializable, which means that if the original object changes, the copy won't.

If we Cut a component, it is serialized to the clipboard, and the original component is disposed. We can't add a disposed component, and we can't add the same component twice. Therefore, we have to find a way to make a copy that can be serialized (although controls can't) and the XML layer does this for us. Generating working source code from the designed form is more important for the user than storing the designed form in XML format. The next section deals with this aspect.

Generating C#/VB.NET Code

Source code generation is similar to loading an XML file. The only difference is that objects are not generated directly. The code is generated, which will generate the objects. However, there is a problem with code generation – which programming language should we use, as the target language? SharpDevelop tends to be a multi-language development environment; therefore, we need more back-ends for language creation.

Instead of writing the back-end ourselves we use a .NET API called CodeDOM. CodeDOM's role is to generate source code from our visual representation of the forms into a language-based format, which tells the runtime to generate our controls, set properties, and so on. CodeDOM currently generates C#, VB.NET and JavaScript code, but it can be extended to support other languages too.

To get an overview of our architecture, take a look at the following diagram:

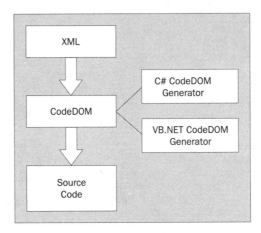

The XML is transformed into CodeDOM data structures by using the code generators (provided by the framework).

Now, we will take a look at the implementation of the `CodeDOMGenerator` class (in the `src\SharpDevelop\FormDesigner\FormDesigner\Xml\CodeDOMGenerator.cs` file). We will also learn a bit about CodeDOM here:

```
public class CodeDOMGenerator
{
  IDesignerHost host;
  AmbienceService ambienceService =
    (AmbienceService)ICSharpCode.Core.Services.ServiceManager.Services.
    GetService(typeof(AmbienceService));

  string acceptButtonName = String.Empty;
  string cancelButtonName = String.Empty;

  int num = 0;
  ICodeGenerator codeGenerator;
  CodeTypeDeclaration codeTypeDeclaration;

  CodeNamespace codeNamespace;
  CodeDOMGeneratorUtility codeDOMGeneratorUtility =
    new CodeDOMGeneratorUtility();

  public CodeDOMGenerator(IDesignerHost host, CodeDomProvider codeProvider)
  {
    this.host = host;
    codeGenerator = codeProvider.CreateGenerator();
```

```
        codeNamespace = new CodeNamespace("GeneratedForm");

        this.codeDOMGeneratorUtility.AddNamespaceImport("System");
        this.codeDOMGeneratorUtility.AddNamespaceImport("System.Windows.Forms");

        codeNamespace.Comments.Add(new CodeCommentStatement
            ("This file was autogenerated by a tool.", false));
    }
```

In the constructor, we generate the code generator, which outputs code in the target language. The caller must provide a `CodeDomProvider`, which generates the code generator. The `CodeDOMGenerator` class does not know about the target language. After that, a namespace called `GeneratedForm` is set up, which will contain the generated type.

The next method will generate the type using an `XmlDocument` that describes the form using the XML format, as seen in the last section:

```
public void ConvertContentDefinition(XmlDocument doc, TextWriter writer)
{
    XmlElement rootComponent = (XmlElement)
        doc.DocumentElement.ChildNodes[0];

    // create class
    codeTypeDeclaration = new CodeTypeDeclaration
        (rootComponent.SelectSingleNode("Name/@value").Value);
    if (ambienceService.GenerateDocumentComments) {
        codeTypeDeclaration.Comments.Add(new CodeCommentStatement("<summary>",
            true));
        codeTypeDeclaration.Comments.Add(new CodeCommentStatement
            ("    Add summary description for " + codeTypeDeclaration.Name,
                true));
        codeTypeDeclaration.Comments.Add(new
            CodeCommentStatement("</summary>", true));
    }
    codeTypeDeclaration.BaseTypes.Add
        (codeDOMGeneratorUtility.GetTypeReference(rootComponent.Name));
    codeNamespace.Types.Add(codeTypeDeclaration);

    // create constructor
    CodeConstructor cc = new CodeConstructor();
    cc.Attributes = MemberAttributes.Public | MemberAttributes.Final;
    if (ambienceService.GenerateAdditionalComments) {
        cc.Statements.Add(new CodeCommentStatement(" Must be called for
        initialization", false));
    }
    cc.Statements.Add(new CodeExpressionStatement(new
        CodeMethodInvokeExpression(new CodeThisReferenceExpression(),
        "InitializeComponents")));
    if (ambienceService.GenerateAdditionalComments) {
        cc.Statements.Add(new CodeCommentStatement("", false));
        cc.Statements.Add(new CodeCommentStatement(" TODO : Add constructor
            code after InitializeComponents", false));
        cc.Statements.Add(new CodeCommentStatement("", false));
```

```
      }
      codeTypeDeclaration.Members.Add(cc);

      // create intialize components method
      CodeMemberMethod cm = new CodeMemberMethod();
      if (ambienceService.GenerateDocumentComments) {
        cm.Comments.Add(new CodeCommentStatement("<summary>", true));
        cm.Comments.Add(new CodeCommentStatement("  This method was
          autogenerated - do not change the contents manually", true));
        cm.Comments.Add(new CodeCommentStatement("</summary>", true));
      }

      cm.Name = "InitializeComponents";
      cm.ReturnType = new CodeTypeReference(typeof(void));

      // set up root component
      SetUpObject(cm, null, host.GetType(rootComponent.Name), rootComponent);

      // set up other components
      Console.WriteLine("Node Count " + doc.DocumentElement.ChildNodes.Count);
      for (int i = 1; i < doc.DocumentElement.ChildNodes.Count; ++i) {
        XmlElement el = (XmlElement)doc.DocumentElement.ChildNodes[i];
        SetUpObject(cm, el.SelectSingleNode("Name/@value").Value,
          host.GetType(el.Name), el);
      }

      cm.Statements.Add(new CodeExpressionStatement(new
        CodeMethodInvokeExpression(new CodeThisReferenceExpression(),
        "ResumeLayout", new CodePrimitiveExpression(false))));
      codeTypeDeclaration.Members.Add(cm);

      // finally generate code
      this.codeDOMGeneratorUtility.GenerateNamespaceImports(codeNamespace);
      codeGenerator.GenerateCodeFromNamespace(codeNamespace, writer,
        codeDOMGeneratorUtility.CreateCodeGeneratorOptions);
    }
```

The next method does the same, but the output is not a stream, but a file:

```
public void ConvertContentDefinition(XmlDocument doc, string fileName)
{
  StreamWriter writer = File.CreateText(fileName);
  ConvertContentDefinition(doc, writer);
  writer.Close();
}
```

The `SetUpObject` method is almost the same as in our `XmlFormReader` class (see the *Loading the XML* section), the only difference is the CodeDOM generation. Its purpose is to set the properties of an object to the contents of `XmlElement`:

```
void SetUpObject(CodeMemberMethod cm, string name, Type currentType,
  XmlElement element)
{
```

```
    bool isThis = name == null || name.Length == 0;

  if (!isThis) {
    cm.Statements.Add(new CodeSnippetStatement(""));
  }
  if (ambienceService.GenerateAdditionalComments) {
    cm.Statements.Add(new CodeCommentStatement("", false));
    cm.Statements.Add(new CodeCommentStatement(" Set up " + (isThis ?
    "generated class " + codeTypeDeclaration.Name : "member " + name),
    false));
    cm.Statements.Add(new CodeCommentStatement("", false));
  }

  // create new member variable
  if (isThis) {
    cm.Statements.Add(new CodeExpressionStatement(new
      CodeMethodInvokeExpression(new CodeThisReferenceExpression(),
      "SuspendLayout")));
  } else {
    codeTypeDeclaration.Members.Add(new
      CodeMemberField(codeDOMGeneratorUtility.GetTypeReference
      (currentType.FullName), name));
    cm.Statements.Add(new CodeAssignStatement(new
      CodeFieldReferenceExpression(null, name), new
      CodeObjectCreateExpression(codeDOMGeneratorUtility.
      GetTypeReference(currentType))));
  }

  foreach (XmlNode subNode in element.ChildNodes) {
    if (subNode is XmlElement) {
      SetAttributes(cm, name, currentType, (XmlElement)subNode);
    }
  }
}
```

The SetAttributes method is implemented the same way as in XmlFormReader (see the *Loading the XML* section):

```
void SetAttributes(CodeMemberMethod cm, string name, Type currentType,
  XmlElement el)
{
  CodeExpression nameReferenceExpression = name == null || name.Length ==
    0 ? (CodeExpression)new CodeThisReferenceExpression() :
      (CodeExpression)new CodeTypeReferenceExpression(name);
  if (el.Attributes["value"] != null) {
    string val = el.Attributes["value"].InnerText;
    try {
      SetValue(cm, name, currentType, el.Name, val);
    } catch (Exception) {}
  } else {
    PropertyInfo propertyInfo = currentType.GetProperty(el.Name);
    bool isList = false;
    if (propertyInfo != null) {
```

```
      Type[] interfaces = propertyInfo.PropertyType.GetInterfaces();
      foreach (Type i in interfaces) {
        if (i == typeof(IList)) {
          isList = true;
          break;
        }
      }
    }
  if (isList) {
    foreach (XmlNode subNode in el.ChildNodes) {
      if (subNode is XmlElement) {
        XmlElement subElement = (XmlElement)subNode;
        Type collectionType = host.GetType(subElement.Name);
        if (collectionType == null) {
          continue;
        }
        string objName = null;
        bool isComponent = false;
        Type[] interfaces = collectionType.GetInterfaces();
        foreach (Type i in interfaces) {
          if (i == typeof(IComponent)) {
            isComponent = true;
            break;
          }
        }

        if (isComponent && subElement["Name"] != null &&
          subElement["Name"].Attributes["value"] != null) {
          objName = subElement["Name"].Attributes["value"].InnerText;
        }

        if (objName == null || objName.Length == 0) {
          objName = "createdObject" + num++;
        }

        SetUpObject(cm, objName, collectionType, subElement);
        cm.Statements.Add(new CodeExpressionStatement(new
          CodeMethodInvokeExpression(new CodePropertyReferenceExpression
          (nameReferenceExpression, el.Name), "Add", new
          CodeFieldReferenceExpression(null, objName))));
      }
} } } }
```

Now we will examine the `SetValue` method. This method sets up a property with a given value (as in the `XmlFormReader`):

```
void SetValue(CodeMemberMethod cm, string name, Type currentType, string
           propertyName, string val)
{
  CodeExpression nameReferenceExpression = name == null ||
    name.Length == 0 ? (CodeExpression)new CodeThisReferenceExpression()
    : (CodeExpression)new CodeTypeReferenceExpression(name);
  try {
```

```
        PropertyInfo propertyInfo = currentType.GetProperty(propertyName);

    if (propertyInfo == null) {
      return;
    }
```

Now we are trying to parse {...} values. When the val string has the form {...} it means that the content should be treated differently. It has the form – {Property1=value1, Property2=value2, ...}. This is due the fact that we convert some objects to a string using the ToString method. The ToString method produces strings in the {...} form.

For example, a Size struct can have the value {Width=352, Height=300}, which means that a new Size struct must be created, and the property Width must set to 352 and Height to 300. We are using regular expressions to find PROPERTYNAME = VALUE patterns until we assigned all properties:

```
    if (val.StartsWith("{") && val.EndsWith("}")) {
      val = val.Substring(1, val.Length - 2);
      Type newType =
        host.GetType(propertyInfo.PropertyType.FullName);
      ArrayList parameters = new ArrayList();
      Regex propertySet = new
        Regex(@"(?<Property>[\w]+)\s*=\s*(?<Value>[\w\d]+)",
          RegexOptions.Compiled);
      Match match = propertySet.Match(val);
      while (true) {
        if (!match.Success) {
          break;
        }
        parameters.Add(new CodePropertyReferenceExpression(null,
          match.Result("${Value}")));

        match = match.NextMatch();
      }

      CodeExpression expr = new CodePropertyReferenceExpression
        (nameReferenceExpression, propertyName);
      cm.Statements.Add(new CodeAssignStatement(expr, new
        CodeObjectCreateExpression(codeDOMGeneratorUtility.
        GetTypeReference(propertyInfo.PropertyType.FullName),
        (CodeExpression[])parameters.ToArray
        (typeof(CodeExpression)))));
```

The next case we have to handle is enumerations. Enumerations are handled specially, because CodeDOM has way to assign enumerations (remember that an enumeration value can have the form: value1 | value2. We're using the GetExpressionForEnum helper method to create the expression, which represents the enum value. We will look at this method after we finish with this listing.

```
    } else if (propertyInfo.PropertyType.IsEnum) {
      cm.Statements.Add(new CodeAssignStatement(new
        CodePropertyReferenceExpression(nameReferenceExpression,
          propertyInfo.Name), GetExpressionForEnum
```

```
             (propertyInfo.PropertyType, val)));
} else if (propertyInfo.PropertyType == typeof(Color)) {
  string color = val.Substring(val.IndexOf('[') + 1).Replace("]", "");
  Type colorType = typeof(System.Drawing.Color);
  CodeExpression ce = null;
  if (colorType.GetProperty(color) != null) {
    ce = new CodePropertyReferenceExpression
      (codeDOMGeneratorUtility.GetTypeReferenceExpression(colorType),
        color);
```

Now we convert `Color`, `Font`, and `Cursor` objects. They do have a slightly different `ToString` behavior from other objects. Here we can see a downside of the `ToString` method (we have to take care of 'special cases'):

```
} else if (typeof(KnownColor).GetField(color) != null){
  ce = new CodeMethodInvokeExpression
    (codeDOMGeneratorUtility.GetTypeReferenceExpression(colorType),
    "FromKnownColor", new CodeFieldReferenceExpression(new
    CodeTypeReferenceExpression(typeof(KnownColor)), color));
} else {
  string[] argb = color.Split(',', '=');
  ce = new CodeMethodInvokeExpression
    (codeDOMGeneratorUtility.GetTypeReferenceExpression(colorType),
    "FromArgb", new CodeArgumentReferenceExpression(argb[1]),
    new CodeArgumentReferenceExpression(argb[3]),
    new CodeArgumentReferenceExpression(argb[5]),
    new CodeArgumentReferenceExpression(argb[7]));
}
cm.Statements.Add(new CodeAssignStatement(new
  CodePropertyReferenceExpression(nameReferenceExpression,
  propertyInfo.Name), ce));
} else if (propertyInfo.PropertyType == typeof(System.Drawing.Font)) {
  // TODO : correct font parameters bold, italic
  string[] font = val.Split(',', '=');
  cm.Statements.Add(new CodeAssignStatement(new
    CodePropertyReferenceExpression(nameReferenceExpression,
    propertyInfo.Name), new CodeObjectCreateExpression
    (codeDOMGeneratorUtility.GetTypeReference
    (typeof(System.Drawing.Font)),
    new CodePrimitiveExpression(font[1]),
    new CodePrimitiveExpression(Int32.Parse(font[3]))))));
} else if (propertyInfo.PropertyType ==
        typeof(System.Windows.Forms.Cursor)) {
  string[] cursor = val.Split('[', ']', ' ', ':');
  cm.Statements.Add(new CodeAssignStatement(new
    CodePropertyReferenceExpression(nameReferenceExpression,
    propertyInfo.Name), new CodePropertyReferenceExpression
    (codeDOMGeneratorUtility.GetTypeReferenceExpression
    (typeof(System.Windows.Forms.Cursors)), cursor[3])));
```

The last case is the standard one. We just create a primitive assign statement, and use a primitive CodeDOM expression for creating expressions for primitive types (like `int`, `byte`, `double`, and so on):

```
            } else {
              if (val != null && val.Length > 0) {
                cm.Statements.Add(new CodeAssignStatement(
                  new CodePropertyReferenceExpression(nameReferenceExpression,
                  propertyInfo.Name), new CodePrimitiveExpression
                  (Convert.ChangeType(val, propertyInfo.PropertyType))));
              }
            }
        } catch (Exception e) {
            Console.WriteLine(e.ToString());
        }
      }
```

Finally, we have some helper methods. CodeDOM has an expression called `CodePrimitiveExpression`, which gets an object in its constructor, and represents the value of a primitive data type. Unfortunately, this method does not support enumerations and no other expression class does. Therefore, these helper methods were implemented to work around the missing feature:

```
CodeExpression GetExpressionForEnum(Type enumType, string val)
{
  string[] enums = val.Split(',');
  for (int i = 0; i < enums.Length; ++i) {
    enums[i] = enums[i].Trim();
  }
  return GetExpression(enumType.FullName, enums, 0);
}
```

The next method will take an array of enumerations, concatenated by an OR operation. This is used for enumeration flags:

```
CodeExpression GetExpression(string enumType, string[] enums, int index)
{
  CodeExpression curExpression = new CodeFieldReferenceExpression(
    new CodeTypeReferenceExpression(enumType), enums[index]);

  if (index + 1 < enums.Length) {
    return new CodeBinaryOperatorExpression(curExpression,
      CodeBinaryOperatorType.BitwiseOr, GetExpression(enumType, enums,
      index + 1));
  }
  return curExpression;
}
```

Finally, we look at an example file, which was auto-generated by this class. It is only a plain form with a button in it, but we get an idea of what the generated code looks like:

```
// This file was autogenerated by a tool.
namespace GeneratedForm {
  using System;
  using System.Windows.Forms;
```

```
//     Add summary description for MyForm
public class MyForm : System.Windows.Forms.Form {

  private System.Windows.Forms.Button button;

  public MyForm() {
    //  Must be called for initialization
    this.InitializeComponents();
    //
    //  TODO : Add constructor code after InitializeComponents
    //
  }

  // This method was autogenerated - do not change the contents manually
  private void InitializeComponents() {
    //  Set up generated class MyForm
    this.SuspendLayout();
    this.Name = "MyForm";

    // Set up member button
    button = new System.Windows.Forms.Button();
    button.Name = "button";
    button.TabIndex = 0;
    button.Text = "OK";
    button.Size = new System.Drawing.Size(80, 24);
    button.Location = new System.Drawing.Point(160, 104);
    this.Controls.Add(button);
    this.Text = "MyForm";
    this.Size = new System.Drawing.Size(248, 168);
    this.ResumeLayout(false);
  }
 }
}
```

Now that we have seen how the source code gets generated, it will be nice to examine it the other way around – reading the source code back, to have a designable form again. We will discuss this problem in the next section.

Round-tripping

The only thing we need to implement a full designer is to load our source code back to into the visual designer. This is called round-tripping. We have almost everything for implementing a round trip. The only thing that's missing is a source code reader. However, it's relatively simple to implement this one, because we already have a C# parser (it's described in Chapter 12).

Our C# parser does not parse down to the statement level; therefore we need to use a little trick to make the round trip work. Basically, we need a compiler that will take the source code and translate it into another form. Unfortunately, we do not have a compiler that outputs our XML format, but we can generate the XML format from an object. We do have a compiler that can generate executable code to generate objects – it is delivered with the .NET Framework itself and is called csc.exe. (Currently only C# round-tripping is supported, but for VB.NET it will work similarly with vbc.exe.)

Take a look at the following diagram, showing the round-trip process:

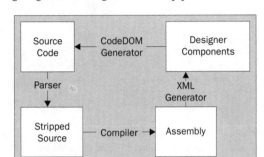

The parser strips the source code to a stripped-source, which can then be compiled by the compiler. We need to do this because we don't want to have dependencies on the project's dll files, or other source code from the project. We only want the 'form' information. The standard compiler makes an assembly, the compiled object gets instantiated, and the XmlFormGenerator then generates an XML definition that can be loaded by the designer. The designer creates the source code by using the CodeDOM generator, and this source is merged back into the starting source code.

First, we have the source code, which is stripped down because the class may depend on custom types. Let's look at the following class skeleton:

```
class CustomType : Form
{
  //components type declaration

  CustomType type1;
  //...more member variables

  public CustomType(int a)
  {
    InitializeComponents();
  }
  //...Stuff
  void InitializeComponents()
  {
  //... area of interrest
  }
  // ... more Stuff
}
```

We only need to know the components (=member types, which are initialized in InitializeComponents); therefore, the rest of the class is not important. The parser is used to get the InitializeComponents method and all fields in the class, to generate a class that looks like:

```
class StrippedClass: Form
{
  //... components type declaration

  public StrippedClass()
```

```
    {
        InitializeComponents();
    }

    void InitializeComponents()
    {
        //... area of interrest
    }
}
```

This class can be compiled because it does not contain references to non-.NET Framework classes, because our designer currently only designs form components. When external components are to be supported, the file must be compiled with the reference of the project, which this file owns (all designable components must be in a referenced assembly).

The compiled file is loaded as an assembly and an object of the `StrippedClass` type is generated. This object is taken, and an XML form is generated using the `XmlFormGenerator`.

We do not take the object directly, because this will require all objects to be generated by the designer host, and this way it is easier (we are just reusing code that it is already written, and don't write new code). The XML can be loaded into the designer just like a file.

The only difficult part is to snip out the old `InitializeComponents` method and field declarations, and to replace them with the new ones, which are generated by a `CodeDOMGenerator` object; but for this task, we need only the parser.

This approach isn't really clean, but it is relatively simple. A better way would have been to let the parser parse to the statement level, and then traverse through the parse tree to generate the XML. This will be less error prone. Users do change the `InitializeComponents` method on their own. They put non-.NET Framework objects inside it, add event handling manually and even other actions they shouldn't, to access objects that aren't part of the .NET Framework.

One solution to this problem will be to just lock this method in the text editor, so that it is displayed but not changeable (some IDEs do that). The best approach is to have an intelligent parser, which tries to read as much code as it can and then merge the generated code back. Note that even with this approach, it is not possible to solve this problem completely; but, it is improvable with this method, and if locking is also done, then the designer should be relatively safe from 'user attacks'.

Now let's go on to the implementation of the round trip. This is done by the `CSharpDesignerDisplayBinding` class, which is defined under `src\SharpDevelop\ FormDesigner\FormDesigner\CSharpDesignerDisplayBinding.cs`.

To understand this part of the source code, we have to know about the tabbed display bindings in SharpDevelop. The display binding contains a tab page that has a source code view and a designer area on its tabs. The problem is how the IDE will know what to do when Cut or Undo is clicked on the menu. The answer is – it won't. The display binding must take care of its contents, and delegate the call to the currently selected component.

The screenshot shows the designer area to demonstrate the tab page at the bottom:

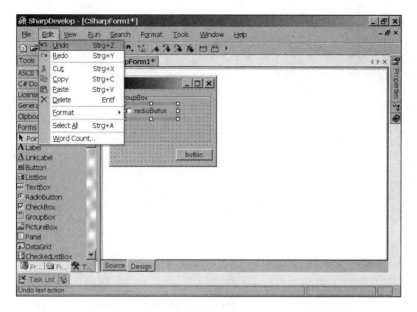

With this information, we will now look at the implementation of the C# round trip:

```
public class CSharpDesignerDisplayBindingWrapper : FormDesignerDisplayBindingBase,
ITextAreaControlProvider
{
  TabControl tabControl;
  TabPage designerPage;
  IViewContent csharpTextEditor;
  bool failedDesignerInitialize;

  public TextAreaControl TextAreaControl {
    get {
      return (TextAreaControl)csharpTextEditor.Control;
    }
  }

  public override IClipboardHandler ClipboardHandler {
    get {
      if (tabControl.SelectedTab.Controls[0] is IEditable) {
        return ((IEditable)
          tabControl.SelectedTab.Controls[0]).ClipboardHandler;
      }
      return base.ClipboardHandler;
    }
  }

  public override Control Control {
    get {
      return tabControl;
    }
  }
```

```
public override void Undo()
{
  if (isFormDesignerVisible) {
    base.Undo();
  } else {
    ((IEditable)csharpTextEditor).Undo();
  }
}

public override void Redo()
{
  if (isFormDesignerVisible) {
    base.Redo();
  } else {
    ((IEditable)csharpTextEditor).Redo();
  }
}
```

Note that the ClipboardHandler property and Undo and Redo methods delegate to the selected component.

The round trip needs the parser to work; therefore, we store the class and the InitializeComponents method as member variables:

```
IClass c;
IMethod initializeComponents;
string fileName;

public CSharpDesignerDisplayBindingWrapper(string fileName, IClass c,
  IMethod initializeComponents)
{
  this.fileName = fileName;
  this.c = c;
  this.initializeComponents = initializeComponents;

  TextEditorDisplayBinding tdb = new TextEditorDisplayBinding();
  csharpTextEditor = tdb.CreateContentForFile(fileName);
  InitializeComponents();
}

public CSharpDesignerDisplayBindingWrapper(string fileName, string
  content, IClass c, IMethod initializeComponents)
{
  this.fileName = fileName;
  this.c = c;
  this.initializeComponents = initializeComponents;

  TextEditorDisplayBinding tdb = new TextEditorDisplayBinding();
  csharpTextEditor = tdb.CreateContentForLanguage("C#", content);
  InitializeComponents();
}
```

Now we look at the method that executes the round trip. First, it generates the tab control and inserts the `csharpTextEditor` in the tab page:

```
void InitializeComponents()
{
  tabControl = new TabControl();
  tabControl.SelectedIndexChanged += new EventHandler(TabIndexChanged);
  tabControl.Alignment = TabAlignment.Bottom;

  TabPage sourcePage = new TabPage("Source");
  csharpTextEditor.Control.Dock = DockStyle.Fill;
  sourcePage.Controls.Add(csharpTextEditor.Control);
  tabControl.TabPages.Add(sourcePage);
```

Then it compiles the source code:

```
string formCode = GenerateClassString(TextAreaControl);
string sourceFile = Path.GetTempFileName();
string exeFile = Path.GetTempFileName();
StreamWriter sw = File.CreateText(sourceFile);
sw.Write(formCode);
sw.Close();

Hashtable options = new Hashtable();
options["target"] = "library";
CSharpBindingCompilerManager compilerManager =
  new CSharpBindingCompilerManager();
CSharpCompilerParameters param = new CSharpCompilerParameters();
param.OutputAssembly = exeFile;
param.CompileTarget = CompileTarget.Library;

ICompilerResult result = compilerManager.CompileFile(sourceFile, param);
File.Delete(sourceFile);

failedDesignerInitialize = true;
StringWriter writer = new StringWriter();
```

This method is programmed defensively (because errors may pop up almost everywhere). The next step is to create an instance of our class and the XML definition for it:

```
if (result.CompilerResults.Errors.Count > 0) {
  MessageBox.Show("Round trip failed due erros in input file: " +
    result.CompilerResults.Errors[0]);
} else {
  Control ctrl = null;
  try {
    Assembly asm = Assembly.LoadFrom(exeFile);
    ctrl = (Control)asm.CreateInstance("Unknown");
  } catch (Exception) {}

  if (ctrl == null) {
    MessageBox.Show("Error creating the type for the round trip");
  } else {
```

```
      XmlElement el = new XmlFormGenerator().GetElementFor(new
        XmlDocument(), ctrl);
      if (el == null) {
        MessageBox.Show("Error while storing to xml");
      } else {
        try {
          XmlDocument doc = new XmlDocument();
          doc.LoadXml("<" + ExctractBaseClass(c) + "/>");

          foreach (XmlNode node in el.ChildNodes) {
            if (node.Name == "Visible" || node.Name == "Location") {
              continue;
            }
            doc.DocumentElement.AppendChild(doc.ImportNode(node, true));
          }
          doc.Save(writer);
          failedDesignerInitialize = false;
        } catch (Exception e) {
          MessageBox.Show("Failed for unexpected reason :\n" +
            e.ToString());
        }
      }
    }
  }
  if (failedDesignerInitialize) {
    writer.WriteLine("<System.Windows.Forms.Form/>");
  }
```

Then we initialize the designer with the generated XML:

```
  InitializeFrom(fileName, writer.ToString());
  designerPage = new TabPage("Design");
  designerPage.Controls.Add(designPanel);
  tabControl.TabPages.Add(designerPage);

  if (failedDesignerInitialize) {
    sourcePage = new TabPage("Generated");
    TextEditorDisplayBinding tdb = new TextEditorDisplayBinding();
    IViewContent newTextEditor = tdb.CreateContentForLanguage("C#",
      formCode);
    newTextEditor.Control.Dock = DockStyle.Fill;
    ((SharpDevelopTextAreaControl)newTextEditor.Control).Document.ReadOnly
      = true;
    sourcePage.Controls.Add(newTextEditor.Control);
    tabControl.TabPages.Add(sourcePage);
  }
  csharpTextEditor.DirtyChanged += new EventHandler(TextAreaIsDirty);
}

void TextAreaIsDirty(object sender, EventArgs e)
{
  base.IsDirty = csharpTextEditor.IsDirty;
}
```

Note that, when the designer initialization fails (if `failedDesignerInitialize` is `true`), an empty form is displayed, and a new tab is inserted, which shows the stripped source code for debug purposes.

Now we will look at the method, which generates the class string for the class that is compiled by the compiler:

```
string GenerateClassString(TextAreaControl textArea)
{
  Reparse(fileName, textArea.Document.TextContent);

  StringBuilder builder = new StringBuilder();
  // generate usings
  foreach (IUsing u in c.CompilationUnit.Usings) {
    foreach (string usingString in u.Usings) {
      if (usingString.StartsWith("System")) {
        builder.Append("using " + usingString + ";\n");
      }
    }
  }

  builder.Append("class Unknown : ");
  builder.Append(ExctractBaseClass(c));
  builder.Append(" {\n");
  ArrayList fields = GetUsedFields(textArea.Document, c,
    initializeComponents);
  foreach (IField field in fields) {
    LineSegment fieldLine =
      textArea.Document.GetLineSegment(field.Region.BeginLine - 1);
    builder.Append(textArea.Document.GetText(fieldLine.Offset,
      fieldLine.Length));
    builder.Append("\n");
  }

  builder.Append("\tpublic Unknown() {\n\t\t");
  builder.Append(initializeComponents.Name);
  builder.Append("();\n");
  builder.Append("\t}\n");
  string initializeComponentsString =
    GetInitializeComponentsString(textArea.Document,
      initializeComponents);
  builder.Append(initializeComponentsString);

  builder.Append("}");
  return builder.ToString();
}
```

The `InitializeComponents` method is created by this method:

```
string GetInitializeComponentsString(IDocumentAggregator doc, IMethod
  initializeComponents)
{
  LineSegment beginLine =
    doc.GetLineSegment(initializeComponents.Region.BeginLine - 1);
```

```
LineSegment endLine =
  doc.GetLineSegment(initializeComponents.Region.EndLine - 1);

int startOffset = beginLine.Offset +
  initializeComponents.Region.BeginColumn - 1;
int endOffset = endLine.Offset +
  initializeComponents.Region.EndColumn - 1;

string initializeComponentsString = doc.GetText(startOffset,
  endOffset - startOffset);
int idx = initializeComponentsString.LastIndexOf('}');
if (idx > 0) {
  initializeComponentsString = initializeComponentsString.Substring(0,
    idx + 1);
}
return initializeComponentsString;
}
```

Currently, we only have two base classes, which are supported by the SharpDevelop designer – Form and UserControl. This method returns the correct base class of a given IClass object:

```
string ExctractBaseClass(IClass c)
{
  foreach (string baseType in c.BaseTypes) {
    if (baseType == "System.Windows.Forms.Form" ||
      baseType == "Form" ||
      baseType == "System.Windows.Forms.UserControl" ||
      baseType == "UserControl") {
      return baseType;
    }
  }
  return String.Empty;
}
```

The next method gets all fields from a class that get used inside the initialize components method:

```
ArrayList GetUsedFields(IDocumentAggregator doc, IClass c, IMethod
  initializeComponents)
{
  string InitializeComponentsString = GetInitializeComponentsString(doc,
    initializeComponents);

  ArrayList fields = new ArrayList();
  foreach (IField field in c.Fields) {
    if (field.IsPrivate) {
      if (InitializeComponentsString.IndexOf(field.Name) >= 0) {
        fields.Add(field);
      }
    }
  }
  return fields;
}
```

The `DeleteFormFields` method deletes all fields inside the class member field that gets used inside the class member `initialiseComponents` IMethod:

```
void DeleteFormFields()
{
  TextAreaControl textArea = TextAreaControl;
  ArrayList fields = GetUsedFields(textArea.Document, c,
    initializeComponents);
  for (int i = fields.Count - 1; i >= 0; --i) {
    IField field = (IField)fields[i];
    LineSegment fieldLine =
      textArea.Document.GetLineSegment(field.Region.BeginLine - 1);
    textArea.Document.Remove(fieldLine.Offset, fieldLine.TotalLength);
  }
}
```

The next method is used to merge the form changes back into the source code. It generates the source code of the Designer area, and puts it in the `InitializeComponents` method and fields in the source code, overwriting the old ones with the new:

```
void MergeFormChanges()
{
  IParserService parserService = (IParserService)
    ICSharpCode.Core.Services.ServiceManager.Services.GetService
      (typeof(IParserService));
  // generate file and get initialize components string
  string currentForm = GetDataAs("C#");
  IParseInformation generatedInfo = parserService.ParseFile(fileName ==
    null ? "a.cs" : fileName, currentForm);
  ICompilationUnit cu = (ICompilationUnit)
    generatedInfo.BestCompilationUnit;
  IClass generatedClass = cu.Classes[0];
  IMethod generatedInitializeComponents =
    GetInitializeComponents(cu.Classes[0]);
  IDocumentAggregator newDoc =
    new DocumentAggregatorFactory().CreateDocument();
  newDoc.TextContent = currentForm;
  string newInitializeComponents = GetInitializeComponentsString
    (newDoc, generatedInitializeComponents);

  TextAreaControl textArea = TextAreaControl;
  Reparse(fileName, textArea.Document.TextContent);
  DeleteFormFields();

  // replace the old initialize components method with the new one
  Reparse(fileName, textArea.Document.TextContent);
  LineSegment beginLine = textArea.Document.GetLineSegment
    (initializeComponents.Region.BeginLine - 1);
  int startOffset = beginLine.Offset +
    initializeComponents.Region.BeginColumn - 1;
  textArea.Document.Replace(startOffset,
    GetInitializeComponentsString(textArea.Document,
      initializeComponents).Length, newInitializeComponents);
```

```
      Reparse(fileName, textArea.Document.TextContent);

      // insert new fields
      int lineNr = c.Region.BeginLine - 1;
      while (true) {
        if (lineNr >= textArea.Document.TotalNumberOfLines - 2) {
          break;
        }
        LineSegment curLine = textArea.Document.GetLineSegment(lineNr);
        if (textArea.Document.GetText(curLine.Offset,
          curLine.Length).Trim().EndsWith("{")) {
          break;
        }
        ++lineNr;
      }
      beginLine = textArea.Document.GetLineSegment(lineNr + 1);
      int insertOffset = beginLine.Offset;
      foreach (IField field in generatedClass.Fields) {
        LineSegment fieldLine = newDoc.GetLineSegment(field.Region.BeginLine -
          1);
        textArea.Document.Insert(insertOffset,newDoc.GetText(fieldLine.Offset,
          fieldLine.TotalLength));
      }
    }
```

The Reparse method parses the source file again with the given content. It puts the class and initialize components method in the IClass and IMethod field of this object:

```
  void Reparse(string fileName, string content)
  {
    if (fileName == null) {
      fileName = "a.cs";
    }
    // get new initialize components
    IParserService parserService =
      (IParserService)ICSharpCode.Core.Services.ServiceManager.
      Services.GetService(typeof(IParserService));

    IParseInformation info = parserService.ParseFile(fileName, content);
    ICompilationUnit cu = (ICompilationUnit)info.BestCompilationUnit;
    foreach (IClass c in cu.Classes) {
      if (BaseClassIsFormOrControl(c)) {
        initializeComponents = GetInitializeComponents(c);
        if (initializeComponents != null) {
          this.c = c;
          break;
        }
      }
    }
  }
  bool BaseClassIsFormOrControl(IClass c)
  {
    foreach (string baseType in c.BaseTypes) {
```

```
      if (baseType == "System.Windows.Forms.Form" ||
         baseType == "Form" ||
         baseType == "System.Windows.Forms.UserControl" ||
         baseType == "UserControl") {
           return true;
         }
    }
    return false;
}

IMethod GetInitializeComponents(IClass c)
{
    foreach (IMethod method in c.Methods) {
      if ((method.Name == "InitializeComponents" ||
          method.Name == "InitializeComponent") &&
          method.Parameters.Count == 0) {
          return method;
        }
    }
    return null;
}
```

The `TabIndexChanged` method is used to determine which designer is visible, and to merge the designer changes back to the source code, when the view is switched from the designer to the source code view:

```
void TabIndexChanged(object sender, EventArgs e)
{
    switch (tabControl.SelectedIndex) {
      case 0:
        if (!failedDesignerInitialize) {
          bool dirty = IsDirty;
          MergeFormChanges();
          IsDirty = dirty;
          TextAreaControl.Refresh();
        }
        break;
    }
    isFormDesignerVisible = tabControl.SelectedIndex == 1;
}
```

Note that currently source code changes are not merged back to the designer because the `InitializeComponents` method should not be altered (and to make the forms designer faster).

The `SaveFile` method saves an XML form if the specified file extension of the filename is `xfrm`. Otherwise, it stores the source code. If the designer is selected, it needs to merge the form changes to the source code before writing:

```
public override void SaveFile(string fileName)
{
  ContentName = fileName;
  if (Path.GetExtension(fileName) == ".xfrm") {
    base.SaveFile(fileName);
    return;
  }
  if (tabControl.SelectedIndex == 0 || failedDesignerInitialize) {
    csharpTextEditor.SaveFile(fileName);
  } else {
    MergeFormChanges();
    csharpTextEditor.SaveFile(fileName);
  }
}
}
```

Using this approach, the implementation is relatively easy. But one problem remains – invisible components, which can be obtained by analyzing the InitializeComponents method for the usage of fields that are initialised, but whose types don't inherit from Control.

With this approach, round trips for other languages besides C# are possible too but still need to be implemented.

Summary

In this chapter, we examined how to store and restore the designer components using XML. We have seen the code that stores all components to XML, and have a good understanding of the XML format used. We now know how to determine the important properties and those that aren't changed, and therefore, are unnecessary to write to disk. We have seen the loading routine that reads it back and knows its inner workings.

We have looked at another place where the XML store/restore routines get used – serialization. We know that it is used as a designer service, which gets called by the clipboard operations.

We have seen how to utilize the CodeDOM API from the .NET Framework to generate executable source code from the XML format. Finally, we looked at the round trip, which reads the generated source code back. This is used to store and restore the designer status to executable source code, without letting the user know that the XML routines are used in background.

INDEX

Index

A Guide to the Index

The index is arranged hierarchically, in alphabetical order, with symbols preceding the letter A. Most second-level entries and many third-level entries also occur as first-level entries. This is to ensure that users will find the information they require however they choose to search for it.

519

T

ASPToday - Your free daily ASP Resource . . .

A discount off your ASPToday subscription with this voucher!!! see below for more details.

Expand your knowledge of ASP.NET with ASPToday.com - Wrox's code source for ASP and .NET applications, with free daily articles!

Every working day, we publish free Wrox content on the web:

- Free daily article
- Free daily tips
- Case studies and reference materials
- Index and full text search
- Downloadable code samples
- 11 Categories
- Written by programmers for programmers

And for just-in-time, practical solutions to real-world problems, subscribe to our Living Book - our 600+ strong archive of code-heavy, useable articles.

Find it all and more at http://www.asptoday.com

This voucher entitles you to a discount off your annual ASPToday subscription; to claim your reduced rate please visit:

http://www.asptoday.com/special-offers/

If you have any questions please contact customersupport@wrox.com

C# Today

The daily knowledge site for professional C# programmers

C#Today provides you with a weekly in-depth case study, giving you solutions to real-world problems that are relevant to your career. Each one is written by a leading professional, meaning that you benefit from their expertise and get the skills that you need to thrive in the C# world. As well as a weekly case study, we also offer you access to our huge archive of quality articles, which cover every aspect of the C# language at www.csharptoday.com.

Tony Loton, one of the authors of this book, has written a related case study: "Build a Better Design Tool with Automation", for C# Today, and exclusively for readers of this book, a free PDF copy is available from http://www.csharptoday.com/info.asp?view=ProfessionalUML. In his case study, Tony shows how any Microsoft application can be driven via automation from a C# application, and how Visio can be used to extract information from diagrams (and not just UML) as a more interesting alternative to the usual Word or Excel automation demonstrations. This piece also comes will fully working code.

By joining the growing number of C#Today subscribers, you get access to:

- A weekly in-depth case study
- Code-heavy demonstration of real-world applications
- Access to an archive of over 170 articles
- C# reference material
- A fully searchable index

Visit C#Today at: www.csharptoday.com

p2p.wrox.com
The programmer's resource centre

A unique free service from Wrox Press
With the aim of helping programmers to help each other

Wrox Press aims to provide timely and practical information to today's programmer. P2P
is a list server offering a host of targeted mailing lists where you can share knowledge
with your fellow programmers and find solutions to your problems. Whatever the level of
your programming knowledge, and whatever technology you use, P2P can provide you with
the information you need.

ASP
Support for beginners and professionals, including a resource page with hundreds of links,
and a popular ASP.NET mailing list.

DATABASES
For database programmers, offering support on SQL Server, mySQL, and Oracle.

MOBILE
Software development for the mobile market is growing rapidly. We provide lists for
the several current standards, including WAP, Windows CE, and Symbian.

JAVA
A complete set of Java lists, covering beginners, professionals, and server-side programmers
(including JSP, servlets, and EJBs)

.NET
Microsoft's new OS platform, covering topics such as ASP.NET, C#, and general
.NET discussion.

VISUAL BASIC
Covers all aspects of VB programming, from programming Office macros to creating
components for the .NET platform.

WEB DESIGN
As web page requirements become more complex, programmer's are taking a more important
role in creating web sites. For these programmers, we offer lists covering technologies such as
Flash, Coldfusion, and JavaScript.

XML
Covering all aspects of XML, including XSLT and schemas.

OPEN SOURCE
Many Open Source topics covered including PHP, Apache, Perl, Linux, Python, and more.

FOREIGN LANGUAGE
Several lists dedicated to Spanish and German speaking programmers; categories include:
NET, Java, XML, PHP, and XML.

How to subscribe:
Simply visit the P2P site, at http://p2p.wrox.com/

Wrox Press
Web Services

A selection of related titles from our Web Services Series

Professional Java Web Services
ISBN:1-86100-375-7
Professional Java Web Services concisely explains the important technologies and specifications behind web services. The book outlines the architecture of web services, and the latest information on implementing web services.

Professional C# Web Services: Building Web Services with .NET Remoting and ASP.NET
ISBN: 1-86100-439-7
This book covers building web services and web service clients with both ASP.NET and .NET Remoting. We also look at the generic protocols used by web services: SOAP and WSDL.

Professional XML Web Services
ISBN: 1-86100-509-1
The technologies presented in this book provide the foundations of web services computing, which is set to revolutionize distributed computing, as we know it.

Professional ASP.NET Web Services
ISBN: 1-86100-545-8
This book will show you how to create high-quality web services using ASP.NET.

Early Adopter Hailstorm
ISBN: 1-86100-608-X
Hailstorm Preview of Version 1.0 - Using SOAP and XPath to talk to Hailstorm - Hailstorm Data Manipulation Language (HSDL) - Practical Case Studies.

Professional Java SOAP
ISBN: 1-86100-610-1
Organized in three parts: Distributed Application Protocols, Sample Application, and Web Service, this book is for all Java developers and system archictects.

Got more Wrox books than you can carry around?

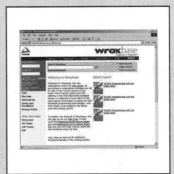

Programmer to Programmer™

Registration Code: 81713IG714223J01

Wrox writes books for you. Any suggestions, or ideas about how you want information given in your ideal book will be studied by our team. Your comments are always valued at Wrox.

Free phone in USA 800-USE-WROX
Fax (312) 893 8001

UK Tel.: (0121) 687 4100   Fax: (0121) 687 4101

Dissecting a C# Application: Inside SharpDevelop – Registration Card

Name _____

Address _____

_____

_____

City _____ State/Region _____

Country _____ Postcode/Zip _____

E-Mail _____

Occupation _____

How did you hear about this book?

☐ Book review (name) _____

☐ Advertisement (name) _____

☐ Recommendation _____

☐ Catalog _____

☐ Other _____

Where did you buy this book?

☐ Bookstore (name) _____ City _____

☐ Computer store (name) _____

☐ Mail order _____

☐ Other _____

What influenced you in the purchase of this book?

☐ Cover Design   ☐ Contents   ☐ Other (please specify):

_____

How did you rate the overall content of this book?

☐ Excellent   ☐ Good   ☐ Average   ☐ Poor

What did you find most useful about this book? _____

_____

What did you find least useful about this book? _____

_____

Please add any additional comments. _____

_____

What other subjects will you buy a computer book on soon?

_____

What is the best computer book you have used this year?

_____

Note: This information will only be used to keep you updated about new Wrox Press titles and will not be used for any other purpose or passed to any other third party.

wrox

Programmer to Programmer™

Note: If you post the bounce back card below in the UK, please send it to:

Wrox Press Limited, Arden House, 1102 Warwick Road,
Acocks Green, Birmingham B27 6HB. UK.

Computer Book Publishers

BUSINESS REPLY MAIL

FIRST CLASS MAIL   PERMIT#64   CHICAGO, IL

POSTAGE WILL BE PAID BY ADDRESSEE

WROX PRESS INC.,
29 S. LA SALLE ST.,
SUITE 520
CHICAGO IL 60603-USA